Advance Praise for

Towers of Deception

Even skeptics like myself will find much in Barrie Zwicker's book to ponder, enjoy, and, yes, even embrace. Interestingly researched and well written, a valuable aid to correct thinking about "conspiracy theory."

— *Michael Parenti, author of* Culture Struggle *and* The Assassination of Julius Caesar

If a significant portion of the evidence summarized here holds up, the conclusion that the attacks of 9/11 succeeded because of official complicity would become virtually inescapable.

— *David Ray Griffin, author of* The New Pearl Harbor: Disturbing Questions about the Bush Administration and 9/11 *and* The 9/11 Commission Report: Omissions and Distortions

Barrie Zwicker has been a courageous and insightful pioneer in the fight to free humanity from Bush's fantastic nightmare vision of the events of September 11, 2001. Barrie's new book is a tour de force, and nowhere more than in his treatment of Noam Chomsky and the left gatekeepers, whose embrace of the government 9/11 story has crippled opponents to the wars in Afghanistan, Iraq, Iran, and beyond. Barrie's critique of Chomskyism is devastating, and bids fair to deprive the warmongers of their secret weapon: an impotent opposition. Bravo, Barrie!

— *Webster Griffin Tarpley, author of* 9/11 Synthetic Terror: Made in USA *and* George Bush: The Unauthorized Biography

One cannot lose sight of the reality: There has been no rational explanation from the White House, the 9/11 Commission or the media as to what happened that day on a number of levels. Zwicker's book asks that obstruction, silence and obfuscation be replaced by honest investigation. *Towers of Deception*, by Canada's most effective media observer and critic deserves to be read and pondered.

— *Walter Pitman, President of Ryerson University, and Director of the Ontario Arts Council, Member of the Order of Ontario, Officer of the Order of Canada, and author of* Music Makers: The Lives of Harry Freedman and Mary Morrison

TOWERS of DECEPTION

THE MEDIA COVER-UP OF 9/11

BARRIE ZWICKER

NEW SOCIETY PUBLISHERS

Cataloging in Publication Data:
A catalog record for this publication is available from the National Library of Canada.

Printed in Canada. First printing June 2006.

New Society Publishers acknowledges the support of the Government of Canada through the Book Publishing Industry Development Program (BPIDP) for our publishing activities.

Paperback ISBN 13: 978-0-86571-573-8
Paperback ISBN 10: 0-86571-573-4

Inquiries regarding requests to reprint all or part of *Towers of Deception* should be addressed to New Society Publishers at the address below.

To order directly from the publishers, please call toll-free (North America) 1-800-567-6772, or order online at www.newsociety.com

Any other inquiries can be directed by mail to:
New Society Publishers P.O. Box 189,
Gabriola Island, BC V0R 1X0, Canada
1-800-567-6772

New Society Publishers' mission is to publish books that contribute in fundamental ways to building an ecologically sustainable and just society, and to do so with the least possible impact on the environment, in a manner that models this vision. We are committed to doing this not just through education, but through action. We are acting on our commitment to the world's remaining ancient forests by phasing out our paper supply from ancient forests worldwide. This book is one step toward ending global deforestation and climate change. It is printed on acid-free paper that is **100% old growth forest-free** (100% post-consumer recycled), processed chlorine free, and printed with vegetable-based, low-VOC inks. For further information, or to browse our full list of books and purchase securely, visit our website at: www.newsociety.com

NEW SOCIETY PUBLISHERS   www.newsociety.com

To Rev. Wilfred Grenfell Zwicker, my father, a ceaseless champion of peace and of environmentalism and ecumenism before those words were in common use; to my mother, Norah Hall, for all her gifts; and to our granddaughter, Leah Emelia Zwicker, who will understand this book in a way none today can.

"What is your take on the events of 9/11?"

When, in early 2002, I began filling public speaking engagements about 9/11, I learned that audiences appreciated being asked this question. Universally, people – whatever view they held — were very interested to learn where others in the room stood on this.

Through trial and error I developed the questionnaire below. If you choose to involve yourself in this, check only one box — the one that comes closest to your "take" on the events of 9/11. This questionnaire appears again at the back of the book, in case you want to check your views on 9/11 now with your views after you read the book. This is also intended to stimulate your feedback to the author. It's welcome at any time, about the questionnaire or anything else in or related to this book. Email me at the address below.

The Four-Box 9/11 Questionnaire
Check the box that comes closest to your take on 9/11:

[ ] 1 I believe that 19 fanatical Muslim terrorists, members of Al Qaeda led by Osama bin Laden, caught all of the U.S. intelligence, military and political establishments totally off guard.

[ ] 2 I believe that enough advance information had been received by U.S. agencies that the "attacks" could have been prevented or ameliorated, but that incompetence at various levels enabled the events to proceed as they did.

[   ] 3 I believe that a great deal of advance information had been received by US agencies, enough that the events could have been prevented, but that people at the top deliberately allowed the events to unfold as they did.

[   ] 4 I believe that the alleged 19 hijackers, if there were that many, were dupes and patsies, that the events of 9/11 were planned at the highest levels in and around the White House, that it was an inside job.

* * *

As you read this book, you'll see that:

Box 1 equates to The Official Story of 9/11
Box 2 equates to The Incompetence Theory
Box 3 equates to the Let It Happen On Purpose (or LIHOP) theory and
Box 4 equates to The Inside Job theory, or Made It Happen On
        Purpose (MIHOP) theory.

Barrie Zwicker
bwz@rogers.com

Contents

Acknowledgments

A lengthy tribute would be needed to do justice to the contributions to this book of each of my two closest collaborators, Ian Woods and Terry Burrows. Both backed the project morally from the day it was conceived and continued to believe in it during years of changes and deferments. Both offered wise criticisms of almost all the chapters. Ian, editor and publisher of *Global Outlook: The Magazine of 9/11 Truth,* offered free access to any images and text from the magazine for which he owns copyright. He exhaustively researched the Chapter 2 exhibits and loaned his employee, Jennifer Hopp, to track down images. (A deep tip of the hat to Jenn.) Terry applied his formidable research skills to most of the chapters, especially Chapter 7, to the point of "pulling all-nighters." His belief that his Christian God deeply approves of this book is not something that I, an atheist Christian humanist, am willing to shrug off entirely. Yet he insists that all the thanks he needs is this: "Research, editorial assistance and transcription supplied by Terry Burrows' Citizens' Audio Report, of Toronto, Ontario, Canada (tburrows@idirect.ca)." So you know who in the main I'm referring to when I say "we" here.

We owe an immense debt of gratitude to David Ray Griffin. Time after time, as we surveyed the literature and the internet for facts, interpretations, and logical analyses, we found we could not improve on Griffin's. This was well after I decided this book required a chapter entitled "Dr. David Ray Griffin: Modern Day Prophet." Griffin was repeatedly helpful and repeatedly patient in reading drafts and offering precious suggestions, responding so quickly each time it was hard to believe he was working on four other books at the same time.

Then there are the Special Thanks. To my wife Jeanie whose tolerance is again and again tried to the extent I would not be surprised to one day find her reading the Book of Job. Without her cutting me the seemingly endless slack needed for this project, it could not have been completed. To Terry O'Connor, who proves a 50-year friendship need not stand in the way of sharp editorial scrutiny. To Ulli Diemer and Elaine Farragher for their steady support. I know of no one who indexes better than Ulli. The solitude of their rent-free cottage north of Kingston, Ontario for ten weeks late in 2005 and early 2006 without question enabled me to complete the manuscript (and proved the truth that "9/11 conspiracy theorists are a small cottage industry.") To the constant support of Roy and Karen Harvey of Snowshoe Films, documentarists to the 9/11 Truth movement, whose next film is being produced on a schedule that will dovetail with promotion of this book. To my lawyer, Marian Hebb, General Counsel for the Writers Union of Canada, a fellow descendant of the "Foreign Protestants" of Nova Scotia and a most gentle and generous soul. To my writing coach Joyce Nelson, whose devotion to logic and clarity was sorely tried as she struggled with my drafts. Whatever the lack of these attributes within these pages, it in no way lies on her doorstep, quite the contrary. To Chris Plant, one half of the co-publishers team at New Society Publishers, for his interest in this book from the moment he heard about it, and for his and Judith Plant's effective continuing support in so many ways all through the process. To Barry Silverthorn, my long-time video editor supremo, friend and confidante, who finds so many ways to help me, whatever project I am working on, no matter how much work is already on his platter.

I am indebted also to each of the 9/11 Truth activists profiled in this book, for her or his unique support, as well as for their collective inspiration. To my editor Ingrid Witvoet; to Phil ("You've gotta write a book") Desjardins, whose generosity and easy-going wisdom are always a gift; to friends Mike and Olja Muller who took all of five minutes back in autumn 2001 to grasp what I was talking about when I told them 9/11 was "a Reichstag Fire 2001," and who have supported all my work since; and to cousin Bob Oxley who, again in 2001, urged me to "break new territory."

To Carolyn Beck, my bookkeeper-accountant-confidante, an author too; to Steve Bhaerman, aka Swami Beyondananda, as wise as he is funny; and to Hans Burgschmidt, whose support emanates from his political and spiritual journey and his deep concern and decency. To Michele Landsberg, once Canada's leading newspaper columnist and always a fearless and superbly-grounded leader for social and political justice; to John McMurtry, a philosopher whose concern for humankind is as profound as his intellect, for his occasional "deep crystals;" and to neighbour and graphic artist Brett Simms, for pitching in.

To other members of my family not included in the Dedication: daughter Xena-Linda whose passion for justice is intense and endless; son Gren-Erich and daughter-in-law Beth, whose interest and support is unflagging; my brother Richard, both younger and wiser than me and my late aunt Florence ("Aunty Fleur") Zwicker of Falmouth, Massachussetts, who remembered me in her will, even though she knew I could not share her enthusiasm for Ronald Reagan.

None of the above are to be considered co-conspirators in all that I have written, especially those whose counsel to remove words, passages and whole chapters I have had to respectfully decline.

Toronto, Ontario, April 2006

It isn't what we don't know that gives us trouble;
it's what we know that ain't so.

— Will Rogers

Never lie to yourself.
— Bertrand Russell's First Commandment

Preface

This book includes "9/11 Media Diary" entries; profiles of 9/11 Truth activists; about 100 illustrations; and a DVD. A word about these. The diary entries are a few of the reactions of an habitual media critic to coverage of 9/11 and the ensuing so-called "war on terrorism." The diary entries are mainly in the present tense, but I have added some later reflections based on subsequent events and developments. Only the last two are fictional.

The profiles are included for several reasons. The leaders of the 9/11 Truth movement — and I have met them all — are role models of deep and benign citizenship and vision. They provide hope. People in the vanguard of a new movement seldom receive the recognition they deserve until much later. The profiles are intended also to add an important human dimension that otherwise would be difficult to include, and I found the commonalities that emerged important and fascinating. My regret is that I could not include even more, equally worthy of being recognized. Time, space and miscellaneous considerations cause this gallery be far less inclusive than it should be.

The illustrations are mainly clustered, close to the relevant text, in Chapter 2 (evidence of complicity), and Chapter 7 (evidence of the history of false flag operations). We decided therefore that a list of illustrations would be superfluous.

The DVD, *The Great Conspiracy: The 9/11 News Special You Never Saw*, is complementary to the book. Overlap is minimal. If you have not seen the DVD, you can view it before, during or after reading this book. If you already have purchased this DVD, the one enclosed could make a great gift.

Where possible I use "Kean-Zelikow commission" for what the media call "the 9/11 Commission," the "Kean Commission" or sometimes the "Kean-Hamilton Commission." This usage is borrowed from David Ray Griffin because "Kean-Zelikow" is more accurately descriptive of the nature and functioning of that deeply compromised and controlled body than the usual designations. The power of naming is important. In this book you will find no reference to "the independent 9/11 commission," because that is a condensed lie.

Introduction,
to a Bad End or a New Beginning

It's an out-of-the-blue, in-your-face, screaming-horror surprise. A nuclear weapon blows up in the harbor at Charleston, South Carolina. It's another 9/11. It's Nuclear Jihad. A repulsed and confused world shudders at the burning devastation. A radioactive cloud drifts off over the Atlantic. The death toll is unknown. Hundreds of thousands of survivors evacuate. This time the White House is in charge. No more Katrinas. The military is your friend. The president addresses the nation and the world: a "suitcase nuke" from the old Soviet arsenal has been obtained by Islamic terrorists, almost certainly Iranian, he intones. Iran must be neutralized. A nuclear strike on that country now is necessary, appropriate and just. Because some people, even in America, may oppose this action and "choose to side with the terrorists," new measures are required to "safeguard the homeland." An unknown number of Americans, and citizens abroad, are rounded up and transported to detention centers. Thousands on FBI and other "watch lists" are permanently denied internet access.

Or maybe the nuke is discovered aboard a freighter in Galveston harbor. As a team of bomb dismantlers works feverishly to defuse the device, a fixed video camera feeds the world's news organizations a close-up image of the inevitable red digits dramatically counting down to detonation time. The nation and the world are riveted in horror. Finally, to a planetary sigh of relief, they succeed! Or fail! Are blown up! The scenarios are as numerous as they are appalling.

All have one thing in common: all are fake. Whatever the unthinkable outrage, it is, in fact, a covert Western operation. Any of the scenarios advances the monopoly capitalist and neo-conservative agenda of seizing Iran's oil reserves, it is another notch in the belt of global resource theft and world domination. Fiction? Let us pray so. But make no mistake, nuclear — or biological or chemical — false flag-operations can be staged. If they are not, it won't be for a shortage of plans at the Pentagon, the CIA and MI6. False flag operations since 9/11 have been the basic engine of the "war on terror," for which the 9/11 false-flag operation is the linchpin. False-flag ops are key in hastening the desired destabilization and dismantling of Iraq, where one British false-flag op was discovered in the making and briefly reported upon (see Chapter 7).

The most effective rhetoric from the mouths of demagogues cannot compete with — but can reinforce — heart-wrenching images of bloodied schoolchildren, wedding guests dismembered, planes flying into buildings. These "flashbulb moments" bypass rational thought. They are informational atomic bombs compared to the regular gunplay of lies from governments. An actual atomic false-flag op is the perverted dream of the Dr. Strangeloves currently infesting the White House, Number 10 Downing Street, the Pentagon and Langley. The ones who brought us 9/11.

The American Empire's Weapon Number One in imposing "full spectrum dominance" is psychological warfare. Without brainwashed populations, the world domination project will unravel. The most indispensable ingredients of psychological warfare today are false flag bombings and assassinations. These inject a continuous supply of fuel for the fear campaign now targeting everyone on Earth. Where would George W. Bush be today without the word "terror?" asks Mike Adams of *Counter Think*. "That single word, it seems, is solely responsible for Bush's continued popularity among simple-minded Americans. Without the word 'terror,' Bush would have no war, no foreign policy, no justification for decimating the Constitution, and nothing to talk about in his speeches." In one of those speeches, on March 20, 2006 in Cleveland, reported Sidney Blumenthal in the *Guardian*, Bush used the word terror 54 times.

"For a long time," Norman Solomon wrote in 2005, for truthout.org, "the last refuge of scoundrels was patriotism. Now it's 'the war on terror.'

The ultimate demagogic weapon is to exploit the memory of September 11, 2001." *The New York Times* reported, regarding a May 17, 2006 speech by George W. Bush, "As he did in 2002 and 2004, he repeatedly invoked the memory of the attacks of Sept. 11."

"The news" consumed by most people in North America and Europe is a cocoon of manufactured facts, distractions and personalities forming an almost seamless web of invented reality — including invented history — obscuring the power of money and other resources in the hands of the few, even while cleverly masking its own unreality. Fake events are a key component of the illusion, a Truman Show writ large.

The mainstream media remain mute in the face of mounting evidence that Western covert operators were behind Bali, Madrid, London 7/7, mosque bombings in Iraq and elsewhere and, of course, 9/11. Because the mainstream media are integral to the Industrial Military Academic Intelligence Media complex (I MAIM), the cold-blooded technicians of death face no journalistic scrutiny. Without moral, legal, technical or financial constraints, the black operators range freely, executing the orders of the global oligarchies — what I call the Invisible Government.

It is those who profit from the arms industry globally — the merchants of death — who finally have the deepest stake in perpetual war. All the grandly wrought outpourings of that ultimate neo-con think tank, the Project for a New American Century, inevitably offer only one answer to every problem or alleged problem: more armaments.

Despite the media blackout, growing numbers of citizens have been developing well-grounded suspicions. In March 2006, when the program *Showbiz Tonight*, on the CNN Headline News channel, aired actor Charlie Sheen's opinions that 9/11 was an inside job, 83 per cent of the 54,000 people who emailed the program agreed. The mainstream media are not necessarily a 100 per cent hopeless cause. But such hope as there is for the mainstream to wake up rests on the shoulders of brave and effective individuals, most likely in unexpected places such as *Showbiz Tonight*.

In the meantime, the main hope for historic change is at the grassroots level. It's true that the mainstream media first ignored, then mocked, the resurgent women's movement and environmental movement. Remember "bra burners" and "tree huggers?" Over time, however, because those grassroots grew into plants that could not be eradicated, the media were forced to discontinue marginalizing these movements.

It is at the grassroots level that the 9/11 Truth movement continues to make stubborn headway, aided by the growing evidence of government lies, corruption, and incipient fascism. Evidence that 9/11 was an inside job continues to accumulate in the *samizdat* of the new Millennium — the internet, DVDs, videos — and in books the mainstream media refuse to review. I take hundreds of direct phone orders for my DVDs from across the US. The most common phrases I hear from these callers: "They're capable of anything" or "They'll stop at nothing."

All of us wrestling with our planet's dire situation have a powerful ally. That ally is crisis. Crisis, more than anything else, forces individuals and organizations to learn and change quickly and profoundly. Once the ongoing synthetic crisis of "terrorism" is revealed for the sham that it is, it will boomerang on its authors. The over-the-top brazenness of the neo-cons who masterminded 9/11 is a gift, because of the mountain of telltale evidence they left behind, including the biggest lie in print, the report of the 9/11 Kean-Zelikow commission. With 9/11, the oligarchy has, with reckless hubris, fashioned the largest Achilles Heel in history.

Crisis is also the best friend of planets in distress. The current crisis is potent because it's multi-dimensional. Each dimension is growing quickly or even exponentially: global warming, energy depletion, hyper-militarism, increasing pollution, human population overshoot, growing inequality, technologies out of control. And dinosaurs *in* control.

Many people will tell you they feel or detect a "growing awareness," "growing consciousness," or "a great awakening." In her book *The Great Transformation,* Karen Armstrong writes that the founding of the great religions followed a period of terrible violence. Compassion — evidenced by the universality of The Golden Rule — lies at the heart of all these religions. We may be undergoing a tweaking of the survival instinct, experiencing the fear of worse to come. Surely there's a weariness at the lies, the waste, the crime, the corruption. An inner stirring for peaceful transformation. As Victor Hugo wrote: "An invasion of armies can be resisted, but not an idea whose time has come."

The most powerful idea of all is a realistic, encompassing and inspiring new story, one that takes into account all we can grasp about the depths to which our species can fall, and the heights to which it can rise. One that includes a full understanding of the powers arrayed against us and the powers at our command. One that incorporates — better than ever before — the learnings to be gleaned from the history of humankind and from the latest research on the inner workings of ourselves.

The story must forward track the inspiring and dangerous but realistic steps on the path to a world finally and permanently set free from the scourges of war, rampant greed and fatal short sightedness. A world in which the energy released by the lifting of fear and the release of goodwill exceeds that of all the nuclear weapons ever built by the blind technicians of death and their masters. A world in which it is recognized that we are all victims and all perpetrators, if not equally so. Such a world — not a utopia (belief in utopia has been one of our snares and delusions) — but a much better world, is possible.

The shortest and most exciting route to that world cuts directly through the Big Lie of 9/11, itself the culmination of centuries of deceit by greedy oligarchies bent on war for privilege, profit and power. Let's gather the number of people on that route into such a large and dedicated throng of the best and brightest, the meek and the fearful, those with nothing to lose and everything to lose, that it — that we — cannot be denied. And then let us be so wise as to deserve the challenge of saving the planet.

* * *

Diary of 9/11 and the Media

How 9/11 Started for Me

Downtown Toronto, September 11, 2001 — Around 8:45 a.m., my wife calls on the intercom from the kitchen. I'm at my computer in my writing studio on the third floor. "Chris says something's going on in New York you'll probably be interested in," she says. Chris is our next door neighbour. She's been talking to him over the back fence. I thank her, click on the TV in my writing studio and start seeing what millions are seeing.

Shortly after the second plane hits I go downstairs. In our living room are my wife and Ken, the male half of the young couple to whom we rent our basement apartment. He's Portuguese Canadian. His wife is American. By now I agree with TV commentators that this amounts to war on the USA. It seems obvious to me the impacts of the planes and the ensuing fires brought down both towers of the World Trade Center. I say: "Perhaps there's one silver lining to this horrible event. Perhaps now some percentage of people in the United States will finally look into their country's foreign policy, and into their hearts, and perhaps gain a little insight or humility. Maybe this could be a blessing in a big disguise."

"Nah," replies Ken. "All that's going to happen is that they're going to bomb the shit out of somebody." Of course, he turned out to be completely right and me almost completely wrong. Now I'm asking out loud: "Where the hell is the US Air Force? I can't believe this." There are reports of errant airliners all over the place, even heading toward Washington and presumably the White House.

I've always been interested in aviation. In the Royal Canadian Air Cadets I reached the rank of Flight Sergeant and was offered an RCAF scholarship to learn to fly Sabre jets in the Korean War. I turned it down, deciding I "didn't want to kill someone I didn't know." (It never occurred to me I might be killed.) Now I'm on my feet, jumping up and down and shouting: "C'mon US Air Force. C'mon you guys! Get going! Migawd, where the hell is the US Air Force? This is unbelievable." A few minutes later the penny drops. Something is *terribly* wrong in the lack of scrambled jet interceptors. The term "inside job" doesn't come to mind; what does is "Reichstag fire," the startling event of 1933 in Germany that was shown later to have been arranged by Hitler to boost his power, then declare war. I say: "This has gotta be Reichstag fire 2001."

At some point it occurs to me with a jolt that our friend (and former tenant) George Murray, an up-and-coming poet and author, works in a building directly across from the WTC south tower. Through the afternoon, with increasing concern, I try to reach him at his office and home. All lines are down. By suppertime I just stand by the phone and cry a little after not getting through for the seventh or eighth time.

Not entirely sure of my sanity on the enormity of what I think has happened, I talk with our son in the early evening. "I thought the same thing," he says. "Something's very fishy about all this."

Shortly before midnight George calls. He and his wife are okay; he spills out his full amazing story "for the 13th time; I know it's therapy." He says: "You know I'm a very peaceful person but I'm sorry, they should nuke the bastards that did this." Months later he reconsiders.

* * *

Diary of 9/11 and the Media

The Instant Myth That "Everything Has Changed."

September 17, 2001 — Tonight, the first *MediaFile* program of the season on Canada's Vision TV airs. It's my first opportunity to comment on the events of six days ago. Looking back on this script, I recall that although I personally did not believe the official story about 9/11, I could not see how I could say that, on air, six days after the events. In retrospect, I think it was wise to stay my hand until later, enabling myself to break loose in January, with a seven-part series questioning the official 9/11 story, still perhaps earning a footnote in some history book as the first journalist in the world to go on national TV and do so. A slightly edited transcript:

* * *

A myth was born in the wake of last Tuesday's events. It is this: "Everything has changed." At first, I did agree. I was one of those for whom Tuesday's shocking news was overlaid with personal dread and foreboding. A wonderful friend, Toronto poet George Murray, worked across from the World Trade Center. His wife is a Fulbright scholar at New York University uptown. It wasn't until mid evening I learned they were both alive.

Upon reflection, it seems to me it may be closer to the truth to say not that "Everything has changed," but that "Little has changed." The same fuels for the world's burning hatreds remain stockpiled. What's changed is that they're higher octane. Many fuels feed the fires. First, the word "terrorism" itself. It's used by US political and military leaders and the media in a profoundly one-sided, hypocritical, way. Never with reference to violent, often illegal US actions past and present around the world. These actions are at the root of violent anti-Americanism. It so happens that last Tuesday was the 28th anniversary of the American-engineered coup in Chile, on September 11, 1973. Masterminded by Henry Kissinger, it toppled a democratically elected government, assassinated its leader and left thousands "disappeared" to this day.

What the mainstream media have failed to put into context is that US forces have unilaterally bombed or invaded Libya, Panama, Cuba, Grenada, Nicaragua, the Sudan — 23 countries in all. For years the US has trained and supported death squads. Until last Tuesday, wanton destruction of innocent civilians had been the fate of the Iraqi, Yugoslav and other peoples, and on a larger scale. At least three million Vietnamese, mostly civilians, died when US planes dropped a greater tonnage of bombs on their tiny country than was dropped by all sides in the Second World War.

Now, none of this justifies the kind of retaliation we witnessed last Tuesday. But at White House press conferences you'll hear no questions about US wrong-doing. The suicide bombers' operation may well have been, in the minds of its planners, revenge for US policies and actions. Polls now show millions of Americans now will support almost any conceivable counter revenge.

Another example of how little the world has changed: the media fan the vengeance flames. One Washington press corps question was: "There are those who say the USA doesn't have the belly for massive retaliation. What's your reaction?" I dream — in technicolor, I grant you — of a day when reporters shout questions such as: "In the Middle East, retaliation upon retaliation has led to escalating violence that has undermined possibilities for true peace. Why do you think retaliation will work at the global level?"

Perhaps most important by far on the list of what hasn't changed is that Western governments and media almost totally ignore the only really effective means to win the war against terrorism. In a truly changed world, governments and media would launch a sustained debate as to how to achieve lasting national security in the twenty-first century. In a truly changed world, they would listen, they would understand and they would address the roots of anger and despair in the third world. Media would urge governments to narrow the now-widening gap between rich

and poor on the planet, to pass fair wage laws, eradicate poverty, eliminate human rights violations, reduce racism, and fund health services.
Some diseases can be healed for pennies a day.

Instead governments are focusing, as usual, on exterminating those
at the demented end of despair. Through, possibly, a repeat of the death-
dealing Gulf War coalition. And most media buy this focus. This is not a
world in which "everything has changed." This is the same world of
selective amnesia and reliance on violence to solve problems that existed
before September 11. What is changing is that the old counter-productive ideas are hardening. Resources are being assembled for even more
violent solutions. The fuel tanks of retaliation are being filled.

* * *

Diary of 9/11 and the Media

Who's anti-American?

September 24, 2001 — Tonight my commentary about "anti-
Americanism" aired on Canada's Vision TV. An edited transcript:

* * *

It seems to me an expanded debate is overdue about the term "anti-
American." Its use as a verbal club amounts to an attempt to suppress
legitimate viewpoints. Some media commentators suggest it's both
wrong-headed and mean-spirited to be less than 100% supportive of
George Bush. A *Globe & Mail* editorial says: "The anti-Americans" — a
putdown in the context — "are always careful to hide their barbs in a
cloak of sympathy." I take deep offence. The sympathy police pontificate
that anyone whose sympathy is encompassing enough to embrace victims of decades of US terror, or of man-made horrors in general, are
insincere. How dare they!

Some suggest that being anti-American is against Canada's interests.
That to be anti-American is anti-Canadian. How weird! Let me first
reflect personally. My life — like that of every Canadian — has been and
continues to be, shaped in important ways by the US. I am enriched forever by the 18 months I studied, then worked, in the US. I studied
American literature, history, politics, journalism and humour. I became

and remain inspired by giants of the American spirit. By Thomas Jefferson. By Abraham Lincoln. Were they anti-American? By Thomas Paine. By American journalists such as Benjamin Franklin, Mark Twain. Were they anti-American?

My heroes include crusading American TV newsman Edward R. Murrow, who dared to confront McCarthyism. Was he anti-American? Or was McCarthy, with his "Un-American Activities Committee?" Another hero of mine: the legendary I.F. Stone who with his little weekly exposed Washington lies and hypocrisy. And the likes of filmmaker Michael Moore, who, of September 11 charges: "I'm angry. I'm an American citizen, and my leaders have taken my money to fund mass murder. And now my friends have paid the price with their lives." Is he anti-American?

I'm nourished immensely by the American weekly *The Nation,* based in New York City. It's been questioning authority since 1865. It consistently opposes American militarism and abuse of US corporate power worldwide. Has it been anti-American for 126 years?

All these people and institutions — and indeed millions of like-minded Americans — are the most patriotic Americans. They uphold the founding principles of their country — legality and justice for all. Call that true Americanism. I am totally pro-American in that sense. What I call real Americans don't see George W. Bush and his oil billionaire and arms manufacturing backers as "a force for good in the world, a beacon of liberty," as *The Globe and Mail* does. Real Americans vehemently dissent from their government breaking international law, training and supporting death squads, practicing might-makes-right on so many fronts.

Count me as one media person who doesn't need any lessons from *The Globe and Mail* or anyone else about what America originally stood for, should stand for, and can stand for, to be true to its founding principles. That would include the rule of law, including international law. Not constantly flouting it, as the present US political leadership does. That would be siding with the oppressed, not adding to their oppression in so many ways — as a sequence of US administrations has done. Now the leadership is further betraying American principles by removing the prohibition on state-sanctioned assassinations.

Thank goodness Canada's tradition is to debate in the middle of crisis. For many of us this is a source of pride in Canada. Which is not the same as anti-Americanism. A frightening tendency south of the border is to have everyone fall into line. It was an American, the late Justice Hugo Black of the US Supreme Court who said "the widest possible dissemination of information from diverse and antagonistic sources is essential to the welfare of the public." Especially in time of turmoil. That's why my dissenting American friends need support at this time, in their grieving and in their sacred principles. To tell the truth I'm tired of being lectured by media barons or anyone else about anti-Americanism. The way I see it, the lecturers are the ones who are truly anti-American.

* * *

Diary of 9/11 and the Media

In Which the Author Tries to Interest a Major Newspaper in a 9/11 Exposé

The Globe and Mail offices, the afternoon of November 6, 2001 — This morning I call Victor Malarek, head of *The Globe's* team of investigative reporters. I say: "I think there's a tremendously important story out there that no one's covering yet. Would you be willing to meet me about this?" He says: "How about this afternoon?" Now I'm in his office.

In the almost two months since September 11 I'd believed — it seems incredible in retrospect that I could be so naïve — that teams of investigative reporters from major media outlets would be hard at work (but quietly, in light of the patriotic hysteria) chasing down the reason the US Air Force went AWOL and other huge anomalies of that day. I'd been waiting, first in excited anticipation, then with growing unease, for the *Washington Post, The New York Times* or one of the American TV networks to break the story wide open. Now I feel a responsibility to find out whether "Canada's National Newspaper" is onto this and if not, to encourage it to go after this incredible story and get the world scoop that the American media are blowing. Victor and I know each other from the more than eight years I worked for *The Globe and Mail*.

I begin by saying: "I know I'm widely identified as a left winger, and that what I'm about to say may seem preposterous, but I hope you respect my body of journalistic work and know I would not waste your time." He assures me I have his full respect and attention. I tell him I've had suspicions about 9/11 from day one, and am seeing more and more evidence from sources I trust on the internet confirming my suspicions. I give him a few printouts from Stan Goff, Jared Israel and Michael Ruppert. He seems genuinely interested, gives me an hour and 20 minutes, and takes a few notes (I wondered later at how few). As I leave he says: "I think you're onto something. We should be looking into this. I'm going to speak to our team about it."

I had asked if I could send him limited amounts of additional material. He said he would welcome that. Subsequently I mailed him two packets of printouts of some of the most solid evidence about 9/11 anomalies. As I revisit this diary in January 2006, four years and two months later, I can report that I never heard another word from him. *The Globe and Mail,* along with every other mainstream medium in the world, has failed to "break" what is probably the most important story of our time.

* * *

Diary of 9/11 and the Media

The Birth of the Leading 9/11 Truth Magazine and a National Movement

Toronto City Hall, the evening of November 20, 2001 — The city government's "clamshell" central chamber, lying between the two semi-circular towers, is jammed. People line the walls. It's a citizen-organized public meeting focused on the erosion of civil liberties endangered by new "anti-terrorism" laws being rushed through the Canadian Parliament (as well as most others in the "Western world"). I've been asked to moderate. The discussion is lively, impassioned and intelligent. Leading lawyers, civil libertarians, representatives of Muslim communities and others share their concerns.

From a 9/11 Truth point of view, two things stand out in my mind. One is that I'm sorely tempted to use the podium to ask for a show of hands as to who in attendance thinks there was something fishy about the events of 9/11. I decide it wouldn't be fair to the organizers of the meeting, who had established a clear focus. I did not have a mandate to introduce a potentially explosive question. The other thing that stands out is that I meet others who already believe as I do. One is Ian Woods from Shanty Bay, Ontario (profiled on page 354). He hands out about 150 leaflets asking "Was September 11 an Inside Job?" On the reverse side are listed several contradictions about 9/11.

It was very reinforcing to find someone else whose take on 9/11 was identical to mine and who was already getting active about it. In autumn 2002, Ian founds *Global Outlook: The Magazine of 9/11 Truth.* This becomes an international journal with a circulation of 15,000. As of early 2006, it's going into its 11th issue. The 10th issue is 100 pages. In a doorway I encounter Jean Smith and John Valleau, longtime citizen activists. He's a chemistry professor emeritus, she a retired teacher. I ask them, a bit apologetically and quizzically, in the way that was required at that time, if they think there was "anything fishy about September 11." "Oh sure," they respond almost in unison. "The White House did it." (Later, they would become strong supporters of the six-day Toronto International

City Hall, Toronto, Canada

Citizens' Inquiry Into 9/11, not yet a gleam in anyone's eye. I proposed the Inquiry in October of 2003, became the director in December and it was held at The University of Toronto at the end of May 2004, with 40 presenters from three continents.)

Starting in late 2001, about a dozen like-minded individuals begin meeting informally to plan actions to reveal 9/11Truth. In addition to the Inquiry we mount several well-attended events at the Bloor Cinema. By the end of 2003, we have incorporated as Skeptics' Inquiry For Truth (SIFT), and at the time of writing, Ian remains president.

That evening at Toronto City Hall, we realized later, marked the birth of the Canadian 9/11Truth movement in Canada.

✳ ✳ ✳

Diary of 9/11 and the Media

A Television Series Questioning the Official 9/11 Story is Conceived

December 20, 2001 — Today, at the weekly *Vision TV* in-house producers' meeting, I blurt out my grave suspicions about the official story of 9/11 and that I want to do a series of six commentaries questioning that official story.

A few weeks ago I came to realize, very belatedly, that the mainstream media are dead in the water on this issue. Also belated was the realization I could launch such questioning myself, on my own half-hour weekly program, *Vision TV Insight: The MediaFile Edition*. Defending my own slowness, now, I think: why should I have dreamed this task should fall to a tiny crew on a Canadian specialty channel? This is the job of big newspapers and big networks with vast resources.

Vision TV is not a news channel. It is Canada's and the world's first and only multi-faith TV network, available in 8 million Canadian households on basic cable and DTH satellite. *Vision* has been unique in Canada, from its inception in September 1988, in featuring regular media criticism. I've been privileged to be the channel's media critic all that time.

Once it became clear to me that I have a responsibility to initiate something, I wonder how to pitch it to my fellow producers so as to minimize the risk of my proposal getting the kibosh. For a few weeks I planned my approach but failed to come up with one I was satisfied with. Today I think: blurt it out and take your chances.

The result is interesting, and soon, thank goodness, successful. One producer says the reason the US Air Force failed to respond on 9/11 was that "the pilots hadn't had their coffee that morning." She feels one commentary should be more than enough. But reaction is generally supportive. "Go for it, Barrie" is the consensus. The senior producer, a Muslim, decides: "Let's agree to three and see how it goes." I'm elated. The series begins in January and does go to six.

* * *

Diary of 9/11 and the Media
"Important — If True"

December 24, 2001 — Say you're back in the 1770s in the American colonies. You're fighting a war of independence against Britain. The British Empire is *the* world empire of the day. But for news from Europe, your colonial newspapers rely on dispatches from untrustworthy London, seat of the empire. So your pro-independence colonial newspaper editors keep on hand a "standing line" of type that they place atop certain stories. It reads: "Important — If True."

Fast forward to the Osama bin Laden videotape unleashed December 16 in Washington, DC, seat of *the* world empire of today. It consists of images stated to be bin Laden and his buddies, yukking it up semi-audibly about death and destruction, praise be to Allah, etc. Most media immediately accept the tape as authentic.

The *Toronto Sun,* that bastion of judicial restraint, accepts the evidence and pronounces the verdict in Second Coming of Christ-size type: "Guilty Bastard." The Canadian Broadcasting Corporation's polysyllabic contrarian Rex Murphy, a scourge of government duplicity, accepts the tape — hook, story line and sound track. Well, call me the Question Man here. Because I have lots of questions about that tape.

How can a man be videotaped for hours, yet we seldom see his lips move? Previous videotapes of him were quite different in this respect.

Some speculate bin Laden had the tape made to impress powerful clerics in Saudi Arabia. Considering he's a multi-millionaire with proven access to high-quality video gear, why would he rely on amateurs using low-grade equipment producing much inaudible audio? Are Muslim clerics impressed by bad audio and video?

If this is such a damning piece of evidence, why have the Pentagon and White House not produced the person who found it? Why have they not hosted a tour to the apartment in Jalalabad where that person could say: "I found it right here, in this drawer with the socks." Who did find it? When did the person realize it was the tape it's claimed to be? Why was the tape released just as George Bush announced he'll scrap the ABM treaty, which gets pushed off the front pages? For this.

No medium provides satisfying details. We're told details can't be revealed for security reasons. What are these reasons? The Pentagon and White House want everyone on Earth to know about the tape. Is the security to prevent Martians from finding out details? A true believer in the Boy Scout honesty of the Pentagon and White House may find no reason to be skeptical. But the media are not supposed to be true believers. They're supposed to be true skeptics.

So I have another question. Why did the mainstream media not perform their skeptical duties? Only one that I saw did. Thomas Walkom in the *Toronto Star* writes: "We are told that while some lunatic Muslims may think the tape was faked, anyone who is not a paranoid conspiracy theorist knows that it proves bin Laden's guilt. But is it inconceivable," Walkom continues, "that the bin Laden tape was doctored? Would a government that once contemplated blowing up Fidel Castro with an exploding cigar balk at faking a video? Would a government that during the Vietnam War concocted a fake attack on one of its [own] naval vessels in order to justify an escalated military campaign, be squeamish about doing a little digital wizardry? To ask these questions is to answer them."

Remember the Hollywood movie *Wag the Dog?* An American president orders the concoction of a whole illusory video war. One with high production values. A shoot involving a single murky interior is considerably less demanding. There are scores more questions. Those arising, for instance, from the long and close relationship of the bin Laden and Bush families are now conveniently dispatched down the memory hole.

Let's go back to where we started. In this age of digital video manipulation you can make a dog say "It's History 101, remember?" Maybe something very low-tech might be brought back. News editors, when they decide to print or air stories about politically-potent tapes with murky origins, might position the reminder "Important — If True" at the top of the story or screen.

The foregoing is an unedited transcript of my Vision TV commentary of this date. I should have mentioned that in an initial, earlier, audio tape said by Al-Jazeera to be Osama bin Laden, the speaker insisted he had nothing to do with 9/11.

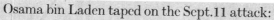

Osama bin Laden taped on the Sept. 11 attack:

'They were overjoyed when the first plane hit the building, so I said to them: Be patient'

TERROR TALK: Osama bin Laden, left, is seen in this TV photo of an amateur video released yesterday by the Pentagon.

No doubt that he's the mastermind, Powell says

By WILLIAM WALKER
WASHINGTON BUREAU

WASHINGTON — With a chilling grin of self-satisfaction, Osama bin Laden raises his hand and mocks the image of a jumbo jet slamming into the World Trade Center.

With that, the world finally had a chance to view first hand the videotape President George W. Bush hopes will lay to rest any doubts that the Al Qaeda leader masterminded the Sept. 11 terrorist attacks.

The men sitting with bin Laden on pillows are rapt. Even the chatty Saudi sheik who had been in danger of mo

nopolizing the conversation falls silent as bin Laden speaks, at least for a bit. "This event made people think," bin Laden says, "which benefited Islam greatly."

Describing the reaction of a roomful of his followers on Sept. 11, bin Laden says: "They were overjoyed when the first plane hit the building, so I said to them: Be patient.

"The difference between the first and the second plane hitting the towers was 20 minutes. And the difference between the first plane and the plane that hit the Pentagon was one hour."

The hour-long tape, dated Nov. 9, sparked a wide range of global reaction yesterday after it showed bin Laden extolling the fact the death toll exceeded even his most optimistic hopes.

"We calculated in advance the number of casualties from the enemy who would be killed based on the position of the jumbo jet striking the World Trade Center," bin Laden says in Arabic, translated into English by both

War on Terrorism

■ Full transcript of the tape, A2-3
■ Al Qaeda surrounded, A12
■ PM defends Ralston Saul, A14
■ Experts: Tape authentic, A20
■ Shock and skepticism, A21
■ Chantal Hébert, A33

Pentagon and four outside expert translators.

"We calculated that the floors that would be hit (by the plane) would be three or four floors. I was the most optimistic of them all."

Key information the tape reveals about the attacks, which killed almost 3,300 people, includes:

■ They were more destructive than bin Laden thought they would be. He believed only the floors of the World Trade Center towers above the point of impact would collapse, not the entire

buildings. "This was all we had hoped for," he says.

■ He believed the success of the attacks would bring more worldwide converts to Islam.

■ He was notified by his Al Qaeda operatives in America on the Thursday before the attacks that they would occur Tuesday, Sept. 11.

■ That on that day, he listened eagerly on radio for reports of the strikes, including radio from Washington.

■ That his supporters were "overjoyed" when the news of the first World Trade Center tower being struck was heard.

■ That the hijackers knew only they were involved in a "martyrdom operation" but not much else, not even who the hijack pilots were.

"How can there be any doubt, any doubt, in anyone's mind any longer that he was the mastermind?" U.S. Secretary of State Colin Powell said.

The White House and Pentagon went

➤ Please see Pentagon, A20

Diary of 9/11 and the Media ⌇⌁

The TV Series is Born and Surprises Everyone

January 15, 2002 — The morning after first commentary. The senior producer tells me later she almost sick to her stomach with fear as she checks her e-mail for response from the previous evening's MediaFile program. "The first comment was positive," she said. "I thought to myself: 'Well, at least we will have one lone positive reaction.'" The surprise for her and everyone, including me, is that the reaction after this first commentary is overwhelmingly positive — in fact, of the nearly 100 initial e-mails, precisely *one* is derogatory.

This pattern continues through the 6 weeks of the series, which attracts the largest audience response in the 15-year history of the channel. (By the end of the series more than 1,000 e-mails were received; I have hard copies of them, which occupy a foot of space in a filing cabinet drawer. Although each and every one is different, this is typical: "Thank goodness for a TV channel that will tell it like it is. Keep up the good work.")

This pattern of viewer, listener and reader response to questioning of the official 9/11 story has been universal ever since 9/11, on those few occasions when media have raised questions. The huge questioning constituency among Joe and Jane Public has always been there.

But flying in the face of that, flying in the face of "giving what the readers, viewers and listeners want," the media have instead almost completely ignored or scorned the evidence the public sees or senses, rather than displaying editorial independence and courage.

As we move toward June 2006 there are signs around the edges of the mainstream media — a five-minute interview here, a few fugitive paragraphs there — that this questioning, and the existence of growing numbers of questioners, won't go away and could eventually become very big.

If it does, it will be interesting to see how these same media will explain (if they deign to do so) their five years of deadly slumber that enabled illegal wars, tens of thousands of deaths, stripping away of civil liberties, and squandering of obscene amounts on armaments — all done in the name of the so-called "war on terror" with 9/11 being the linchpin for it all, and the media by and large being spear carriers for the emperor.

1

Your Sunday Puzzle — Three Amazing Secrets About 9/11

The process [of doublethink] has to be conscious, or it would not be carried out with sufficient precision, but it also has to be unconscious, or it would bring with it a feeling of falsity and hence of guilt .... To tell deliberate lies while genuinely believing in them, to forget any fact that has become inconvenient, and then, when it becomes necessary again, to draw it back from oblivion for just so long as it is needed, to deny the existence of objective reality and all the while to take account of the reality which one denies — all this is indispensably necessary.

— George Orwell, *1984*

AUGUST 22, 2005 — This morning I submit an article "on spec" to Peter Scowen, editor of the "Ideas" section of *Sunday*, the Sunday edition of Canada's largest-circulation newspaper, the *Toronto Star*.

The focus of the article, 9/11, is timely. It's 20 days before the fourth anniversary of the event, and it happens to fall on a Sunday, which won't happen again until 2011. At 4,500 words the article is within the range *Sunday* publishes.

While writing the article I enlisted the help of distinguished writer colleagues more than I usually do. Several are more accomplished writers than I am. They contributed improvements.[1] They all praised the article in its near final form.

Scowen's response is as promising as it is prompt:

From: Scowen, Peter
To: Barrie Zwicker
Sent: Monday, August 22, 2005 11:25AM
Subject: RE: Proposed article for *Sunday*'s Sept. 11 issue

Barrie,
Thanks for this. I'm blown away. I need to run this by several other people to get their take on it. And then I will have some questions and suggestions.
I think the strength of it is that you focus on the reasons for the media avoiding so-called conspiracy theories, and not on the conspiracies themselves.
I will be in touch.
Peter

I'm not going to spill the beans and divulge here whether *Sunday* published the article that follows (unedited; exactly as submitted). I want you first to read it and decide, were you the "Ideas" editor of a Sunday paper, whether you would publish it.

The 3 Biggest Secrets About 9/11

By Barrie Zwicker

On the fourth anniversary of 9/11, three amazing secrets about the official version of what really happened that history-changing day lie relatively unexamined in the public domain.

Secret #1 is the size of the constituency of disbelievers in the official story. It's huge, as I am confident will be further proven by reader response should *Sunday* choose to publish this article.

Secret #2 is the body of evidence and questions upon which the constituency of disbelievers is built.

Secret #3 is why mainstream media, with honourable exceptions, including some examples from this newspaper, have almost entirely steered clear of this evidence, when it is easily accessible.

In the conventional field of judgment about 9/11, those who question the official version are typically dismissed as believing in "conspiracy theories." But the official story, as concretized in the *Final Report of the National Commission on Terrorist Attacks Upon the United States, Authorized Edition*, is also a conspiracy theory. It is one not investigated but rather assumed *a priori* by the Commission: that 19 fanatical Arabs, organized by a small group of co-conspirators, Osama bin Laden being the most notorious, planned and executed the entire operation.

According to this conspiracy theory (nothing has been proven) the Al Qaeda conspirators caught the whole of the US intelligence, military, political and diplomatic establishments off guard to the extent that they were unable to prevent or even ameliorate the events.

Within this a secondary narrative emerged from official and unofficial sources in the months following. This can be called "the incompetence theory." It is again a theory because no one to date has been charged with incompetence. (*9/11 Commission Report*, page xvi: "Our aim has not been to assign individual blame.")

According to the incompetence theory there were warnings. There are two variations on the number and severity of the warnings. One variation (main proponent, Condoleezza Rice, who said "no one could have guessed" that planes would be used as weapons) is that the warnings were insufficient to enable prevention or amelioration of the events. The other variation is that the warnings should have been sufficient ("the system was blinking red," CIA director George Tenet testified) but there were "failures."

Either way, the nub of the official story stands. The official story permits no other interpretation than that the USA was attacked by its enemies. All discussions about whether a history of bloody US foreign policy, unacknowledged by most, was the motivation (the view of Noam Chomsky), whether Islam is a peaceful religion but a few evil-doers pervert it (see op ed pages everywhere), whether Canada is "a haven for terrorists," "how to balance civil liberties while fighting terror," and many others, are beside the point. Those on both sides of all such discussions accept the framing of the official story. And this is exactly the story, I submit, huge numbers of people do not accept and many have not accepted for a long time, even going back to the very day of the events.

One group that does not accept the official story sees evidence of a darker theory, now abbreviated as LIHOP, standing for Let It Happen On Purpose. This theory posits that when those atop the US power structure learned of the planned attack, they saw it would suit their agenda and let the plotters go ahead.

Another group, count me in, sees abundant evidence of the darkest scenario of all: that 9/11 was an inside job, a false flag operation, "Reichstag Fire 2001" executed by a network of covert agents under orders from the neocons, those whom Bill Moyers of PBS calls "the shadow government." To us it appears clearly to be the most brazen of dozens of similar iconic events through history calculated to stampede public opinion into support of the rulers' agenda — in this case resource theft and global domination. In this scenario, such Arabs as were involved were patsies, dupes.

Where do we obtain our information? From original research, from the books referred to in this article and others, through DVDs and videos, from Internet sites, periodicals such as Canada's *Global Outlook* (current issue, 100 pages, *www.globaloutlook.ca*), from isolated stories, occasional columns and fugitive paragraphs in the mainstream media, and from face-to-face and email conversations and public meetings (such as one at 4 p.m. today at the Bloor Cinema).

Secret #1

Consider some evidence about the size of the "secret" constituency I assert exists.

On May 11, 2003, the *Sunday Star* published a column by Michele Landsberg headed "Conspiracy crusader doubts official 9/11 version." That "conspiracy crusader" was me. After Ms. Landsberg examined some clanging anomalies surrounding the official story of 9/11, she concluded: "And if you call him a conspiracy theorist, call me one, too, because I agree with Zwicker when he says, 'I don't know exactly what happened, but something smells very fishy.' Even [fishier] is the refusal of most

Canadian journalists to ask ... questions about one of the worst catastrophes of our time."

"Last January, I wrote a column about American declassified documents that verify a long history of top-level conspiracies," Ms. Landsberg wrote. "The US government, its military and its secret service have plotted to justify wars and impose their control on other countries through intricate secret schemes of drug-running, gun smuggling and assassination. They even considered rigging fake terrorist attacks that would cost American lives in order to stir the public to war-ready outrage. Immediately, I was deluged with hundreds upon hundreds of approving e-mails from American citizens. Some of them praised the TV work of Barrie Zwicker — a *Globe and Mail* colleague of my youth." So back in early 2003 this constituency was already large, as suggested in the pages of this paper by one of its most respected columnists.

In dozens of speaking engagements in Canada, the USA and Europe, I've found belief in the official story a mile wide and an inch deep. Speaking to an audience of 200 in Denver, Colorado last November [2004], I asked how many people believe the official story. Not a single hand went up. It was not the first or last time.

But these are public occasions where the audience is self selected. Is there better proof? Would polls count? Although the Canadian poll reported below is the only one so far taken in North America that has dared to include the "inside job" option for responders, there's a clear pattern to the polls. A few of them:

On April 17, 2002 when the *Atlanta Journal-Constitution* asked "Are you satisfied the Bush administration had no advanced warning of the Sept. 11 attacks?" 46 percent of responders chose "No, I think officials knew it was coming." In other words, let it happen on purpose (LIHOP).

On July 23, 2003 a Reuters report datelined Berlin reported "Almost one in three Germans below the age of 30 believes the US government may have sponsored the September 11, 2001, attacks on New York and Washington." (Inside Job.)

Here in Canada in May 2004 Maritz Research reported 63% of respondents strongly or somewhat agreed "Individuals within the US government including the White House had prior knowledge of the plans for the events of September 11 and failed to take appropriate action to stop them." (LIHOP.) Sixteen per cent strongly or somewhat agreed "Individuals within the US government including the White House were involved in the planning and execution of the events of September 11." (Inside Job.) In the interests of full disclosure I must mention the Maritz poll was commissioned by the International Citizens' Inquiry Into 9/11, Phase 2, held at The University of Toronto in May 2004. I was the director of the Inquiry.

In a Zogby International poll conducted Aug. 24-26, 2004 on the eve of the Republican National Convention, 50% of New York City residents said some US leaders "knew in advance that attacks were planned on or around September 11, 2001, and that they consciously failed to act." (LIHOP.)

On Nov. 11, 2004 CNN conducted an online poll asking "Do you believe there is a US government cover-up surrounding 9/11?" Of the 10,641 responses, 89% were yes and 11% no.

True, internet polls are unscientific. But they should be taken together with a great deal of anecdotal evidence and another category of evidence: large sales of books contradicting the official theory. These sales (some figures are reported below) are all the more impressive in that the books involved have been almost totally ignored by the book review sections of the mainstream media.

Secret #2

The second secret is the compelling body of evidence which so dramatically and widely undermines belief in the official theory in the minds of so many. Consider just ten of these puzzling anomalies concerning the official story:

1. How could it be that during a drama in the skies lasting almost two hours not a single US jet interceptor turned a wheel until it was too late? It's a matter of historical record.

2. Why did the Secret Service not whisk George Bush out of that school classroom moments after Andrew Card, his chief of staff, informed him: "A second tower has been hit. America is under attack"? Instead the Commander in Chief continues reading a story about a pet goat for at least eight minutes and it's half an hour later he's taken from

the school to Air Force One which takes off unaccompanied by any fighter escort. Lots of people can imagine Bush didn't know what to do, but are we expected to believe the Secret Service did not? Its mission is to protect the president. His whereabouts were well known; he could have been the main target for the alleged foreign terrorists.

3. Why did George Bush claim twice, on the record, that while waiting to go into that classroom he saw, on ordinary television, the first plane hit? The footage of that event, taken by a French documentary film crew that happened to be in New York City, was not aired on ordinary television until the next day, Sept. 12, 2001.

4. At 5:25 p.m. on Sept. 11, 2001, World Trade Centre Building 7, a 47-storey structural steel edifice only very slightly damaged by the events of earlier that day, suddenly collapsed. How could this be? Why, on a PBS documentary titled "America Rebuilds" would Larry Silverstein, who had leased the WTC complex a few months before 9/11, state that he agreed to "pull" the building. "Pull" is an industry term for "demolish." Controlled demolitions of large buildings take weeks to prepare. Interestingly, Building 7 contained large CIA and Secret Service offices.

5. Why was all the steel from the WTC towers rushed away on freighters to India and China to be melted down, when an examination of that steel would show whether it had been exposed to demolition explosives, and when it's a federal offense to remove evidence from a crime scene?

6. How could a Boeing 757 have hit the Pentagon when all pictures of the Pentagon after the event showed a hole much smaller than would be made by a 757? Where were the huge amounts of wreckage there should have been, and why — except for five frames showing an explosion — have videotapes of this event seized by the FBI not been released to this day?

7. Why did the White House resist calls for an independent investigation into 9/11 for more than a year, until families of victims made such a fuss that it became politically impossible to refuse?

8. Why did George Bush initially refuse to testify before the supposedly-independent 9/11 commission, then agree only if he could do so in the Oval Office with him not under oath, accompanied by Dick Cheney, with no opening statement, no tape recorders or transcript allowed

Event	Number of days after event that an independent investigation was ordered:
Sinking of the Titanic	6
JFK assassination	7
Challenger disaster	7
Pearl Harbor attack	9
Events of 9/11	441

and with everyone present taking notes having to submit them to security personnel?

9. Would Osama bin Laden have the power to neutralize the US Air Force, make George Bush say odd things about what he saw on television, demolish a high rise building late on the day of 9/11, cause the White House to drag its feet so dramatically on an independent investigation or cause the 9/11 Commission to omit embarrassing connections between the Bush and bin Laden families?

10. Why did the 9/11 Commission also omit to mention scores of other relevancies? For instance that some of the alleged hijackers, such as Mohamed Atta, did not behave like devout Muslims; that alleged hijacker pilot Hani Hanjour did not have the piloting skills to fly flight 77 the way it allegedly flew; Larry Silverstein's statement about WTC building 7; advance warnings evidently received by Attorney General Ashcroft, San Francisco Mayor Willie Brown and several Pentagon officials; FBI agent Robert Wright's serious allegations about obstruction at FBI headquarters; Minneapolis agent Collen Rowley's accusation of sabotage by FBI headquarters in the Moussaoui case; all of the damning details presented by FBI employee Sibel Edmonds during her 3½ hours of testimony, and the statement made by the neocons' Project for a New American Century (PNAC) in its September 2000 paper *Rebuilding America's Defenses* that the American public would not likely support the military buildup PNAC was calling for "absent a catastrophic and catalyzing event — like a New Pearl Harbor."[2]

Those of us who reject any versions of the official story, including incompetence, do not believe the 9/11 ball is in our court. We believe the onus is on those who cling to the official theory to respond to these ten and numerous other deeply troubling questions.

The evidence that elements of the US government were complicit in 9/11 is, frankly, overwhelming. It can be found in the growing number of well-referenced books by authors with excellent bona fides. The first of these books appeared in 2002. The most respected include: two superb volumes by California philosopher and theologian David Ray Griffin, *The New Pearl Harbor: Disturbing Questions about the Bush Administration and 9/11* and *The 9/11 Commission Report: Omissions and Distortions* (both published by Olive Branch Press, www.interlinkbooks.com), Michael C. Ruppert's *Crossing the Rubicon: The Decline of the American Empire at the End of the Age of Oil* (New Society Publishers, Gabriola Island, B.C., www.newsociety.com) and two titles by Nafeez Mosaddeq Ahmed, *The War on Freedom: How and Why America was Attacked September 11th, 2001* (Tree of Life Publications) and his follow-up study *The War on Truth: 9/11, Disinformation, and the Anatomy of Terrorism* (Olive Branch Press).

Two other titles of significance, exhaustively researched, are *The Terror Timeline: Year by Year, Day by Day, Minute by Minute* by Paul Thompson and the Center for Cooperative Research (HarperCollins, www.reganbooks.com) and *9/11 Synthetic Terror: Made in USA* by Webster G. Tarpley (Progressive Press, www.progressivebooks.com). *The Terror Timeline* is based entirely on excruciatingly-referenced reports published in the mainstream press. Taken together, these mainstream media reports cast serious doubt, to say the least, on much if not most of the official 9/11 story.

And these books, taken together, blow the official story out of the water.

Secret #3

This is a secret, or puzzle, foremost in the minds of this huge constituency of skeptics. It's reflected in questions I'm repeatedly asked at public meetings. "Why are the mainstream media closing their eyes to all the evidence? Why are they refusing to review the books? Why aren't they covering this meeting? Why are they censoring all the hard questions?

Why don't we see our views reflected in the mainstream media? Why aren't the media telling the people the truth?"

As a media critic for 35 years, I recognize this is a challenging bundle of questions. For instance, it is curious on the surface that the book editors at mainstream media outlets would overwhelmingly choose not to review *The Terror Timeline*. All but 83 of its 594 pages are directly-quoted news reports. You'd think newspapers would commission a reviewer who would have to point out that this book reveals that a judicious selection of information published in the mainstream about 9/11 adds up to an expose: the official story is full of contradictions, absurdities and impossibilities, thereby proving that mainstream media are in fact doing their job of speaking truth to power.

But a search of the Internet fails to turn up a single mainstream review. Why the big chill on this particular book? A clue may be found in British philosopher Bertrand Russell's 1967 book *War Crimes in Vietnam*. The first chapter is "The Press and Vietnam." The first paragraph reads: "The role of the Western press in the Vietnam controversy has been important and revealing. It is from Western newspapers that I derived my earliest understandings of the involvement of the United States, and it is from these same reports that I first became aware of the barbarous character of the war." So far, so good — for the media.

But then Russell continues: "I was soon to discover that although some newspapers were prepared to publish isolated pieces of horrifying information, they had no intention of forming a coherent picture of the war from these reports — and every intention of preventing others from doing so."

In other words, when a coherent picture — surely what readers, viewers and listeners want — is needed on a really controversial topic, something as huge as the Vietnam War, the assassination of John F. Kennedy or in this case 9/11, the media buy quickly into the initial official version (dominoes will fall, lone gunman, 19 crazed Arabs) issued by officialdom. Tons of images and verbiage follow. All new information is interpreted within the framework of the initial official story. The picture rapidly fills in. Contradictory facts and interpretations begin to be sidelined or dismissed altogether; like light trapped in a black hole, they're not allowed to escape. The investment of the media in the official story becomes too large to abandon, even when alarming contradictions — even books full of them — surface.

David Ray Griffin's *New Pearl Harbor* has been reviewed to his knowledge by only two daily newspapers in the English-speaking world, *The Vancouver Sun* and the conservative *Daily Mail* of London. Douglas Todd, the *Sun*'s religion specialist, wrote: "So why did this soft-spoken professor from the high-ranking Methodist-rooted School of Theology at Claremont, Calif., feel it necessary to risk his hard-earned reputation as a religion scholar to write one of the most incredible — in all senses of the word — political books of 2004? Because no one else in mainstream America seemed prepared to do it .... The result? Griffin's book has already sold an astonishing 80,000 copies despite receiving virtually no reviews in North America's mainstream media. That's unlike in Britain, where he's had solid coverage, including a three-page spread in London's mass-circulation *Daily Mail*."

Todd, like anyone trying to write about the gaping holes in the official 9/11 story, cannot evade the apparent mystery of the mainstream boycott of the topic. Griffin's second book has not been reviewed at all. (Recently the *Daily Mail*, an exception among newspapers that seems to prove the rule of *de facto* censorship of 9/11 skepticism, published a fair review of the just-released book *9/11 Revealed: Challenging Facts behind the War on Terror* by Ian Henshall and Rowland Morgan. The review runs 4,400 words, the length of this article.)

Author Nafeez M. Ahmed reports that *War on Freedom*, the first of his two books, "within about a month after its release in July 2002, became an instant underground bestseller, rocketing to the top several hundred of Amazon.com, and fluctuating occasionally within the top hundred. Later on in the year, the book was translated and published in German and Italian, again reaching bestseller status. There were a number of mainstream media reviews in Germany and Italy from some of the daily broadsheets; the most prominent being a review article by Gore Vidal in Rome's *la Repubblica*. Vidal's piece was also published in English by our major British newspaper, *The Observer*. *The Observer* was the only major mainstream media outlet in the Anglo-American market to discuss the book. In Canada, a short review appeared in *Now* magazine (Toronto). But otherwise, there were only reviews in small and/or alternative publications."

As for his second book, *The War on Truth*, out in July, "there has been dead silence from the entire mainstream media apparatus, both in the US and here in the UK. This is perhaps not surprising given that for the first time, *The War on Truth* explores in detail the *modus operandi* of the manipulation and subversion of Al Qaeda in the Middle East, Central Asia, Asia-Pacific, Caucasus, and Balkans. Al Qaeda is found to be the outgrowth of a coordinated network of highly secret sub-units of state-intelligence services operating under the overarching strategic direction of the most clandestine parallel structures of western military-intelligence services, especially those of the US and UK. Clearly, that kind of conclusion is not commensurate with the official narrative."

Michael C. Ruppert reports that *Crossing the Rubicon* "has sold approximately 50,000 copies and is one of the best-selling books about 9/11 after the Kean Commission report. It has never been reviewed by ANY major media anywhere." (This includes Canada, the country of publication.) "In fact, it has been diligently and stridently ignored."

Finally, Webster Tarpley reports of *9/11 Synthetic Terror* simply: "I am not aware of any book reviews in major mainstream media."

The underlying reasons for the generalized mainstream media blackout on information known to millions of people are several, intertwined, often subtle, and complicated, the outcome of a unified amalgam of mutually-reinforcing factors.

Journalists are not outside the over-arching sense of reality shared by most people from acculturation and education — life experience. This is and always has been largely determined by the church, various forms of government, and in our day, corporate culture. And what is the "reality" of world events? Nowadays more than ever it is synthetic, fashioned in each person's brain heavily from indirect inputs, especially from the instantaneous global "infosphere."

Amateur media critics frequently bemoan, as they see it, "establishment propaganda" pouring out of the newsrooms. These critics overlook that this stream pours *into* newsrooms, that journalists must cope with it, that it has its cumulative effect. The content of much of the text and images making up the infosphere is determined by corporations and governments.

Much overlooked to our peril is that there's an 800-pound gorilla in our synthetic perceptual environment: the increasing "invention of reality" by covert agents working for "invisible governments." The ultimate is what Bakunin called "the propaganda of the act." Recall Ms. Landsberg's words.

This undeniable aspect of the reality of our world is dangerously under-reported, even as clandestine operations, by definition undemocratic and deceitful in the extreme, receive ever more funding. In *9/11 Synthetic Terror* Webster Tarpley claims reality today is "over-determined" by fake events. One example is the incubator baby murders allegedly carried out by Iraqi soldiers during Iraq's 1990 invasion of Kuwait. The mainstream media uncritically bought, and the world believed, emotional testimony about babies being "thrown on the cold concrete floor to die," delivered in a Washington, DC Congressional hearing room by a 15-year-old Kuwaiti girl who "could not be identified for fear of reprisals." The testimony helped sway the US public in favour of land war against Iraq, Operation Desert Storm. But the CBC's investigative program *the fifth estate* later revealed the girl to be the daughter of the Kuwaiti ambassador to the US, coached in acting by the giant US public relations firm Hill & Knowlton. It was a $10-million joint White House-Kuwaiti conspiracy of deception, *the fifth estate* proved.

Many "terrorist" events, sure to garner headlines all over the world, are similarly "false flag" operations, Tarpley writes, based on his 30 years of study of the Red Brigades, the Baader-Meinhof group and Al Qaeda. Tarpley is not alone in asserting that "international terrorism" — including 9/11 — is overwhelmingly the product of Western intelligence agencies. He provides considerable detail on the roles of patsies and fall-guys, networks of moles inside governments and the media, assassinations and mass murders carried out by the "anonymous cold technicians of death" who actually carry out, for the "invisible governments," the atrocities the public sees.

Within the media there's a natural tendency to turn away from consideration that corruption that profound and that high up, deception that brazen, intentions that murderous, could exist. I've heard otherwise well-informed journalists say "I just don't want to go there." Then there's the study required to follow the money or the contradictions, to look into this abyss. There's the fear of being wrong: "If all the other papers haven't tackled this kind of thing head on, they must have a reason." Everybody thinks that and does nothing.

Fears of stepping out of line, being laughed at, losing out on a promotion, facing a demotion, being seen as "a conspiracy nut." On and on go the interlaced fears, none the less real for sometimes being half-conscious or totally unacknowledged.

The culmination of this process of denial was succinctly expressed by a person overheard by US social critic Steve Bhaerman: "Well, that may be true, but I don't believe it." Believe. Belief systems. The battlefield on which the struggle for our survival, or not, is taking place.

The stakes could hardly be higher. The official story of 9/11 is the linchpin for the so-called "war on terror," being sold 24/7 as the imperative reality of our time. The "war on terror" has replaced the Cold War template as the justification for the escalation of already obscene squandering of Earth's precious resources on militarism, the gutting or endangerment of every worthy goal from social equity to social justice to civil liberties, peace and the very survival of the life support system of our planet.

At the same time the so-called "war on terror" is transparently self-serving for those who promote it. It reaps profits for the arms and security industries, bestows power on the "intelligence community," the "counter terrorism experts" and the military, and boosts poll numbers for politicians. Spikes in George Bush's popularity track "terrorist" incidents exactly. "Terrorist events," and warnings of them, are his main source of political strength. Unlike Franklin Delano Roosevelt, who said "We have nothing to fear but fear itself," George Bush and those behind him traffic in fear. "Fighting the terrorists" is the only issue on which the majority of voters fall in line behind the US president.

The "war on terror" is really a war *of* terror against domestic populations. Everything harks back to "remember 9/11." What could be more important than to have mainstream media lead an extended critical public analysis of the official story?

I await the results of the editors' decision whether to publish this article with trepidation. If it's published, I'll await the comments of readers with confidence.

Award-winning journalist Barrie Zwicker was director of the International Citizens' Inquiry Into 9/11, Phase 2, held in Toronto in May 2004. He is writing a book, 9/11: The Media, and Our Future.[3]

✂⟋⟍

This article was rejected.

The decision was ironic, since right off the top, *Sunday*'s "Ideas" editor Peter Scowen found the main strength of the article was that it included "reasons the media avoid" articles like this.

I'll be the first to admit this article can be improved. Almost all writers find in retrospect their work can be improved. On the other hand, it was the best effort of a person who has earned his living in journalism for 55 years, including a year as education editor of the *Toronto Star*.

The rejection sheds light on the cover-up in mainstream media everywhere of any serious questioning of the official 9/11 narrative, from the very day of 9/11 until now, as I write this book. The official 9/11 narrative is that 19 fanatical Arabs, directed from a cave in Afghanistan, caught the whole of the US intelligence and military, the whole of US political and diplomatic establishments, and NORAD (North American Aerospace Defense Command) completely off guard. This narrative is, on the face of it, ludicrous. Only Zacarias Moussaoui has been convicted, on flimsy grounds bordering on the ludicrous. Osama bin Laden is still missing. The more one looks at the evidence, some of which is presented in the next chapter, the more obvious it becomes that the evidence points to 9/11 as an inside job, carried out by the White House to advance its agenda of resource theft, world domination and domestic control.

Sunday's rejection of this article is a case history of media cover-up of 9/11, the subtitle and focus of this book: the extent of the cover-up, the reasons for it, who's ultimately behind it, the tragic stifling of history that the cover-up accomplishes, and what we can and cannot do about it.

My presenting this article and its rejection is not sour grapes. Something much, much worse is involved — a fine paper's missed opportunity to "speak truth to power." This is a phrase of Quaker origin meaning to muster the courage to tell the truth in the face of potential adverse reaction from authorities. *Sunday*'s opportunity was perhaps historic. Because if there ever was a country, a city, a paper, an editor and timing that could create a stir over the anomalies of the official 9/11 story, it would be Canada, Toronto, *Sunday*, Peter Scowen and the fourth anniversary of 9/11.

To begin with, Canada is to the left of the USA. (Of course, what country isn't?) If Canada were a US state (there are those who say it already is in many respects, but that's another story), it would have voted against George Bush almost as overwhelmingly as did the voters in New York City, only 15% of whom voted for him in 2004. The war on Iraq? Canada stayed out of that from the beginning, with the support of 75% of Canadians.

Toronto is Canada's largest city, and progressive by Canadian standards. Torontonians enjoy a greater diversity of English-language newspapers than do citizens of any other city in North America, including New York (if you do not include Long Island's *Newsday* as a New York paper). A Torontonian can subscribe, as I do, to all four dailies: *The Globe and Mail*, the *Toronto Sun*, the *National Post*, and the *Toronto Star*.

Within Toronto, in turn, the *Star* is the most left wing paper, and has been since it's founding by "Holy Joe" Atkinson more than 100 years ago. Within the *Star* organization, *Sunday* is further to the left again, being in the hands of a separate editorial team that not infrequently publishes articles discomfiting to the establishment. Two examples: the September 4, 2005 skewering with consummate detail and fairness of Michael Ignatieff, an apologist for US exceptionalism and a "white-haired boy" being groomed as a potential future Canadian Prime Minister. On Sunday, November 27, 2005, *Sunday* published an article by Markham lawyer Paul Bigioni headed "Fascism Then. Fascism Now?" In the lengthy piece Bigioni wrote: "North America is on a fascist trajectory. We must recognize the threat for what it is, and we must change course." He commented: "By exploring the disturbing parallels between our own time and the era of overt fascism, we can avoid the same hideous mistakes." Among the parallels he sees: the "exaltation of big business," just as happened in Hitler's Germany. Also, Germany's and Italy's fascist dictatorships "were preceded by years of reactionary politics, the kind of politics that are playing out (here) today." Economic power is in fewer and fewer hands, as was the case in fascist Germany and Italy. "Economic power," he continues, "when sufficiently vast, becomes by its very nature political power. The political power of big business supported fascism in Germany and Italy."

This is nervy stuff in the context of mainstream media offerings, and brings us back to Peter Scowen, a rare media gatekeeper who let Paul

Bigioni's article through. Obviously not your average North American newspaper editor. Another thing: Scowen has written his own book entitled *Rogue Nation: The America the Rest of the World Knows.*[4] (Not to be confused with *Rogue State*, by William Blum.)

Rogue Nation documents terrorism, murder and societal destabilization inflicted for decades by forces of the US and their surrogates around the world. Two representative passages:

> No one likes a bully, especially one who hides behind empty claims of moral superiority. But that is the United States of America in the twenty-first century. (page 268) When judged by anyone other than itself, the US is seen not as the noble protector of the free world but as something of a rogue nation, mining international waters, breaching the sovereignty of foreign countries for political purposes, organizing hit squads to terrorize innocent, non-military populations, and lying to its own people about its activities. (page 119)

Scowen is a citizen of both Canada and the United States. This may help explain why his book was written, it appears, in the hope the US will become the force for good the author believes it once was and could again be. Nevertheless, a search of the Internet fails to turn up mainstream media reviews of his book.[5] Scowen has felt the chill of *de facto* censorship himself.

We still have not yet identified all the significant differences between Peter Scowen and the vast majority of his fellow ink-stained wretches. In an e-mail to me reassuring me my article was scheduled for publication, he wrote "I always get my way." I didn't take that as arrogance, but rather that he enjoyed an unusual amount of autonomy and a good working relationship with his fellow editors. Few editors have that much clout and say it.

In short, when Peter Scowen, of all editors working on all papers, received the article you've just read, three weeks before the fourth anniversary of 9/11, it was journalistically speaking a rare conjunction of the stars.[6]

Peter Scowen

DENNIS PAQUIN

But they must have been the wrong stars. There was some conventional back 'n' forth between us before Scowen took a week off in early September. By Tuesday, September 6, five days before the 9/11 anniversary, I had heard nothing for ten days. Not a good sign. I e-mailed him to say that if there still was an intention to publish, I knew of two small changes that should be made, and included them. The next day Scowen left me this voice message:

Hi Barrie. It's Peter Scowen. Well, the upside is I'm not going to run the piece this Sunday. I have been thrown very much by the New Orleans thing. [Here he is referring to the disastrous Hurricane Katrina.] Perhaps it is possible for them to be that incompetent and it's not unusual in politics for extremely incompetent politicians to be rewarded for their incompetence rather than punished or fired. I also think that you yourself are a believer in the idea that they staged this but provide no evidence of that. You do mention books that apparently show that, and I think you know … it's just that I don't think you convince anybody of your own beliefs. You do convince people of the Let It Happen On Purpose theory, and I think that could work. But I think just the way the piece is framed now and in light of New Orleans I'm not prepared to run it this Sunday. Although I think we can still talk about some kind of version of it or changes to it for the future. Alright? I'm at (416) 000-0000.

As his voice mail suggests, it was not Katrina that washed away this article. For one thing it was much too early for *Sunday,* let alone its "Ideas" section, to be looking back on Katrina, which was in its early stages. And the fourth anniversary of 9/11 was immovable. Moreover as I noted to Peter, links could be made between Katrina and 9/11, if anything adding to the attractiveness of my piece. One of the links was the contrast in George Bush's reactions to the two large events, links which, we shall see,

Scowen made. Scowen said we could "still talk." I was grateful and now looking forward to salvaging something. I responded:

> Hello Peter:
>
> Good of you to call even if the immediate word's disappointing from my point of view.
>
> Picking up on your final reference ("I think we can still talk about some kind of version of it or changes to it for the future") I'll certainly want to approach you again; already I have a couple of ideas that might make sense to you .... I still believe I have something to offer your readers on this history-changing topic that is different, well-based, interesting and important. In other words, in the tradition of the "Ideas" section.
>
> Best wishes,
>
> ---B

Almost immediately I received this e-mail:

> We will definitely talk. There is some really good stuff in your piece.
>
> Peter

September 11, 2005 — Even had I *not* known that *Sunday* on the fourth anniversary of 9/11 might have published an impressively illustrated article (the paper is outstanding graphically) questioning the official story of 9/11, that *Sunday*'s edition would have been a disappointment for me. The first section carried a desultory, repetitive and superficial feature about 9/11 widows. Summary: they support one another. Touching but unsurprising. In the opinion of a respected colleague *Sunday*'s "Ideas" section was "unreadable." It consisted of four pieces given equal play:

Insurgents, bombers, and us. This story assumes all insurgents are genuine radicals, a naïve assumption when covert actions by paid mercenary killers are rampant. (See Chapter 7.)

Tall buildings, tall target, tall ambitions. This article informs us tall buildings are still being built in spite of 9/11. Timely, but fails utterly to mention that never in the history of the world before or after 9/11 did any structural steel structure collapse due to aircraft impact, fire or a combination of the two. (See Chapter 2.)

Broken guns: A soldier's life in Iraq. A soldier's life is different than we might think. Hardly a revelation, connected less than tenuously to an anniversary of 9/11.

How the terror president blew it in Biloxi. This last piece was Scowen's. He is scathingly and sarcastically critical of George Bush for not handling Katrina the way he handled 9/11, to make maximum political hay from it. The next day I emailed Scowen to praise his "wry take on Bush, 9/11 and Katrina" and added:

> ... It still seems to me *Sunday* can land a punch on the 9/11 front. A solid peg may show itself, or if you decide to go with a version of my piece in the near future, it could be related to "the recent fourth anniversary of the events." I would enjoy the chance to meet you and discuss possibilities face to face. I'll have some adaptation in mind by then but mainly am interested in where you're willing to go. I can make myself available for an hour or two pretty well anytime, anywhere.
> Best wishes,
> ---B

No response. On September 20 I left Scowen a brief and friendly voice message saying I still hoped we could talk as he had suggested, and followed up four times. But the article, and the conversation, died there.

Why? Scowen said the article "failed to provide the evidence" to back up the Inside Job theory about 9/11, but "you do convince people of the Let It Happen On Purpose theory." Well, I wondered, wouldn't *Sunday*'s readers be interested — to say the least — in a lengthy well-illustrated article suggesting the US government *deliberately allowed the events of 9/11 to unfold as they did*? Scowen's dropping this particular journalistic ball — one he himself identified — is part of the puzzle that I try to solve in this book.

Part of the puzzle's solution must be the phenomenon, clarified by George Orwell in the quote that opens this chapter, of Doublethink. In this phenomenon — to which we all are vulnerable — we allow what we know to shift in or out of our consciousness very subtly. It's also been described as looking at something while looking away. It's not accurate to understand Doublethink as two conflicting ideas consciously held in the mind simultaneously, with one or the other chosen knowingly to suit purposes. It's far more subtle than that.

Remember: "The process has to be conscious, or it would not be carried out with sufficient precision, but it also has to be unconscious, or it would bring with it a feeling of falsity and hence of guilt ...." Orwell writes. "To tell deliberate lies while genuinely believing in them, to forget any fact that has become inconvenient, and then, when it becomes necessary again, to draw it back from oblivion for just so long as it is needed ..." "... and all the while to take account of the reality which one denies — all this is indispensably necessary."

In Chapter 3, I'll explore this phenomenon in depth. Is this essentially what was happening with Peter Scowen, and what is happening every day in newsrooms? (We don't know what reactions he got from his fellow editors about my article, but we know he has clout, and he made no reference in his voice mail to being overruled.) Maybe his book, *Rogue Nation*, contains clues. We know he knows that "joint efforts of the American government and a mainstream media overcome by fits of jingoism" imposed "a largely artificial patriotism" on the US following 9/11.[7] We know he knows that American journalists have a tendency to accept what their government tells them. An example he gives is the lies about Hiroshima that they "swallowed whole."[8] We know that he knows that information that does not enter the arena of public discussion nevertheless exists and can be important, because he uses the following quotation: "... what is unspoken is no less real, nor does it lack consequence just because it is not part of any ongoing domestic discussion."[9]

We know that he knows of huge and nasty covert operations carried out by the CIA and other agencies. His example (all of his Chapter 8) of the CIA's role in overthrowing the democratically-elected Iranian leader Mohammed Mossadegh[10] in 1953 was also published as a one-page article in the *Star*.

We know that he knows about false flag operations in which CIA agents "terrorize people and bomb their homes and make it look like someone else had done it,"[11] and also "create martyrs of our own followers, someone who is well-liked that gets killed in a way that looks like the government did it."[12]

Throughout his book, though, Scowen firmly accepts the official story of 9/11 — that Osama bin Laden masterminded the "terrorist attacks." He believes Americans need to understand that their government has been so blood-drenched for so long that "blowback" was all but inevitable.

Had Peter Scowen's mind changed about 9/11 since he wrote his book in early 2002? If not, this could account for his saying that in my article I "don't convince anybody" of the Inside Job theory. On page 266 of *Rogue Nation*, however, he writes "If a wacky conspiracy theorist believed the widespread American intelligence failures that allowed the attacks to happen were *deliberate* [emphasis added], and he was looking for a motive to support his accusation, the policy and its enthusiastic public acceptance ... might stand up in court." This comes close to LIHOP and could explain why he did not reject that contention in my article. (The "policy" Scowen referred to is one primarily promoted by Dick Cheney for ten years to boost military spending and to advance a "larger scheme" for the USA to be "global policeman.")

The most germane reference of all in his book regarding 9/11 is the edited transcript of a telephone interview he recorded with his sister Amy on September 11, 2001. She was an office worker on the 54th floor of the south tower. In the transcript we find Amy telling Peter this:

> And then we were walking up Broadway and went into a store to get a battery for our cell phones and we heard a radio broadcaster describe how she had been at the base of the building when a huge fireball exploded out of the basement of the building. She was implying there was a bomb in the basement of the World Trade Center, as well.

As we see in the next chapter a large amount of evidence is known to millions of people in New York — and beyond — that prove the Twin Towers, and WTC Building 7 were brought down by controlled demolition (see Chapter 2, Exhbits H-K.) Peter Scowen knows what his sister told him and should be aware of reams of supporting evidence especially since civil libertarians and *The New York Times* were successful in having many of the New York oral histories tapes released. On the tapes, numerous firefighters and other emergency workers testify as to the explosions in the towers. This evidence clearly contradicts the "pancake" collapse theory and in fact shows the towers were brought down through controlled demolition.

Meanwhile I could not learn which evidence in my piece he thought "convinces people" of the LIHOP theory, or why he thought some or all of that evidence fails to "convince anyone" of the Inside Job theory. I couldn't convince him to discuss anything further. But his reactions and non-reactions illustrate how important is the question of evidence in connection with the events of 9/11. That's the subject of the next chapter.

2

9/11 is a Number, Here are the Facts:
Evidence Proves White House Complicity

> The law says a person is presumed innocent until found
> guilty. But it should be realized this concept is applica-
> ble only in a courtroom. As individuals we have the
> right to form our own judgments at any point we
> become convinced, one way or another.
>
> — Noel Twyman, in *Bloody Treason*

Two persuaders battle in the fields of 9/11.

The first is the Official Story. It was put into play the day of 9/11. It is the story of crazed Arab terrorist hijackers who fly planes into buildings. Seemingly backing up that story were the images of planes indeed flying into buildings — iconic images we'll never be able to erase from our memory banks — images reinforced by movies such as *United 93* and *The Last Hour of Flight 11*.

Stories are powerful, and easy to remember. We're suckers for stories. The essence of every story, writes two-time Pulitzer Prize winner Jon Ferry in *Writing For Story*, is that "a sympathetic character encounters a complication." In the official 9/11 storyline, "America" is the sympathetic character.

Fighting a rearguard action against the official 9/11 story is Evidence. Evidence that the official story is a fiction, evidence that leads to another story, the much less known, much more explosive, much more difficult story: White House complicity in 9/11. The sympathetic character in the story that Evidence tells is the America that rejects massive lying, militarism, corruption, resource theft and lawlessness.

We pay lip service to Evidence with a capital "E," but in real life generally arrange evidence to support the Story we're already in thrall to — in the case of 9/11, a story laden with powerful emotions: fear, sympathy, anger, revenge, patriotism.

A common mistake concerning 9/11 is to confuse great sympathy for the victims with great certainty about the identity of the perpetrators. You see it in on-line chat rooms: One person says he's convinced that the WTC towers were brought down by controlled demolition. Immediately, someone responds with "Don't you understand that 3,000 innocent people died that day?!" This mother of all non sequiturs is encouraged by the dark forces behind the demolitions. False-flag operations are designed to inflame emotions and overcome rational thought. The confusion reinforces the Big Lie.

Getting back to the facts: the existence of this confusion is hidden — perhaps from themselves, too — by editors who censor out factual evidence that fails to conform to the "emotional evidence." In Chapter 4 we'll see a big city editor declare that questions about the 9/11 Official Story cannot be pursued if the "information that comes to the attention of the newspaper ... [cannot] be properly substantiated through sources and documents that would stand up in a court of law." That's an impossibly demanding standard that would disqualify most stories most days. It certainly would have squelched printing most of those stories about WMDs in Iraq in the period leading up to the US invasion of that country. So there's a double standard when it comes to proof, to evidence.

Once a storyline has taken hold, two universal tendencies emerge. One is to downplay or even dismiss facts that don't fit the story, along with the arguments brought forward to support it. The second tendency is to play up and make central anything that fits the story. Whole police forces have been known, once they decide who the guilty party is, to twist everything to gain the conviction, and later be shown to be wrong. Judges and juries are not immune from the phenomenon. Nor are the rest of us.

In this chapter, we tackle the issue of evidence with two overlapping groups in mind. One is simply "us," people in general. The other group is those who work in the media. Accepting or dismissing information or evidence is more important in the case of those who work in the media than it is with the rest of us. If inconvenient facts, or even just questions about 9/11 don't get past the media gatekeepers, the public does not get its chance to judge on the "admissibility" or "inadmissibility" of those facts or questions. The facts and questions might as well not exist.

My colleagues and I are the first to admit it's not within our power to definitively declare who did what on 9/11. We possess no warehouse full of physical exhibits. We have no team of lawyers, are not in a position to cross-examine witnesses. But having acknowledged our limitations, we nevertheless argue that, because of the large amount and the nature of evidence freely available, it is beyond a reasonable doubt that 9/11 was an inside job, perpetrated by elements of the US government.

The Official 9/11 Story Can Fail With One Proven Falsehood

In his introduction to *The New Pearl Harbor: Disturbing Questions About the Bush Administration and 9/11*,[1] David Ray Griffin makes a distinction critical in the field of 9/11, between *cumulative* and *deductive* arguments. The exhibits in this chapter show *cumulatively* that 9/11 was an inside job. Only one exhibit needs to be proven true (beyond a reasonable doubt) for the "Inside Job" theory to be strengthened, or even proved (the "smoking gun"). If more than one holds up, the case for an Inside Job becomes even more substantive. If a clear majority hold up, the argument for Inside Job becomes nearly invincible.

What if, on the other hand, one exhibit (or a part of one exhibit), fails to hold up? Does this mean all the others are undermined or rendered null and void? Not at all. It simply means that particular exhibit can be set aside for further scrutiny or turn out to be entirely wrong. This holds true for more than one exhibit. All exhibits need to be examined on their own merits. Each *bona fide* exhibit on its own supports the cumulative evidence of an inside job on 9/11. To maintain the credibility of the official 9/11 story *all the evidence that follows must be proven wrong.*

The approach of the Bush White House, *The 9/11 Commission Report* and supporters of the official 9/11 story, is entirely different. Supporters must employ *deductive* reasoning to maintain the official story of 9/11. In deductive reasoning, each step in the argument depends upon the truth of the previous step. For example, to logically believe in the official story you have to believe there were 19 kamikaze Arab hijackers who could hijack four commercial airliners all at once *and* outsmart the $44-billion-a-year US intelligence apparatus *and* outwit NORAD, the FAA and the US Air Force *and* fly the airliners with pinpoint accuracy into the Twin Towers and Pentagon *and thus* bring the towers down (a first in architectural history) *and* that all this was orchestrated by Osama bin Laden or some other member of al Qaeda. The truth of each part of this official story is essential in holding up the whole story. For instance, if there is no credible evidence that the 19 individuals the White House claims boarded the airliners actually did so, the rest of the official narrative is seriously damaged and would collapse in a court of law. In deductive reasoning, the whole chain can fail if one link fails.

Types of Evidence: Means for Weighing Them Individually and "at the End of the Day"

The most persuasive treatise we've encountered on the subject of evidence is by Noel Twyman. He's neither a judge nor a lawyer, but a retired businessman and a concerned American citizen. He was forced to study the subject of evidence in depth after he began to take an interest in the assassination of President John F. Kennedy, long after JFK's death. Twyman pursued evidence surrounding the assassination with dogged determination, thoroughness and a keen mind. The result is his long and excellent book, *Bloody Treason*.[2] "This is a very important subject if we are to keep our bearings, while maneuvering through the JFK quagmire," Twyman writes. His learnings on evidence transcend any individual's views on the JFK assassination, and they also apply to 9/11.

Twyman writes that he was forced to accept the reality that "no evidence ... in any complex crime is of absolute certainty." Doubts can be raised about any piece of evidence "if one is willing to search long enough." In fact this is the method of courtroom lawyers: their job is to create doubts in the minds of jurors or of a judge. They will go so far as to "manufacture doubt out of thin air," Twyman notes.

Toronto lawyer Peter Rosenthal says "The two main criteria for admissibility of evidence are that it be reliable and shed light on the ultimate issue. The decision on the ultimate issue must be based on the totality of the reliable and relevant evidence." In other words, the *cumulative* evidence.

Over centuries of jurisprudence it has developed that the most important evidence is called the *best evidence*. It's called that because it's primary, as distinguished from secondary; original, as distinguished from substitutional, "the best and highest evidence of which the nature of the case is susceptible."[3] It can also mean there's nothing better. If an original document has been destroyed or lost, the next "best" thing is a photocopy. When best evidence is available, other evidence can and should be discarded.

Best evidence includes photographic, so long as it has not been tampered with. Evidence that has been tampered with constitutes powerful evidence in itself, and tampering with evidence is a serious charge for good reasons. Conviction on a tampering charge is tantamount to proof of involvement in the crime to which the evidence relates. When the tampering reveals the *pattern* of cover-up, the likelihood of guilt for the crime in question escalates.

Fresh oral testimony is better than later oral testimony. In the first 24 or 48 hours after a massive event such as JFK's assassination or 9/11, numbers of people who have not yet understood what the official storyline is going to be, or who have not been leaned on, will speak in an unconstrained way about what they saw or heard.

DIRECT AND INDIRECT EVIDENCE

The law recognizes a difference between direct and indirect evidence. Direct evidence involves one step. It does not require any inferences. A piece of debris or an undoctored videotape are examples of direct evidence. Direct evidence provides an instant path to the issue at stake.

Indirect evidence (also known as circumstantial) involves two steps. It is one step removed from the issue at stake. Indirect evidence comprises information "about a related fact from which the existence of an ultimate fact can be deduced or inferred," writes Twyman. Circumstantial evidence can be more solid than its popular reputation would have it (we so often hear "Oh, that's just circumstantial evidence" in a certain tone of voice). "The tryer of fact," notes Rosenthal, "whether a judge or a jury, must consider all the evidence, direct and indirect, and must decide the case based on the totality of the admissible evidence. If it is a criminal matter, it must be determined if that totality establishes guilt beyond a reasonable doubt."

REASONABLE DOUBT AND PREPONDERANCE

One of the most fascinating areas of the law is the concept of *proof of guilt beyond reasonable doubt*. It's a mainstay of the criminal justice system. Yet once again the public notion of it leaves much to be desired. In his book *Shadow of a Doubt* [4], US Federal Judge William J. Caughlin writes: "A reasonable doubt is a fair doubt, growing out of the testimony, the lack of testimony, or the unsatisfactory nature of the testimony. It is not a mere imaginary or possible doubt, but a fair doubt based on reason and common sense."

"This should be a doubt," Rosenthal says, "based on the totality of the evidence at the end of the inquiry." The reasonable-doubt standard, writes Twyman, "is considered by the legal system to be the highest standard." While its main purpose is to prevent the conviction of innocent parties, it also cuts the other way, in and out of the legal system. In and out of courts, persons strongly suspected or even otherwise shown to be guilty, should not be exonerated because of imaginary or concocted doubts. Adds Twyman: "Critics of pro-conspiracy evidence have demonstrated they will stop at nothing to create 'reasonable doubt' out of imaginary doubt to avoid facing the truth of a conspiracy." In my opinion, this applies equally to 9/11.

HOW THE EXHIBITS WERE SELECTED

Out of the hundreds of pieces of evidence that could be brought forward, why do we select the few that follow? Few, because this book is not focused on attempting to prove 9/11 was an inside job; many other books on that specific topic have already been published. But this book would be incomplete without devoting a full chapter to evidence. Each reader of this book should be offered an opportunity to say "I see there's a serious problem here," or "Aha, this really nails it for me" — if that's how the reader's mind works. The number 26 is arbitrary; we chose the alphabet to set our limit.

These particular 26 are among the "best," legally speaking. They also fit a bias toward the pictorial. Pictures can provide "at a glance" proof, and are a relief from text.

Summary of Exhibits A-Z

If a significant portion of the evidence summarized here holds up, the conclusion that the attacks of 9/11 succeeded because of official complicity would become virtually inescapable.

— David Ray Griffin, author of *The New Pearl Harbor*

A – WTC 7 Collapsed at Near Free-Fall Speed at 5:20 p.m. on 9/11

B – Standard Operating Procedures Were Not Followed by NORAD on 9/11

C – Otis Fighter Jets Were Put into a Delaying Holding Pattern over the Atlantic

D – Langley Fighter Jets Were Ordered Out over the Atlantic

E – Fighters at Andrews AFB Did Not Protect Nation's Capital or Pentagon

F – NORAD Has Been Well-Prepared for Major Emergencies Since 1961

G – War Games on 9/11 Helped Paralyze the US Air Force

H – WTC Collapses Reveal Eleven Features of Controlled Demolitions

I – WTC Twin Towers Were Designed To Withstand Impact of a Boeing 707

J – Proof Steel-Framed High-Rise Towers Don't Collapse Due to Fires

K – Oral Evidence from Firefighters: the WTC Towers Were "Demolished"

L – Federal Government Broke the Law by Rapid Removal of Steel Debris

M – Bush Remaining in Florida Classroom Inconsistent With All Protocols

N – Lies in the Pentagon's Alleged Ignorance about Flight 77

O – Anomalies in the Official Story of What Struck the Pentagon

P – Flight 93 Was Shot Down: Debris Covers Five Square Miles

Q – Cell Phones Don't Work Above 8,000 feet or Over Areas Without Cell Relay Transmitters

R – 9/11 Commission Delays and Obstructions = Bush Administration Cover-Up

S – Executive Director of 9/11 Commission Closely Tied to the Bush White House

T – *The 9/11 Commission Report*: "A 571 Page Lie" — Evidence of a Cover-Up

U – CIA Creates, Trains and Runs Terrorists Around the World Including 9/11 Patsies

V – FBI Involved in Protecting Persons Connected to Terrorism and 9/11

W – CIA-Linked Pakistan ISI Financed "Lead Hijacker" Mohammed Atta

X – 9/11 "Put" Options Prior to 9/11 Showed Advance Knowledge by Insiders

Y – Osama bin Laden Has Long and Close Ties to CIA

Z – Leading Neo-Con Organization called for "A New Pearl Harbor"

What happened to media curiosity about the collapse of World Trade Center Building 7 at 5:20 pm on September 11, 2001?

A

IMAGE RESTORATION BY KEN JENKINS

B

IMAGE RESTORATION BY KEN JENKINS

C

IMAGE RESTORATION BY KEN JENKINS

EXHIBIT A

World Trade Center Building 7 Collapses at Near Free-Fall Speed at 5:20 p.m. on 9/11

The exhibits that follow are generally presented in chronological order. But the sudden collapse at 5:20 p.m. on September 11, 2001 of World Trade Center Building 7 (WTC7) is so outstandingly bizarre, on so many fronts, that it deserves to be Exhibit A. This collapse alone — admitted to be a controlled demolition — constitutes virtually indisputable proof that the whole of 9/11 was an inside job.[5][6]

No evidence has been produced to date to link Osama bin Laden or al Qaeda with the wiring of this 47-story steel-framed skyscraper for controlled demolition or to provide a motive for them to risk devoting resources to this aspect of 9/11. If al Qaeda did it, why would officialdom and the media make so little mention of Building 7 as to make it a "non-building" from the very day of 9/11?

The 9/11 Commission's 571-page *Report*, which accepts *a priori* the official White House story of 9/11, mentions WTC Building 7, a 47-story steel-framed skyscraper, only a few times and never refers to its demise.[7]

Located one block from the Twin Towers, WTC7 was barely scratched by the collapse of those structures. Photographic evidence shows that a few small and not very hot fires burned for some time on the 7th and 12th floors. When the structure suddenly imploded, it fell straight down at near free-fall speed, landing in a compact pile of rubble, barely damaging any of the surrounding buildings. These are just a few of the 11 controlled-demolition characteristics to which Building 7's collapse conformed (see Exhibit H). The steel debris from Building 7 was rapidly and illegally removed and shipped overseas to be melted, just as was the debris from the Twin Towers (see Exhibit L).

Some have argued that tanks of diesel fuel in the basement of Building 7 caught fire causing the collapse.[8] The problems with this contention include the fact that no one can point to any photographic evidence of excessive smoke or fire, and the fact that even raging fires have never before been responsible for the collapse of a steel-framed high-rise (see Exhibit J).

Larry Silverstein: After three years, a "clarification."

No one refers to evidence that anyone smelled burning diesel fuel coming from WTC7. According to the Federal Emergency Management Agency (FEMA), the notion that diesel fuel leaked, burned and heated the building's steel supports to the point of failure "has only a low probability of occurrence." The official report on WTC7's collapse comes to no specific conclusion.[9]

Larry Silverstein, the building's leaseholder, said on a PBS documentary in September 2002 that he suggested to the NYC fire department commander that they "pull" Building 7. "Pull" is an industry term meaning "demolish." Silverstein's exact words on PBS:

> I remember getting a call from the, er, fire department commander, telling me that they were not sure they were gonna be able to contain the fire, and I said, "We've had such terrible loss of life, maybe the smartest thing to do is pull it." And they made that decision to pull and we watched the building collapse.

He said nothing about burning tanks of diesel fuel. On September 9, 2005, Silverstein issued a "clarification" that what he meant by "pull it" was to remove a contingent of firefighters remaining in the building.[10] But this makes no sense in the context of his videotaped remarks on the record. Also there is no evidence there were any firefighters in the building.[11]

Relevant to the issue of a government conspiracy on 9/11 is the fact that Building 7, according to NYC 9/11 Truth activist Michael Kane, "effectively ... was a military building." In the DVD *The Great Conspiracy: The 9/11 News Special You Never Saw*, he states: "The CIA had a clandestine bunker on the 25th floor of World Trade Center 7. The Secret Service had offices there too. And Mayor Rudolph Giuliani's Office of Emergency Management was also located there."[12]

This emergency command center, ordered built by Mayor Rudolph Giuliani about a year earlier, had its own separate air and water supply and windows that could withstand gales of 160 mph. It should have been "command central" during the emergency. But it was abandoned earlier in the day.

BY ORDER OF THE COMMANDER

AIR COMBAT COMMAND

ACCI 13-SAOC

VOLUME 3

30 MAY 1997

Includes HQ ACC/DIS IC 98-1, 131718Z Mar 98

Space, Missile, Command, and Control

AIR DEFENSE COMMAND AND CONTROL OPERATIONS

COMPLIANCE WITH THIS PUBLICATION IS MANDATORY

2.1. General:

2.1.1. **Air Defense System (ADS).** The mission of the ADS is to provide Commander-in-Chief, North American Aerospace Defense Command (CINCNORAD)/Commander-in-Chief, United States Atlantic Command (CINCUSACOM) with the means to detect, monitor, identify, intercept, report, and, if necessary, destroy an airborne object that may pose a threat to North America and/or Iceland, in fulfillment of the tactical threat warning/attack assessment (TW/AA) and collateral missions of NORAD. The ADS also supports the drug interdiction mission of the operational CINCs. The ADS provides CINCNORAD and CINCUSACOM the capability to integrate CONUS air defense forces with other service components and allies. To accomplish the mission of the ADS, associated units/elements perform functions that may be generally categorized as Air Surveillance, Force Management, and Airspace Control.

Detect, intercept and destroy orders in NORAD operations documents did not and do not exclude US airspace.

```
    1.  Air Defense Emergency.  An emergency condition which exists
    when attack upon the continental United States, Alaska, Canada,
    or U.S. installations in Greenland by hostile aircraft or
    missiles is considered probable, is imminent, or is taking
    place.
```

The definition of an emergency is inclusive and unambiguous.

EXHIBIT B

Standard Operating Procedures Were Not Followed by NORAD on 9/11

Standard operating procedures (SOP) dictate that if a Federal Aviation Administration (FAA) flight controller notices anything that suggests a possible hijacking (for instance, if radio contact is lost, if the plane's transponder switches off, or if the plane deviates from its flight plan) the controller is to contact a superior. If the problem cannot be fixed quickly — within minutes — the superior is to ask NORAD (North American Aerospace Defense Command) to scramble jet fighters to find out what is going on. NORAD then issues a scramble order to the nearest air force base with fighters on alert.[13]

According to General Ralph Eberhart, the head of NORAD, after the FAA senses that something is wrong, "it takes about one minute" for it to contact NORAD, after which, according to a spokesperson, NORAD can scramble fighter jets "within a matter of minutes" to anywhere in the United States.[14]

Intercepts by jet fighters occur about 100 times a year[15] and commence in well under 30 minutes, as the 9/11 commission itself acknowledges.[16] In the ten months "between September 2000 and June 2001 fighter jets were scrambled at least 67 times in the United States."[17]

On 9/11, even though *four* commercial airliners were hijacked all at once, jet interceptors did not appear until one hour and 18 minutes after the first hijacking had been reported (at 8:20). And by that time, all the damage had been done (at 9:38).

The 9/11 Commission Report explains the fiasco by claiming NORAD had only nine minutes' warning for the first flight.[18] However, Laura Brown, the FAA's Deputy in Public Affairs, told the media that the National Military Command Center (NMCC) in the Pentagon had set up an air threat teleconference call at about 8:20 that morning.[19] Her statement establishes that the military knew about Flight 11's erratic behavior shortly after 8:15, which indicates the FAA had followed standard procedures, whereas NORAD and the US Air Force had not.

NORAD also claims it had no warning about the other three hijackings until they had crashed. An FAA clarification memo from Laura Brown flatly contradicts that.[20]

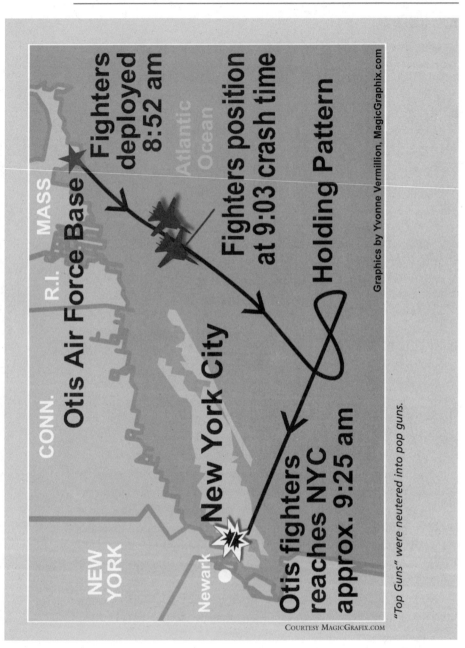

CONN.

R.I.   MASS

Otis Air Force Base

Fighters deployed 8:52 am

Atlantic Ocean

Fighters position at 9:03 crash time

Holding Pattern

Graphics by Yvonne Vermillion, MagicGraphix.com

NEW YORK

Newark

New York City

Otis fighters reaches NYC approx. 9:25 am

COURTESY MAGICGRAFIX.COM

"Top Guns" were neutered into pop guns.

EXHIBIT C

Otis Fighter Jets Put into a Delaying Holding Pattern over the Atlantic

On 9/11, all the alleged hijackings occur in NORAD's Northeast Air Defense Sector (NEADS). According to *The 9/11 Commission Report*, "NEADS could call on two alert sites, each with one pair of ready fighters: Otis Air National Guard Base in Cape Cod, Massachusetts, and Langley Air Force Base in Hampton, Virginia."[21]

The 9/11 Commission Report claims the air defense of America began with a call from NEADS to Otis AFB to scramble the two F-15s that were on alert (at 8:46 a.m.), for duty in New York City 153 miles away.[22] There are at least nine conflicting accounts of urgency and destination for the Otis F-15s that appear in *The 9/11 Commission Report* and are detailed in *The Terror Timeline*.[23]

In one account, NORAD commander Major General Larry Arnold "states that the fighters head straight for New York City at about 1,100 to 1,200 mph." According to "an Otis spokeswoman" quoted in the account, "An F-15 departing from Otis can reach New York City in 10 to 12 minutes," just before Flight 175 hit WTC 2. Yet according to a NORAD timeline developed just after 9/11, the fighters take about 19 minutes to reach New York City (arriving at about 9:11 a.m.), 8 minutes too late, because they were traveling at less than 600 mph.

In another account, NEADS did not know where to send the alert fighter aircraft, and the officer directing the fighters pressed for more information: "I don't know where I'm scrambling these guys to. I need a direction, a destination." Radar data allegedly show the Otis fighters were airborne at 8:53. Lacking a target and to avoid New York area air traffic, they were vectored toward military-controlled airspace off the Long Island coast to "hold as needed," from 9:09 to 9:13 until it was too late.[24] [25] (See diagram opposite.)

Two conclusions are justified. Whatever the takeoff time and whatever the speed of these F-15s, their flight path is bizarre. Even if the account of the tainted 9/11 commission is correct, it is a scandal of planned "failure." Still other accounts make the Kean-Zelikow story seem even more bizarre.[26]

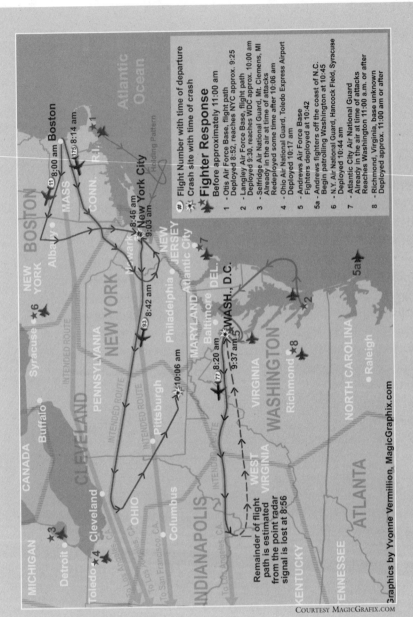

Fighter Response

Before approximately 11:00 am

1 - Otis Air Force Base, flight path
    Deployed 8:52, reaches NYC approx. 9:25
2 - Langley Air Force Base, flight path
    Deployed 9:30, reaches WDC approx. 10:00 am
3 - Selfridge Air National Guard, Mt. Clemens, MI
    Already in the air at time of attacks
    Redeployed some time after 10:06 am
4 - Ohio Air National Guard, Toledo Express Airport
    Deployed 10:17 am
5 - Andrews Air Force Base
    Fighters deployed at 10:42
5a - Andrews fighters off the coast of N.C.
    Begin patrolling Washington at 10:45
6 - N.Y. Air National Guard, Hancock Field, Syracuse
    Deployed 10:44 am
7 - Atlantic City Air National Guard
    Already in the air at time of attacks
    Reaches Washington 11:00 a.m. or after
8 - Richmond, Virginia, base unknown
    Deployed approx. 11:00 am or after

Flight Number with time of departure
★ Crash site with time of crash

Graphics by Yvonne Vermillion, MagicGraphix.com

COURTESY MAGICGRAFIX.COM

"Deliberate time-delaying misdirection" coordinated from above.

EXHIBIT D

Langley Fighter Jets Were Ordered Out over the Atlantic

The convoluted flight paths of the "hijacked planes" of 9/11 — over a two-hour time span from Flight 11's takeoff from Boston at 7:59 a.m. to Flight 93's crash near Shanksville at 10:06 a.m. — highlight the total failure of military protection on 9/11. (See map opposite.) Even more bizarre than the account of the Otis jet fighters is the jumbled story of the Langley fighters. According to the 9/11 Commission, it looked as if the Otis jets might run out of fuel doing their holding pattern, so NEADS scrambled (at 9:24) a pair of jet fighters from Langley AFB in Virginia to fly to New York to provide backup, or so the story goes.[27] Radar data allegedly show the Langley jets airborne at 9:30 and thought to be heading towards Washington (and later Baltimore) to intercept "a reported southbound American 11" before it gets to the nation's capital. (This is just before the Pentagon is to be hit at 9:38, but allegedly by Flight 77, not Flight 11, which had crashed in NYC at 8:46.) The startling news of this "unknown plane" prompted the mission crew commander at NEADS, according to the commission, to take immediate control of the airspace to clear a flight path for the Langley fighters.[28] [29] By the 9/11 Commission account, he then discovered, to his surprise, that the Langley fighters were not headed north toward the Baltimore area as instructed, but east over the ocean.[30]

The whole mess, even by the tortured account of the 9/11 Commission, represents one of the largest failures in US military history, on a par with Pearl Harbor. It is not uncharacteristic non-performance, however, but deliberate time-delaying misdirection, evidence of an inside job plus cover-up, deserving of a separate inquiry.

Researcher Jared Israel sums it up: "Some of what happened on 9/11, such as planes flying into buildings, is unusual. But most of what happened, such as commercial jets flying off course, transponder failures and possible hijackings, are common emergencies. On 9/11 the emergency systems failed despite, not because of, the extreme nature of the emergency. This could only happen if individuals in high positions worked in a coordinated way to make them fail."[31]

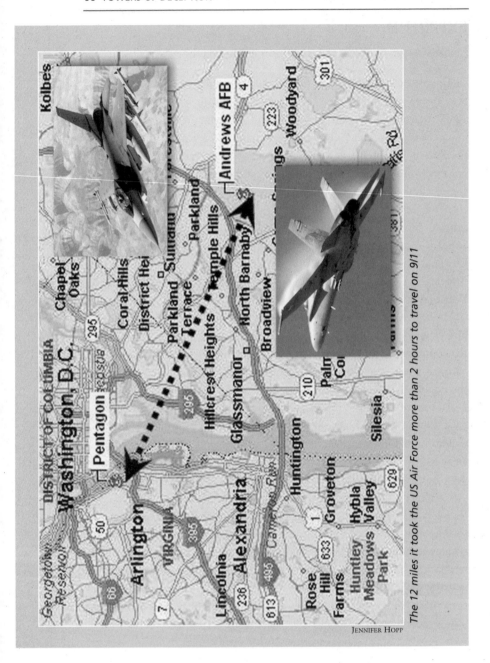

The 12 miles it took the US Air Force more than 2 hours to travel on 9/11

JENNIFER HOPP

EXHIBIT E

Fighters at Andrews AFB Did Not Protect Nation's Capital or Pentagon

Andrews Air Force Base is 12 miles from the Pentagon and the White House. According to its own website on 9/11, it had at least two squadrons of jet fighters whose task was the protection of Washington, DC.[32] [33] Yet the 9/11 Commissioners claim that in order to protect the Pentagon the scramble order had to go to Langley Air Force Base, 130 miles away, because Andrews had no fighters on alert. The Andrews AFB website was altered September 12, 2001 in a way that deleted mention of fighter jets,[34] further proof of tampering with evidence.

The Commission claim is contradicted by a report in *Aviation Week*[35] that three F-16s from Andrews AFB were on a training mission in North Carolina when the North Tower was hit at 8:46 a.m. Being only 207 miles from Washington, they could have been back by 9 a.m. to establish CAP (Combat Air Patrol) until replacements were sent. And yet they did not begin flying over Washington until 10:45.[36]

Aviation Week also states that at 10:42 Andrews fighters finally did take off, but without missiles (or shoot down orders), and that two more F-16s, armed with AIM-9 missiles (and shoot down orders), took off 27 minutes later, at 11:09 a.m. ... after it was all over.[37]

According to David Ray Griffin, "Andrews AFB has primary responsibility for protecting the nation's capital. Can anyone seriously believe that Andrews, given the task of protecting the Pentagon, Air Force One, the White House, the houses of Congress and the Supreme Court would not have had fighters on alert at all times? If Andrews had fighters on alert, it would seem likely that McGuire AFB in New Jersey did too, meaning that fighters to protect New York City did not have to be scrambled from Otis Air Force Base on Cape Cod."[38]

National security expert and former ABC producer James Bamford says, moreover, that NEADS was also able to call on "alert fighter pilots at National Guard units at Burlington, Vermont; Atlantic City, New Jersey; and Duluth, Minnesota." In that case, there were at least seven bases from which NEADS could have scrambled fighters, not merely two, as the official story has it."[39] [40]

Civilian Planes to Be Grounded 12 Hours Today in Defense Test

By McCANDLISH PHILLIPS

All civil aircraft, commercial as well as private, will be forbidden to fly over the United States or Canada for twelve hours beginning at 1 P. M. today.

The ban will give military aircraft freedom of the skies for a massive test of the ability of the two allies to repel or diminish an enemy bombing attack.

Though 250 bombing planes will attempt to penetrate continental defenses and 1,800 fighter planes will rise to oppose them, there will be little for the public eye to see. Most of the action will be carried out at altitudes above 30,000 feet.

The public ear, however, will at times be filled with man-made thunderclaps, called sonic booms, as planes enter the supersonic speed range. The frequency of these and the points over which they will occur were not predictable, military authorities said.

For the air-minded but earth-bound public, the major domestic and overseas airlines will hold open house from 2 P. M. to 6 P. M. at New York International Airport. Similar hospitality will be offered at Newark Airport, but there will be little happening at La Guardia Airport.

At Idlewild, jet and piston aircraft will be open to inspection. Pilots and mechanics will give brief talks and answer questions. Visitors will be taken behind the scenes at the terminals to see hangars, weather stations, dispatching offices and the like.

Two taxiways at Idlewild will be thrown open for parking at $1 a car and complementary bus

Continued on Page 4, Column 4

Sonic booms in airspace over US soil showed NORAD and the US Air Force to be robustly ready for any threat — in 1961. This clipping is from the front page of The New York Times for October 14, 1961.

EXHIBIT F

NORAD Has Been Well Prepared for Major Emergencies Since 1961

On October 14, 1961, with US President John F. Kennedy at Hyannis Port and the "Soviet threat" the bogeyman of choice, it might seem that evidence relating to September 11, 2001 would be scarce on the ground or in the air. But on this day, almost 45 years before 9/11, the largest air defense exercise to date begins. As reported in *The New York Times*,[41] for 12 hours, residents of the United States and Canada heard repeated sonic booms as 1,800 fighter planes flew 6,000 sorties, intercepting hundreds of "enemy" bombers and missiles attempting to attack North American targets, including 250 missile sites. During Operation Sky Shield II, personnel at 106 radar consoles scanned — as they do every day — an area of 10 million square miles as intruders, singly and in threes, "attacked." The intruders released aluminum "chaff" to confuse domestic radars, and sent out "energetic electronic counter signals" to jam the same radars.

Domestic defenders sent out "counter counter measures," even while tracking hundreds of flights and identifying them as friendly (F), hostile (H) or fake (K). Defenders, *The New York Times* reported, had two minutes to make identification before deciding whether to issue a scramble order. Interceptor flight crews, their "quick don" boots nearby, occupied lounge chairs a 30-second sprint from their aircraft. "One F-106 Delta Dart pilot, Capt. Harmon A. Dungan of the 539th Fighter-Interceptor Squadron," the *Times* stated, "... had been on five-minute alert since 7:20 A.M. At 4:47 P.M. the 'scramble' order came and he was airborne at 4:52."

Commanding officers at combat centers in the Pentagon, at NORAD headquarters at Colorado Springs and at Strategic Air Command headquarters in Omaha shared live secure telephone conference links. All followed developments on electronic "Iconorama" screens occupying two walls. All information was fed into a giant computer (it weighs 275 tons; this is 1961) at McGuire AFB in Wrightstown, N.J. President Kennedy was informed that the exercise was a success.

How does this relate to 9/11? If North American air defenses were this capable in 1961, would they be any less capable 45 years later?

The Games of 9/11

1. **Northern Vigilance (aka Northern Guardian):** A mock Cold War hijack exercise in Alaska and Northern Canada. (Not mentioned by 9/11 Commission.)

2. **Vigilant Guardian:** Involved the insertion of false radar blips onto radar screens in the NE Air Defense Sector. (Mentioned by 9/11 Commission.)

3. **Vigilant Warrior:** A live-fly hijack drill being conducted by the Joint Chiefs of Staff and NORAD to test national air response systems — involving hijacking scenarios using at least one real commercial airliner. (Not mentioned by 9/11 Commission.)

4. **Tripod II:** A non-military bio-warfare exercise was being set up by FEMA at Pier 29 in Manhattan on 9/11, under the immediate control of US Vice President Richard Cheney. (Not mentioned by 9/11 Commission.)

5. **National Reconnaissance Office (NRO) Drill:** Another potential drill was being hosted by the NRO "... for the scenario of an errant aircraft crashing into its NRO headquarters [coincidentally, located only four blocks from Dulles airport in Washington D.C.]" (Not mentioned by 9/11 Commission.)

— Source: Michael C. Ruppert,
Crossing the Rubicon: The Decline of the American Empire at the end of the Age of Oil, New Society Publishers, 2004, Chapter 19.

EXHIBIT G

War Games on 9/11 Helped Paralyze the US Air Force

The following insight into what else was happening on 9/11 is explained by author Michael C. Ruppert, in a speech delivered at the Commonwealth Club in San Francisco in 2004:[42]

> The mysterious and inexplicable failure of the nation's air defenses on 9/11 remains the most glaring and gaping hole in the [Kean-Zelikow] account and in the government's version of events. For me, the pivotal evidence absolutely demonstrating direct government complicity in, and management of, the [alleged terrorist attacks] was found in a number of undisputed, yet virtually unaddressed war games that were being conducted, coordinated and/or controlled by Vice President Dick Cheney or his immediate staff on the morning of September 11.
>
> The names of those war games are known to include: Northern Vigilance, Vigilant Guardian, Vigilant Warrior and Tripod II. All have been reported on by major press organizations relying on undisputed quotes from participating military personnel.[43] [44] [45] They have also been confirmed by NORAD press releases.[46] [47] [48] [49]
>
> All, except for Northern Vigilance and Tripod II, involved scenarios of hijacked airliners within the Northeast Air Defense Sector (NEADS) where all four 9/11 hijackings occurred. In some cases false blips were deliberately inserted onto FAA and military radar screens ....

Other exercises, specifically Northern Vigilance, had pulled significant fighter resources away from the northeast US, just before 9/11, into northern Canada and Alaska.

Since Ruppert's speech, researchers working for Paul Thompson's "Terror Timeline" website have identified at least four more. The injection of this flood of "noise" caused what Ruppert calls "a paralysis of fighter response."[50] [51]

ERIC HUFSCHMID

Simple pancaking would not produce a series of outbursts of explosive "squibs" (see arrow), nor would it produce this enormous mushroom cloud of finely pulverized debris.

EXHIBIT H

WTC Collapses Reveal Eleven Features of Controlled Demolitions

The collapses of the Twin Towers and WTC Building 7 exhibited distinct features associated with controlled demolitions:[52]

1. The towers fell straight down through themselves.

2. The Twin Towers' tops mushroomed outward into vast clouds of pulverized concrete and shattered steel.[53]

3. The collapses exhibited demolition "squibs" (puffs of dust) shooting out of the towers well below the zones of total destruction.

4. The collapses generated dust clouds that expanded to many times the towers' volumes — much more than occurs in typical controlled demolitions. This indicates that far more explosives were used to destroy the towers than are used in typical demolitions.

5. The towers came down suddenly.

6. And completely.

7. The towers fell at a rate only slightly slower than free-fall in a vacuum. The steel superstructures of the towers provided no more resistance to the falling rubble than air, impossible unless demolition charges going off were systematically removing the building's structure ahead of the falling rubble.

8. There was oral testimony published on the *NYT* website[54] of people hearing synchronized explosions, characterized by intense blast waves that shattered windows in buildings 400 feet away.

9. The steel skeletons were consistently shredded into short pieces, common in sophisticated demolitions, so they could easily be carried away by the equipment used to dispose of debris.

10. Eyewitnesses reported explosions before and at the outset of the collapses.

11. Molten steel (still liquid) was found at the base of the Twin Towers *three weeks* after 9/11, indicating much more energy was involved in the destruction than that associated with aircraft impact, burning jet fuel and a mechanical "pancaking" collapse.[55] [56]

COURTESY DON PAUL AND JIM HOFFMAN

Forty-seven giant, immensely strong "over-designed"
central steel vertical girders would remain standing if the
floors they supported had simply pancaked down around
them. Instead the vertical girders were found in 30-foot
lengths, ready for rapid removal.

EXHIBIT I

WTC Twin Towers Were Designed To Withstand Impact of a Boeing 707

Robert MacNamara, president of the engineering firm MacNamara and Salvia, was quoted on ScientificAmerican.com (October 9, 2001) as saying "The World Trade Center was probably one of the more resistant tall building structures. Nowadays they just don't build them as tough." The online article reports: "Despite the expert panel's preliminary musings on the failure mechanisms responsible for the Twin Towers' fall, the definitive cause has yet to be determined ... The details of how the frame members failed remain under contention." [57] [58]

Defenders of the official story say the collapses were caused not simply by the fire but by the fire combined with the damage caused by the airliners. However, Leslie Robertson, who was a member of a firm involved in designing the Twin Towers,[59] said that they were designed to withstand the impact of a Boeing 707, which at the time, 1966, was the largest airliner in commercial operation, and about the size of a Boeing 767.[60]

In 1945, a B-25 bomber struck the Empire State Building at the 79th floor, creating a hole 20 feet high. There was never any indication this accident would cause the building to collapse.[61]

Hyman Brown, the construction manager of the Twin Towers, said: "They were over-designed to withstand almost anything, including hurricanes ... bombings and an airplane hitting [them]." [62]

Thomas Eagar, an MIT professor of materials engineering who supports the official theory, says nevertheless that the impact of the airplanes would not have been significant, because "the number of columns lost on the initial impact was not large and the loads were shifted to remaining columns in this highly redundant structure." [63]

A report by the National Institute of Standards and Technology (NIST) — the official US government standards body — says: "The towers withstood the impacts and would have remained standing were it not for the dislodged insulation (fireproofing) and the subsequent multi-floor fires." The official theory of the collapse, therefore, is essentially a fire theory. Yet fire never caused large steel-frame buildings to collapse before or after 9/11.[64] (See Exhibit J.)

Left: First Interstate Bank building in Los Angeles (1988).
Right: One Meridian Place in Philadelphia (1991).
These structural steel buildings burned for 3½ hours and 18 hours,
respectively. Neither building sustained significant structural damage.

EXHIBIT J

Steel-Framed High-Rise Towers Don't Collapse Due to Fires

Kevin Ryan was site manager of the Environmental Health Laboratories[65] which certified the steel components used in construction of the WTC buildings. He wrote an open letter[66] to a government scientist, Frank Gayle, at NIST, questioning NIST's October 19, 2004 report that fuel fires caused the three towers to collapse.

The letter pointed out that the steel in the towers tested up to its certified standard and so would easily withstand temperatures caused by burning jet fuel. A chemist by profession, Ryan said he was acting in the hope of receiving a public response from Gayle. "Given the impact of September 11 on events around the world," Ryan said, "everyone needs to know the full truth of what really happened on that day." One week later Ryan was fired by his employer.[67]

Ryan later wrote: "The three WTC buildings in question weren't all designed the same way and weren't all hit by airplanes. The only thing they seemed to have in common were relatively small and manageable fires. From the government's report we know that only a small percentage of the supporting columns in each of the first two buildings were severed, and that the jet fuel burned off in just a few minutes."

Ryan continues: "To follow the latest 'leading hypothesis' from the NIST, what are the odds that all the fireproofing fell off in just the right places, even far from the point of impact? Without much test data, let's say it's one in a thousand. And what are the odds that the office furnishings converged to supply highly directed and (somehow) forced-oxygen fires at very precise points on the remaining columns? Is it another one in a thousand? What is the chance that those points would then all soften in unison, and give way perfectly, so that the highly dubious 'progressive global collapse' theory could be born? Finally, what are the chances that the first, second and third incidents of fire-induced collapse would all occur on the same day? Let's say it's one in a million. Considering everything, we're looking at a one in a trillion chance."[68]

The report put out by NIST in 2005 implies that fire-induced collapses of large steel-framed buildings are normal events.[69] Far from being

WWW.LMC.EP.USP.BR

WWW.FIRETACTICS.COM

As bad as it gets: If ever a skyscraper were going to collapse due to fire, it would be Madrid's Edifico Windsor (top), which burned for 16 hours in February 2005. It didn't collapse. Nor did this 50-story building in Caracas, Venezuela (inset), which blazed for 17 hours in 2004.

normal, however, such collapses have never occurred, except — allegedly — on a single date in history: September 11, 2001. Contrast the havoc allegedly caused by the short-lived fires in the twin WTC towers with the damage caused by comparable fires elsewhere.

In 1988, a blaze in the First Interstate Bank Building in Los Angeles raged for three and a half hours and gutted four and a half of the building's 62 floors, but there was no significant structural damage.[70]

In 1991, a huge fire in Philadelphia's One Meridian Plaza lasted for 18 hours and gutted 8 of the building's 38 floors but, said the FEMA report, although "beams and girders sagged and twisted … under severe fire exposures … the columns continued to support their loads without obvious damage."[71]

In 2004, a fire in a 50-story building in Caracas, Venezuela raged for more than 17 hours, gutting the building's top 20 floors, yet the building did not collapse.[72]

In 2005, another spectacular high rise fire occurred when the Edificio Windsor in Madrid turned into a raging inferno for 16 hours on February 12 with only the top floors partially collapsing. The building is only partially comparable to the WTC towers in that it was built of reinforced concrete. But, by the same token, the WTC towers, being steel-framed, were even stronger.

The fires in Los Angeles, Philadelphia and Caracas were hot enough to break windows. The WTC towers fires were not.[73]

Kevin Ryan, in his letter to Frank Gayle, wrote in criticism of NIST's preliminary report[74]: "This story just does not add up. If steel from those buildings did soften or melt, I'm sure we can all agree that this was certainly not due to jet fuel fires of any kind, let alone the briefly burning fires in those towers …. Please do what you can to quickly eliminate the confusion regarding the ability of jet fuel fires to soften or melt structural steel."

Firefighters at Ground Zero with an inset of Louie Cacchioli.

EXHIBIT K

Oral Evidence from Firefighters: The WTC Towers Were "Demolished"

Most of the eleven features of controlled demolitions mentioned in Exhibit H are features that could have been observed by people in the area. In fact, testimonies about some of these phenomena have been available, since shortly after 9/11, from "fresh" oral evidence captured on tape from reporters, firefighters, police officers and people who worked in the towers.

These testimonies were withheld, however, by the New York City Fire Department. On August 12, 2005, following a Freedom of Information Act lawsuit filed by *The New York Times* and some family members of victims,[75] the fire department was forced to release the transcripts and tapes.[76]

Among those testifying is firefighter Louie Cacchioli, 51. With his arm he gestures in a series of downward movements to illustrate what he's saying: "We were about two blocks away ... floor by floor it started popping out ... It was as if they had detonators and they planned to take out a building, boom, boom, boom." Firefighter Cacchioli reported that upon entering the north tower's lobby, he saw elevator doors completely blown out and people being hit with debris. "I remember thinking ... how could this be happening so quickly if a plane hit way above?"

When Cacchioli reached the 24th floor, he encountered heavy dust and smoke, which he found puzzling in light of the fact that the plane had struck the building more than 50 stories higher up. Shortly thereafter, he and another fireman "heard this huge explosion that sounded like a bomb. It was such a loud noise; it knocked off the lights and stalled the elevator." After they pried themselves out of the elevator, he reported "another huge explosion like the first one hits. This one hits about two minutes later ... [and] I'm thinking, 'Oh. My God, these bastards put bombs in here like they did in 1993! ... Then as soon as we get in the stairwell, I hear another huge explosion like the other two. Then I heard bang, bang, bang — huge bangs."[77]

Paramedic Daniel Rivera also mentioned "pops." Asked how he knew that the south tower was coming down, he said: "At first I thought it was — do you ever see professional demolitions where they set the charges on certain floors and then you hear 'Pop, pop, pop, pop, pop'? ... I thought it was that."[78]

These pictures were taken in the basement of one of the twin WTC towers peior (obviously) to the towers' collapse. They were delivered anonymously to Janette MacKinlay, an artist, 9/11 Truth activist and a survivor from a building directly across from the towers. They are irrefutable photographic evidence of demolition within the building prior to its collapse and put "paid" to the "pancake" theory.

Firefighter Richard Banaciski said: "[T]here was just an explosion. It seemed like on television [when] they blow up these buildings. It seemed like it was going all the way around like a belt, all these explosions." [79]

A *Wall Street Journal* reporter said: "I heard this metallic roar, looked up and saw what I thought was just a peculiar sight of individual floors, one after the other exploding outward. I thought to myself, 'My God, they're going to bring the building down.' And they, whoever they are, ... I saw the explosions." [80]

BBC reporter Steve Evans said: "I was at the base of the second tower ... that was hit .... There was an explosion .... [T]he base of the building shook .... [T]hen when we were outside, the second explosion happened and then there was a series of explosions." [81]

Stationary engineer Mike Pecoraro, who was working in the north tower's sixth sub-basement, stated that after his co-worker reported seeing lights flicker, they called upstairs to find out what happened. They were told that there had been a loud explosion and the whole building seemed to shake. Pecoraro and Chino then went up to the C level, [which is still "way underground"], where there was a small machine shop, but it was gone. "There was nothing there but rubble," said Pecoraro. "We're talking about a 50 ton hydraulic press — gone!" They then went to the parking garage [still far below ground], but found that it, too, was gone. Says Pecoraro, "There were no walls." Then on the B Level, they found that a steel-and-concrete fire door, which weighed about 300 pounds, was wrinkled up "like a piece of aluminum foil." Finally, when they went up to the ground floor, "The whole lobby was soot and black, elevator doors were missing. The marble was missing off some of the walls." [82]

Terri Tobin, a lieutenant with the NYPD public information office, said that during or just after the collapse of the south tower, "all I heard were extremely loud explosions. I thought we were being bombed." [83]

A story in the London *Guardian* said: "In New York, police and fire officials were carrying out the first wave of evacuations when the first of the World Trade Center towers collapsed. Some eyewitnesses reported hearing another explosion just before the structure crumbled. Police said that it looked almost like a 'planned implosion.'" [84]

Profile: William Rodriguez

"9/11 is Just a Big Magic Trick"

"When William Rodriguez was a young man," writes Russ Wellen, "the Amazing Randi hired him as an assistant — to help expose faith healers and psychics." Two decades later," writes Wellen, an editor with freezerbox.com, "Rodriguez's life has come full circle and once again he's taken on the task of unmasking what he sees as the truth behind a spectacle."

The "spectacle" is 9/11. As an employee of the World Trade Center Rodriguez was in the North Tower before it was hit. He knows the first explosive event was not a plane hitting the tower. The first thing he experienced that morning was completely at odds with the official story: he was on sub-level one, and along with 20 others experienced a massive explosion — from below. Seconds later, he heard another — from above (Flight 11).

A custodian with keys to every floor, he accompanied firefighters up the stairs, enabling hundreds to escape to safety. He heard more explosive sounds in the North Tower. They also resounded from the South Tower. He was turned back at the thirty-ninth floor, and was the last person out of the North Tower. He scrambled for refuge under a vehicle as the structure collapsed. He was recognized as a hero and photographed with George Bush.

On the Jimmy Walter 9/11Truth tour of Europe in May 2005, Rodriguez showed me his WTC master key, the only one remaining. "I have to tell the truth about how the towers came down, to be true to those who died, and because I've been given a second life. You have two options. Stand for the truth or be part of the game. I didn't want to be part of the game." He found out about the game after he and others pressed for an independent inquiry about 9/11, and found that his hours of testimony behind closed doors was ignored in the Commission's *Report*. Rodriguez was also rebuffed by the National Institute of Safety and Technology (NIST) and the FBI. But he successfully pressed Congress, the Legislature and Senate for many of the benefits that the families finally received. He is the President of the Hispanic Victim's Group and lobbied successfully to obtain an amnesty for undocumented Hispanic workers who perished.

His experience with Spanish-language media has been very different from his experience with English-language media. Once he was out of harm's way on 9/11, he was interviewed by CNN and became the designated Spanish-speaking eyewitness for Spanish TV, including Telemundo and Univision, and for newspapers like *Hoy* and *El Diario*. "English-language media ignore or twist what I have to say."

In early 2006 Rodriguez is traveling the world "just telling what I know, nothing else," and is greeted as a hero by, for instance the government of Venezuela. The president of that country's national assembly ordered a video documentary of Rodriguez's life be made. It took a week, and was filmed on the grounds of the presidential palace. "The president has one of the largest collections of 9/11 materials anywhere," Rodriguez notes.

Wellen asked Rodriguez how he would describe 9/11 to a child. He responded without hesitation: "I was a magician for thirty years. . . It is very easy to do misdirection, to make you look into one place while you're doing the magic with the other hand. 9/11 is just a big magic trick. It's an illusion."

"We are treating the steel removed from the site like garbage, not like crucial fire-scene evidence." — Fire Engineering magazine

EXHIBIT L

Federal Government Broke the Law by Rapid Removal of Steel Debris

Steel from the WTC buildings was removed[85] before it could be examined.[86] Virtually all of was sold to scrap dealers. Most of it was shipped to Asia.[87] Removing evidence from a crime scene is a federal offense; in this case, federal officials facilitated the removal.[88]

The removal evoked protest. On Christmas Day 2001, *The New York Times* said: "The decision to rapidly recycle the steel columns, beams and trusses from the WTC in the days immediately after 9/11 means definitive answers may never be known." [89] The next week, *Fire Engineering Magazine* said: "We are literally treating the steel removed from the site like garbage, not like crucial fire scene evidence…"

New York City mayor Michael Bloomberg defended the decision to dispose of the steel. He said: "If you want to take a look at the construction methods and the design, that's in this day and age what computers do.[90] Just looking at a piece of metal generally doesn't tell you anything." [91] His statement is false. An examination of the steel could have revealed whether it had been cut by explosives.

The May 2002 FEMA *World Trade Center Building Performance Study* stated some of the steel was "rapidly corroded by sulfidation." [92] FEMA appropriately called for further investigation of this finding, which *The New York Times* called "perhaps the deepest mystery uncovered in the investigation." Evidence of a continuing cover-up on the part of NIST is shown by its superficial treatment of this provocative finding. A closely related problem, expressed by Dr. Jonathan Barnett, Professor of Fire Protection Engineering at Worcester Polytechnic Institute, is that "fire and the structural damage … would not explain steel members in the debris pile that appear to have been partly evaporated." The NIST report fails to mention either evaporation or sulfidation.[93]

The officially ordered rush removal of crucial forensic evidence from a crime scene itself is evidence of a systematic and deliberate cover-up.[94] On September 26, 2001, then-mayor Rudolph Giuliani banned tourists from taking photos at the World Trade Center site on the basis that it was a crime scene.[95]

The curiously calm, succinct, whisper of White House chief of staff Andy Card into the president's ear: "A second plane hit the other tower, and America is under attack." The wording shows the president knew of the first plane. Additionally, Bush said later that he had seen, on regular TV, the first plane crash. (This was an impossibility since the footage was not released to the world on TV until the next day — September 12th, 2001.) These and other major contradictions of the morning indicate that the president and his close associates possessed prior knowledge of what was going to happen, and that they play-acted according to a prepared script.

EXHIBIT M

Bush Remaining in Florida Classroom Inconsistent With All Protocols

At 8:35 a.m. on 9/11, President Bush's motorcade leaves for the Emma E. Booker Elementary School in Sarasota, Florida for a photo opportunity. Captain Deborah Loewer, director of the White House Situation Room, is traveling in the motorcade and receives a message about the first tower being struck. As soon as the motorcade reaches the school, at 8:55, she runs to Bush's car and passes on the message. When Bush enters the school, Karl Rove takes him aside and tells him about the situation.[96] National Security Advisor Condoleezza Rice updates Bush as well, by phone.[97]

Bush and his staff decide he will stay in a reading class at the school, despite the fact that the FAA, NORAD and some of his staff know that three domestic airliners have already been hijacked by the time he enters the classroom at around 9:00 a.m.[98]

Meanwhile, three Secret Service agents and a Marine, traveling with Bush, turn on the television in a nearby front office just as Flight 175 crashes into Tower 2. "We're out of here," the Marine tells Sheriff Bill Balkwill, who's standing by. "Can you get everyone ready?"[99] But Bush remains in the classroom.

At 9:06 a.m., White House Chief of Staff Andrew Card enters the classroom and whispers into Bush's ear, "A second plane hit the other tower, and America is under attack."[100] In the video footage seen around the world, Bush remains reading with the children for at least another seven or eight minutes.[101] Why didn't the Secret Service remove him?[102] Terrorists wanting to attack the symbols of America would quite likely target the President. His whereabouts had been well publicized.[103]

The public record shows the president and his associates failed to act appropriately under the circumstances. Their behavior strongly suggests they knew what was going to happen and therefore did not fear for their own lives nor the lives of any of the others present at the Booker Elementary School that day.[104] [105]

The primary question regarding the Pentagon strike on 9/11 is how any aerial vehicle — an airliner, a missile, a warplane, or warplane fitted with a missile, a small plane, or a blimp — could have penetrated such restricted airspace. If it was a Boeing 757, it would have looked like this.

COURTESY DON PAUL AND JIM HOFFMAN

EXHIBIT N

Lies in the Pentagon's Alleged Ignorance about Flight 77

It is absurd, on the face of it, to think that the central headquarters of the greatest military power in history could be caught both unaware and undefended by an attack from the ground or from the air, whether by hijacked aircraft, warplane or missile, or any combination of these.

Yet the Kean-Zelikow Commission claims in its report that Pentagon officials were in the dark about the hijacking of Flight 77,[106] which, according to the official story, hit the Pentagon at 9:38 the morning of September 11, 2001. This being in the dark is flatly contradicted by the memo distributed to the media on May 21, 2003 by Laura Brown, FAA's Deputy in Public Affairs. She stated the FAA had established a teleconference call with military officials "within minutes" of the first WTC strike. She said that the FAA shared "real-time information" about "all the flights of interest, including Flight 77." [107]

Brown's statement was known by the Commission. Richard Ben-Veniste, after reading Brown's memo into the record, said: "So now we have in question whether there was an informal real-time communication of the situation, including Flight 77's situation, to personnel at NORAD."

The Commission's final report simply resorts to an outright lie when it says the FAA had not notified the military about Flight 77 formally or informally.[108]

Also contradicting the official story is the open testimony given to the 9/11 Commission by Secretary of Transportation Norman Mineta. Mineta testified that at 9:20 that morning, he went down to the shelter conference room under the White House, where Vice President Cheney was in charge.[109] Mineta told the commission that the vice president knew of the approaching aircraft at 9:26, at least ten minutes before the impact on the Pentagon. The 9/11 Commission ignored Mineta's testimony in its final report.

Mineta's testimony undermines the official 9/11 story in two serious ways. It indicates there was knowledge in the White House of the approaching aircraft at least 10 minutes before the Pentagon was struck. It also implies that Vice President Cheney was involved in a *de facto* standdown. Mineta's testimony suggests that the attack on the Pentagon was desired, as in "a New Pearl Harbor."

So-called new video of 9/11 from the Pentagon, released by the Pentagon in late May 2006: These three of the multiple frames released are neither new nor are they video as normally understood (30 frames per second), but instead a series of stills, as was the Pentagon's earlier "video."

Mainstream TV anchors solemnly stretched cognitive dissonance to near the snapping point when they introduced this "new video" as "showing the plane that hit the Pentagon" that "would surely lay to rest conspiracy theories that no plane hit the Pentagon."

As they spoke these words, no plane could be seen hitting the Pentagon. According to these "news" people, the Emperor's airplane was well dressed. Most viewers, however, were in the position of the little boy who not only could not see an emperor's naked airplane, but no airplane whatsoever.

The Pentagon holds footage of the crime scene from an admitted 84 cameras. Even with this much footage to choose from, the "best evidence" the Pentagon has provided that a Boeing 757 hit the Pentagon is these three frames. Since these totally unrevealing images cannot end legitimate conjecture by anyone, the larger question raised is what game the Pentagon is playing in its using disinformation as a weapon against the American public and the world.

EXHIBIT O

Anomalies in the Official Story of What Struck the Pentagon

Two main theories compete concerning the strike on the Pentagon on 9/11. One is that American Airlines Flight 77, a Boeing 757, struck the building. The other is that a warplane or a missile struck. In considering these theories, numerous anomalies in the official 9/11 story should be considered. Here are just seven:

1. The alleged pilot of Flight 77, Hani Hanjour, was so incompetent that he was refused rental of a single-engine Cessna.[110]
2. The Pentagon is 11 miles from Andrews Air Force Base, which housed two combat-ready fighter wings. Despite scramble times of under five minutes, no interceptors made it into the air before the strike.[111]
3. The Pentagon is surrounded by restricted airspace and presumably, being the pre-eminent military headquarters in the world, is protected by suitably-placed surface-to-air missiles ready to fire at any aerial vehicle failing to identify itself as friendly.
4. The plane Hanjour was allegedly flying, encountering no resistance from Andrews AFB, proceeded into the restricted airspace, unfired upon by defensive missiles, made a spiral dive, turning 270 degrees and dropping 7,000 feet in 2½ minutes,[112] then was piloted into the west wing so low that it clipped lamp posts on the highway about 500 feet from the Pentagon.
5. An air traffic controller from Washington testified, "The speed, the maneuverability, the way that he turned, we all thought in the radar room ... that that was a military plane."[113]
6. Surveillance camera videotapes and debris were immediately confiscated by FBI or Pentagon personnel.
7. To early June 2006, the US government has refused to release other than the "new video" referred to in Exhibit N, which does not show an airliner.

Competition between the two main theories could be resolved if the Pentagon released, undoctored, all its videotapes. But the competition between the two theories is strictly secondary. The primary issue is how the Pentagon got hit at all. The airliner *vs.* missile debate distracts from the primary issue. It will remain the primary issue even if the Pentagon releases 84 doctored videos of an airliner.

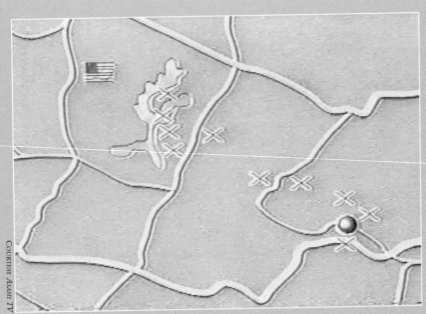

This map is a frame grab from a 90-minute special "Seven Questions About 9/11" aired on Asahi TV, Japan's second largest network. The Xs mark places where Asahi investigators found people who testified about parts from Flight 93 that landed where they saw them on 9/11. In all, the investigators found debris spread over seven or eight square miles, making the official story of the flight plummeting whole into the ground a bald-faced lie, no matter who repeats it or believes it.

EXHIBIT P

Flight 93 Was Shot Down: Debris Covers Five Square Miles

Flight 93 was the flight that crashed into a field near Shanksville, Pennsylvania at 10:06 a.m. on 9/11, allegedly due to a passenger revolt. According to David Ray Griffin, in his essay "Flights of Fancy:" The Kean-Zelikow Commission "had to convince us that the military did not shoot it down." The Commission makes two major claims about Flight 93. The first one is that: "By the time the military learned about the flight, it had crashed." [114]

The main support for this claim is provided by yet another Commission tale of amazing incompetence by FAA officials. To accept this account, we must believe that, on a day on which there had already been attacks by hijacked airliners, officials at FAA headquarters had to debate whether a hijacked airliner with a bomb on board was important enough to disturb the military. And we must believe that they were still debating this question 13 minutes later, when, we are told, the following conversation between Herndon ATC center and FAA headquarters occurred:

Command Center: "Uh, do we want to think, uh, about scrambling aircraft?"

FAA HQ: "Oh, God, I don't know."

Command Center: "Uh, that's a decision somebody's gonna have to make probably in the next ten minutes." [115]

The Commission's tales about FAA incompetence and worthless tele-conferences are directly contradicted by Laura Brown's memo[116] and in Richard Clarke's book.[117] Their combined testimony implies that the Commission's main claim — that "by the time the military learned about the flight, it had crashed" — is a bald-faced lie.

There is an enormous amount of evidence suggesting that the FAA *did* notify the military about Flight 93; that Cheney went down to the underground shelter about 45 minutes earlier than the Commission claims; that he gave the shoot-down authorization about 25 minutes earlier than the Commission claims; and that military jets went after and shot down Flight 93. If some committee had set out to construct a fable about Flight 93, every part of which could be easily falsified, it could not have improved on the Commission's tale. Yet the mainstream media have not reported any of these obvious falsehoods.[118]

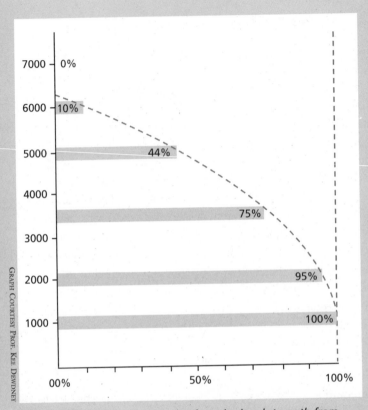

The curved dotted line shows the decay in signal strength from the strongest of several cell phones to the ground, from aboard a Piper Apache. Large commercial jets have much lower ceilings. Above 6,500 feet altitude, cell phone calls from airplanes on 9/11 were impossible anywhere. Over countryside such as rural Pennsylvania, without cell phone transmitters, service is unavailable at any altitude.

EXHIBIT Q

Cell Phones Don't Work Above 8,000 Feet or
Over Areas Without Cell Relay Transmitters

According to Canadian mathematician and computer scientist, Professor Emeritus A.K. Dewdney of the University of Western Ontario, a key element in the emerging story of the 9/11 terror attacks was the use of cell phones aboard high-flying passenger aircraft on the morning in question.[119] The calls would confirm the presence of Arab terrorists aboard the aircraft. The alleged use of cell phones aboard these aircraft was reported in virtually all the media and is referred to in several speeches by administration figures, including George W. Bush. Just two of the calls from Flight 93 are reported to have been via AirFone, the back-of-the-seat handset which operates through the aircraft's antennae.[120]

In a series of experiments conducted in 2003 and 2004, Dewdney tested a variety of cell phone equipment in light aircraft flying out of his home airport in London, Ontario, Canada.[121] The experiments show the cell phone service decayed more quickly with altitude and with heavier engine mass. There is ample anecdotal evidence to suggest that in larger aircraft such as the Boeing 767 and 757, the operational ceiling for cell phones is between 1,000 and 2,000 feet altitude. Indeed, service usually drops within a few minutes of takeoff. On the morning of September 11, 2001, all aircraft from which calls were allegedly made were at verified altitudes of more than 25,000 feet. Under these conditions, the cell phone calls were physically impossible.[122]

According to Professor Michel Chossudovsky of the University of Ottawa, "A large part of the description regarding the 19 hijackers relies on cell phone conversations with family and friends. While a few of these calls (placed at low altitude) could have got through, the wireless technology was not available [for cellular phones to work over 8,000 feet]. On this issue, expert opinion within the wireless telecom industry is unequivocal.[123] In other words, at least part of the Commission's *Report* on the cell phone conversations is fabricated. The planners of 9/11 found "cell phone conversations" about "Arab hijackers" necessary, as a real-time channel for lies necessary to the official story's "Script."[124]

Profile: Kee Dewdney

The PhD in Mathematics
Who Calls for a Scientific Jihad

Professor A. K. Dewdney, with a Ph.D in mathematics, taught computer science for more than 26 years at the University of Western Ontario and at the University of Waterloo. He is the author of 15 books on mathematics, science, and nature, more than 100 papers and more than 80 columns for *Scientific American* magazine.

Dewdney's suspicions were aroused on the morning of 9/11 by the official story of Muslim suicide bombers. "As a Muslim I was aware that suicide under any circumstances whatever is strictly ruled out by Islam, as are attacks on innocent civilians. The hijackers would be purchasing one-way tickets to a very unpleasant place." So much for the virgins in heaven. Since 9/11, thanks to his own experiments and the enormous amount of research available from working groups, he has come to believe the "war on terror" is an "extended false-flag" operation. "This investigative work is what *I* call jihad," he says.

The 64-year old Dewdney took early retirement in 1995, enabling him to devote more time to writing, research, and his first love — nature. Following 9/11, he decided to test elements of the official story for fakery. He tested the idea of cell phone calls from high-flying jetliners by conducting a number of experiments in light aircraft. His findings demonstrated conclusively that the cell phone calls allegedly made by passengers from the doomed aircraft were bogus. (See Chapter 2, Exhibit Q. He has also ruled out Airfones as the source of the calls.)

Kee Dewdney

In 2003 he formed a still-growing organization of some 35 scientists, engineers, scholars, intelligence officers, and others from relevant professions. The website of the Scientific Panel Investigating Nine-Eleven (SPINE) is at Physics911.net. This website includes thorough analyses of the cell phone calls, the Pentagon strike and the collapse of the WTC towers. A section is devoted to subsequent false-flag operations, including Madrid, Bali and London.

Dewdney supported — morally, financially and with his presence — the International Citizens' Inquiry into 9/11, Phase 2, at The University of Toronto in May 2004. He has also been active in spreading the word to Canadian Islamic communities, enjoining Muslims to be clear about the real purpose of the "war on terror."

Like most other 9/11 researchers and truth activists, Dewdney has a deep concern for the planet. His stewardship activities include owning and operating a 114-acre conservation area deep in southwestern Ontario. He and his wife have been working to restore a lush river line forest habitat there for the last six years. The couple has won many conservation awards for this and similar work.

His sense of humor is never far away, whether he's discussing scientific propositions, 9/11 research, or his beloved outdoors. "My wife Pat and I have discovered that it is possible to have a personal relationship with wild raccoons," Dewdney observed, "as long as the terms are set in advance: whatever they want, they get." Reminds one of the neocons. Dewdney's personal website (www.ced.uwo.ca/~akd/) can be visited for further details.

"In a post-9/11 (Truth Revealed) world, the citizens of our planet might turn again to what ought to be our main business — saving the planet while there is still time," he says. Dewdney's skills will be as welcome then as they are now, as he conducts his scientific and intellectual jihad on two fronts for the security of the human homeland.

COMMONDREAMS.ORG © NYT/SUCHAT PEDERSON

The "Jersey Girls," who pressured the White House into forming a 9/11 commission. Front to back: Kristen Breitweiser, Lorie VanAuken, Patty Casazza, Mindy Kleinberg.

EXHIBIT R

9/11 Commission Delays and Obstructions
Equal Bush Administration Cover-Up

A major obstacle for anyone wanting to find out what really happened on 9/11 was the delay in the setting up of a commission of inquiry. Most commissions of inquiry into major disasters have been appointed a few days after the disaster or precipitating event. In the case of the sinking of the Titanic it was six days. In the cases of the JFK assassination and the Challenger disaster it was seven. The first of four inquiries into the Pearl Harbor disaster was set up in just under ten days.[125]

The White House, on the other hand took 441 days after 9/11 to set up a commission of inquiry. This was after four determined 9/11 widows from New Jersey, who became known as "The Jersey Girls," pressured President Bush into creating the 9/11 Commission. Even so, two years after the Commission's final report, more than half of the questions the Jersey Girls asked the Commissioners remain unanswered. For example: Why has no one in any level of our government yet been held accountable for the countless "failures" leading up to and on 9/11? And: Was there a reason for Air Force One lifting off on 9/11 without a military escort, even after ample time had elapsed to allow military jets to arrive?[126]

The second obstacle to an honest inquiry was President Bush's initial appointment of Henry Kissinger to be its chairman. This appointment triggered a widespread negative reaction. *The New York Times* commented editorially: "It is tempting to wonder if the choice of Mr. Kissinger is not a clever maneuver by the White House to contain an investigation it long opposed." [127] It was only after this appointment failed that Bush appointed Thomas Kean and Lee Hamilton as co-chairmen but with Bush insider Philip Zelikow as the executive director. (See Exhibit S.)

The final budget given to the Kean-Zelikow Commission to investigate the biggest US disaster since Pearl Harbor was $14 million, compared to $40 million for Ken Starr's investigation into President Clinton's real estate and sex scandals, $50 million to investigate the 2004 *Columbia* disaster, and $75 million for the 1986 *Challenger* disaster.[128]

WWW.OTTAWAINDYMEDIA.CA

WWW.SANDLOPER.ORG

Condoleezza Rice and Philip Zelikow: "Essentially, the White House was investigating itself."

EXHIBIT S

Executive Director of 9/11 Commission
Closely Tied to the Bush White House

Although the *Report* of the 9/11 Commission was completed in July 2004, many Americans still had, and have, questions. Dr. Philip Zelikow, executive director of the Commission, acknowledged that questions remain in the minds of some. He has claimed that official reports and photos exist which would lay to rest the lingering unanswered questions of the official story. He said he has seen them but the public will not be allowed to view them. Zelikow's message: You can't see the evidence, just trust me.[129]

Zelikow has close ties to the Bush White House. David Ray Griffin, in his book *The 9/11 Commission Report: Omissions and Distortions,* makes the case that Zelikow was far from being "independent" in his work as the Commission's executive director. Zelikow accepted the official 9/11 story *a priori* and worked backwards to prove it, says Griffin. It is on this basis that Griffin believes the most accurate description of the commission is the Kean-Zelikow Commission.

Zelikow was a member of the Bush I administration. He got to know Condoleezza Rice very well there — they both served on the National Security Council in the 1980s. When they were between administrations during the Clinton years, they wrote a book together.[130] When the Bush II administration was coming into power Rice brought Zelikow in to help with the transition; he was then appointed to the foreign advisory board, so he is essentially a member of the Bush White House.

"And yet," Griffin notes, "as executive director, he ran the Commission. He had a staff of 70-some; he decided which topics were worth looking into, and which ones were not. When people would come and say, I want to testify to the Commission, I have something important to say, he would decide who would take that testimony." [131] At the Commission hearings there was testimony about the war games (see Exhibit G). Later the commissioners were asked: "Why didn't you deal with the war games in your report?" The commissioners replied: "Well, we were told that was unimportant." Well, by whom were they told? Philip Zelikow. "Essentially," Griffin says, "the White House was investigating itself."

THE
9/11
COMMISSION REPORT

Omissions and Distortions

by DAVID RAY GRIFFIN
author of The New Pearl Harbor

Author Griffin found "more than 100 lies" in the 9/11 Commission's Report.

EXHIBIT T

The 9/11 Commission Report:
"A 571 Page Lie" — Evidence of a Cover-Up

A study of the *Report,* according to author David Ray Griffin, will show it is entirely constructed to support the official 9/11 story. The 9/11 Commission accepted the official story lie *a priori.* In the process of embellishing this overall lie, the *Report* publishes many specific lies about particular issues. Many lies are outright, as when it claims the core of each of the Twin Towers consisted of a hollow steel shaft, instead of the 47 immensely strong, multiple solid steel columns that were actually there (see picture in Exhibit I). Another explicit lie is the *Report's* claim that Vice President Cheney did not give the Flight 93 shoot-down order until after 10:10 the morning of 9/11.

Other lies were told through omission, such as the Commission's leaving out almost all reference to the multiple war games that were both suspicious and detrimental on 9/11 (see Exhibit G). And when the Commission in its discussion of the 19 alleged suicide hijackers skips the fact that at least six of them have credibly been reported to be still alive[132], or when it fails to mention the fact that Building 7 of the World Trade Center collapsed (see Exhibit A), it is lying through omission.

The omissions show that the Commission failed to honor its stated intention "to provide the fullest possible account of the events surrounding 9/11." They are also lies insofar as the Commission could avoid telling explicit lies about particular issues only by avoiding any mention of them, which Griffin believes was the case in most instances.

Given these two types of lies, it might be wondered how many lies are contained in *The 9/11 Commission Report.* Griffin says he does not know. "But, deciding to see how many lies I had discussed in my book, I found that I had identified [more than] 100 ..."[133]

COURTESY MICHAEL SPRINGMANN

Michael Springmann, 20-year veteran of the US State Department, Foreign Service: The CIA was "complicit" in 9/11.

EXHIBIT U

CIA Creates, Trains and Runs Terrorists
Around the World Including 9/11 Patsies

In 1987, Michael Springmann, a practicing lawyer in Washington, DC, was chief of the visa section at the US Consulate in Jeddah, Saudi Arabia. He had worked for the US State Department's foreign service for 20 years. He says that back then the Consulate was a front for recruiting terrorists. In an article in *Covert Action Quarterly*[134] of Washington, DC, he detailed the recruiting of Arabs, "rounded up by [the CIA] and Osama bin Laden, to [be sent to] the U.S. for terrorist training by the CIA." He wrote: "The State Department did not run the Consulate in Jeddah. The CIA did. Of the roughly 20 Washington-dispatched staff there, I know for a certainty that only three people (including myself) had no ties, either professional or familial, to any of the U.S. intelligence services." He protested when his superiors repeatedly overruled his turning down unqualified applicants for entry to the USA. He was dismissed.

In October 2001, US attorney David Philip Schippers, former Chief Investigative Counsel for the US House Judiciary Committee and head prosecutor responsible for conducting the impeachment against former President Bill Clinton, revealed that several months prior to September 11, three FBI agents came to him informing him of "impending attacks." According to Schippers, these agents knew the names of the hijackers,[135] the targets of their attacks, the proposed dates, and the sources of their funding, along with other information, many months in advance of the "attacks." Schippers attempted to contact US Attorney General John Ashcroft without success. The FBI command cut short the investigations of the agents, threatening them with prosecution under the National Security Act if they publicized information pertaining to their investigations.

Springmann was asked on July 3, 2002, by CBC Radio host Rick MacInnes-Rae:[136] "If the CIA had a relationship with the people responsible for September 11, are you suggesting ... they are somehow complicit?" Springmann replied: "Yes, either through omission or through failure to act ... By the attempts to cover me up and shut me down, this convinced me more and more that this was not a pipedream."

WWW.MESINFOS.CANALBLOG.COM

Sibel Edmonds, former FBI translator of top-secret documents, accuses FBI translation services of "sabotage, intimidation, corruption and incompetence."

EXHIBIT V

FBI Involved in Protecting Persons Connected to Terrorism and 9/11

Sibel Edmonds[137] began working for the FBI shortly after 9/11. Until the spring of 2002 she worked in the FBI's Washington field office translating top-secret documents pertaining to suspected terrorists. When she witnessed many irregularities she began to speak out.

On February 11, 2004 Edmonds testified before the Kean-Zelikow Commission for three and a half hours. She told the Commission of an incident in which her colleague Behrooz Sarshar was participating in translating a message from Iran. The FBI had an asset in Iran, who told them prior to 9/11 that Osama bin Laden was planning to attack the United States; Edmonds said they (Behrooz Sarshar and the agent who received the message) were told to shut up and just keep quiet about it. Behrooz testified for two and a half hours, confirming Edmonds' testimony. None of the testimony of either is contained in *The 9/11 Commission Report*. She is mentioned in two footnotes as one of four people who recommended the FBI should "tighten up its procedures." [138]

Edmonds wrote a lengthy letter to Commission co-chairman Thomas Kean on August 1st, 2004, in which she asked detailed questions concerning issues ignored by *The 9/11 Commission Report*.[139] One was why a very significant pre-9/11 intelligence warning had not been mentioned in the report. She has received no satisfactory reply to any of her questions.

Earlier, on October 18, 2002, Attorney General John Ashcroft imposed a gag order on Ms. Edmonds, citing possible damage to diplomatic relations and national security. Shortly afterwards, she appeared on CBS's *60 Minutes*[140] and charged that the FBI, State Department and Pentagon had been infiltrated by agents of a Turkish intelligence officer suspected of ties to terrorism. She also accused members of the FBI's translation services of sabotage, intimidation, corruption and incompetence.

In August, 2004, Edmonds founded the National Security Whistle Blowers' Coalition. Edmonds, a woman who has faced an unprecedented level of government secrecy, gag orders and classification over 9/11 cover-ups, explains: "Trust me; they would not go to this length to protect some 'nobody' criminal or terrorist." [141] Her website is justacitizen.com

COURTESY AL JAZEERA

WWW.ALJAZEERA.COM

General Mahmoud Ahmad   *Mohamed Atta*   *George Tenet*

3AR.COM

3AR.COM

Representative Porter Goss   *Senator Bob Graham*

Pakistan's ISI (Inter Services Intelligence) agency was set up by the CIA. Starting upper left, clockwise: ISI head General Mahmoud Ahmad arranged for $100,000 to be wired to alleged lead hijacker Mohamed Atta shortly before 9/11, and met with CIA head George Tenet shortly before 9/11. Senator Bob Graham and Representative Porter Goss (a long-time CIA agent) breakfasted with Ahmad the morning of 9/11. Goss was later appointed head of the CIA by George W. Bush.

EXHIBIT W

CIA-Linked Pakistan ISI Financed "Lead Hijacker" Mohamed Atta

ISI stands for Inter Services Intelligence Agency, Pakistan's intelligence service. It was set up by the CIA; the two have long had close links.[142] So if there were evidence that the ISI was involved in 9/11 that would suggest a CIA link also.[143]

General Mahmoud Ahmad, the head of the ISI, was in Washington the week prior to 9/11, meeting with George Tenet, then head of the CIA.[144] This went unmentioned in the Kean-Zelikow *Report*.

Little reported by mainstream media was the fact that Sen. Bob Graham and Rep. Porter Goss had breakfast with General Ahmad on September 11.[145] Three years later, Porter Goss was named by Bush as the new "Intelligence Czar"[146] to head up the CIA, replacing Tenet.

Shortly before 9/11 the leader of Afghanistan's Northern Alliance, Ahmad Shah Masoud, was assassinated. Five days previous to the assassination Ahmad and Tenet met. According to the Northern Alliance, the assassination was carried out by the ISI. One outcome of this assassination was that control of the domestic situation in Afghanistan after the post-9/11 invasion was somewhat easier for the US; there were no established popular leaders left to challenge those the US administration arranged to be put into place. Michael C. Ruppert answered, when I asked him why Masoud was assassinated, that Masoud was "charismatic and incorruptible."[147]

Ahmad, according to a report in the *Times of India*, ordered another ISI agent to wire $100,000 to Mohamed Atta shortly before 9/11[148]. None of this evidence is referred to in *The 9/11 Commission Report*, whose authors said that they "found no evidence of any foreign government funding."[149] Among the report's recommendations is continued cooperation and funding of Pakistan and continued cooperation with Saudi Arabia.

Profiting from a loss

The stocks of United and American airlines fell sharply following the Sept. 11 terrorist attacks, which used hijacked jets from the two airlines. But unknown investors made a bundle using a financial derivative that increases in value when a stock goes down.

United Airlines
Daily closes

$30.82
$18.26
$17.50

SEPTEMBER

American Airlines
Daily closes

$29.70
$19.14
$18

SEPTEMBER

KEY: ■ Sept. 10 ■ Sept. 17 ☐ Yesterday
⋮ 4-day market closure after Sept. 11 attacks

Source:
Yahoo Finance

Chronicle Graphic

YAHOO! FINANCE

"Put" options are investments that pay off when a stock drops in price. Between September 6 and September 10, 2001, put options on UAL (United Airlines) jumped 90 times over average, and 285 times (not 285%) on the Thursday prior to 9/11. Similar activity was registered for American Airlines' stock.

EXHIBIT X

9/11 "Put" Options Prior to 9/11
Showed Advance Knowledge by Insiders

In the days just before 9/11, unusual volumes of trading had occurred in certain 9/11-related stocks. CBS *News* reported on September 19 that "alarm bells were sounding over unusual trading in the US stock options market." This involved "put options" – investments that pay off only when a stock drops in price.

On September 26, CBS reported that, in fact, there had been "a jump in UAL (United Airlines) put options 90 times [not 90 percent] above normal between September 6 and September 10, and 285 times higher than average on the Thursday before the attack." Similarly, there had been "a jump in American Airlines put options 60 times [not 60 percent] above normal on the day before the attacks." [150] Dylan Ratigan of *Bloomberg Business News* said: "This could very well be insider trading at the worst, most horrific, most evil use you've ever seen in your entire life." [151]

The CIA monitors stock trading in real time. Such highly unusual trading, therefore, would constitute a clear advance warning that United and American Airlines aircraft are going to be used on 9/11. [152] Darker possibilities are suggested by the fact that CIA Executive Director A. B. ("Buzzy") Krongard formerly managed the company that handled the "put" options on United Airlines. [153]

The 9/11 Commission says, in effect, as David Ray Griffin puts it: "Well there's been a lot of hullabaloo about the put options but we checked it out and we found that there was no advance knowledge because we found the agency that bought 95% of the United Airlines shares and it was somebody who had 'no conceivable ties to al Qaeda.' [154]

"So you see the circular argument. The official story is that the operation was pulled off entirely by al Qaeda and that nobody else knew about it. So if a speculator didn't have a pipeline to al Qaeda, he couldn't have possibly had anything to do with it." [155]

According to Michael C. Ruppert there was also "the fact that a *single* $2.5 million put option trade on United Airlines went unclaimed after the attacks which is appallingly clear evidence of criminal insider knowledge." [156]

The US "systematically" turned down numerous offers by the Taliban to extradite "and even assassinate" Osama bin Laden. — Leili Helms, niece of former CIA director Richard Helms, and unofficial US liaison to the Taliban in clandestine oil pipeline negotiations.

EXHIBIT Y

Osama bin Laden Has Long And Close Ties to CIA

Nafeez Ahmed, author of *The War on Truth*, writes that, "According to the conventional wisdom, US officials had consistently been attempting to encourage the Taliban to hand over Osama bin Laden, but the regime consistently refused to do so. But according to Leili Helms, niece of former CIA Director Richard Helms and the unofficial US liaison to the Taliban in relation to the clandestine oil pipeline negotiations, the US systematically turned down numerous offers by the Taliban to extradite — and even assassinate — bin Laden." [157]

Michel Chossudovsky, author of *America's 'War on Terrorism'*, writes: "Since the Cold War era, Washington has consciously supported Osama bin Laden, while at same time placing him on the FBI's 'most wanted list' as the world's foremost terrorist." [158] [159]

Richard Labeviere, a Swiss journalist,[160] wrote that bin Laden was reported to be receiving kidney dialysis at the American Hospital in Dubai in the United Arab Emirates in July 2001, just before 9/11. Not only that, but he was visited by the local CIA agent and members of the Saudi Royal Family.[161] Also, just *one day* prior to 9/11, he underwent kidney dialysis in Rawalpindi, at a military hospital in Pakistan (which has close ties to the Pentagon).[162] In *The 9/11 Commission Report* there is no mention of these two remarkable sightings.

According to David Ray Griffin, "They do not mention that the British press decided that the whole hunt for Osama bin Laden in Afghanistan was a charade. Remember, this was when he was in the Tora Bora Mountains and we were bombing this road and yet somehow he escaped into Pakistan? They didn't tell us that there were two roads and we only bombed one road, and he escaped using the other road. The preface of the Kean-Zelikow *Report* says, 'Our intention was to give the fullest possible account of the events surrounding 9/11.' Yet there is no mention of Saudi funding of al Qaeda. Former Senator Bob Graham's book[163] said this was clearly about Saudi government funding of al Qaeda." [164]

"A new Pearl Harbor" would be helpful in the "imperial effort" to control the vast petroleum reserves of central Asia. — Zbigniew Brzezinski

EXHIBIT Z

Leading Neo-Con Organization called for "A New Pearl Harbor"

The main objective of the new American Empire is full-spectrum dominance. That includes the weaponization of space. It is estimated by some this would cost at least a trillion dollars.[165] But now that the Cold War is over, how could the neo-conservatives get the American taxpayer to pay for it? They formed The Project for the New American Century (PNAC).[166]

Donald Rumsfeld, Dick Cheney, Richard Perle, Paul Wolfowitz and many other prominent Republicans who became central members of the Bush II administration were members of this organization. In September 2000, they issued a document called *Rebuilding America's Defenses*. In that they discuss the US playing "a more prominent role in Gulf regional security." And that "the process of transformation [of the US military] ... is likely to be a long one, absent some catastrophic and catalyzing event — like a new Pearl Harbor." The PNAC document asserts that "while the unresolved conflict with Iraq provides the immediate justification, the need for a substantial American force presence in the Gulf transcends the issue of the regime [change] of Saddam Hussein." [167]

There's no mention in Kean-Zelikow's *Report* of the fact that this same group was looking for an excuse to attack Iraq after Bush Senior stopped half way to Baghdad in 1991. In the 9/11 *Report* there's no mention of an interest in oil. However, Chalmers Johnson in his book *Sorrows of Empire* [168] makes clear that it's all or very largely about oil — and the necessary military bases to secure American corporate interests. According to the Kean-Zelikow Commission, the main US interests were "regime change" and encouraging democracy.[169]

As David Ray Griffin points out, in his list of 115 omissions from the 9/11 *Report* [170], there is no mention of Zbigniew Brzezinski's concept that the United States, in order to secure global primacy, needed to gain control of Central Asia. This is spelled out in Brzezinski's 1997 book, *The Grand Chessboard*. Brzezinski, co-founder of the Trilateral Commission, also pointed out the need to control the vast petroleum reserves of Central Asia, and wrote that a "new Pearl Harbor" would be helpful in getting the US public to support this "imperial effort." [171]

Closing Argument:
Where is The Evidence — for The Official Story?

The preceding 26 exhibits provide evidence showing beyond a reasonable doubt that 9/11 was an inside job perpetrated by elements of the US government and coordinated by the White House.

What evidence, on the other hand, has been provided by the US government — or anyone else who supports the official story — to back up the claim that 9/11 was an authentic "terrorist attack" carried out by Osama bin Laden and his al Qaeda network?

On October 2, 2001 what was alleged to be such evidence was provided to a meeting of the NATO Council by the US representative to NATO. Lord Robertson, the Secretary-General of NATO, stated in a press release that day: "We know that the individuals who carried out these attacks were part of the world-wide terrorist network of al Qaida, headed by Osama bin Laden and his key lieutenants and protected by the Taleban." He added that US representatives met officials of all NATO members in their capitals where they were presented with "evidence" regarding these charges.[172] [173] This evidence, or alleged evidence, was not made public.

NATO

Lord Robertson, Secretary-General of NATO, 1991.

On the basis of this unpublicized alleged evidence, NATO decided for the first time to invoke Article 5 of the NATO Charter which reads: "The Parties agree that an armed attack against one or more of them in Europe or North America shall be considered an attack against them all and consequently they agree that, if such an armed attack occurs, each of them, in exercise of the right of individual or collective self-defense recognised by Article 51 of the Charter of the United Nations, will assist the Party or Parties so attacked by taking forthwith, individually and in concert with the other Parties, such action as it deems necessary, including the use of armed force, to restore and maintain the security of the North Atlantic area."

Canada is a NATO country. On October 3, 2001, Alexa McDonough, at the time leader of Canada's New Democratic Party, rose in the House of Commons asking that the Canadian government make public the proof supplied by the US of bin Laden's and al Qaeda's involvement in 9/11. The proof was not forthcoming then, nor has it been to the time of writing, to Canada or any other NATO country, nor to the citizens of the US.

Canada, nevertheless, began contributing materially to the war in Afghanistan on the basis of the NATO decision. In late 2005, Canadian forces personnel in Afghanistan numbered 700. The number has increased to 2,000 as of March 2006, and the mission has been expanded to include search-and-destroy missions in the Kandahar area, freeing a similar number of US troops for other duties, such as in Iraq. In all, 12,000 soldiers in Afghanistan from 36 NATO countries have freed as many US soldiers to fight in Iraq. In Afghanistan, 8 Canadian soldiers had lost their lives by January 15, 2006, the day senior Canadian diplomat Glyn Berry was killed near Kandahar in a suicide bombing which injured three servicemen, two seriously. By May 20, 17 Canadians had been killed.

On September 12, 2001, prior to the NATO meeting, the UN Security Council adopted hastily-written resolution 1368 (2001) in which the Council condemned "in the strongest terms the horrifying terrorist attacks which took place on September 11, 2001 in New York, Washington, D.C. and Pennsylvania and regards such acts, like any act of international terrorism, as a threat to international peace and security." The resolution called on "all States to work together urgently to bring to justice the perpetrators, organizers and sponsors of these terrorist attacks and stresses that those responsible for aiding, supporting or harbouring the perpetrators, organizers and sponsors of these acts will be held accountable."

The resolution did not name Osama and al Qaeda, but nevertheless a "white paper" for the UN was promised by then Secretary of State Colin Powell proving Osama bin Laden's and al Qaeda's guilt for 9/11. Such a white paper, if proved valid, would enable all member nations at the UN to proceed with this urgent priority of tracking down the 9/11 perpetrators, since the resolution is binding on all UN members. But there's a problem blocking this potentially much-expanded "war on terrorism." The promised white paper has never been produced.

Profile: Elias Davidsson

"A New Mass Movement for True Democracy Could Emerge"

As I was departing Iceland's Keflavik airport in June 2005 a pleasant lady handed me a questionnaire. Why did I choose Iceland as a destination, how was the service, and so on. And what did I think of the proposed motto "Pure Energy" for Iceland? As a motto for the country I wasn't sure, but I was sure it could be the motto of Elias Davidsson, who had just been my and my wife's host for three days.

Besides setting up a successful screening of my DVD at Nordic House, Davidsson arranged a lunch with two Members of Parliament, two radio interviews and one newspaper interview. All were successful. There were two visits to the spacious basement headquarters in Reykjavik of the Icelandic 9/11Truth movement. Oh, yes, the full day of sightseeing. Even though it was daylight for 24 hours, we had no trouble sleeping.

Davidsson, 65, is mentor and inspiration to a talented group of Icelander activists most of whom are hardly half his age. When he is deep into the theory and details of 9/11Truth and organization it's hard to imagine he's also a composer of note and a long-time human rights researcher and

Elias Davidsson

activist. Where these converge is in his insistence on a fact-based approach, rigorous logic, rationality and a sense of justice. It is because he does not hold forth until he is sure of his facts that he can be so passionate when he does. He is sharply opposed to the idea of "toning down" one's beliefs so that they will be more acceptable. "Truth may be bitter, but it heals," he believes.

He was born in Palestine in 1941 of a German father who moved there ten years earlier for religious reasons. His mother left Germany because of Nazi persecution of Jews. As a young man in France, Elias was a member of a Zionist youth movement but left it, "disillusioned with Zionist ideology which I recognized as based on racist premises." At age 21 he moved to Iceland which until the 60s required new citizens to adopt Icelandic names. He worked for 22 years as a computer specialist, 14 of them with IBM. He then returned to his once-cherished field of music, becoming a music school director, church organist, composer and arranger. He has published about 20 volumes of original compositions.

For many years, Davidsson has engaged in research and activism for social and global justice, peace, anti-racism and human rights. He is co-founder of the Association Iceland-Palestine and a supporter of a united democratic state in Palestine for both Jews and Arabs. As a response to the deadly sanctions against the Iraqi people he began researching international law. With the aid of a research grant from the Icelandic Red Cross Society he studied economic sanctions and published his findings in peer-reviewed journals.

In 2002, after he read Thierry Meyssan's books on 9/11 "and checked his (Meyssan's) sources," he was convinced that the truth about 9/11 must be exposed.

Davidsson contemplates two opposing scenarios for the future. In the first the truth about 9/11 will be exposed and "those who conceived, planned, organized, perpetrated and covered up the crime" will be brought to justice and "a new mass movement for real democracy will emerge." In the second the truth about 9/11 "will remain underexposed, those who conspired in 9/11 and its cover-up will feel confident to set up national security states in which no true opposition will be permitted, and human rights and democracy will wither for a long time."

Such a paper would need to include, for instance, some basic information such as the names of the supposed hijackers on the passenger lists of the four airliners. But the publicly released flight manifests contain no Arab names. And so it goes with aspect after aspect of the official story.

Iceland is a NATO country. On October 4, 2004, Elias Davidsson, a 9/11 Truth activist living in Reykjavik (see profile, page 112), wrote a letter to the Icelandic Ministry of Foreign Affairs requesting that the Ministry publish the evidence it had received from NATO on the alleged guilt of bin Laden and al Qaeda for the events of 9/11. In particular, the author requested that evidence be provided that al Qaeda members had actually boarded the four planes that crashed on 9/11, a prerequisite for committing the crimes they were alleged to have committed.

The Icelandic Ministry of Foreign Affairs did not respond to the letter, nor to a reiterated request in December. Davidsson then turned to the Icelandic Ombudsman who, in turn, asked the Ministry to reply before January 4, 2005. The Ministry did not abide by this request. The Ombudsman's office repeated its request to the Ministry. Finally in a letter to Davidsson dated February 18, 2005 the Ministry invoked its "duty of secrecy towards NATO" as the main reason for refusing to provide the requested information. As a secondary reason, the letter invokes the fact that Iceland's Public Information Act can be used to limit information to ordinary citizens. The Ministry refuses to further justify its refusal.

Closer to home, why has the public not been informed of the data on three black boxes that, according to Nicholas DeMasi, firefighter, Engine Co. 261 FDNY,[174] were found at the WTC site, and then confiscated by the FBI? Why have the video tapes of the Pentagon confiscated by the FBI from the CITGO gas station and Sheraton Hotel across the road from the Pentagon not been released? Why have the Pentagon's own tapes not been made public except for five video frames (See Exhibit N), in which no airliner can be seen?

With the approach of the fifth anniversary of 9/11, there has been time for US government investigators and lawyers to assemble sufficient evidence for numerous charges against Osama bin Laden and members of al Qaeda. Many alleged al Qaeda members have been held in Guantanamo Bay, and others have been held elsewhere around the world. Many trials should be underway and plenty of convictions registered, in light of the US government's unwavering and strident insistence as to who the culprits are, and given the vast resources of the US government. Where are these charges, these trials, these convictions? On August 31, 2004, 9/11 researcher Michael C. Ruppert stated: "To date, the case that 9/11 was perpetrated solely by Osama bin Laden and al Qaeda has never been proven even to the most rudimentary standards. In fact, some 35 months after the attacks there has not been a single successful 9/11 prosecution anywhere in the world. The only conviction that had been secured, a German prosecution against Mounir el Motassadeq, charged with aiding the so-called Hamburg cell of Mohammed Atta, was overturned in 2004 because the US government refused to produce key witnesses such as Khalid Shaikh Muhammad or Ramzi bin al-Shibh and other evidence relevant to the charges." [175]

As I was writing this in early 2006, a sentencing hearing was being held for Zacarias Moussaoui, to determine solely whether he should be executed or receive life in prison. He's been convicted of lying to investigators about his alleged knowledge of alleged plans of al Qaeda to fly planes into buildings. While incarcerated he confessed, the government prosecutors said, to conspiracy charges in connection with 9/11. Moussaoui's arrest, custody, confessions, trial, conviction and sentencing hearing have been marked by absurdities and controversies. For instance, Harry Samit, one FBI agent involved in the case, testified under oath on March 20, 2006 that he believed his superiors at the FBI in Washington were guilty of "criminal negligence" in the way they failed to follow up on urgings by Samit that Moussaoui be fully investigated prior to 9/11.

The suspect conviction of Moussaoui in a "show trial" worthy of Stalin is the sole and fragile connection between 9/11 and any alleged "terrorist", almost five years after 9/11. On May 3, 2006, Moussaoui was sentenced to life in prison. He has since recanted his "confession" and is appealing.

The wars on Afghanistan and Iraq, nevertheless, are based largely on the official story of Osama bin Laden and al Qaeda being responsible for 9/11. The Iraq war as of January 2006 has cost US$236 billion,[176] and more than 2,400 American[177] and 250,000 Iraqi civilian lives.[178] Lives, justice and history are at stake in determining the true criminals behind 9/11.

We have provided our evidence that elements associated with the White House perpetrated 9/11. What evidence has been provided by the US government — or anyone else — to prove that Osama bin Laden had the power to:

- Neutralize the US Air Force?
- Make George Bush say odd things about what he saw on television?
- Demolish WTC 7 late in the day of 9/11?
- Cause the White House to drag its feet for 441 days before setting up a commission of inquiry into his amazing powers?
- Cause the 9/11 Commission to omit embarrassing connections between his family and the Bush family, and between the CIA and al Qaeda, in addition to more than 100 other omissions, distortions and falsehoods?

In short, where is the evidence that — in the words of the big city editor quoted previously — "can be properly substantiated through sources and documents that would stand up in a court of law," to prove 9/11 was an authentic "terrorist attack" carried out by Osama bin Laden and his "al Qaeda network?"

Only a truly independent judicial or quasi-judicial international inquiry mandated to hear all evidence from all interested parties — including the US regime — can provide trustworthy answers to questions such as these.

3

9/11 Truth is Hidden in Plain Sight: 2001 Tricks for Avoiding the Obvious

"The conscious mind ... is a spin doctor, not the commander in chief."

— Steven Pinker in *How The Mind Works*

"How much truth can this world stand?"

— Mose Allison, song

Washington, D.C. July 23, 2005 — We are six, enjoying pre-dinner drinks in a warm and friendly restaurant pub near American University. Five of us, attending the three-day DC Emergency Truth Convergence, are familiar with the evidence in the preceding chapter that 9/11 was an inside job. The sixth person in our party is a friend of one of us, invited to join us for dinner, a pleasant woman in her late forties, an architect.

A binder of information relating to 9/11 has been brought by hummux, the former Star Wars engineer profiled on page 120. He opens it to a page featuring a pair of images he thinks will interest an architect. On the left is a picture of the Madrid high-rise building (see Chapter 2, Exhibit J), fully ablaze on February 12, 2005. It burned out of control for 17 hours but never collapsed. The other photo is of one of the WTC towers collapsing after a much smaller fire burned for about an hour.

He shows the photos to the architect. Why, he asks her, would the WTC tower collapse so quickly while the Madrid tower remained standing? Without missing a beat she answers: "Because the Madrid tower was fireproofed." I say to her: "You just made that up, didn't you?" Without missing a beat she replies: "Yes!" We all laugh.

It *was* funny. Laughter is involuntary, a reflex. The meaning of laughter often is insignificant. But in this case I think it *was* significant, especially in the context of this book. It was added evidence of the latest research findings about how our minds so often function to short-circuit rational thought, without our consciously planning for this to happen.

The essential transaction is that hummux introduces threatening information: there's something fishy about the way the WTC towers came down — with all that implies. The architect's mind instinctively, if you will, searches for an explanation to prove the threat is not real. In the flash of the moment, her mind decides there's no time to grapple with the implications of the suddenly-introduced visuals, but there's time to protect the "truth" of the fire-and-pancaking theory pre-established in her mind. This is typical of a great deal of "thinking" that takes place every day in all our minds, on a wide variety of topics.

These mental processes are of great relevance in the struggle between 9/11 Story and 9/11 Evidence discussed in the previous chapter. Let's analyze further this little exchange in the restaurant. Steven Pinker in his book *How The Mind Works*[1] devotes a section to "reverse engineering" humor. He first turns to Arthur Koestler's work in the field. Koestler said humour begins with a train of thought in one frame of reference, that bumps up against an anomaly: an event or statement that makes no sense in the context of what went before.

One of the many contradictions of 9/11 is that no steel-framed high-rise prior to 9/11 had ever been felled by fire (and none since, either). But for someone who has accepted the official story, the fire-and-pancaking explanation for the Twin Towers' collapses will be that person's established, or at least current, truth on the matter.

Koestler's analysis of humour continues: The anomaly bumped up against can be resolved by shifting to a different frame of reference, one in which the event does make sense. In our restaurant-pub scenario, the architect shifts to a (ludicrous, in hindsight) frame of reference: some sprayed-on asbestos keeps a flaming Madrid office tower standing for 17 hours. In New York no asbestos, buildings burn down. Anomaly resolved (except the NY buildings did have asbestos and lots of it!).

The frame shift, Koestler says, involves someone's dignity being down-graded. In our little example, at this point, it's hummux's. For a moment it appears the implication behind his question doesn't have a leg to stand on.

But then I question the architect's frame-of-reference shift. Now it's her dignity that's on the line. Things are moving too quickly for her mind to protect her new explanation; her mind figures out the fastest way to pre-serve her dignity is a strategic retreat to a truth that will stand an immedi-ate test: that her frame-of-reference shift was concocted. In this particular give-and-take, no one's dignity was much damaged, as the involuntary laughter all 'round confirms.

Other interpretations of the exchange are available. One begins with Pinker's observation: "The mind reflexively interprets other people's words and gestures by doing whatever it takes to make them sensible and true." "If [they] are sketchy or incongruous, the mind charitably fills in missing premises or shifts to a new frame of reference in which they make sense."

In this interpretation, the architect's mind, not being embedded in a hard-edged or confrontational person, reaches for a far-fetched explanation to make hummux's anomaly "sensible and true." That process is based on the "principle of relevance," without which language itself would be impos-sible. Explains Pinker: "The thoughts behind even the simplest sentence are so labyrinthine that if we ever expressed them in full our speech would sound like the convoluted verbiage of a legal document." (Or like this part of this book.)

We Make Up Facts on the Spot

If we recognize that other people (and ourselves) involuntarily make up "facts" on the spot, this equips us better to challenge them (nicely, of course) when they hold forth on 9/11 without knowing what they're talk-ing about. Failure to recognize that we make things up involuntarily robs us of some valuable humility, and makes us less likely to retract quickly when we've slipped into invention.

We're still not finished with the role of humour here. The role I played was also involuntary. The question "You just made that up, didn't you?" just popped out of my mouth. Involuntarily, I played the role of jester. "The jester," Pinker explains, "manipulates this mental machinery to get the

Profile: hummux

"Enlightenment is a Full Time Job!"

It's especially appropriate to consider the trajectory of the life of hummux (pronounced who-mook, lower case). Born in 1940, he earned his Ph.D. in physics at California Institute of Technology. His first "real job" was helping design the intercontinental ballistic "Missile X" and harden its silos, "even before it was named the Minuteman Missile." He "happily participated in underground tests in Nevada," thinking "this was my patriotic contribution to the Vietnam war effort." He ultimately participated in the Cold War, working on Star Wars (Strategic Defense Initiative). He had "become more disgruntled by what was going on; when the Berlin Wall fell, I assumed the Cold War was over and got out of the business."

"White Wolf" hunting audio at Toronto's International Citizens' Inquiry into 9/11.

Shortly after he left the military-industrial complex something guided him to a native teacher, with whom he studied for ten years, and he became a wilderness guide. The single name of the missile guide turned wilderness guide was given him by his teacher. It means White Wolf in the Esselen language. His concerns have become deep and several. They all come, he says, "from the center of my being — the place where each of us can find our truth, and all meet at the One Center."

For hummux the light bulb on 9/11 was "no scramble of fighter jets." After that it took a lecture by Ken Jenkins discussing the psychological aspects of 9/11, "and seeing the collapse of WTC building 7, to spark my activism." Once involved, he learned about "the string of war pretext events and military interventions from Pearl Harbor through the JFK and Martin Luther King assassinations, Waco, WTC '93 and the CIA supporting military dictators worldwide." This heightened his resolve "to subvert this paradigm," and led to the comment in the headline. Although a light bulb in effect went off in his head on 9/11, he had to work to get the larger picture. "You have to work on finding your center and staying balanced."

His has joined Jenkins in producing "a continuous string of 9/11Truth videos" based on 9/11Truth events including international 9/11 inquiries in San Francisco, Toronto and New York. Hummux identifies this work "and (Ken's) focus on the psychological aspects of 9/11 and the 9/11Truth movement in a gentle and practical way" the most positive experiences from his involvement.

His primary motivation, he says, is to stop what he helped create, "the militarization of the planet. I don't want lingering doubt about what happened on 9/11 to confound my children, the way the murder of JFK confounded my generation." The fuel to keep him going is "slow but sure progress. Anybody who 'gets it' never goes back." He's heartened at the "slow but sure leaking of 9/11 information into the mainstream." He cites the C-SPAN coverage of a talk in Madison, Wisconsin by David Ray Griffin and of Cynthia McKinney's congressional briefings (see chapter 8), and Steven Jones' outspoken lectures at Brigham Young University. But overall he sees the media as being held "in a stranglehold by the military, industrial, intelligence community." He cites "the total media suppression of the blatantly stolen 2004 election." He sees the way forward as 'being the media.'"

The future, hummux believes, holds "great change, and ultimate success in deflating the Global Domination Project of the neocons, with the emergence of an America that is peaceful and sharing, while surviving in a world devastated by global warming."

audience to entertain a proposition — the one that resolves the incongruity — against their will. People appreciate the truth of the disparaging proposition because it was not baldly asserted as a piece of propaganda they might reject, but was a conclusion they deduced themselves."

This explains, he continues "the feeling that a witty remark may capture a truth that is too complex to articulate, and that it is an effective weapon that forces people, at least for a moment, to agree to things they would otherwise deny." It would be pleasant to believe I'm that brilliant but as I say it was involuntary. What made it possible? What triggered it? The key is that my mind's field of pre-judgment was different from the architect's. My mind's orientation was and is that 9/11 was an inside job. My mind saw a threat, too, but that threat was the official story — and by extension all protections of it, including instantaneous unconscious ones, such as the architect's.

The brief exchange was more a manifestation of two minds automatically defending their organizing belief systems than two people having a conversation. The architect and I were in that brief instant, essentially puppets in a contest between our minds. It's interesting territory for those who truly seek to remain truth-seekers and truth-tellers.

The Illusion of the Unified Self

If you've stuck with me this far, you may be more willing than most to go deeper into the brief exchange we've been considering. Going deeper is threatening to that part of us that believes — because we are wired to believe this way — that we're in control of our consciousness, that we are captains of our thoughts. It's an ongoing human conceit that we are always in charge of what we think. We pay a price if we do not explore this conceit. The price is foregone self-knowledge. Pinker, in his latest book, *The Blank Slate: the Modern Denial of Human Nature*[2] writes that "the unified self is an illusion." He builds on new research into the two hemispheres of our brains. The left is the so-called logical, rational, intellectual side. The right is the so-called artistic, pattern-recognizing, "emotional," side.

"One of the most dramatic demonstrations of the illusion of the unified self," Pinker writes, "comes from the neuroscientists Michael Gazzaniga and Roger Sperry, who showed that when surgeons cut the corpus callosum joining the cerebral hemispheres, they literally cut the self in two, and each hemisphere can exercise free will without the other one's advice or consent. Even more disconcertingly, the left hemisphere *constantly weaves a coherent but false account of the behaviour chosen without its knowledge by the right.*" [Emphasis added]

British medical journalist Rita Carter in *Mapping the Mind*[3] addresses the same phenomenon: "The idea that our actions may be irrational is peculiarly unacceptable to the left hemisphere," she writes. "A series of famous experiments showed that people hardly ever admit to making arbitrary decisions. In one of the experiments, for example, a selection of nylon stockings was laid out and a group of women were invited to choose a pair. When they were asked why they had made their particular choice all the women were able to give detailed and sensible reasons, citing slight differences in colour, texture or quality. In fact, all the stockings were identical — the women's 'reasons' for choosing them were actually rationalizations constructed to explain an essentially inexplicable piece of behaviour."[4]

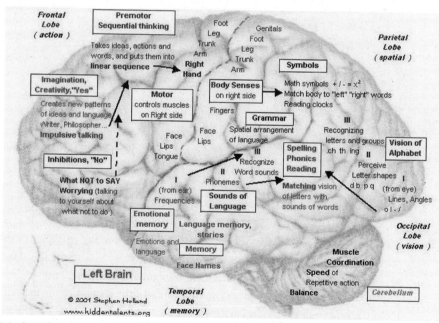

In Stephen Holland's layperson's guide to the function of the brain, the "imagination, creativity, 'yes'" section is the "spin doctor." Note the "impulsive talking" where rationalizations are generated.

The "spooky part," Pinker writes, "is that we have no reason to think that the baloney-generator in the left hemisphere [of a patient whose left and right hemispheres have been separated surgically] is behaving any differently than our baloney generator .... The conscious mind ... is a spin doctor, not the commander-in-chief."

Let's apply this to everyday life. A story becomes in effect our commander-in-chief. Our "baloney-generator" says: "Yes, sir! I'll back that up." Our "baloney generator" will invent reasons to prove true a story we've been pre-programmed with.

A stunning example of such a story is one I've heard repeated which is supposed to explain the sudden collapse of World Trade Center Building 7 (WTC7) into its own footprint at 5:20 p.m. on September 11, 2001 (see Chapter 2, Exhibit A). This particular story must be close to a baloney generator buster. The story is that there were tanks of diesel fuel in the basement and they caught fire. Anyone loading this baby into his brain has to overlook that there is zero evidence of blazing diesel fuel in WTC7. No one can point to any photographic evidence of fire or smoke near the base of the building. No one can cite any eyewitness evidence. No one can refer to evidence that anyone smelled burning diesel fuel. No one can point to any forensic evidence. (This is all apart from the fact that even if the *whole building* was soaked in burning diesel fuel *that* would not have brought it down.) The official report on WTC7's collapse comes to no conclusion. The report of the 9/11 Commission does not mention WTC7 falling. Anyone accepting the burning diesel fuel "explanation" has an out-of-control baloney generator.

When We Reject Unwelcome Information the Brain's Pleasure Center Lights Up

But the psychological trouble we're in — and therefore the challenge faced by those who are striving to introduce evidence to change preconditioned beliefs — is much greater than that presented by denial alone. Recent American research shows that "we derive positive pleasure from irrationally sticking with beliefs against evidence."[5] The research, done at Emory University, was presented in January 2006 to the Society for Personality and Social Psychology, in Palm Springs, CA. It showed "there are flares of activity in the brain's pleasure centers when unwelcome information is being rejected," said psychologist and lead author Dr. Drew Westen. "... activity spiked in the circuits involved in reward, a response similar to what addicts experience when they get a fix," Westen explained. The study points to a total lack of reason in political decision-making. And make no mistake: 9/11 *is* political. "None of the circuits involved in conscious reasoning were particularly engaged," Westen said.

The "cold reasoning" regions of the cortex were relatively quiet. For partisans, political thinking is often predominantly emotional. "It is possible to override these biases," Dr. Westen said, "but you have to engage in ruthless self reflection, to say, 'All right, I know what I want to believe, but I have to be honest.'" He added: "It speaks to the character of the discourse that this quality is rarely talked about in politics."

Into this discouraging mix we must introduce interests. The brain of a person whose livelihood derives largely or wholly on belief in a particular story or worldview will be rationalizing on steroids to protect that story or view. This factor alone makes it quite understandable to me why an Ethopian Canadian cab driver can "get it" about 9/11, where a university-educated editor at a major daily newspaper cannot. Or for that matter, a Ph.D in psychology. Intellect is little involved and insofar as it is, intellect is at the service of emotional automatism and interests.

This muddle of factors determining our beliefs about 9/11 should be kept in mind when we are talking with family, friends, neighbors and colleagues about 9/11. Our best chance is to try to understand what they think is fact, what is their worldview, what values they think are at issue and what interests are at stake for them. Openings to share the truth as we see it will tend to appear. For instance if "security" is a big issue for someone, a discussion as to whether the Bush regime's "reactions" to 9/11 increased or decreased domestic security could be interesting and fruitful. If a person is patriotic but values honesty in government, trying to find out which ranks higher and then relating that to lies of 9/11 could be useful.

9/11 as Macro Psychological Event

In this chapter, we've been dealing with what might be called the micro side of denial. This includes the events of 9/11, which were received at a very personal level, invading our psyches, our emotions, our dreams. At the same time, 9/11 was obviously a macro event. It was planned to exert maximum psychological effect on the population as a whole, and on history. It was planned to hugely advance the interests of its planners, the neo-con cabal atop the American Empire, and the vast financial, corporate, and especially military interests they serve, and that currently predominate on Earth.

It doesn't help that in previous times our tendency to believe the guff dished out by the powers-that-be made sense. As Carter writes in *Mapping the Mind:*

> The urge to rationalize behavior probably has considerable survival value. The human species got where it is largely by forming complex social constructs — from the hunting party to the political party — and making them work. To work they require that we have confidence in them and to have confidence we need to believe that the actions of these organizations are based on sound, rational judgments. At one level, of course, we know we are kidding ourselves. For example, all governments, in all societies, have some policies that are demonstrably irrational. We may see through it, but basically we like things this way — it makes us feel safe. Similarly, rationalizing our own actions gives us confidence in our sanity.[6]

In late 2000, media guru Douglas Rushkoff, a professor at NYU and an Esalen Institute teacher, wrote *Coercion: Why we Listen to What "They" Say.*[7] It received good reviews and went on to win the 2002 Marshall McLuhan Award for best media book. What Rushkoff did was actually listen to advertisers, marketers, public relations specialists, Hollywood filmmakers, salespeople, pyramid scam artists and cult leaders to find out how they get us to "listen to them," that is, *believe* what they say. Rushkoff came to the conclusion that the ways they accomplish this go beyond persuasion, hence the title of his book. He believes what they do is much more muscular, that it is a form of coercion. Ominously, the methods used are the same as those developed and gradually perfected by CIA interrogators and psychological warfare experts.

Secrets of Mind Control are Well-Understood

Fortunately, the mind-control secret Rushkoff learned is so simple it can be summed up in one sentence: "In whatever milieu coercion is practiced, the routine follows the same basic steps: generate disorientation, induce regression, and then become the target's transferred parent figure."[8] As soon as I read that, I recalled the testimony of a Canadian recently held in a Syrian prison and tortured for ten months after US authorities illegally seized and "renditioned" him with the collusion of Canadian authorities. He said: "The first full slap on the face changed everything."

In early 2006, Kevin Barrett, coordinator of the US-based Muslim-Jewish-Christian Alliance for 9/11 (MUJCA-NET), wrote a brilliant essay

on 9/11 as a psychological operation (psyop). He praises Rushkoff's work as his inspiration. His essay is entitled "Apocalypse of Coercion: Why We Listen to What 'They' Say About 9/11."[9] Rushkoff emailed Barrett that he thought his essay "terrific." Barrett begins: "Rushkoff's *Coercion* is a sizzling exposé of mind control, American style. Unlike Chomsky's *Manufacturing Consent*, Rushkoff's book provides a detailed guide to the nuts-and-bolts techniques employed against us every day ..."

The techniques, Barrett says, "disable rational thought and manipulate behavior at the unconscious and emotional levels." Here he seems to be assuming that people think rationally to begin with. As we have seen, this is simply not the case. But his apparent unawareness of the fragility of the human reality-generating apparatus serves to emphasize our vulnerabilities to the planned deceptions by those behind the really dark curtains. Both

Barrett and Rushkoff underline the extent to which we are sitting ducks. Our strength to resist and overcome the manipulators depends on our knowledge of *their* methods and *our* vulnerabilities. In understanding our vulnerabilities lies our strength. As Barrett puts it:

> Anyone curious about why so many otherwise rational people have believed the official story of 9/11 for so long, in the teeth of overwhelming evidence against it should start by reading *Coercion*. Under coercion, millions of otherwise rational people can be persuaded to act against their own interests — whether by shelling out big bucks for overpriced lemons, betraying a comrade and a cause, or allowing a gang of criminals to destroy their nation's Constitution and launch criminal wars of aggression.[10]

The Infantalization of the American Public

A CIA interrogation manual obtained by Rushkoff takes the location of the coercion back to the micro level. As he explains in *Coercion*, as the minutes, hours or days go by for the person being interrogated, the "sights and sounds of an outside world fade away, [and] its significance is replaced by the [windowless] interrogation room, its two occupants, and the dynamic relationship between them .... The subject becomes completely dependent on the interrogator for all external stimuli and, accordingly, his sense of self."[11] The "disruption of the familiar emotional associations" of the "target," the manual explains, "induces a ... stage of radical confusion. When this aim is achieved, resistance is seriously impaired. There is an interval — which may be extremely brief — of suspended animation, a kind of psychological shock or paralysis ... that explodes the world that is familiar to the subject as well as

Douglas Rushkoff

his image of himself within that world. Experienced interrogators recognize this effect when it appears and know that at this moment the source is far more open to suggestion." [12]

This is the moment the interrogator encourages the subject to regress to a childlike state of mind and the interrogator "becomes the subject's transferred parent figure." Students of language will notice that in this CIA manual, the person being interrogated is never described as a person. He or she is described as a "target," a "subject" or "a source."

Barrett then draws the parallel with the 9/11 false-flag operation. "The images of planes crashing into landmark buildings ... created a state of extreme confusion, a kind of psychological shock or paralysis. They literally exploded the world that was familiar to us, and our images of ourselves in that world." He postulates that "we experienced a moment of dissociation, which is why we can ... recall where we where and what we were doing when we learned of the attack." [13] In *Mapping the Mind*, Rita Carter suggests our memories became imprinted on 9/11 because of fear. She writes: "During a trauma attention is very narrowly focused and whatever happens to be the center of attention — whether it is relevant or incidental — will be laid down as a particularly sharp 'flashbulb' memory." [14]

My reading is that neither of these two words — dissociation or fear — adequately captures what most of us experienced on 9/11. Putting Carter's and Pinker's insights together we can postulate that our minds instantly assessed the situation (in the limbic system, what Carter describes as "the cerebral underworld of raw emotion," at a deeper level than words: "Something huge is happening that is fearful, confusing and extremely threatening. All other considerations must be shoved aside to permit laser-like focus on this to decide what I should tell my host body to do." [15] Call it massive alertness suspending normal brain function; openness to further data to make the fight, flight or appease decision. The Buddhist "gap moment."

Psywar Experts Planned 9/11 as Mass Hypnosis

As Carter writes: "Our conscious control over emotions is weak, and feelings often push out thinking, whereas thinking fights a mainly losing battle to banish emotions." [16]

However we might describe our collective state of mind and emotions, "the psychological warfare experts who designed the operation knew very well," Barrett says, that the events of 9/11 "left us radically open to suggestion — to mass hypnosis. Our old world had been annihilated, and we were ready to be hypnotized, and to have a new world created for us. The psywar planners had a complete narrative — the official 9/11 story — prepared, to explain everything. Additionally "we" — our minds — were manipulated into "desperately [needing] a parent figure to tell us how to make sense of the madness."[17] In the US the presidency is "a paternal institution." Even George W. Bush "could briefly become our idealized national daddy." The American public was infantilized and manipulated. Thus the official story was powerfully imprinted on the collective consciousness.

On the day, the equivalent of the windowless interrogation room for the public at large was its dependence on the mass media — especially television. Marshall McLuhan pointed out that TV tends to disable our left brain and leave us more open to suggestion in the right. So our brains were doubly vulnerable to suggestion as the official story was fed to us. As Barrett puts it: "They say suicidal Muslim fanatics did it. They say those radical Muslims hate our freedoms. They say the country is full of sleeper agents who could wake up and kill us at any moment, as soon as their little red-white-and-blue 'I hate the USA' wristwatch alarms go off. They say anybody who questions what they say is a conspiracy theorist."[18]

The number 911 may have been deliberate as well, Barrett speculates. It has emotional associations because it's "the magic number we can call in the event of an emergency ... a benevolent figure, the government, will come rushing to help us. It's these emotional associations, not facts, that condition how we think."

Brainwashing is Simple

The hypnotic inculcation of thoughts — brainwashing — is simple. As Barrett states: "The key is repetition: Repetition, repetition, *repetition*. In the Alice-in-Wonderland world of the so-called war on terror, 'what I tell you three times is true.'" It's important to note that the story does not have to make rational sense entirely. In this case it includes such patent absurdities as observant Muslim fanatics drinking at bars the night before 9/11, a hijacker's passport miraculously floating down from the inferno in the towers, alleged Arab hijacker Hani Hanjour who could not fly a Cessna training aircraft flying an amazing stunt maneuver in a 757 in order to hit an empty, newly reinforced wing of the Pentagon and cause minimal damage — instead of just diving into the roof and killing thousands. The baloney generator will defend this story.

Even firmly-planted fictional stories, however, can be cracked open if a sufficient number of questions about them are permitted to prosper. The baloney generator can be overcome. But only by questioning. Enter the mainstream media: before the day is out on a critical story they will be performing the most crucial function of all: suppressing questioning. At the same time they will be reinforcing the existing establishment-oriented prejudgments about how the world works and, within that, disseminating the "new normal" official story. The synthetic surround for the official story is comprised of zero questioning but immense repetition of emotional buzzwords such as *terror, terrorism, the war on terror, hate our freedoms, hate our values, patriot, patriotic, Patriot Act, evildoers, extremists, security, anthrax, homeland, biological weapons, Islamo-fascists, dirty bombs, weapons of mass destruction, mushroom cloud.*

Return now to our nature as imperfect human beings. We negotiate reality in an interplay between the internal dynamics of our nervous systems and what is happening in the outside world — or more properly our perceptions of what is happening in the outside world. The manipulations of the psywar operators intersect with our psyches. Once we understand this dynamic we gain much more control over our beliefs, identity, confidence and effectiveness.

Why Bad Beliefs Won't Die

In his article "Why Bad Beliefs Don't Die,"[19] psychologist Gregory W. Lester points out that "because beliefs are designed to enhance our ability to survive, [our brains] are biologically designed to be strongly resistant to change."

Why, Lester asks, "do so many people's beliefs ... not change in the face of disconfirming evidence?" The key to understanding, he says, lies in recognizing that "the brain is a tool for survival. Even the difficulty of successfully treating such behavioral disorders as obesity and addiction can only be understood by examining their relationship to survival. Any reduction in caloric intake or in the availability of (an addictive substance) is always perceived by the brain as a threat to survival. As a result the brain powerfully defends the overeating or substance abuse, producing the familiar lying, sneaking, denying, rationalizing and justifying commonly exhibited by individuals suffering such disorders."

Again, our conceit that we are in conscious control of our thinking takes a few knocks from Lester. "When data and belief come into conflict, the brain does not automatically give preference to data. This is why beliefs — even bad beliefs, irrational beliefs, silly beliefs, or crazy beliefs —often don't die in the face of contradictory evidence. [The brain] is extremely reticent to jettison its beliefs."

Although written before 9/11, Lester's words seem particularly applicable to the tendency of people to cling to the official 9/11 story provided by "daddy" (President Bush), when so much about that story is absurd. So when George Bush presses the "evildoers" button, the "national security" button, and the "protect our homeland" button, the overall belief system is reinforced. "Thus, trying to change any belief, no matter how small or silly it may seem, can produce ripple effects through the entire system and ultimately threaten the brain's experience of survival." Any one of the Exhibits provided in the previous chapter could comprise a significant threat to an individual whose brain has a deep investment in the official story. In the case of Americans in particular, the official 9/11 story is embedded in the official myth of an entity called "America," which essentially can do no wrong no matter how much contrary evidence exists.

This is why, as Lester says, "challenging beliefs must always be done with care and compassion." The "truly amazing part of all this," he says, "is that anyone's beliefs ever change at all." But they do. The lesson that Lester doesn't address directly is that when we are communicating with others about 9/11 we must listen carefully to hear what fears they may be experiencing and to grasp the underlying belief system within which the fears live. Listening is a tremendously important part of encouraging a change in belief — about 9/11 or any other. This can be seen more clearly when we recall that it is when *others* listen to *us* that we become more reasonable, more opening to questioning or rational argument.

JFK's Assassination and 9/11

In 1996, Boston psychologist and playwright E. Martin Schotz approached the nature of belief in a slightly less psychological and slightly more political way in his book, *History Will Not Absolve Us: Orwellian Control, public denial, and the murder of President Kennedy.*[20] He writes: "It is so important to understand that one of the primary means of immobilizing the American people politically today is to hold them in a state of confusion in which anything can be believed but nothing can be known, nothing of significance, that is. And the American people are more than willing to be held in this state because to *know* the truth — as opposed to only *believe* the truth — is to face an awful terror and to be *no longer able to evade responsibility.* [emphasis added] It is precisely in moving from belief to knowledge that the citizen moves from irresponsibility to responsibility, from helplessness and hopelessness to action, with the ultimate aim of being empowered and confident in one's rational powers."[21]

For several reasons the JFK assassination is psychologically and politically almost perfectly analogous to 9/11. First, a high-level government conspiracy was behind both monstrous events. Second, in 1963 the belief was widespread in America — and around the world — that America and its government were benign. This is less so today — especially around the world — but large sections of the American public cling to it. Third, powerful vested interests of money, the military, the corporations and intelligence agencies constituted a powerful Invisible Government then and are even more powerful now. The role of the media in both events is almost completely analogous. Much of the research, thinking and the political activism that grew out of the outrage of Kennedy's assassination therefore is applicable to the outrage of 9/11. Not many wheels have to be re-invented.

By his own account, Schotz remained puzzled for many years, despite his best efforts to understand, as to why so many people — from ordinary citizens up through the echelons of the elite —

E. Martin Schotz

could essentially accept that John F. Kennedy was assassinated by powerful forces within the state, while simultaneously accepting that the essence of America is "democracy." The contradiction was resolved for him with his realization there is a widespread *unconscious acceptance* that it is precisely through these forces holding final power, that American "democracy" works.

He does not for a moment accept this state of affairs. He writes in his introduction that his book "is written expressly for people motivated by a desire to inform themselves through study so as to be capable of discharging their responsibilities as citizens of a true social, economic and political democracy." Like every other person whose work I have encountered who is deeply concerned about the justice of society and the future, and specifically about state-executed outrages, Schotz is forced to focus on the role of the media in the cover-up of seemingly obvious truths about these events.

"I imagine," he begins, "that at the moral center of our culture is a black star [I translate this into "black hole"] which absorbs all light .... If you write something which impinges too closely [on] the center and send it to someone well-situated in the bureaucracy, you will rarely receive a reply. The existence of this black hole is an essential element in the working of our society; everyone relates to it in one way or another. When an individual accommodates this black hole, accepts it as morally valid, relinquishes the search for the truth, ceases to struggle against it, this process is reflected as a central moral blindness in the personality of the individual."[22]

One Way Journalists Delude Themselves

In the book, Schotz includes some letters he has written to colleagues. One is his friend of 25 years, Philadelphia lawyer and writer Vincent J. Salandria. "By what psychological processes," he asks Salandria, "can competent journalists" be exposed to [your] carefully documented evidence pointing to government involvement in the murder of the President "and yet deny to themselves and the public (this) obvious truth?" Schotz speculates that "the process occurs as an automatic response beyond the awareness of the journalist. That the process goes on beyond the journalist's awareness makes it that much easier for him to engage in it."

If we substitute "9/11" for the murder of JFK and the 9/11 Commission report for the Warren Commission report, Schotz's explanation fits like a glove. I am going to take the liberty of making that substitution in Schotz's letter so as to apply his insights to the media and 9/11:

Consider the following: A journalist is seriously looking into [9/11]. He starts talking to people and one way or another [turns up documentary evidence pointing to an inside job]. He reads this evidence. Now the immediate, inescapable conclusions ... are that: (1) There is no doubt there was a conspiracy; (2) The [9/11 Commission report] is fraudulent; (3) The government of the United States is engaged in a criminal conspiracy after the fact to shield the true perpetrators. There is one further conclusion, depending on the point in time this is happening. The journalistic establishment is by now more or less involved in the cover-up ....

These are very powerful conclusions which, if accepted, would shatter the journalist's identification with the government. These conclusions are very disturbing. There is the sense that a system which one looked to for security and protection has turned against one. There is a sense of betrayal and danger, which is very painful ... the more identified the person is with the system, the more disturbing will be these three conclusions.

Drawing on his experience in psychiatry, Schotz observes that one of the ways a person with a horrible obsession continues to function "is to keep the thoughts secret. Just as a dream tends to fade from memory if it is not written down or told to someone, so waking thoughts of a terrible nature which are not shared have only a partially conscious quality. Talking about such thoughts or writing them down stabilizes them by giving them existence beyond the internal psychology of the person. Once this occurs they cannot be so easily erased or forgotten." The letter continues:

So the journalist, having read [the documents], is not likely to talk to anyone about them. If the journalist can keep from doing that, the experience which the [documents] created initially with time will begin to fade like a dream. The exact arguments and details will become blurred. [The proof in the documents] that there was a conspiracy will be transmuted into [a] "theory" there was a conspiracy — one theory among many competing theories. There's a tendency not to look at the documents again. On a conscious level the journalist may be thinking [they] were not that important. On an unconscious level the mere thought of the articles sets off [a] response which is likely to set in motion an avoidance reaction.

The journalist, Shotz observes, "may well believe there was a conspiracy;" may even be sympathetic to the researchers who produced the documents.

But he will only *believe* that there was a conspiracy; he will have avoided *knowing* that there was a conspiracy. And in that transmutation lies the transformation of a person who was on the verge of investigating the truth ... into [a person who becomes] part of the cover-up.

Shotz writes that what is true of the journalist is true also of the audience.

They do not want a reporter who knows there was a conspiracy and explains it to them. Rather, the typical citizen is much more content to have a journalist who believes there was a conspiracy, but at the same time indicates there is doubt, room for debate, and thus one is not in a position to draw any firm conclusions *and there is nothing to be done*. [emphasis added]

To the perpetrators of 9/11 involved in the psychological warfare aspects of it, all this is well known. This they depend upon as they exercise their powers to stifle any moves by independent-minded citizens or journalists to break out of the partly self-created ghetto of half-knowing. "The 'powers that be,'" writes Schotz, "can count on the fact that the more important the person or institution which commits a crime and the more serious the crime in regard to the system, the more central will be the threat of knowledge of the truth to the ordinary citizen, the more [a psychological tendency toward] uncertainty and confusion."

The [black hole], says Schotz, "organizes and perpetuates its tyranny of confusion, by threatening people with isolation and being labeled insane if they aren't willing to compromise."

A value in studying denial and associated phenomena is that we will be better prepared to identify and offset the psychological warfare being practiced on us by the likes of the CIA, the military and the White House, with their disinformation and fear-mongering. It is not just advertising agencies that study our minds in pursuit of our wallets. Right-wing political machines study our minds to keep us a fearful and bewildered herd, ceding more and more of our rights and liberties to them so they will become ever more powerful.

The Relationship of War, 9/11 Psychology, and Hope

An intriguing and hopeful take on 9/11 was published in the Winter 2005 issue of *The Journal of Psychohistory*[23] In the lead article, "The New 9/11 Scandal," Matt Everett devotes 24 pages to establishing for readers, with carefully assembled evidence, that 9/11 was an inside job perpetrated by elements of the US government. In the final seven pages he analyzes 9/11 as psychohistory. First he deals with wars, because in his conclusions he suggests that the huge psychological impact that exposure of the 9/11 fraud would have would be similar to the impact of war on the society. He quotes Lloyd deMause to the effect that "wars have generally occurred after periods of increased prosperity and social progress, especially when accompanied by more personal freedom." These wars "not only occurred far more frequently after prosperous periods, but were longer and bigger after prosperity, six to twenty times bigger as indicated by battle fatalities." The underlying reason, deMause suggests, for a degree of popular support for a war after prosperity is that "personal achievement and prosperity often make individuals feel sinful and unworthy of their success." This goes back to Freud's first case studies of people "ruined by success."[24]

The basic formulation here is that in a psyche burdened by feelings of unworthiness and low self-esteem, success stirs up unconscious guilt, which seeks expiation through punishment. This is complicated by co-occurring conflicting feelings of anger and resentment that the success also might be taken away, and that any "enemy" which threatens this must be punished.

According to deMause, the essential psychological purpose served by war in these circumstances has been one of "purifying the nation's polluted blood by virtue of a sacrificial rite identical to the rites of human sacrifice so common in early historical periods, when the blood of those sacrifices was believed to renew all people."

The psychological ill-health of the American and other First World populations is well known to mental health professionals. Mental health associations have told us for years that one in four will seek professional help for mental health problems in their lifetime. Clearly, this underlying psycho-morbidity is understood *in depth* by the psywar planners, including those behind 9/11. They manipulate our vulnerabilities through the repeated traumas of false flag "terrorist" incidents, repeated triggering of cognitive dissonance (the contradictory official cover-ups) and fear mongering — to induce psychological paralysis and social docility for political control.

As this book will continue to assert, 9/11 is the capstone, to the time of writing, of covert intelligence-designed, state-sponsored terrorism. From a psychological point of view 9/11 is "reverse psychotherapy," a psyop of malevolent brilliance.

Would Public Revelation of 9/11 be the Emotional Equivalent of War?

But a new element, Everett says, has been introduced into psychosocial history. That is improvements in parenting practices. These now can be measured in decades rather than centuries. Sweden banned hitting children in 1979. In 1992 more than 90 per cent of American parents hit their children; by 1999 only 57 per cent of American parents reported hitting their children.[25] "Consequently," Everett writes, "there are now more and more people in the higher 'psychoclasses:' individuals who, due to their more loving childhoods, have a higher level of psychological health. As a result they will have less ... desire for war." Everett takes the massive and unprecedented peace demonstrations *prior* to the Iraq war throughout the Western world as an indication that the existence of these individuals in greater numbers is a political reality of contemporary history.

Everett suggests: "Maybe the improvements in childrearing over recent decades that account for this unprecedented opposition to war, will also mean there are now enough people less afraid to challenge authority and face unpleasant truths, so as to help bring about a 9/11 scandal." He continues:

> While a 9/11 scandal would be a sufficiently large public crisis to help ease the particularly high level of public anxiety ... among the lower psychoclasses, unlike a massive war it ought also be acceptable to the more peaceful higher psychoclass individuals. If we do have such a scandal, the emotional effect will undoubtedly be intense.

He asks how the general public will feel if open accusations are leveled at the Bush administration of complicity in the 9/11 attacks. "I can imagine many people finding such events devastating." What if security camera footage of the attack on the Pentagon was forced into public and showed something *other* than a Boeing 757 hitting the Pentagon?

> Surely millions of people would feel horrified. The full implications of a 9/11 scandal would be colossal. It would be the *emotional equivalent* of a massive war. So maybe instead of the war "of a force and scope and scale that has been beyond what has been seen before," that Donald Rumsfeld promised back in 2003, there is going to be a scandal of "a scope and scale that is beyond what has been seen before."

We are left with an awesome question: is it possible that incremental improvements in the psychological well-being of developing generations could be the seedbed for an unprecedented breakout from denial? If so, it demands the planting of seeds of 9/11Truth by everyone with access to them, in the most effective and ongoing ways. The 9/11Truth story must be told repetitively by all who share it. We cannot afford to wait for the answer to the question. We must provide it.

4

While Sleeping Watchdogs Lie, Other Watchdogs Are Lied To

The Central Intelligence Agency owns everyone of any significance in the major media.
— William Colby, former director of the CIA

As 2001 came to a close and the world was being exposed to images of the horrors of the war on Afghanistan, most Americans were still in shock over 9/11. Editors and reporters were serving at their battle stations as usual, manning the gates of perception.

On the day of 9/11, I had intuited — and then became convinced — that 9/11 was an inside job. This became the lens of my perception, completely at odds with the official story the gatekeepers were reflecting and promoting. As I watched, read and listened to the reverberating coverage of 9/11, four particular news stories caught my attention for reasons I didn't fully understand until later. I've chosen to dissect these, rather than attempt an across-the-board survey of the unprecedented cascade of 9/11 coverage. (There is, however, buried in this chapter a "9/11 Media Diary" entry describing a survey of the ideas of 100 big city newspaper editors about 9/11 coverage.) These four case histories, to a great extent, reflect it all.

Some of the coverage promoting the official story is deliberate, pipelined from the storyboards of the psychological warfare masters. That is the case with the *New York Times* and *National Post* stories we look at here. The *Post* stories are by a Canadian "terror beat" reporter, Stewart

Bell. His techniques are typical of those reporters whose main sources are within spy agencies. On the other hand, some of the coverage promoting the official story is the outcome of sophisticated spin pawned off on honest journalists doing their jobs to the best of their ability. That is the case with the *CBC News* story. In the case of ABC, it may be a combination. In all cases, the outcome is nearly identical.

Not a great deal more could be learned, I think, from surveying minutely the hundreds of thousands of stories about 9/11 in thousands of media outlets. Because there has been so much coverage, I've been asked: "How can you say the media haven't covered 9/11 when so much has been reported, some of it pointing out contradictions?" My answer is that the really important contradictions, such as the non-appearance of the air force on 9/11 and the fate of WTC 7 building that day, are hardly touched. When they are dealt with, it's inside the framework of the official story. The coverage is overwhelmingly unquestioning and unskeptical. No coherent analysis or criticism based on the available evidence about the massive anomalies is even hinted at, let alone presented; let alone investigated; let alone blown wide open.

This mass of 9/11 coverage, when accessible through a good index (as in the case of Paul Thompson's book *The Terror Timeline*) can be useful for purposes of analysis. But as coverage comes at the public on a daily basis, it is less than useless in providing a coherent picture. The total output amounts simply to variations of the official story.

Case #1: NORAD Spins a Tale

November 27, 2001 — Host Alison Smith introduces a special "NORAD in Cheyenne Mountain" documentary on the Canadian Broadcasting Corporation's flagship 10 o'clock TV newscast, *The National*. "Americans and Canadians work side by side there to protect us all," says Smith. "Here's the CBC's Jo Lynn Sheane now with a rare glimpse inside the mountain." The 13-minute documentary follows.

Sheane and her colleagues had contacted North American Aerospace Defense Command (NORAD), in October 2001 with a simple question: "Where was NORAD on September 11?" At the time she was Saskatchewan correspondent for *The National*. She teamed up with colleagues from Calgary after the story idea was approved. They worked hard on the story and felt they did a good job.

This was one of NORAD's earlier 9/11 "public relations challenges." In responding to Sheane and her colleagues, NORAD brass had to decide on a story line. Embarrassingly, they already had at least three to choose from. Just two days after 9/11, General Richard Myers, acting Chairman of the

COURTESY CBC TV News

Jo Lynn Sheane

US Joint Chiefs of Staff, appeared before the US Senate for hearings (which had been scheduled weeks earlier) to consider his appointment as his country's supreme military officer.[1] Myers told the Senate "after the second tower was hit, I spoke to the commander of NORAD, General (Ralph) Eberhart. And at that point, I think the decision was at that point to start launching aircraft." That would be shortly after 9 a.m.

But on September 18, 2001 NORAD General Eberhart contradicted Myers, issuing a statement that NORAD was alerted by the FAA about each of the four errant flights and responded by scrambling two squads of interceptors. On that date NORAD stated the first fighters were scrambled even before the first WTC hit.[2] The story now was that these arrived too late to intercept.

On September 23 the Armed Forces Press Service published a different version again. In this account Myers sees, on a TV in an outer office of Senator Max Cleland, that the first WTC building has been hit. He is quoted as saying: "They thought it was a small plane or something like that," so he goes ahead with the meeting with Cleland. He says: "Nobody informed us" about the second WTC crash, and he remained oblivious to the emergency until after the meeting with Cleland ended, as the Pentagon explosion took place, at 9:37. Then he spoke to General Eberhart.[3] That would be a full hour and 20 minutes after the first of the 9/11 planes was diverted from its flight path.

Both of Myers' statements were incredible, given standard operating procedures (SOP) for both the Federal Aviation Administration (FAA) and NORAD. Fighters had been scrambled at least 67 times in the year prior to June 1, 2001. That was the date the scramble protocols had last been changed. But scrambling remained automatic, as it always had been. No authorization from the President or anyone else was needed for SOP to be followed. (See Chapter 2, Exhibit B.)

General Richard Myers

General Ralph Eberhart

Making it Up: NORAD was "Blind"

A dissection of what the CBC crew was shown and told provides a glimpse of official storymaking, in the making. The contradictions were glossed over and a main theme was settled upon to dispense to Sheane and her colleagues. That was that NORAD on 9/11 had no capability for seeing what was going on in US air space. "All the military radar equipment was watching the borders and beyond," she reported to her CBC audience, reflecting not only what she was told, but also what she was shown. She and her crew were taken on a flight in an Airborne Warning and Control System (AWACS) aircraft, she told me in an email in early 2006. "I was on one of those planes as part of the research for our documentary and talked about the fact that the AWACS [this in October 2001] were giving NORAD radar images not available through ground radar [which is of course what an AWACS does]. At the time, NORAD didn't have any of its own dedicated AWACS, we were told, and did not perform AWACS missions over North America. We did not uncover any information to disprove this." NORAD, she was told, had to depend on CNN for information. "Inside the mountain

NORAD watched it all on CNN," she reported on air. "What the military saw happening that day (on CNN) was a complete surprise and hence difficult to respond to."[4]

"Since 9/11, however," she reported, there had been an "historic change." NORAD "now has … added critical responsibility to watch for threats originating from within North America." Sheane's report and other reliable reports that changes took place post-9/11 nevertheless do not confirm that NORAD was "blind" on 9/11. The record could not sustain most of what Sheane and her colleagues were told in that respect. NORAD has maintained radar surveillance in US domestic air space since its inception. "The idea that the military was prepared to respond only to threats coming from abroad was put forward primarily by General Myers," David Ray Griffin states in his book *The 9/11 Commission Report: Errors and Omissions*. Griffin notes that Myers called it "a posture, by law, by policy and in practice" to respond only to "threats originating outside our borders." He said: "[We] were clearly looking outward. We did not have the situational awareness inward because we did not have the radar coverage." [5]

But even at the Commission, which itself was a monumental whitewash, some commissioners felt Myers needed to be challenged. One was Commissioner Jamie Gorelick, former general counsel for the US Department of Defense. "… if you go back and you look at the foundational documents for NORAD, they do not say defend us only against a threat coming in from across the ocean, or across our borders. It has two missions, and one of them is control of the airspace above the domestic United States, and aerospace control is defined as providing surveillance and control of the airspace of Canada and the United States." Griffin says Myers replied with "an absurd argument" relying on reference to the *Posse Comitatus*[6] and "whether the military should be involved in domestic law enforcement." Gorelick "quickly pointed out the absurdity of this argument,"

9/11 Commissioner Jamie Gorelick

Griffin notes. She said "*Posse Comitatus* says you can't arrest people. It doesn't mean that the military has no authority, obligation, or ability to defend the United States from attacks that happen to happen in the domestic United States." Nevertheless, Griffin notes, "although Gorelick had thoroughly undermined Myer's case, Myers' view became that of the Kean-Zelikow Report."

NORAD In Fact All-Seeing — When it Wants to Be

Apart from official statements, including such a "finding" of the 9/11 commission, an ordinary person might ask how NORAD would watch "the borders" and beyond without seeing some domestic air space? Do radar beams know where the 49th parallel is? One small indication that domestic airspace was always a NORAD responsibility is found in a memo issued on February 9, 1976, by John P. Stenbit, acting director, Department of Defense Instruction. The memo concerned changes to Security Control of Air Traffic and Air Navigation Aids, well-known through the military as SCATANA and applying to domestic airspace. Inquiries about his memo, Stenbit said, "should be addressed to: North American Air Defense Command, Ent Air Force Base, Colorado 80912."

The guiding document for the military is *ACC1 13-SAOC, Volume 3, U.S. Air Defense Command and Control Operations.* At the top of the first page it reads: "Compliance with the order is mandatory." The first paragraph reads: "The ADC (Air Defense Command) is to provide ... North American Aerospace Defense Command [NORAD] ... with the means to detect, monitor, identify, intercept, report and if necessary destroy any airborne object that may pose a threat to North America ...." (See a reproduction in Chapter 2, Exhibit B.) So the means were always there, and the extensive document says nowhere that only airspace outside the continental USA is to be monitored. This is in line with what Commissioner Gorelick said.

Further underscoring that NORAD's mission has always included US airspace is the report on April 18, 2004 in *USA Today,* stating that "In the two years before the· September 11 attacks, the North American Aerospace Defense Command conducted exercises simulating what the White House says was unimaginable at the time: hijacked airliners used as weapons ... One of the imagined targets was the World Trade Center. [Another] was the

Pentagon ..."[7] These buildings were widely reported to be located on US soil. The *Boston Globe*, on April 14, 2004, reported: "Concerns that terrorists might use hijacked airliners as missiles dates back to the 1996 Olympic games in Atlanta, when jets were placed on patrol to guard against such a threat." Sources in Atlanta report that city also remains on US soil.

NORAD

These reports and others give the lie not only to statements made to Sheane and her colleagues concerning the "we could only see outward" theme, but also the second theme of the official-story-in-the-making — that what happened on 9/11 was so unimaginable that preparations could not be made for such events. As it was put to the CBC by Lieutenant General Ken Pennie: "The general thinking, the probability of a terrorist indi-vidual or group of individuals

Lieutenant General Ken Pennie

taking over an airliner [full] of innocent people and actually driving that into a building filled with innocent people was just something that was considered too horrific to think credible. Even though a few thought it might be, many, most in fact, thought it wouldn't be."

But delivering the *coup de grace* for both themes was that NORAD, *on the very day of 9/11*, was involved in at least five war games exercises, most of which involved US air space. Sheane recalled in early 2006 that she was told about Russian war games and also about a game involving NORAD called Vigilant Guardian. "We chose not to talk about [Vigilant Guardian] in the documentary," she said in an email to the author, "because we were told that the exercise never interfered with the reaction to the events of 9/11 and at the time we had no reason to doubt that." [8]

As reported in *Aviation Week and Space Technology* on June 2, 2002: "Senior officers involved in Vigilant Guardian were manning NORAD command centers throughout the US and Canada, available to make immediate decisions."[9] These decisions involved hijacked airliners (not Russian missiles or bombers). NJ.com, a New Jersey-based service that summarizes all major stories published by New Jersey press outlets, reported in December of 2003: "NORAD also has confirmed it was running two mock drills on September 11 at various radar sites and command centers in the United States and Canada, including air force bases in upstate New York, Florida, Washington, and Alaska."[10]

In October 2001, thanks to the CBC's initiating a story about why NORAD failed on 9/11, the CBC news crew was rewarded with some of the earlier lies which later would be woven into the overall lying themes of the Kean-Zelikow cover-up report.

Games NORAD Plays

In her e-mail of early 2006, Sheane recalled: "About Vigilant Guardian, we were not told what the exercise involved, but various people in headquarters told us it was one of the two annual major exercises they conduct. They prepare for them well in advance and know exactly what all the 'injects' are because they're responsible for injecting the scenarios into the exercises. So, when they got word of a 'real world' scenario, they immediately knew it had nothing to do with their exercise. The comment from the … director of the air warning centre was: as soon as the FAA notified NORAD of a possible hijacking, they abandoned the exercise."

This would suggest that some of the people Sheane talked with were dupes in a larger game, but that some were in on that larger game to one extent or another. The researcher who has looked most closely at the role of the multiple war games on 9/11 is Michael C. Ruppert. He observes the games had a "paralyzing effect" on military defenses.[11] This would appear to be at least partly self-evident, yet Sheane was told that Vigilant Guardian "never interfered with the reaction to the events of 9/11."

This sub-theme of the official story later was escalated by General Eberhart before the 9/11 commission, into the claim that Vigilant Guardian had actually enhanced the nation's air defenses, a claim Ruppert describes as "ludicrous." [12]

Sheane further recalls, regarding the war games "... and what had been practiced before 9/11, we actually spent a great deal of time in our interviews asking about this. We were told they had done table-top exercises [not full-scale exercises] on scenarios similiar to 9/11. But even the table-top exercises were quite different from what actually happened in New York, Washington and Pennsylvania, according to what we were told." That could well be, since as Ruppert found out, while some of the exercises involved the injection of false radar blips, others were "live-fly."

"Various people told us," Sheane recounted, "that the imagined attacks always originated with planes from outside of North America. So part of the table-top exercise involved having far more time to digest the problem and make decisions. And those table-tops never advanced to full-scale exercises because the 'general thinking' was that it would never happen. We short-handed this in our documentary ..., again for time purposes. Because ultimately they were telling us they never imagined a coordinated attack, originating from within North America ... and we had no evidence to the contrary."

The Awful Truth:
Dick Cheney was in Charge of the NORAD Paralysis

The CBC crew was not the only one that did not understand what was going on. Most people didn't, and most people still don't today. That's because what is really unimaginable for many people is what Ruppert sums up categorically in *Crossing the Rubicon:* "I have absolutely no doubt that on the day of September 11 Richard Cheney was in full and complete control of a properly functioning and parallel command and communications system ...." [13]

Those who coach the NORAD officers in media relations obviously encourage them to put the most positive spin on everything. Major General Rick Findley took this as far as it could go when he told Sheane: "... getting it all airborne, getting it all co-ordinated, was an enormous achievement." To call an abject failure of military interceptors to respond during a nation's

COURTESY CBC TV NEWS

Major General Rick Findley

greatest air crisis "an enormous achievement" reminds me of the Orwellian "war is peace." The enormous achievement was Findley saying this with a straight face.

Findley, clearly of the Pennie school of "we didn't think it credible," told Sheane there was "nothing they could have done differently." Apparently thinking differently prior to the events doesn't count as "differently."

Sheane told me she recalls feeling Lt. Gen. Pennie "was holding something back," and "was not entirely forthcoming." She said the visit of her and her TV crew was "extremely well-managed. We had multiple people with us at all times. It's a very secretive organization." NORAD's secrets about 9/11 are being kept from the people of the US and Canada, who might decide the organization's budget is badly inflated considering what the public gets back for its investment of tax dollars. Speaking of budget, Sheane reported that "the organization says it needs additional money and resources." This is a familiar, if incredible, official 9/11 refrain. The organizations that failed most miserably were all given more money, and the individuals who failed most miserably were all promoted.

A Growth Industry: Cover-Up Stories About 9/11

Since Sheane's report was aired, more varying accounts of NORAD and the failure of air response on 9/11 have been tried on for size. In early May 2003, a fourth version of the events was provided by General Larry Arnold of NORAD to the 9/11 Commission. He said the FAA had become increasingly slow in delivering alerts to NORAD, thereby shifting blame for the debacle to the civilian agency. On May 21, 2003, the FAA disputed Arnold's claims, stating that phone bridges were established immediately after the first plane hit the World Trade Center at 8:46 a.m. and that NORAD was informed in real time of all developments "concerning all flights of interest, including flight 77," the plane that allegedly hit the Pentagon.[14]

In mid-2004, NYC 9/11Truth activist Nick Levis wrote: "For more than a year the FAA has been in open dispute with NORAD on who informed whom, and when, about the September 11 hijackings; unfortunately, this has never become the major media story it deserves to be." As of August 1, 2004, Levis could find only one story on charges made on July 30 by Sen. Mark Dayton, D-Minn., that the FAA and NORAD have "covered up catastrophic failures" on 9/11. The story was filed by Greg Gordon of the *Minneapolis Star Tribune*'s Washington bureau.

Gordon's story began by quoting Dayton: "For almost three years now, NORAD officials and FAA officials have been able to hide their critical failures that left this country defenseless during two of the worst hours in our history." This was at a Senate Governmental Affairs Committee hearing. Dayton charged that "a NORAD chronology made public a week after the attacks was grossly misleading."

In early 2006 Sheane told me she was still puzzled and disappointed that their story was ignored by her own news organization, the CBC, and by other media. "A lot of questions didn't get answered. They should have been followed up."

Case #2: The *NYT* Spins a Tale

Sunday, December 30, 2001 — *The New York Times*, on its front page this morning, publishes a 7,237-word narrative about the events of 9/11 and what led up to those events, under the headline "A Nation Challenged: The Response; Planning for Terror but Failing to Act."

It is one of the self-imposed tasks of "papers of record," none more so than *The New York Times*, to report what governments are up to. *Times* readers are trained, through seeing pages of dense type excavating minutiae under a headline such as "Military's Information War is Vast and Often Secretive," (top of page 1, December 11, 2005) to believe the *Times* does this — digs out dark government secrets, then plays them on page one. Today's story in its front page play, length, quotations from authoritative sources and timing would seem to fulfill this mandate on arguably the most significant event of our time.

The last thing you would expect of this story from the *Times* is that it be the same simplistic 9/11 official story fed to the masses via commercial TV — the "absurd cartoon," as author and 9/11 researcher Don Paul of San Francisco calls it, "made up of physical impossibilities, incapable pilots, hard-drinking Muslims, indestructible passports, etc."

But under closer examination this article is indeed a long text version of the cartoon. The *Times* adds panels to the cartoon, introduces more characters, fills the balloons with impressive quotes. The *Times* presents this "cartoon" as the final and crowning article in the three-part series "A Nation Challenged: The Response." The first "examined Saudi Arabia's policies toward militants who left home to wage war" and the second "looked at how militancy took root in Europe and how European governments failed to understand its danger and depth." But a complete reading of the crowning article contains almost no education past the tired cartoon of "Arab terrorists who hate our way of life."

A reading between the lines reveals the *Times* in this case to be a supine pipeline for the official story, albeit with a gloss obtained from interviews with "White House insiders," "former officials" and "counter terrorism experts."

The *Times* is the premiere agenda-setter for the rest of the North American media. The storylines and values of its journalism, while being a cut above that of most of its contemporaries, are reflective of the whole. In Chapter 1, we saw an example of information the mainstream media will *not* run about 9/11. In today's *Times* we see what is understood to be "the best" information the mainstream media do run. It doesn't get better than the *Times*. The *Toronto Star*, for instance, reprinted the series on its front page.

The feature begins dramatically: "Inside the White House situation room on the morning terrorism transformed America,

Franklin C. Miller, the director for defense policy, was suddenly gripped by a staggering fear: 'The White House could be hit. We could be going down.'"

Repetitive Themes that Support the Official Story

The headline and opening help establish four sub-themes and one overall theme of this narrative which — given the timing and the prestige and influence of the *New York Times* — many took to be a definitive account of 9/11. The sub-themes are: First, the events of 9/11 were a complete surprise but should not have been. Second, they might have been avoided if the White House (under both Democratic and Republican administrations) had heeded the warnings of "counter terrorism" experts to the "growing threat of terrorism." Third, intelligence agencies were hobbled by a lack of informants within "terrorist cells" and resources in general. Fourth, Osama bin Laden and his al Qaeda network in retrospect were always the big danger. The overall theme: missed opportunities.

It's a story of "missed signals," insufficient resources, bureaucratic turf wars, lack of will, underestimation of how cunning and powerful Osama bin Laden and his organization were becoming, of politicians distracted by less important issues. In the story's frame of reference, all other issues are less important than "terrorism," the issue that "transformed America," as the first sentence has it, the issue that a "post-9/11 world" faces, the no-alternative, number-one issue of the rest of our lives, no end-date given.

This "takeout," as such definitive stories are referred to in the newspaper business, is by none other than the now-disgraced Judith Miller, along with Jeff Gerth and Don Van Natta Jr. Ms. Miller later gained notoriety for her published lies about the alleged existence of weapons of mass destruction in Iraq and her political

Judith Miller

coziness with, for instance, Donald Rumsfeld, who arranged for her to obtain the highest possible security clearance in order to join the search for those non-existent weapons.

Miller's 37-year career with the *Times* ended unhappily for both on November 9, 2005. This was six months after the *Times* found itself obliged to examine some of her work, and that of others, retroactively. It found, according to its sedate expression in an editorial, that "information that was controversial [was] allowed to stand unchallenged." The editorial refused to blame "individual reporters," but others noted that 10 of the 12 flawed stories discussed had been written or co-written by Miller. She had relied heavily in her stories on Iraq on Ahmed Chalabi, a longtime CIA asset, and the *Times'* examination of its journalism in this regard was reported on May 26, 2004, a week after the US government apparently severed ties with Chalabi.

Diary of 9/11 and the Media

Am I a Boiling Frog?

Tuesday, January 18, 2005 — Information from *The New York Times* and Reuters is included in a story in this morning's Toronto *Globe and Mail* headed "Bush won't rule out attack on Iran." The gist is that the US is saying it reserves the right to attack Iran. In other words, it reserves the right to break international law and offend basic morality by launching an aggressive military operation against another sovereign country.

The rationale or pretext in this case would — or will — be to prevent Iran from working on the manufacture of nuclear weapons. Whether Iran is actually doing so is not clear, but the US president is saying his country is prepared to be judge, jury and executioner on this issue.

Since the US possesses by far the world's largest stockpile of nuclear weapons, is manufacturing more, and is developing new ones, the hypocrisy is easily seen for those not immersed in the same hypocrisy. The enormity of the double standard is underscored for anyone who cares to take into account US arsenals of biological, chemical, high explosive, particle beam, weather-related, psychological, mechanical and electromagnetic weapons.

In paragraph four, the story matter-of-factly states that the Pentagon is conducting reconnaissance missions *inside* Iran. One need only ask the question: "What would be the reaction in the US — from the president on down to the man and woman on the street — if Iran was conducting reconnaissance missions on US soil?" Not to leave that question hanging, the answer is that the whole of the US would go ballistic. Bonkers. Blasting Iran off the map would not be out of the question.

The same certain answer and the same blood-curdling threat has applied equally in scores of cases over the past 50 years in which US leaders threatened and US forces bombed or invaded sovereign countries in flagrant violation of international law and basic morality.

Few informed and fair-minded people would disagree with any of what I've just written. That's why for me, the most alarming and dispiriting aspect of my encounter today with this particular story is that it wasn't until I read it a *second time* that I asked myself the questions about the Gargantuan US Double Standard. Suddenly I realized the extent to which I've been drawn into accepting, literally without question, aggressive US lawlessness. It's as if I were a German or Bulgarian in 1939, not questioning whether Germany had the right to invade Czechoslovakia or Poland.

An assumption, in this case the assumption that any country can be invaded by US forces, can be tyranny. To the extent that I've slipped into accepting this assumption, my mind is becoming a colony of the Pentagon. If that's happening to me, what hope is there for average Americans who seldom if ever hear serious questioning, as the latest invasion rhetoric and disinformation are ramped up by the White House?

The story that a frog in increasingly hot water will continue to sit until he's boiled to death apparently is a fiction, but the metaphor remains too hot for comfort.

* * *

In April 2003, Judith Miller reported, based on secondhand statements from the military unit she was embedded with, that WMDs had been found in Iraq. This was widely reported in the press. "Well, I think they found something more than a smoking gun," Miller said on *NewsHour with Jim Lehrer.* "What they've found is a silver bullet in the form of a person, an

Iraqi individual, a scientist, as we've called him, who really worked on the programs, who knows them, firsthand, and who has led [the search team] to some pretty startling conclusions." It later turned out this individual was an intelligence agent.

By the time of her departure from the *Times,* her journalism had come under intense criticism. It generally followed the line that she reported cherry-picked intelligence favorable to the administration's prewar position prior to the Iraq war, and that she was in an uncomfortable "entanglement" with administration officials.

Later, what could only be called an entanglement was revealed when she refused to appear before a federal grand jury looking into who had leaked information to reporters revealing that Valerie Plame was a covert CIA operative. Miller had been asked to divulge a source in connection with the affair, even though she had not filed a story on it. Miller spent some time in jail, a hero to some, before divulging her source was the now-indicted Lewis Libby, Vice President Dick Cheney's chief of staff.

Miller's 9/11 Journalism is in the Same Dismal Category as her WMD Journalism

Rather than disqualify Miller's feature on 9/11 back in late 2001 as an appropriate subject for study of 9/11 coverage, the subsequent revelations about her close connections with secret agents and high officials make it even more appropriate. The substance and style of her "history on the run" about 9/11 bears the hallmarks of her earlier, and her later, journalism. These hallmarks include an extreme dependence on official sources, especially within the national security state apparatus, a dearth of supporting evidence for numerous assertions, and an ideological through-line in perfect sync with that of the White House, just as her later through-line on alleged WMD in Iraq matched that of the White House.

One example of her adherence to the official line is the curiosity that a word search shows that not once in her article about 9/11 do the words "accountable," "incompetence" and "blame" appear. If these words were used, they would invite ensuing copy dealing with who is accountable or should have been, *what* incompetence there was, whether blame should be laid. In skirting the issue of accountability, and in most other respects, the

Judith Miller-*NYT* version of 9/11 foreshadows the line the White House took and that the 9/11 Commission would take three years later. Commission co-chair Lee Hamilton declared the commission was "not out to blame anyone," and the Commission's report identified the final culprit as "failure of the imagination." In the intervening period, the White House, the legislative branch, and law enforcement could find no one with identifiable responsibility who could be called to account. No one was called on the carpet, no one was reprimanded, no agency was given orders to smarten up, not even an individual scapegoat was dragged into the limelight to be suitably admonished. Articles such as this one written by Judith Miller in the world's leading newspaper make this inaction less surprising than it otherwise would be.

On the contrary, individuals in positions of high responsibility, such as General Richard Myers, acting head of the US Joint Chiefs of Staff on 9/11, were promoted. Shortly after 9/11, in a little-reported move, President Bush personally announced a $1 billion boost in the CIA's budget; subsequent reports suggest the increase was more like $1.9 billion.[15]

It's as if there had been a "story line" from the start, a party line, a message track, a clearly scripted multi-act play to be staged. It's as if there were influential people in place — in politics, in academia, in the military, and in the media — who would disseminate that line, "stay on message," act out their parts. It's as if, in short, there were an organized campaign of psychological warfare, with interlocking players at key points to control the storyline. As if.

The Political Cost of Tainted Journalism: Re-Election of Bush — and War.

This Miller-*NYT* history of 9/11 accepts *a priori* the official White House story just as Miller's later journalism followed the White House line on Iraq. These official line stories, especially when emanating from agenda-setting media, carry political power. An Inter Press Service story by Jim Lobe on April 22, 2004, reported that "US public perception about former Iraqi president Saddam Hussein's alleged ties to al Qaeda and stocks of weapons of mass destruction continues to lag far behind the testimony of experts, boosting chances that President George W. Bush will be re-elected."

Lobe's story was based on surveys and analysis. They showed a "high correlation" between people who believed Hussein was either "directly involved" in the 9/11 attacks or had provided "substantial support" to al Qaeda and people who said they intended to vote for Bush — 57 per cent for Bush. Of people who did not believe there were these connections, only 28 per cent intended to vote for Bush.

We are looking at more than just "pipeline journalism" here; we are looking at a nation being led to war — in Afghanistan based on the official story of 9/11, and in Iraq based on 9/11 as well as on alleged weapons of mass destruction. Judith Miller was a significant player in both campaigns.

The fourth paragraph of Miller's story reads: "Somewhere in the havoc of the moment, Richard A. Clarke, then White House counterterrorism chief, recalled the long drumbeat of warnings about terrorists striking on American soil, many of them delivered and debated in that very room. After a third hijacked jet had sliced into the Pentagon, others heard Mr. Clarke say it first: 'This is al Qaeda.'"

Someone with credentials had to say it first. Who better than the White House counterterrorism chief. Never mind that this conflicts with the version of the official story delivered shortly after by Condoleezza Rice among others, that "no one could have predicted" such an attack. Either, on the one hand, "no one predicted" terrorists striking American soil or, on the other "a long drumbeat of warnings about terrorists striking on American soil had been delivered and debated" right in the White House situation room. It's one or the other. Rice at the time was National Security Advisor, so we have pretty serious differences of opinion being expressed around the same time by two of the top people in the White House responsible for the fear file. This contradiction, which would have to be well known by Miller and her colleagues, presented them with an opportunity to note the contradiction, raise questions, at least suggest follow-up. This was pointedly not done. The exclusion of such differences and contradictions is a hallmark of this piece.

There's another way the above paragraph is typical of the whole. The expert quoted is a "counterterrorism" expert. The *Times* gives a lot of credence to practitioners of this specialty. Richard A. Clarke is a sometime columnist on "security affairs" for the *New York Times Magazine*. "Terrorism experts," "anti-terrorism" experts and "counterterrorism" experts —

Miller's traditional sources — are the main sources for this piece. This may seem reasonable enough on the surface, since the pivotal event is understood — again, according to the official story — as a "terrorist act." But in fact for a newspaper of record there are many problems and pitfalls involved in depending too heavily on this clique for information and interpretation, on 9/11 or any other subject. These "security," "terrorism," "antiterrorism" and "counterterrorism" experts are suspect because of conflict of interest. They live off the avails of insecurity and terrorism.

Miller's Main Sources are Disinformation Specialists

Miller's sources are also suspect for a far more fundamental reason. One of the stocks-in-trade of this cadre is disinformation. It's probably accurate to say it is their main stock-in-trade. A real expert on "counterterrorism," someone like Webster G. Tarpley, author of *9/11 Synthetic Terror: Made in USA*, can shed light on the prime functions of "counterterrorism," one of which is to *mount* fake terror attacks that will be blamed on the chosen enemies of the state paying the salaries of the "counterterrorism" agents. In other words, it is as if Judith Miller is consulting men who have just robbed a bank for the identification of the robbers. They are not going to name themselves as prime suspects. Their specialty is naming others. But to speak of such things in a story in which "counter terrorism experts" are sources is taboo.

In this story as in so many of its kind, denizens of the "intelligence community" are presented as the perspicacious and brave select few who face the facts and gamely try to warn the doltish "leaders" of reality. In this account, leaders — including former president Bill Clinton and president George Bush — lacked sufficient foresight or fortitude to deal with the "mounting threat of terrorism." Those quoted to this effect include the aforementioned Mr. Clarke; Charles Duelfer, a former State Department official; Michael Sheehan, counterterrorism coordinator at the State Department in the last years of the Clinton presidency; Gerry Kauvar, a senior policy analyst at the RAND Corporation; and James Woolsey, a former director of the CIA.

Miller sums up: "... for years before September 11, terror experts throughout the government understood the apocalyptic designs of Osama bin Laden. But the top leaders never reacted as if they believed the country was as vulnerable as it proved to be that morning." The White House did, she admits, undertake "a covert campaign to kill Mr. bin Laden." Typical of the habitually bloodthirsty American corps of pundits, Miller evidently considers the immorality of such a campaign beneath mention. Typically, the law-breaking aspects also are rendered invisible. The contradiction of such a campaign being mounted by a nation that congratulates itself on conforming to "the rule of law" and on its essential goodness, is passed by, as usual. Some days it seems that except for a small minority, the whole of US journalism has lost its bearings and ability to identify immorality, hypocrisy and self-deception.

Miller says it was in connection with the 1993 bombing of the World Trade Center that US investigators first detected "the rising threat of the Islamic jihad movement." The many anomalies surrounding that bombing make it anything but the certainty Miller attached to it. Not long after the 1993 bombing, West Coast radio producer and political activist Ralph Schoenman published a long article in *Prevailing Winds* magazine,[16] pointing out numerous anomalies including close FBI and Mossad ties with some of those — Arabs of course — pinpointed as suspects. Since then questions about the provenance of the 1993 WTC bombing have only mounted.

New Lies Built on Old Ones, Laying Groundwork for More

Casual references to the highly questionable official versions of previous such events are used by Miller in building the new highly questionable version of the events of 9/11. For instance, she goes on to write that the 1993 WTC bombing "revealed weaknesses in the immigration system ... But that hole was never plugged." That was because it was a hole created by and defended by the CIA, as former US State Department immigration officer Michael Springmann has documented.[17] Some of the alleged 9/11 hijackers were imported and trained by the US military, Springmann has written and stated publicly on several occasions. A veteran of 20 years of foreign service, posted at the Saudi Embassy for two years, he has stated: "I was instructed to issue US visas to Saudi terrorists." (See Chapter 2, Exhibit U.)

After citing, always without references, several incidents, Miller concludes: "The government's fight against terrorism always seemed to fall short." *Bad government!* She does not explore how a war can be mounted against a noun. She does not even recognize the existence of the Chomskyist explanation that a long history of bloody US foreign policy outrages was bound to provoke "blowback." Her and the *Times*' account is hermetically sealed against intrusions by facts, interpretations or viewpoints outside the narrow confines of the official story and the lies, half-truths and self-serving interpretations attached to that. This is not journalism. This is *Pravda*, US-style.

The disinformation line spread by intelligence agencies that they lack inside information is faithfully parroted by Miller. The CIA "lacked sources inside al Qaeda." As the creator of al Qaeda, the CIA's "sources inside it" are analogous to the relationship of an adult kangaroo and the baby kangaroo in its pouch.

An Old Refrain (read: cover) The CIA is Bumbling

Just as government is characterized as "never getting it," the CIA is characterized as "never getting its act together." Example: "... the CIA could not provide an exact location for Mr. bin Laden, which was essential to the objective of killing him." Why the CIA could not do this is not explored. Is it short of money, sophisticated equipment, squads of analysts, agents in the field? The most likely explanation for this is that bin Laden has been, all along, a CIA asset. "On at least four occasions, Mr. Clinton sent the CIA a secret 'memorandum of notification' authorizing the government to kill or capture Mr. bin Laden ..." Miller writes. A little further she writes that on at least three occasions between 1998 and 2000, the CIA told the White House it *had* learned where Mr. bin Laden was and where he might be soon. (This contradicts what she wrote earlier but if we were to point out all her contradictions we'd never finish.) She continues: "Each time, Mr. Clinton approved the strike." And each time the operation failed. Although she does not report this, on one occasion cruise missiles hit the cave where he was supposed to be, but he had just left. Either he led a charmed existence all these years or he was being tipped off and protected by forces beyond Clinton's control that wanted bin Laden alive as an arch villain, an asset who could be milked as the poster boy for militant Islam.

Evidence of Osama bin Laden's long and close ties with the CIA and his being assiduously protected by the CIA and other elements of the US government is found, among other places, in *The War on Truth: 9/11,*

Disinformation, and the Anatomy of Terrorism [18] by British researcher and author Nafeez Ahmed. He devotes a full chapter to this phenomenon: "The Anglo-American Axis: Protecting Osama." Toward the end of the chapter, Ahmed includes information showing long and close links between the bin Laden family, the CIA, the Saudi military, and intelligence and financial links involving billions of dollars of Saudi oil money deposited in Western banks. Brad Bouland, chief economist of the Saudi American Bank (one quarter owned by Citibank) confirmed in June 2001 that his bank's best estimate of the value of western investments, mostly in the US, by members of the Saudi royal family "is about $700 billion, with the possibility that it is as much as $1-trillion." Miller, in recounting the activities of that wily "terrorist" Osama, never hints at any complex background involving power centers and the funding and training of terrorists and, in fact, the US encouragement of terrorism. (See also Chapter 2, Exhibit Y.)

Miller and the *New York Times*: Partners in Deception

All in all, the Miller-*NYT* version of 9/11 published on December 30, 2001 went above and beyond what founder and publisher of *Time* magazine, Henry Luce, and his wife Claire Booth Luce, used to call "AmProp." William A. Swanberg, Pulitzer Prize-winning author of *Luce and His Empire*,[19] wrote that Luce's empire could be depended upon, "like a thousand flashing rapiers," to promote the interests of corporate America. Miller and her kind go beyond that pursuit to become partners in corruption, abetting serial deceptions by the American Empire and its military, in the service of global resource theft and global domination.

The editors at the *Times* could re-examine Judith Miller's work on 9/11. Out of this exercise the *Times* could begin to weave a new tapestry of truth, as modern day prophet Dr. David Ray Griffin calls upon the *Times* to do. Should the newspaper undertake this, it could restore its good name and become a powerful impetus to restoring an America of which the vast majority of Americans could be proud. In revisiting Miller's work, however, the *Times* would have to revisit the whole of its output on 9/11. This exercise, if carried out honestly and thoroughly, would develop into the most momentous reversal in the history of journalism. To say it would be historic would be an understatement. It would be a cataclysm, inside and outside of the newspaper.

Case # 3: Stewart Bell's Terror Cells and Other Fearsome Phrases

Toronto, November 23, 2005 — It's pretty alarming, even by today's standards of fear-mongering: "Canadian indicted as terror cell master" is the headline on of a story by Stewart Bell on the front page of the *National Post*, the right-wing daily launched by now-disgraced media mogul Conrad Black.

The lead paragraph: "A suspected kingpin of Canada's jihadist network has been indicted by the United States for his alleged role in a terrorist cell that sent money and recruits overseas to 'murder, maim and kidnap.'" Bell is the Chief Reporter of the paper. His "terrorism" dispatches for the *Post* — detractors refer to it as the *National Pest* — are as numerous as they are journalistically embarrassing when examined closely, even though Bell has won several writing awards.

Bell is constantly on Red Alert; 9 of the 33 words or phrases in that lead paragraph are staples of terrortalk: "kingpin," "jihadist," "network," "indicted," "terrorist cell," "recruits," "murder," "maim" and "kidnap." He has written a whole book about the danger we're in, *Cold Terror: How Canada Nurtures and Exports Terrorism Around the World.*[20] The opening endorsement of the book, by David B. Harris, Director, INSIGNIS International and Terrorist Intelligence Program, asks "Will Canada be the next Bosnia, the next Lebanon? Most intelligence officers think so ... [Canada is in a] catastrophic slide ..." Such histrionics and the so-called "war on terror" are Bell's ticket to fame

Canadian indicted as terror cell master

Former Alberta theatre owner accused of funding, recruiting overseas

By Stewart Bell

TORONTO • A suspected kingpin of Canada's jihadist network has been indicted by the United States for his alleged role in a terrorist cell that sent money and recruits overseas to "murder, maim and kidnap."

Kassem Daher, a Lebanese-Canadian and former Alberta theatre owner, was indicted on three counts for allegedly fundraising, recruiting and supplying equipment for armed conflicts in several countries.

Among those allegedly recruited by Mr. Daher and his associates was José Padilla, a former Chicago gang member whom prosecutors say was sent abroad for terrorist training.

Senior U.S. justice officials held a news conference in Washington yesterday to announce Mr. Daher and Mr. Padilla had been indicted in a case involving three other defendants.

"Mr. Padilla is now a new co-defendant — along with Canadi-

and fortune. If, as a bonus, he were paid a dime for every time he uses the words "allegedly," "suspected" and that new word "believedtobelinkedtoalQaeda," he would be a millionaire.

The jihadist "kingpin" is Kassem Daher, a Lebanese Canadian and former Alberta theatre owner. Daher is back in the news because yesterday in Washington, DC, an American citizen named Jose Padilla, who has been locked up for years by order of President George Bush as an "enemy combatant," got a reprieve of sorts. He had been "suspected by the White House" of "plotting to detonate" a "dirty bomb" to contaminate a US city. It's a fearsome prospect re-raised by Bell and all his colleagues in the media every time they report on this unproven allegation of the White House.

The US Supreme Court was about to examine the legality of the President's jailing Padilla, an American citizen, indefinitely without charge. So US Attorney General Alberto Gonzales announced at a press conference that Mr. Padilla's name was being added to an existing indictment accusing several people, including "kingpin" Daher, of "raising funds for violent acts overseas." Nothing has been proved against any of them. For technical reasons alone Daher is one of those unlikely ever to face trial.

The *Post* story has Daher allegedly recruiting Mr. Padilla, no less. Where that comes from is anybody's guess. Where the "suspected kingpin" designation comes from is anybody's guess. Attorney General Gonzales didn't mention that. Where the existence of "Canada's jihadist network" comes from is anybody's guess. Gonzales said the success of the investigation was "only possible because prosecutors and law enforcement agencies were able to share information" but nevertheless they apparently didn't get wind of "Canada's jihadist network" either.

Stewart Bell

The *Post* Fails to Detect any Setback for George Bush

Other media are treating the twist completely differently. The *Globe and Mail*'s front page headline is: "White

House reverses field on 'dirty bomb suspect.'" Reporters Paul Koring and Alan Freeman write that "… in a stunning climbdown, the Bush administration indicted Mr. Padilla … on charges unconnected with any attack on the United States, thereby short-circuiting the Supreme Court's plan to examine the legality of the President's move …."

It was, the *Globe and Mail* reported, "only the latest in a series of legal retreats by the administration, which has given ground on several fronts, from its open-ended incarceration of hundreds of detainees in Guantanamo Bay to compromises on some of the more Draconian aspects of the PATRIOT Act." The *Globe's* 49-word lead paragraph contains only six terrortalk words or phrases, all connected directly with the development: "terror suspect," "plotting," "detonate," "dirty bomb," "contaminate" and "radioactivity." The catchline on the *Globe's* "jump" on page 14 is "Padilla indictment also names Canadian," but the story continues: "Yesterday's announcement completed a long backtracking by the Bush administration on the case." It reports: "At a Washington news conference yesterday … Gonzales repeatedly ducked questions about the legality, in retrospect, of denying Mr. Padilla almost every civil right and treating an American as an enemy combatant."

White House reverses field on 'dirty bomb' suspect

**BY PAUL KORING
AND ALAN FREEMAN,** WASHINGTON

Jose Padilla — the terror suspect and "enemy combatant" locked up for years by order of President George W. Bush because he was suspected of plotting to detonate a "dirty bomb" to contaminate a U.S. city with radioactivity — will finally face charges unconnected with any attack on the United States.

Yesterday, in a stunning climbdown, the Bush administration indicted Mr. Padilla, thereby short-circuiting the Supreme Court's plan to examine the legality of the President's move to jail an American citizen indefinitely without charge by declaring him an enemy combatant.

It was only the latest in a series of legal retreats by the administration, which has given ground on several fronts from its open-ended incarceration of hundreds of detainees in Guantanamo Bay to compromises on some of the more Draconian aspects of the Patriot Act. Those retreats have occurred amid intense and growing political and public pressures on the administration to come clean about the murkier legal aspects of the so-called war on international terrorism.

See PADILLA on page A14

How does Bell manage to get such a different story generating such a different — and more alarming — headline? Easy. Old news. Long before "terrorism" was expanded by the manipulation of 9/11 to occupy a malignantly-swollen amount of mindspace, it had been noted that criminal charges and convictions generate large headlines, whereas acquittals usually generate smaller ones. When charges are dropped — which is the case with a vast majority of those charged with alleged "terror"-related offences — the headline is usually so small that a magnifying glass helps in spotting it. Or there may be no headline at all. This is the playing field on which the journalistic game Write an Alarming Headline is played.

Bell's 24-paragraph story faithfully regurgitates claims and allegations by Gonzales, but fails to mention any ducking or backtracking by the US attorney general. Bell reports but ignores entirely what most other media saw as the main story: that the indictment was a "climbdown," a reversal, and a major setback for the administration.

Bell should have been reprimanded for missing the story and for recycling old — and suspect — news. Instead he's given space on page one. Bell is a whirling dervish of his kind, the "terrorism beat" reporter, producing big black headline after headline about the fearsome crowd of terrorists who infest Canadian society.

Only three days after his blowing the cover of Daher, the "jihadist network kingpin," Bell announced in the top story on the *Post*'s front page "Bin Laden Deputy Lived in B.C." This alleged deputy, Mubarak Al Duri, an Iraqi, is also allegedly Osama's "chief weapons of mass destruction broker," no less. The story is based on a line in a 105-page ruling by Judge Eleanor Dawson who said "Canadian intelligence investigators had determined that (Al Duri) had once lived in Richmond, B.C." A lot of people have lived a lot of places and not gotten a front page headline out of it.

Earlier, on November 3, a Bell story was heralded by the large black banner of the *Post*'s front page: "CSIS: TERROR CELL BUSTED." CSIS stands for Canadian Security Intelligence Service. Apparently "Canadian counter-terrorism investigators dismantled a suspected terrorist cell in Toronto whose members allegedly included an al-Qaeda-trained explosives expert." As is usual with Bell stories, the "suspected terrorist cell" had solidified by the second paragraph into "the cell," suspected no more.

Diary of 9/11 and the Media

On watching Senator Ted Kennedy Interviewed by Wolf Blitzer on CNN

November 10, 2005 — When we see a Volvo with a Save The Whales bumper sticker, chances are we're going to get it right if we guess the owner/driver recycles, does not vote Republican and opposes the war in Iraq. We have a snapshot of the person's cultural/political DNA. But it's stereotyping. We could be wrong. The person at the wheel could be a car thief who loves whale meat.

But watching Senator Ted Kennedy, not someone who stole his car, on CNN tonight being interviewed by Wolf Blitzer, I hear Kennedy say the Bush administration is making a mistake "by losing its focus on the war on terror." That's all the DNA I need as evidence that Kennedy hopelessly does not "get it" that the whole so-called "war on terror" is a fraud, and that it is the enabling centerpiece of the New World Order. If he did, he could not possibly say what he has just said.

This snapshot of Kennedy's political DNA shows he is trapped in the framing of the Far Right. On the so-called "war on terror," Kennedy is in lock-step with George Bush and the worst of the American Empire. Kennedy might as well be driving a giant SUV with a bumper sticker reading "I love Bush."

This is why so many despair of the Democratic Party. Kennedy's profound blindness fuels the angry observation that there's "no difference" between the Republicans and Democrats. There are in fact differences, one being the voting pattern on the invasion of Iraq. Many more Democrats than Republicans opposed that. But if the parties are united on the fundamentals supporting the Empire and its perpetual war, then forget the whales — and the rest of us.

* * *

There were bonus points for terrortalk in that day's *National Post*, with a page 6 story by Peter Goodspeed headed "Canada seen as having 'soft belly,' terror expert says," topped by a large photo of Osama bin Laden at a lectern over the caption "Osama bin Laden might launch a suicide attack on Canada using a second generation immigrant." In that story Boaz Ganor, founder of the International Policy Institute for Counter-Terrorism in Israel, and described as "one of the world's top counter terrorism experts," warns Canada "to brace itself for a major terrorist attack — possibly using weapons of mass destruction." How one goes about "bracing" for this is not explained by Ganor. He does explain, however, that terrorists think "it is either with us or against us. There is no in-between ...." This apparently did not remind him of any prominent person who ever promoted the categorical "with us or against us" formulation.

Ganor warns that "second generation immigrants, people who are supposed to be very well-blended into society," could well be recruited by Osama bin Laden to perform suicide attacks in Canada. This "second generation scare" has become a favourite of the "counter terrorism" experts, whose output contributes to the constant state of fear engendered by repeated claims that the person next to you in a coffee shop could be a terrorist.

Ganor said the main aim of terrorism "is not to kill or destroy but to maximize anxiety ...." Since Ganor endorses the official story of 9/11, it is odd he doesn't think 9/11 fits the "kill or destroy" category. Goodspeed, the *National Post* stenographer in attendance, apparently did not ask Ganor whether he might be helping the terrorists achieve their "main aim of maximizing anxiety" with his warnings of the terrible things that could happen at the hands of "the terrorists." But irony seemed lost on speaker and stenographer alike.

On December 20, 2005, "TERROR SUSPECT NAMED" was the large black banner running atop a Bell front-pager about a one-legged Algerian former Toronto school bus driver. This soccer-playing married father of one son was, according to Bell's sources, "the ringleader of an alleged Algerian terrorist cell." Bell reported that "Canadian investigators believe" the man "is a seasoned terrorist and explosives expert." Throughout the story, each damning "fact" is based on what "investigators believe." As often Bell's facts are based on what "investigators suspect." Friends of the named suspect said things like: "Honestly, we just talked about soccer."

A Journalist Whose Personal Research Department is the Spy Establishment

The single most noticeable characteristic of Bell's journalism is its dependence on spooks as sources. He has somehow, as the dust jacket of his book says, come into possession of "a vast collection of classified intelligence documents." Bell himself says it "may be the largest collection outside of government." How does a person on "the outside" get all this stuff? In effect, the spy establishment is his personal research department.

He augments his files regularly from "exclusive interviews with senior Canadian counter-terrorism officials." Exclusive means they're feeding him and not other reporters. The situation here is what is sometimes called Source Journalism. Walter Karp wrote in *Harper's* magazine in 1989: "It is a bitter irony of source journalism that the most esteemed journalists are precisely the most servile. For it is by making themselves useful to the powerful that they gain access to the 'best' sources." When journalists depart from the servile role in any significant way, on the other hand, they feel an icy blast. This was described for Karp by Tom Wicker of *The New York Times*. Wicker had written on November 22, 1963, that President John F. Kennedy "was

EXCLUSIVE

TERROR SUSPECT NAMED

CSIS believes Algerian explosives expert drove Toronto school bus

BY STEWART BELL

A former Toronto school bus driver was the ringleader of an alleged Algerian terrorist cell that operated in the city until it was dismantled by Canadian counterterrorism agencies, the *National Post* has learned.

Nourddine Zendaoui, 40, a one-legged Algerian known as Hajji, has been identified as the alleged central figure of a group of Toronto men targeted by the Canadian Security Intelligence Service.

Canadian investigators believe Mr. Zendaoui is a seasoned terrorist and explosives expert affiliated with the Algerian terrorist faction Salafist Group for Call and Combat, which is loyal to Osama bin Laden.

Before coming to Canada in 1998, investigators believe, Mr. Zendaoui was an instructor at the Khaldun terrorist camp in eastern Afghanistan, where several of the 9/11 hijackers were trained.

CSIS officers began showing up at the weekly soccer games in at least 2002 and later met with the players to ask them about the one-legged goaltender, known as Hajji because he had made the Muslim pilgrimage to Mecca.

See SUSPECT on Page A14

9/11 myth about Canada repeated, Page A14

Khadr was dealing in missiles: affidavits

hit by a bullet in the throat, just below the Adam's apple ...."[21] That was before the official story of a lone assassin firing from the rear so important to the cover-up by officialdom was firmly in place. Wicker told Karp that hazards he faced included "lost access, complaints to editors and publishers, social penalties, leaks to competitors, a variety of responses no one wants."

It's a carrot-and-stick situation. Bell is treated to bushels of carrots and no sticks. His "exclusive interviews with senior Canadian counter-terrorism officials" no doubt augment the flow of documents. He then reliably acts as a pipeline to pump this "information" into the public sphere. In Bell's world, all biases favor the US government, the security establishment, and the so-called "war on terrorism." His story of today illustrates this clear pro-Bush agenda, but it's never called that. It's pipeline journalism, serving the psychological warriors intent on keeping our fear levels up to serve the purposes of their masters.

Case #4: The Anniversary Waltz

September 11, 2002 — "From *ABC News*, this is '9/11.'" These simple, authoritative words launch ABC's special 9/11 first anniversary programming, featuring Peter Jennings. "Tonight, behind the scenes on the day America was attacked. Deep inside the corridors of power. From the secret bunkers near the capitol, to the Pentagon war room and on board Air Force One. Exclusive details of what the nation's leaders were thinking and doing in the moment of crisis."

This news special is typical of 9/11 news specials on all the major TV networks, on all anniversaries of 9/11, for four years: the lead-in suggests a full and accurate documentary is to follow. It is also typical in another way: upon closer examination it is neither full nor accurate. The producers fail to deal with important questions about 9/11. Instead, they impress superficially with interviews — mainly with White House figures and other authorities — and high production values. Other details are selected out. Carefully selected details mask other details just as carefully omitted.

Any suggestion of doubt, any suggestion the 9/11 crime case is not closed, that the facts are not all in, that more investigation is needed, that contradictions exist, that people exist who are not satisfied with the official story — is absent. As well, the program serves the White House agenda of making 9/11 the linchpin for the so-called "war on terror," and building on that so-called war to ramp up and maintain a fear campaign targeted at the American people.

Just 3 minutes and 46 seconds into the piece ABC's viewers are told: "You'll be stunned to see how vulnerable we are to nuclear terrorism," later called "the most urgent threat to America today."

Some potentially embarrassing questions are raised. But embarrassing answers are not forthcoming. Questions: "How was Osama Bin Laden allowed to slip away? And where is he now?" Answer to both: Finding bin Laden isn't as important as it once was. Answer provided by establishment figures. Answer accepted.

Peter Jennings

At the One-Minute Mark, The Omissions begin

Jennings' omissions begin exactly one minute into his script: "[9/11] was, in a phrase, a moment of crisis which not a soul that I know of anticipated." This may have been technically true on Jennings' part. But in the context of a significant news documentary produced by a major network, his words were severely misleading. By the time of this broadcast, the least-equipped newsroom had access to overwhelming evidence that numerous individuals, organizations and even governments *had* anticipated the events of 9/11. Not only that, but had warned Washington. The *Washington Post* had reported on May 17, 2002, about CIA director George Tenet's intelligence

summary of June 28, 2001, "that a significant al Qaeda attack is in the near future ...." Paul Thompson's book, *Terror Timeline*, devotes 53 pages to warnings that had poured into Washington, to the point that one official referred to "warning fatigue." All Thompson's reports are culled from open sources such as *Time* magazine.

Charles Gibson

ABC's Charles Gibson does the heavy lifting on reportage in the first hour. Four minutes into the program, he reports that on the morning of 9/11 the USAF is "in the midst of a full-scale training exercise." He says, "Normally there would be only a handful of military fighters on duty across the US," but he's told by Colonel Robert Marr that on the morning of 9/11: "We had 14 aircraft on alert, 7 sites, 2 aircraft at each site."

Marr was in Rome, New York, in command at NEADS, and he is referring only to aircraft available to NEADS.

This excess of fighters — the official story was to be changed dramatically later, to a scenario in which very few fighters were available — did not trigger a single on-air question from Gibson or ABC as to how so many planes could fail all at once to show up in a timely fashion.

Similarly, anomalies about what the president knew and when he knew it were simply not addressed in this ABC special. Gibson reports that Bush's entourage arrived at Booker Elementary School at the same time the first plane hit the WTC. "Simultaneously, the pagers of his aides erupt in a cacophony of beeps and tones," Gibson tells ABC's viewers. In order to arrive at this chronology, the producers of the program had to send down the memory hole some of ABC's own live coverage the morning of 9/11, involving none other than Peter Jennings himself.

ABC Banishes its Own Footage

On the morning of 9/11, Jennings had received this report from ABC reporter John Cochrane, who was traveling with the president: "Peter, as you know, the president's down in Florida talking about education. He got out of his hotel suite this morning, was about to leave, reporters saw the White House chief of staff, Andy Card, whisper into his ear. The reporter said to the president, 'Do you know what's going on in New York?' He said he did, and he said he will have something about it later.

His first event is about half an hour at an elementary school in Sarasota, Florida." So the program producers had to know there were conflicting reports about when the president and his entourage knew of "something going on in New York." But they chose to ignore live footage in their own archives.

Despite the producers' largely successful attempts to produce a question-free, anomaly-free documentary, nevertheless anomalies did pop up during the special. One is after the first WTC tower has been hit, which is when Lt. Colonel Dawne Deskins of the Air National Guard "knows she needs to call NORAD operations in Florida ...." Gibson reports. And exactly who, according to Gibson, does Lt. Colonel Deskins call? She calls "Public Affairs Officer Don Arias." Why would she call a PR flack about an extreme aviation emergency? Gibson and ABC do not consider this question worthy of detaining their viewers.

Equally anomalous are the travels of the two jet interceptors from Otis AFB on Cape Cod. Pilots "Duff and Nasty rocket into the air at 8:52 a.m. just six minutes after the first Tower is hit," Gibson reports. ABC viewers next see Duff say: "As we're climbing out, we go supersonic ...." Says Duff: "I just wanted to get there quickly." Says Nasty: "We're going as fast as we could." The program's producers must have done a bit of research into how fast that would be. *Air Force News* had, on July 30, 1997, reported the not-uncommon knowledge that an F-15 can travel at more than 1,875 mph. NORAD commander Major General Larry Arnold, quoted in this program but not on the subject of the Otis planes' speed, told MSNBC on September 23, 2001, that the Otis fighters were doing 1,100 to 1,200 mph. Even at Arnold's speed Duff and Nasty just might have been able to do something about Flight 175.

But Gibson chooses a different speed, and omits that there are widely conflicting reports about Duff and Nasty's speed. Gibson and ABC fail to share with viewers that there are four speeds to choose from, all on the record, according to different sources. He reports: "The fighters are hurtling toward New York at mach 1.2, nearly 900 miles per hour. They are 153 miles from the World Trade Center." It happens that at 900 mph, it will take Duff and Nasty about 10.2 minutes to get to New York City, just in time to accomplish ... nothing.

Back at Booker Elementary School, ABC's viewers are told, President Bush is informed by Andrew Card, his chief of staff, about the second WTC impact and that "America is under attack." They are also told by Gibson that the president "stays calm and lets the students finish" reading their story about a pet goat. ABC's viewers then see and hear White House Counselor Karl Rove explain: "The President thought for a second or two about getting up and walking out of the room. But the drill was coming to a close and he didn't want to alarm the children." ABC accepts that the president of the country, just when one of the utmost conceivable national emergencies had occurred, could not figure out how to leave a room by saying "Excuse me, I have some urgent business I have to leave to attend to." ABC's viewers are encouraged, almost directed, to think no question exists about the president's behavior at this point.

As the minute-by-minute account of the day unfolds, Gibson and ABC arrive at the Pentagon just as it's struck, at 9:38 a.m. Gibson reports: "High overhead, jet fighters arrive. Just moments too late." An Air National Guard pilot, Major Dean Eckmann, describes how "We get in closer and I can start to see smoke coming up." The coincidences of the country's "top guns" repeatedly arriving just a little bit too late — it would happen yet again according to ABC's account of the fate of Flight 93 — just doesn't strike Gibson, Jennings or ABC as noteworthy or questionable. One full year later their eyebrows remain unraised.

ABC's first-anniversary 9/11 programming fulfills the same function fulfilled by the "docudrama" movie *United 93* and by Arts & Entertainment's "entertainment" programs "Flight 93" and "The Last Hour of Flight 11." The latter production begins with the viewer being told: "This is the most detailed reconstruction yet" of the events that allegedly took place on Flight 11. Flight 11 is the one on which Mohammed Atta allegedly was the lead hijacker and piloted the aircraft. Viewers were treated to a great deal of Atta quoting from the Koran, but nothing inconvenient such as Atta's living with a prostitute, drinking alcohol or the like, documented in the work of Daniel Hopsicker, who interviewed people who knew Atta well.

Relentlessly, on the first anniversary of 9/11, ABC further solidifies and reinforces the official story, and sedulously avoids any questioning of that story. This "news special" is at one with the docudramas that reify the official story and avoid questioning. The difference is that the docudramas do it with professional actors and "documentary type" production values. The "news specials" do it with "real" persons such as Condoleezza Rice playing the roles. Both types of production blend into a seamless "reality." Likewise, over at PBS in early 2006, the *Frontline* "documentary" titled "al Qaeda in Europe," accepts throughout the official version of what al Qaeda is and the threat it represents.

Across the Board: Cover-Up

"News specials," "documentaries," "docudramas," "entertainment programming," in the evening news, on the all-news channels, on PBS, on the specialty channels, it's all the same: official 9/11 story, no questions asked. Media "coverage" of 9/11 with exceedingly rare exceptions, is wall-to-wall cover-up.

Individual readers, listeners and viewers, in order to uncover what's under the cover-up, have to select or chance across scattered bits and pieces of information and reassemble them into a coherent pattern of the reader's, listener's or viewer's own construction. This ABC special, and all its clones on all other channels, because of common selective omissions and lack of ordinary curiosity, can barely be called information. Compared to what could and should be presented, it is disinformation: the viewer has to do a lot of heavy lifting to extract an alternative reality out of the "reality" presented.

On such an important matter, this is not good enough. The media tell us their mandate is to "make sense of the news," or publish "all the news that's fit to print" or provide "fair and balanced" coverage. This requires honesty, thoroughness and coherence. We are receiving virtually none, on the matter of 9/11. We are receiving instead misdirection, controlled serial omissions and myriad elaborations of a fictional construct. A Big Lie, the kind Hitler said works better than small ones.

This program alone, "9/11," is one of scores of "smoking guns" of cover-up — elaborate media fictions that make ABC, and the other networks airing very similar productions, complicit with those who planned and executed the events of 9/11. The seriousness of the cover-up of a crime ranks very closely with committing the crime itself. It's as simple as ABC.

Diary of 9/11 and the Media

Just In — The Results of Douglas Herman's Survey of Editors

Monday, December 12, 2005 — Today, Douglas Herman's report arrives; a survey of 100 US big-city editors about 9/11 coverage.[22] I've been anticipating the results. It's the kind of survey I might have attempted for this book, had I the time. Herman is the author of *The Guns of Dallas*, a novel fictionalizing, through the eyes of reporter David Pilgrim, the demise of the American press. Herman's questions, sent two weeks ago:

1. Do the US media purposely avoid disturbing news stories of 9/11 contradictions (see example below) that conflict with the official government version of events?

2. Has your newspaper ever mentioned any significant news story (or stories) that disagreed with the official Kean Commission version of 9/11 events?

3. Is it treasonous, or patriotic, to claim that 9/11 attacks were partly or completely an "inside job," as internet bloggers claim (see below)?

4. If you personally became suspicious that 9/11 was possibly an inside job — by a rogue element in the government — would you suppress the story rather than inform, and thus distress, your readers?

Herman attached a few 9/11 stories from the alternative press, "really pretty tame stuff for those already in the 9/11 Truth movement," he said earlier. "I mean there is no need to overwhelm them with the WTC-7 controlled demolition right away!" He also "sent along a few links to well-researched 9/11 news … reports of discrepancies that should awaken the skeptical instincts of a good editor." Herman said he would "carefully weigh" the responses he receives against the principles established by Joseph Pulitzer, former owner of the *St. Louis Post-Dispatch*, which for decades was included in an annual ranking of the "elite" newspapers of the world because of the extent to which it maintained Pulitzer's principles. Upon his retirement in 1907, Pulitzer said (and Herman attached this to his questionnaire):

I know that my retirement will make no difference in its cardinal principles, that [the *St. Louis Post-Dispatch*] will always fight for progress and reform, never tolerate injustice or corruption, always fight demagogues of all parties, never belong to any party, always oppose privileged classes and public plunderers, never lack sympathy with the poor, always remain devoted to the public welfare, never be satisfied with merely printing news, always be drastically independent, never be afraid to attack wrong, whether by predatory plutocracy or predatory poverty.

Now I find out why it did not take Herman weeks to sift through the responses and prepare a lengthy report summarizing them. The reason? He received ... just one response.

It was from Jim Wilhelm of the *Toledo Blade*. "Without looking at (the links)," Wilhelm responded to Herman, "I personally don't believe the US media would purposely avoid reporting such stories. There are lots of reasons information that comes to the attention of a newspaper ... (is) not reported, some of them having to do with whether they can be properly substantiated through sources and documents that would stand up in a court of law." In response to Herman's fourth question Wilhelm wrote: "The question — like most of the others, is loaded. If I had the resources (for example, reporters in Washington) I would pursue such a story. I would not willfully suppress such a story if I had substantiated information."

The formula now is clear. We saw it with Peter Scowen in Chapter 1. We see it with the Right Gatekeepers. We'll see it in the next chapter with Noam Chomsky and his fellow Left Gatekeepers. The formula is this: "I need proof but I'm not going to look at the proof." All the rest is from the brain's baloney generator.

For instance, exactly *when* is this verifiable, substantiated, documented information "that will stand up in a court of law" needed? Is it before an editor *decides to start* pursuing a story? Is it *after* pursuit of a story has begun and more information now has been gathered? How will an editor *know*, before deciding to pursue and then in fact pursuing a story, whether the information "will stand up in court of law?" Don't courts decide that? Wilhelm and the other editors surveyed *were given enough information* by Herman to *decide to begin* pursuing the 9/11 anomalies story. In journalism, whether stories might be actionable is something that is dealt with around the time the stories are completed. Papers, such as the *St. Louis Post-Dispatch,* have been known to risk legal action and publish anyway, where the editors and publisher believe the public's need to know is over-riding.

It's not *information* these editors surveyed by Herman lack. It is *will* that they lack. It's worse than that. They have a will to *not* pursue, *not* investigate. They are *anti*-investigatory on 9/11. This makes them pro cover-up. Their decision-making energy is invested in inventing rational- izations to mask their role as *de facto* censors. How many stories — in every paper, every day — meet the exacting standards of being substan- tiated and documented to the extent that they "will stand up in a court of law?" Is each one of those wire stories that flood in followed by 100 pages of affidavits and exhibits? Why wasn't the "information" about Iraq's alleged weapons of mass destruction held back from publication until it could be "properly substantiated through sources and documents that would stand up in a court of law?" These editors are setting new standards in the category of double standard.

Herman concluded his doleful report: "Curiously, guys like [free- lancer] Greg Szymanski, way up in Idaho, without a huge news organi- zation behind them (the *Blade* employs 146 newsroom staff), without a … decent salary … can manage to uncover more substantial bits and pieces of the puzzle of 9/11 than ALL the editors I queried."

Szymanski's freelance work is seen on Arcticbeacon.com and Rense.com. Szymanski has just reported that Joseph Pulitzer "may be turning over in his grave" because his beloved and independent *Post- Dispatch* recently "tumbled into the corporate ownership of media giant Lee Enterprises, that brought the flagship paper from the Pulitzer family for $1.46-billion. Shortly after, more than 130 staff members, including 41 journalists and the editor-in-chief, quit the paper over salary cuts and obvious editorial policy changes inhibiting what were termed 'free speech issues.'"

5

The Shame of Noam Chomsky and the Gatekeepers of the Left

> "Let us never tolerate outrageous conspiracy theories ...."
> — President George Bush, Nov. 10, 2001,
> to the United Nations General Assembly

> "Look, this is just conspiracy theory."
> — Noam Chomsky to author in conversation,
> November 14, 2002

> "There is a principle which is a bar against all information, which is proof against all arguments and which cannot fail to keep a man in everlasting ignorance — that principle is contempt prior to investigation."
> — Herbert Spencer

Thanks for the identical advice, George Bush and Noam Chomsky. But no thanks.

There's something very strange here. You'd expect George Bush, the most visible face of the American Empire, to employ the intellectually-bankrupt put-down phrase "conspiracy theory" as an element of his propagandistic rhetoric in defense of the official story of 9/11. On the other hand, about the last person you'd expect use the same phrase the same way for the same purpose would be Noam Chomsky, known for masterful deconstructions of propaganda.

179

You'd expect Noam Chomsky to be *unmasking* the nature of this phrase and the purposes of George Bush in using it. As we shall see, this phrase (and its muscular friends "conspiracy nut," "conspiracy whacko," etc.) is far more than simply another misleading figure of speech. It's a particularly effective tool for suppressing healthy citizen skepticism about the contradictions and absurdities of 9/11 and further investigation into them.

Chomsky himself at one point issued a strong caution against the use of the term. He had just explained,[1] at a public meeting, how mainstream media stories are skewed to favor vested interests by means of reporters quoting establishment representatives at length while neglecting to quote critics of the establishment. "Would you characterize [your] media analysis as a 'conspiracy theory' at all?" a woman asked Chomsky.

"It's precisely the opposite of conspiracy theory, actually," Chomsky said. "... institutional factors ... set boundaries for reporting and interpretation in ideological institutions." He continued: "Any economist knows

this: it's not a conspiracy theory to point [out] that ... it's just taken for granted as an institutional fact. If someone were to say 'Oh no, that's a conspiracy theory,' people would laugh." He concluded: "For people to call [Chomsky's media analysis] 'conspiracy theory' is part of the effort to prevent an understanding of how the world works, in my view — 'conspiracy theory' has become the intellectual equivalent of a four-letter word: it's something people say when they don't want you to think about what's really going on."

Noam Chomsky

So, when Noam Chomsky repeatedly uses the phrase "conspiracy theory" to describe questioning of the official story of 9/11, he clearly knows its power and the purpose of its use.

Emotional Considerations
Arising from a Study of Chomsky's Work

Among readers of this book's draft form, this chapter became the most controversial. These readers include writer friends, other friends, and colleagues. No one was close to neutral. The chapter — and I — encountered strong praise and strong aversion, hearty congratulations and dire warnings, gratitude, anger and suspicion.

I came to realize how deep for others — and for me — are the feelings associated with this chapter. This caused me to try to separate out the emotional issues. The attempt has helped me think more clearly about Noam Chomsky and the Left Gatekeepers. I hope this sidebar likewise will be useful to you, the reader.

The emotional attitude toward Chomsky on the Right for the most part is simple hatred. A hatchet job on Chomsky in the Saturday Observer section of the *Ottawa Citizen* of November 5, 2005, provides an example. "The Fanatic Professor: As smart as Noam Chomsky is, he can be infuriatingly stupid" reads the teaser box at the top of the section front page. Inside, the attack is titled "Blind genius." The hatchet is wielded by the paper's editorial page editor, Leonard Stern. Chomsky's political views are "crude." Chomsky is a "weird one" who "buys into ideas that would embarrass the flat earth society."

On the Left, the feelings are more complicated. The main emotions are gratitude and admiration — sometimes to the extent of near idol worship. As Daniel Abrahamson puts it: "Noam Chomsky is often hailed as America's premier dissident intellectual, a fearless purveyor of truth ☞

fighting against media propaganda, murderous US foreign policy, and the crimes of profit-hungry transnational corporations. He enjoys a slavish cult-like following from millions [of] leftist students, journalists, and activists worldwide who fawn over his dense books as if they were scripture. To them, Chomsky is the supreme deity, a priestly master whose logic cannot be questioned."[2]

I myself was one of his earliest supporters, from the days when most had not heard of him. My admiration knew almost no bounds. I have a stack of his books more than a foot high. I praised him personally and publicly and in my university teaching. I was honored to interview him for four segments on Vision TV. A friend of mine and I at one time competed to see who could get the larger number of letters to the editor published defending Chomsky against the ill-wishers who twisted his words or called him names such as "anti-American." I assisted in a small way with the film *Manufacturing Consent*.

But I became one of those in the Left puzzled, even mystified, as a result of Chomsky's insistence for more than 40 years that Lee Harvey Oswald was the lone gunman who killed JFK. This puzzling anomaly took on new significance after 9/11 with Chomsky's opposition to questioning the official 9/11 story — which questioning he says is a huge mistake for the Left.

As I studied his work ever more closely under the intense illumination of 9/11, I became increasingly amazed at patterns, dealt with in this chapter, that emerge from his body of work. Disbelief turned to shock. I feel I have been duped. I feel embarrassment that mainly I duped myself, that I had been in denial. With these realizations came anger from feeling betrayed by someone I welcomed into my innermost sanctum of trust.

One of my emotional tasks is not to go overboard, like the jilted lover who seeks revenge. Trying to be reasonable, I attempt to reconcile these new strongly negative emotions with the positive emotion of gratitude that I felt for so long, and that it would seem reasonable that I should continue to feel. Gratitude for all that I did learn from Chomsky, for all the support he has given to causes I support. I still wrestle with these conflicting emotions as I chance across the latest brilliant articulation by Chomsky of the ☞

havoc wreaked by the American Empire. For instance, his comments in an article by Jim McIlroy and Coral Wynter:

> **Caracas** — By sending gas for heating to poor, homeless people for free and at very low prices for those who can pay, "Venezuela is giving a great example of cooperation and solidarity with the people of the United States. And this is being seen by the entire world," Noam Chomsky, well-known US intellectual, told a public meeting of teachers, students, researchers and journalists on February 13 at the Massachusetts Institute of Technology, according to a special report in the February 15 Caracas newspaper *Diario Vea*.
>
> Chomsky also said that the majority of North Americans "receive little or no information of the great achievements of the Bolivarian revolution, that is headed by President Hugo Chavez, because the mass media only emphasise the bad, and are silent about the positive."[3]

But now, even while reading a report such as this, I cannot forget the evidence of his being a major leader of the "controlled opposition" to the American Empire. My feelings of gratitude are hugely diminished and can never rise again.

I decided to disclose my anger and mixed feelings here, but I have reined them in as much as possible in this chapter. My hope is to channel most of my anger into increased research and into understanding better the complexities of the subject matter. I have also been helped by a friend who is a leader in the "Forgiveness First" movement.

You, too, may encounter strong feelings as you read this chapter. I am grateful for the debate that raged among my friends and colleagues, not least for the emotions directed at me. They have made me reconsider, have rekindled my sensitivity for the feelings of others, and have helped me rewrite usefully, I hope. I also hope you have friends as thoughtful and honest as mine with whom to discuss the intellectual, political and emotional aspects of Chomsky and his work. I must say I now find it creepy. ∎

Every person who says or writes "Oh, that's just conspiracy theory" in response to a question or claim about 9/11 should be challenged immediately. The phrase, in that tone, is counterfeit currency. To allow it to stand leaves the person using the phrase the framer of the discourse, and devalues the discourse and the target. Challenging the phrase is not making a mountain out of a molehill. It is to expose its illegitimacy and enable more reasoned discussion to proceed.

Used pejoratively, the phrase fails in at least four ways. First, as a part of speech it includes two words each of which has a legitimate purpose and meaning — as do the two in combination. To entertain a *theory* about a *conspiracy* or possible conspiracy can be eminently reasonable — and usually is.

Second, the phrase as putdown is usually tossed out *in place of* a response to the facts, claims or assertions brought forward in connection with the theory being advanced. As such the phrase is counterfeit, a *non sequitur.*

Third, it's a psychological below-the-belt blow. The essential power of the phrase — especially when rendered as "conspiracy nut" or "conspiracy wacko" — is that it raises for the person who is its target, the spectre of one of our deepest fears: fear for our sanity. No one wants to be thought of as insane, not even slightly.

Fourth, the cumulative use of this putdown forms a psychological and political wall in society that helps protect *actual* conspiracies from being discussed and investigated as they deserve to be. It's a compact but powerful ideological tool to deflect attention away from the reality of the conspiracies' existence. Let's look more closely at each dimension, because it's time to permanently decommission this weapon of psychological warfare.

Real Conspiracies Abound

First, real conspiracies exist, have always existed and always will. In law, a conspiracy is simply two or more people agreeing to an illegal goal, and one of them taking at least one act in furtherance of that agreement. So common is the crime of conspiracy that a keyword search of any newspaper's archives will reveal numerous stories of people charged with conspiracy to commit fraud, conspiracy to commit murder, and so on. For instance, between January 1 and June 30, 2004 a total of 529 articles in the *New York Times* used the word conspiracy.

Three more recent high-profile examples of conspiracy charges being laid are those against Bernie Ebbers of Worldcom, against Martha Stewart, and against Enron defendants.[4] In the American political arena, large conspiracies have been proven in the cases of Iran-Contra and the "October Surprise" that denied Jimmy Carter the presidency. No one can be labeled "paranoid" for saying Richard Nixon and Henry Kissinger conspired to topple the democratically-elected government of Salvadore Allende in Chile in 1973.[5] In the military sphere, the secret 1962 plans by the US Joint Chiefs of Staff to kill Americans and blame this on Cuba to justify war on Cuba qualifies as a conspiracy, or nothing does. (See Chapter 7, Operation Northwoods.)

Webster G. Tarpley, reaching back further into history, points out that the American Revolution "was based on a conspiracy theory which saw the individual actions of George III as all being governed by a singly unifying design, which was to impose tyranny on the UK's North American colonies."[6] Even though the American Founding Fathers could not produce documents proving their case, were they wrong to believe this? Tarpley notes that the US Declaration of Independence signed in Congress in Philadelphia on July 4, 1776 contains "one of the most celebrated conspiracy theories of all time." Toward the beginning it states that "when a long train of abuses and usurpations, pursuing invariably the same object, evinces a design to reduce [the people] under absolute despotism, it is their right, it is their duty, to throw off such government ..."[7] There you have the conspiracy theory and the call to action based on it, in one passage.

No one should ever accept a whiff of criticism for suggesting that conspiracies have existed and do exist. More than that, the existence of conspiracies, especially at the highest levels, is bedrock. It is those who disparage the existence of conspiracies who should be put instantly on the defensive. As Don Paul, a 9/11 Truth activist and author in San Francisco puts it: "We should remember, I think, the following realities. Conspiracies are history. Conspiracies are how ruling elites grab or maintain power."

Theorizing is Inescapable, Useful and Indispensable.

As for theories, they're the foundation of science, and unavoidable in everyday life. Unavoidable because we are hard wired to theorize. If you hear a

PROFILE: Webster G. Tarpley

"International Terrorism is Not Spontaneous; it Requires Expert Terrorist Controllers"

As a by-product of his fluency in more than five languages, his fascination with history and his photographic memory, Webster Griffin Tarpley is a tour guide extraordinaire. In Berlin he led me on an hours-long Metro and walking tour, during which he explained the glories of the Pergamon Museum, the lessons of the Emperor William II memorial church on the Kurfürstendamm, the history of the Reichstag. We took a pedicab to Checkpoint Charlie and along the way "we" talked with ordinary Berliners. He literally knew the history of almost every street, building and monument. It was the same in Paris, London and Madrid. His own favorite travel is "political tourism." If there's an election, a conference or a demonstration, he wants to be there and learn all about it.

More than anyone else I know in the 9/11Truth movement, Webster Tarpley provides a tour of the most important checkpoints of our political world — the powers of the oligarchies, the importance of economic forces, and the specifics of the fake terrorism mounted by oligarchies' covert agents — all of which he situates in the sweep of history as he sees it. His work in these fields is singular, from his 1978 Moro dossier and his famous book *George Bush: The Unauthorized Biography,* which he wrote in 1992 with Anton Chaikin;[8] to his 1998-9 study of the world financial crisis entitled *Surviving the Cataclysm;* through his *9/11 Synthetic Terror: Made in USA* published in March 2005, and now in its third edition. He frequently uses the term "rogue network" to describe the machinations of "the huge and pervasive

Webster Griffin Tarpley

intelligence agencies ... whose cumulative effect is to over-determine observed reality."

As it happened, he was in Berlin on September 11, 2001. "I concluded more or less instantaneously that the 9/11 events were a provocation by this rogue network ... in order to provide a new enemy image to organize the internal social order of the US and other NATO states, and to provide a pretext for military attacks on Arab and Islamic countries."

He's also an activist. "My most important long-term commitment is to work to improve the intelligence and world awareness of the anti-regime political forces in the United States and around the world," he says. He recognizes the importance of media. "On the positive side, I would cite the talk radio people like Jeff Rense and the Lennie Bloom/Sherman Skolnick cloakanddagger.de, as well as Alex Jones, Jack Blood, Meria Heller, the Dave von Kleist Power Hour, Keidi of LIB network in Los Angeles, and others. Free speech lives in these anti-establishment radio and internet radio outlets, be they leftist, conservative, centrist." On the other hand, he cites his disappointment, as an example, of the failure of the *New York Times,* the *Washington Post,* and the *Los Angeles Times* — or any other mainstream paper — to review *9/11 Synthetic Terror.* He observes: "Even a slanderous review would be better than total silence."

Tarpley foresees new political upsurges on the agenda for the decade and a half ahead, along the lines of 1968. "Bush, Blair and the neo-cons are in the process of creating bureaucratic-authoritarian police states. The emerging opposition to those oppressive regimes will need epistemology, economic program, political strategy, international focus and networking, and much more." Tarpley hopes to be able to help on many of these fronts, "including the serious matter of identifying agents of influence the US-UK finance oligarchs [are deploying to] try to wreck emerging opposition."

loud bang right now, you cannot stop your brain from launching an instantaneous scan of your memory chips. You cannot prevent possibilities from flashing into your mind: Is it a car backfiring, a gunshot, a car crash, an electrical transformer exploding? You rush to the window with at least four theories in mind. Smoke and sparks flying from a hydro pole validate the exploding transformer theory. In science, the process is more refined. Theorizing is inescapable, useful and, indeed, indispensable as a means of making sense of the world. It is the heart of the scientific method. The word *theory* and the idea it encapsulates should be put on a pedestal, not besmirched in an illegitimate slogan.

Second, the phrase as *non sequitur.* The first sentence of a review in *The Nation* of David Ray Griffin's book *The New Pearl Harbor* was: "Conspiracy theories are hard to kill." The review was by longtime CIA operative Robert Baer. In his response to the review, Griffin wrote: "... by declaring 'Conspiracy theories are hard to kill' [Baer] pretends not to know that in the book's introduction, I pointed out that the question is not whether one accepts or rejects a conspiracy theory about 9/11, but only whether one accepts the government's conspiracy theory or some other one. By pretending not to know this, Baer suggests that to take issue with the book one needs only to put it in the 'conspiracy theory' genre, thereby dismissing it *a priori.*" [9]

A Below-the-Belt Blow

Third, the phrase as psychological below-the-belt blow. It is justified to describe the term "conspiracy wacko" as a weapon of psychological warfare. Psychologist Floyd Rudmin writes:

> The power of this pejorative is that it discounts a theory by attacking the motivations and mental competence of those who advocate the theory. By labeling an explanation of events "conspiracy theory," evidence and argument are dismissed because they come from a mentally or morally deficient personality, not because they have been shown to be incorrect. Calling an explanation of events "conspiracy theory" means, in effect, "We don't like you, and no one should listen to your explanation." [10]

Op-ed page pundits sometimes deliver the blow more gently, but to the same pejorative effect. They attempt through amateur psychologizing to explain away the evidence of those they label "conspiracists." Some people, the line goes, have a "need" to believe conspiracies and so they "invent them."

Fourth, the cumulative exercise of this phrase in its putdown mode performs an ideological function in society. It endorses the idea that only a nutty minority could actually think our leaders would lie to us, or that there are very real and powerful interests that secretly engage in crimes of various sorts to protect and expand their power, control and wealth. The demeaning notion that those who are suspicious of power are few and mentally unstable can only benefit the powerful. You can bet that the person who thought up the term "You can't fight city hall" was a mayor.

The Descriptive, Non-Putdown, Use of the Phrase Conspiracy Theory

It may be that a larger percentage of the population today is concerned about conspiracies than was the case in, say, the 1950s. Despite the official "lone gunman" explanation for the assassination of President John F. Kennedy, 78 per cent of Americans believe a high-level conspiracy did him in. The eventual unraveling of the lie — put out by the White House and dutifully amplified by the mainstream media — that Iraq possessed WMDs has increased the knowledge that a powerful network can collude in inventing a countrywide, even worldwide, bogus reality. Suspicions linger about the plane crash that killed Senator Paul Wellstone, a much-respected politician poised at the time of his death to play a key role in holding the Bush administration to account. And of course there are the contradictions of 9/11. As already noted, almost half of New Yorkers believe the White House was complicit in 9/11.

If more people than before suspect high-level conspiracies, Rudmin puts forward an intriguing theory as to why. Conspiracy theorizing arises, he says, when:

a. Significant political or economic events change power relationships in society;

b. Contradictions in the explanations of these events are noticed by ordinary citizens;

c. Curiosity and then concern are aroused, and

d. Further information is sought under the presumption that power is being abused and *deception is being deployed* [emphasis added][11]

This swings a spotlight onto the media. Rudmin continues:

Conspiracy theory is "deconstructive history" because it is in rebellion against official explanations and against *orthodox journalism* [emphasis added] and orthodox history.

Conspiracy theory by ordinary people is radically empirical: tangible facts are the focus, especially facts that the standard stories try to overlook. There is a ruthless reduction down to what is without doubt real, namely, persons. Conspiracy theory presumes that human events are caused by people acting as people do, including cooperating, planning, cheating, deceiving, and pursuing power. Thus, conspiracy theories do not focus on impersonal forces like geo-politics, market economics, globalization, social evolution and other such abstract explanations of human events.

To call conspiracy theory "naïve" does not mean that it is uncritical or stupidly innocent. In fact, that is what conspiracy theorists ... say about orthodox explanations of events promoted by government sources, by *mainstream journalism*, [emphasis added] or by school-book history.

Conspiracy theories arise when dramatic events happen, and the orthodox explanations try to diminish the events and gloss them over. In other words, conspiracy theories begin when someone notices that *the explanations do not fit the facts.*[12] [emphasis added]

Noam Chomsky on Conspiracy Theory

Noam Chomsky is inconsistent in dealing with the term "conspiracy theory" and in using it. As we have seen, in one instance — one in which his own work was under threat of being tarred with the "conspiracy theory" brush — he warned that the term in its putdown mode is "something people say when they don't want you to think about what's really going on."

But as we shall see, Chomsky has used the term in its putdown mode repeatedly to describe those who question the official stories of JFK's assassination and 9/11. These are the extremes of his relationship with the phrase and concept. Between these extremes, Chomsky engages in some convolutions. In light of the influence of Chomsky and the importance of the topic, they deserve to be examined closely.

The most sustained deconstruction by Chomsky of the term "conspiracy theory" I can find is in his book, mentioned earlier, *Understanding Power*[13]

The venue, again, is a public meeting. Chomsky had been asked whether "corporate elites can't turn the environmental crisis to their benefit" so that "the public will now pay them [through subsidies] to salvage the environment they've been primarily responsible for destroying." Chomsky essentially answered "Yes."[14]

As a follow-up another questioner asked: "How much of this do you attribute to a conspiracy theory, and how much would you say is just a by-product of capital near-sightedness and a shared interest in holding onto power?"

"Well, this term 'conspiracy theory' is kind of an interesting one," Chomsky begins. He continues:

> For example, if I was talking about Soviet planning and I said, "Look, here's what the Politburo decided, and then the Kremlin did this," nobody would call that a "conspiracy theory" — everyone would just assume that I was talking about planning. But as soon as you start talking about anything that's done by power in the West, it's not allowed to exist. So if you're a political scientist, one of the things you learn — you don't even make it into graduate school unless you've already internalized it — is that nobody here ever plans anything: we just act out of a kind of general benevolence, stumbling from here to here, sometimes making mistakes and so on. The guys in power aren't idiots, after all. They do planning. In fact, they do very careful and sophisticated planning. But anybody who talks about it, and uses government records or anything else to back it up, is into "conspiracy theory."[15]

Since the nature of "conspiracy theory" was raised in the context of a question about the true motives of big business, Chomsky's response can't be faulted for remaining in that context. But his response within that context can be faulted. He claims that "anybody who talks" about planning being done by corporate interests is accused of being a "conspiracy theorist." In my experience, this is untrue on two counts. First, stories about long-term planning by business abound. An example are those dealing with investment in the development of the Alberta tar sands for the future extraction of petroleum. Second, I can't think of an instance where "anybody who talks about" long-term business planning is labeled a "conspiracy theorist." He continues:

> It's the same with business: business is again just operating out of a generalized benevolence, trying to help everybody get the cheapest goods with the best quality, all this kind of stuff. If you say: "Look, Chrysler is trying to maximize profits and market share," that's "conspiracy theory." [16]

One of Chomsky's Many Straw Men

I strongly doubt most people would agree that critics of excess corporate profits have very often been dubbed "conspiracy theorists" for that criticism. My experience is that they are labeled "anti-business" or sometimes "allergic to profits (or the profit motive)." If their tormentors are out for blood they're accused of being "socialistic," or of in fact being "socialists" or "communists." They may also be called "tree huggers," "knee jerk liberals" or "opposed to the American way of life." Although this list does not exhaust the list of epithets, "conspiracy theorist" is noticeably absent from the list. Plainly put, Chomsky has created a straw man. He continues:

> In other words, as soon as you describe elementary reality and attribute minimal rationality to people with power — well that's fine as along as it's an enemy, but if it's a part of domestic power, it's a "conspiracy theory" and you're not supposed to talk about it. [17]

Now, we're getting somewhere. Chomsky's generic deconstruction here is relevant and persuasive. It's articulated by Chomsky as a pretty effective

defense of himself in a situation where he's facing the sting of the suggestion that he himself is a "conspiracy theorist." He follows with a practical
suggestion: "So, the first thing I would suggest is, drop the term." He
then, however, continues with an unduly limited duality:

> There are really only two questions. One is how much of this is *con-
> scious* planning — as happens everywhere else. And the other is, how
> much is *bad* planning [his emphases].[18]

This is a false choice, the kind Chomsky warns against in different con-
texts. In the context of the concerns of ordinary people over outrageous
events such as JFK's assassination or 9/11, it is easily demonstrable that
there are many more than "only two questions." Indeed, the two he raises
are not even the most important among several. To agree to pursue only
these two is to be directed down a dead-end.

The most important questions include *what* was planned (on the one
hand, assassinations and brazen false-flag ops; on the other, maximizing
profits?); *who* did the planning (how high up is the responsibility or culpability?); *how criminal or unconstitutional* was the planning (determining
this could be a foundation for impeachment or other forms of calling to
account); and *which agenda has benefited* from the conspiratorial planning?
Overlooking all these, Chomsky goes on to answer his own question:

> Well, it's all conscious planning: there is just no doubt that a lot of
> very conscious planning goes on among intelligent people who are
> trying to maximize their power. They'd be insane if they didn't do
> that.
>
> I mean I'm not telling you anything new when I tell you that top
> editors, top government officials, and major businessmen have meet-
> ings together — of course. And not only do they have meetings,
> they belong to the same golf clubs, they go to the same parties, they
> went to the same schools, they flow up and back from one position
> to another in the government and private sector, and so on and so
> forth. In other words, they represent the same social class: they'd be
> crazy if they didn't communicate and plan with each other.[19]

He continues his exposition on conscious planning (as opposed to "bad" planning — also, these are not opposites):

So of *course* the Board of Directors of General Motors plans, the same way the National Security Council plans, and the National Association of Manufacturers' PR agencies plan. I mean, this was a truism to Adam Smith: if you read Adam Smith [classical economist], he says that every time two businessmen get together in a room, you can be sure there's some plan being cooked up which is going to harm the public. Yeah, how could it be otherwise? And there's nothing particularly new about this — as Smith pointed out over two hundred years ago, the "masters of mankind," as he called them, will do what they have to in order to follow "the vile maxim;" all for ourselves and nothing for anyone else." Yeah, and when they're in the National Security Council, or the Business Roundtable [a national organization composed of the CEOs of 200 major corporations], or the rest of these elite planning forums, they have extreme power behind them. And yes, they're planning — planning very carefully.[20]

Who could disagree? And this is vintage Chomsky. But he then turns to what he has laid down as *the only other question that can be asked of this situation:* "Now, the only significant question to ask is, is it *intelligent* [his emphasis] planning?" He answers his own second, final, and most important question in the negative:

Okay, that depends on what the goals are. If the goals are to maximize corporate profits for tomorrow, then it's very intelligent planning. If the goals are to have a world where your children can survive, then it's completely idiotic. But that second thing isn't really part of the game. In fact, it's institutionalized: it's not that these people are stupid, it's that to the extent that you have a competitive system based on private control over resources, you are forced to maximize short-term gain. That's just an institutional necessity.[21]

He continues at length with valuable analyses of, for instance, rifts within the Right between corporate types who are socially progressive, on the one hand (being in favor of abortion rights and opportunities for their daughters), and Christian fundamentalists on the other ("who think women ought to be driven back to the home and shut up, and who want to have twelve assault rifles in their closets, and so on"). He even points out that "major class war" requires the oligarchy to "appeal to the population" on the bases of "jingoism, racism, fear, religious fundamentalism: these are the ways of appealing to people if you're going to organize a mass base of support for policies that are really intended to crush them." [22]

But he never — it should not be controversial to point this out — connects the jingoistic, racist, fear-based so-called "war on terror," heavily reliant on fear of (Muslim) religious fundamentalism, with the events of 9/11, even though the events of 9/11 are the linchpin for the so-called "war on terror." In other words, he provides a masterful analysis of the overall problem generically, while avoiding engagement with the specific toxic core that fuels it. And this avoidance is unbending. The contradiction is total.

The Ostensible Mystery of Chomsky, JFK and 9/11

Like many on the Left, for years I lived in puzzlement as to why Chomsky could not or would not recognize the mountain of evidence that JFK could not have been killed by lone gunman Lee Harvey Oswald. I had encountered many others on the Left who said they were "mystified" and "bewildered" as to his decades-long obstinacy and adamancy on the JFK assassination, especially because their belief was that Chomsky valued evidence above all.

Then a friend gave me a little-known book by E. Martin Schotz, *History Will Not Absolve Us*,[23] which contains evidence that Chomsky indeed was exposed to a coherent collection of evidence undermining the official *Warren Report* version of what happened to JFK. In one of the appendices was a first-person account by citizen investigator Ray Marcus, detailing his attempts to have Noam Chomsky seriously study evidence Marcus had assembled. In early 1969, Marcus met Chomsky with "a portfolio of evidence, primarily photographic, that I could present briefly but adequately in 30-60 minutes."

He believed this evidence "carried sufficient conviction to impress most intelligent and open-minded people." The one-hour meeting was extended to between three and four hours when Chomsky had his secretary cancel the rest of his appointments for that day. Chomsky showed "great interest in the material. We mutually agreed to a follow-up session later in the week." Marcus then met with Gar Alperovitz. At the end of their one-hour meeting Alperovitz said he "would take an active part in the effort if Chomsky would lead it." The "effort" would be an attempt to reopen questioning about the provenance of JFK's death. A long second meeting with Chomsky and a colleague, MIT philosophy professor Selwyn Bromberger, followed. After the meeting Bromberger said: "If they are strong enough to kill the president, and strong enough to cover it up, then they are too strong to confront directly ... if they feel sufficiently threatened, they may move to open totalitarian rule."[25]

Marcus provided further information to Chomsky, which Chomsky acknowledged. Chomsky then left on an extended trip abroad, saying in a final note, "I'm still open-minded (and I hope will remain so)." Marcus reports: "I never heard from him again. In recent years he has on a number of occasions gone on record attacking the critics' position and supporting the *Warren Report*."[26]

There's a great deal of supporting evidence in *History Will Not Absolve Us* from author Schotz, from Vincent Salandria, from Ray Marcus and from legendary investigative reporter Fred Cook that, following JFK's assassination, Chomsky and other leading lights of the Left simply would not acknowledge the evidence that interests opposed to Kennedy's stands for peace, rapprochement with the USSR, normalization of relations with Cuba and other progressive policies had the means, motive and opportunity to kill him. If these leaders of the Left were overcome with fear, then I for one cannot continue to honor them for bravery. But I shoved my disappointment and puzzlement off to one side and returned to my state of denial.

Chomsky can be Illogical and Unfair

Then someone recommended Chomsky's book *Rethinking Camelot*.[27] There I found abundant proof that Chomsky could be illogical, contradictory and unfair in ways I could not previously have imagined. I was attempting to resolve for myself (no one in my circle could explain it) the mystery of why Chomsky would dismiss the now even larger mountain of evidence that JFK was executed by elements of the state. But in *Rethinking Camelot* Chomsky, 30 years after JFK's assassination, takes great pains to study documents concerning Vietnam policy circa 1963, rather than rethinking the central event. His conclusions smack of a mind made up and a certain meanness. "The belief that JFK might have responded differently ... is an act of faith, based on nothing but the belief that the President had some spiritual quality absent in everyone around him, leaving no detectable trace," he says. "The extensive record of newly-released documents ... undermine much further the already implausible contention that [JFK's assassination] caused dramatic changes in policy (or indeed, had any effect)."[28]

He thus dismisses the trajectory of Kennedy's policies, condensed well by Michael Parenti in his book *Dirty Truths:*[29] "JFK's enemies in the CIA, the Pentagon, and elsewhere fixed on his refusal to provide air coverage for the Bay of Pigs, his unwillingness to go into Indochina with massive ground forces, his no-invasion guarantee to Khrushchev on Cuba, his overtures for a rapprochement with Castro and professed willingness to tolerate countries with different economic systems in the Western hemisphere, his atmospheric-test-ban treaty with Moscow, his American University speech calling for reexamination of US cold war attitudes toward the Soviet Union, his antitrust suit against General Electric, his curtailing of the oil-depletion allowance, his fight with US steel over price increases, his challenge to the Federal Reserve Board's multibillion-dollar monopoly control of the nation's currency, his warm reception at labor conventions, and his call for racial equality. These things may not have been enough for some on the Left but they were far too much for many on the Right."[29]

Yet Chomsky claims to this day that US policy on Vietnam would have been no different had Kennedy lived. This claim is flawed for four reasons. First, no one can prove beyond reasonable doubt such a thing one way or another, so at the best he is no better than those he criticizes for claiming the opposite. Second, on the balance of probabilities, everything we know about JFK (see the passage above) suggests that he was already following and would have continued to follow the more peaceful and sane directions he had established for himself, which could hardly exclude Vietnam. Third, his general trajectory was away from escalation of the war. The *Pentagon Papers*[30] document Kennedy's intent to withdraw. They refer to "the

Accelerated Model Plan ... for a rapid phase out of the bulk of US military personnel" and note the administration was "serious about limiting the US commitment ..." But "all the planning for phase-out ... was either ignored or caught up in the new thinking of January to March 1964." Parenti notes that this "new thinking" was the reversion to a war course that came "after JFK was killed and Lyndon B. Johnson became president." [31]

On page after page of *Rethinking Camelot*, Chomsky inserts assertions where examination of evidence is called for. He states on page 38 that those who reject the lone assassin thesis of JFK's death "have recognized that credible direct evidence is lacking ...." This is *a priori* rejection of large amounts of evidence, including direct, such as the wound in the front of Kennedy's throat, to name just one example. A good deal of this evidence is even found in the appendices to the Warren Commission's *Report*. Chomsky's usual diligence in finding obscure contradictory information fails him on the Kennedy assassination. But even after making scores of admittedly angry marginal notes in *Rethinking Camelot*, I reverted to a stance of total respect for Chomsky's work. I see now that I was in deep denial, no different from that of someone who adulates George Bush and dismisses successively all reasons to fault him.

It took 9/11 to shake me out of my denial. Even then, I see in retrospect, the process was painfully slow. Finally Chomsky's sustained rejection of evidence, his sustained use of the term "conspiracy theory" to describe the work of those seeking the truth about JFK's assassination (and the other assassinations of the 1960s), and 9/11, and his diminishment of the role of leaders such as JFK and his brother, and of Dr. Martin Luther King Jr., became a pattern I could no longer ignore. Writing this book opened my eyes further.

The Role of Structuralism

Chomsky has described himself as a structuralist although curiously there's little about this in the 14 Chomsky books in my library. Michael Parenti, also interested in this concept, writes: "A structural analysis, as I understand it, maintains that events are determined by the larger configurations of power and interest and not by the whims of happenstance or the connivance of a few incidental political actors." [33] Parenti's description might be considered a bit ascerbic, until one realizes that Chomsky has come close to arguing that whatever Lyndon B. Johnson did, John F. Kennedy would have done!

Chomsky insists that ideological institutions are the most powerful determinants of what those who operate within them will do. Few on the Left or the Right would disagree that there's a great deal of important truth to this contention. But Chomsky is dogmatic in his dismissiveness of the power or influence of individual leaders (or say a group of world leaders cooperating in some field), or the good that great leaders can accomplish. Chomsky's insistence has the effect of diminishing hope as well as demeaning the visions and the efforts of such people as JFK, his brother Robert Kennedy, Dr. Martin Luther King, Jr., or Malcolm X — all wiped out in a decapitation of the US Left in the 1960s. He does not think these people would have "made a difference." It's surprising that more people have not challenged Chomsky on his theory of structuralism on the basis that it is, in a word, ludicrous. President Harry Truman ("The buck stops here") did not have to make the decision to drop the atomic bomb on Hiroshima. Did Franklin Delano Roosevelt have no impact on the course of US history? Was Winston Churchill just a replaceable cipher? History books are filled with detailed descriptions of major decisions made, one way or the other, within overall existing structures of power, changing the lives of millions and sometimes leading to vast changes in those structures as well. A recent case would be the interaction between Mikhail Gorbachev, perestroika and the transformation of the former Soviet Union. Who could deny that Chomsky himself has "made a large difference?" Claims from him to the contrary must be counted as false humility.

There's a parallel between Chomsky's claim that JFK wouldn't make a difference and his claim that whoever killed JFK didn't make a difference. If the leaders don't make history, then neither do their assassins. Somehow, no one's in charge. So no one's responsible, accountable. To refuse to examine available evidence that state conspiracies ended the lives of charismatic progressive leaders is to protect, almost absolve of historical responsibility, their killers. It is a template Chomsky applies to the events of 9/11. He does admit that 9/11 made a difference. But he has said "it doesn't matter" who carried out 9/11, and that he's not interested.[34] If the perpetrators are within the state apparatus, this stance is protective of those perpetrators.

In any event, the existence of ideological, financial and other structures on the one hand, and the existence of pivotal decisions by individuals on the other, are not mutually exclusive. But even in unduly emphasizing, in my opinion, the structural, Chomsky is evasive. "However unpleasant and difficult it may be, there is no escape from the need to confront the reality of institutions and the polices and actions they largely shape," he wrote in Z Magazine in 1992.[35] Michael Parenti rightly selects the CIA as an example of an institution marinated in conspiracy by its very nature. "As I pointed out in published exchanges with [Alexander] Cockburn and Chomsky (neither of whom responded to the argument), conspiracy and structure are not mutually exclusive dynamics. A structural analysis that *a priori* rules out conspiracy runs the risk of not looking at the whole picture," writes Parenti. "In investigating the JFK conspiracy, researchers are not looking for an 'escape' from something 'unpleasant and difficult,' as Chomsky would have it, rather they are raising grave questions about the nature of state power in what is supposed to be a democracy." Parenti adds: "In sum, national security state conspiracies are components of our political structure, not deviations from it."[36]

The Events of 9/11 as a Touchstone Issue

A criticism can be leveled against me that the truth about 9/11 is my touchstone, my compass, the litmus test by which I measure all individuals, organizations and institutions. I plead guilty. I cannot imagine a more legitimate test. The events of 9/11 were specific and yet universal. They involve murder, deceit, abuse of power, the role of government, perpetual war, the life of the planet. They are similar to the test at the height of the Vietnam War that faced every individual, organization and institution. Once the brutality of the war became known (which was very early on, as early as 1961, for those who did not avert their eyes), it stood as a test of moral systems and political stances. Daniel Ellsberg met the test by risking a lengthy jail term, public disgrace, personal harassment, and more, in changing his mind about the war, then putting himself on the line in effective opposition to that war. Dick Cheney failed the test by evading the draft.

There *are* defining issues. As Richard Falk says, to examine the evidence about 9/11 with "even a 30 per cent open mind," is to see it is an issue "almost certain to change the way we understand the workings of constitutional democracy in the United States at the highest levels of government."[37] And that is an understatement. Add to that the expansion of hyper-militarism and the further destruction of Earth's environment that are among the outcomes of the acceptance of the official 9/11 story and it can surely be seen that we face a issue against which everyone's moral and political approach can be measured on an historical yardstick. I am not saying agreement about this must be universal. I am saying this seems inescapably valid to me.

Because he is so adulated on the Left, Chomsky's slim book *9-11*,[38] issued soon after 9/11, sold heavily. Many — if not most — Left and liberal people looked to Chomsky and specifically that book to explain the events to them. But it turned out to be an echo of his 40-year denial of the possibility of conspiracies involving the state and, indeed, an endorsement of the official 9/11 story, albeit almost invisibly because of his facility with word evasion, which we shall examine more closely.

On the first page of the first chapter he suggests that it is "misleading" to draw an analogy between the events of 9/11 and Pearl Harbor. The reason, he says, is that Hawaii in 1941 was "in effect a colony." Pearl Harbor was not "national territory." The continental USA "was never threatened." He is geographically correct. But in the much more important territory of national emotions, it is Chomsky who is being misleading. The attack on Pearl Harbor seared the nation, mobilized it overnight to enter World War II — a complete turnaround at the time. It remains embedded as one of the iconic events of American — not just Hawaiian — history.

By the third page of the first chapter he has accepted (as he has consistently has since), the essential line of the official 9/11 story, that the "likely perpetrators" are from the Middle East and "draw support from a reservoir of bitterness and anger over US policies in the region...." Later: "it was assumed, plausibly, that the guilty parties were bin Laden and his al Qaeda network." Plausibly and yet, he admits, contradictorily, "the evidence is surprisingly thin." Surprisingly thin evidence he finds plausible. Further: "it was assumed, plausibly, that the guilty parties were bin Laden and his al Qaeda network."[39] He loves this word, *plausibly*, which usually he ascribes to no one.

Chomsky's Evasiveness Dissected

Who assumed this? What is the source of the finding of "plausible?" It's the equivalent of "everyone knows." An odd source of authority for Chomsky. This is a typical Chomsky construction: he reinforces the official story but seems at the same time to be distancing himself from it. He seldom says anything as direct as "Yes, I think bin Laden did it." But repeatedly he accepts the reality of the 19 Muslim hijackers as the genuine criminals by using terms such as "terrorist atrocities" and "radical Islamists." (See discussion of the alleged hijackers in Chapter 2, Exhibits T and U.) Even in the course of explaining that the evidence is weak, Chomsky supports the case by saying, for instance, "for all we know, most of the perpetrators may have killed themselves in their awful missions."

During "An Evening with Noam Chomsky: The War on Terror," held at MIT October 18, 2001, just five weeks after 9/11, when many people would be looking to him for wisdom about 9/11, he devoted perhaps 10 minutes to 9/11 as such, during which he clearly accepted the official story. Of the "likely perpetrators" he says "it is astonishing to me how weak the evidence was. And it ended up about where it started, with a *prima facie* case." He continued: "So let's assume that it is true. So let's assume that, it looked obvious the first day, still does, that the actual perpetrators come from the radical Islamic, here called, fundamentalist networks of which the bin Laden network is undoubtedly a significant part." So he is buying into the official story totally, without providing any evidence, in fact while agreeing that if there is any evidence it is weak. He also does not suggest where this "weak" evidence comes from, namely the White House and the media. But in case anyone might decide to pursue his contradictions, Chomsky adds dismissively: "Whether [Islamic terrorists] were involved or not nobody knows. It doesn't really matter much." This quietly arrogant dismissiveness is a recurring theme or ploy with Chomsky. As it flies by, it is a thought stopper. It discourages questioning or further discourse.

Chomsky accepts in *9-11* that the alleged audio and video tapes of bin Laden are authentic, an odd stance for a skeptic, especially since bin

Laden's voice, comport and even looks have varied quite widely from tape to tape. (See 9/11 Media Diary entry for December 24, 2001, p. 15.) And although Chomsky will refer from time to time to "the bin Laden network and other graduates of the terrorist forces set up by the CIA and its associates 20 years ago to fight a Holy War against the Russians," he steers away from any suggestion that links could remain between the CIA and bin Laden or that he could be a CIA asset now. Or that the CIA would fabricate tapes.

Chomsky says, "Scholarship is virtually unanimous in taking the terrorists at their word." Whatever one's definition of the vague term "scholarship," this generalization is unsupportable. Unanimity at taking "terrorists" at their word? Unanimity about who the "terrorists" are? Yet Chomsky leaves no room for evidence that the terrorists are genuine, and no room for even suspicions, according to his word in this context, that many of the terrorists are valuable assets on the payrolls of covert Western agencies, pawns useful to keep the "war on terror" simmering, to the benefit of Western intelligence and military interests, and the interests of the American empire that he otherwise criticizes for its depredations. Chomsky's reading is curiously selective in that it seems to exclude, for instance, books such as *The War on Truth: 9/11, Disinformation, and the Anatomy of Terrorism,* by Nafeez Mosaddeq Ahmed, which explores in detail the *modus operandi* of the manipulation and subversion of al Qaeda in the Middle East, Central Asia, Asia-Pacific, Caucasus, and Balkans, and in which, as Ahmed writes, "Al Qaeda is found to be the outgrowth of a coordinated network of highly secret sub-units of state-intelligence services operating under the overarching strategic direction of the most clandestine parallel structures of western military-intelligence services, especially those of the US and UK." Chomsky would prefer to "take terrorists at their word."

In sum, Chomsky's book *9-11* has had the effect of selling the official story about 9/11 to the Left in general, and even to a wider public which might be suspicious of his politics but respect him as a thinker. When one of the world's leading critics of the US Empire accepts the official story, it's a powerful boost for the official story — and brings to the fore questions about Chomsky's agenda.

The Selective Relationship of Chomsky and Evidence

Chomsky's reputation rests heavily upon the alleged care he takes to always present evidence in support of his contentions. He has earned that reputation through the huge body of work he has produced documenting the "state terrorism" of the American Empire. His notations are prodigious. In his 441-page *The Washington Connection and Third World Fascism,*[40] there are 74 pages of notes in small type. Thus, when he makes statements to which no evidence is attached — which he does all the time — people *assume* he has evidence to back up those statements as well. An analysis of his statements on 9/11, JFK's assassination and on other subjects we shall touch upon, however, shows that on the crucial matters at the center of this book, he consistently fails to provide evidence.

But his *modus operandi* goes far beyond failing to provide evidence for most of his assertions surrounding 9/11. More tellingly, he does not seek out evidence. Furthermore, he consistently refuses to engage with the evidence offered to him. And finally, he caps his rejection of evidence by his use of the epithet "conspiracy theorists" to disparage those who do engage with the evidence.

As author Michael Parenti puts it in relation to Chomsky's track record on the JFK assassination: "[He] is able to maintain his criticism that no credible evidence has come to light [to suggest anyone other than Lee Harvey Oswald killed JFK] only by remaining determinedly unacquainted with the mountain of evidence that has been uncovered."[41] Parenti's statement applies equally to the mountain of evidence surrounding the events of 9/11; evidence uncovered much more quickly than in the case of JFK.

Herbert Spencer wrote: "There is a principle which is a bar against all information, which is proof against all arguments and which cannot fail to keep a man in everlasting ignorance — that principle is contempt prior to investigation." When a figure as towering on the Left as is Chomsky rejects the need for further investigation, it's a distinct setback for the cause of further investigation. I have repeatedly encountered this stopper effect. One day I was speaking on the phone with a woman from Tennessee who was ordering one of my DVDs. Typically, she said: "I'm convinced the Bush Administration was behind 9/11, but I can't get my husband to even consider it." "Why is that?" I asked. "He says if it was true, Noam Chomsky would have said so. And he says that until Noam Chomsky comes out and questions the official story, it's good enough for him."

Chomsky Engages in Scare Campaign Against the Left

Chomsky actually *warns* the Left not to examine the evidence: "If the left spends its time on this, that's the end of the left, in my opinion: the mainstream would be utterly delighted. It is highly likely that nothing significant will be found. And if — which I very greatly doubt — something is found that would quickly send everyone in Washington to the death chamber, the left is unlikely to emerge triumphant." [42] Coming from Chomsky, this amounts to a scare campaign against the Left.

On the subject of 9/11 Chomsky routinely flouts the practices he constantly preaches to others: provide the evidence, examine the evidence, search for more evidence. His techniques for evading the evidence are many. They are, in effect, tools for protecting official stories. We encounter a panoply of propaganda techniques that one would expect Chomsky to be familiar with. But many would be surprised to learn how consistently he practices these arts of obfuscation himself, without disclosure, in support of an agenda clearly at odds with the one most people believe he consistently follows. A partial list of his propaganda techniques:

Absurdities	Framing to exclude contrary
Ad hominem sallies	outlooks
Bald assertions that are mis-statements	Ignorance flaunted as admirable
Bandwagon psychology	Inappropriate selectivity
Bizarre non-sequiturs	Insinuation
Bullying	Internal contradiction
Diminishment of the importance	Major premises hidden in passing
of the important	Misdirection
Dismissiveness	Misleading asides
Diversions (e.g., not answering	Mixing apples and oranges
the question)	Obfuscation
Failure to provide minimal evidence	Restriction of options
Fake humility	Scare tactics
Fake open-mindedness	Setting up straw men
False parallels	Sweeping generalizations
False syllogisms	Word inflation

When he deploys any of these throughout a fairly short statement the effect is a kind of word magic or doubletalk. Take this, one of his posts to the ChomskyChat Forum (zmag.org/chomsky/other/chomchatarch.htm):

It's true that I know very little about the assassination [of JFK] [ignorance flaunted]. The only thing I've written about it is that the claim that it was a high-level conspiracy with policy significance is implausible [internal contradiction: he admits knowing "very little" so on what basis does he find any claim "implausible?"] to a quite extraordinary degree [adding to the internal contradiction, word inflation, failure to provide minimal evidence.] History isn't physics [obfuscation] and even in physics nothing is really "proven" [misdirection, vis a vis the laws of physics] but the evidence against this claim is overwhelming [internal contradiction, word inflation, bald assertion, failure to provide minimal evidence] from every testable point of view [sweeping generalization, bald assertion,] remarkably so for a historical event [word inflation, failure to provide minimal evidence.] Given that conclusion, which I think is very well founded [bandwagon psychology, failure to provide minimal evidence,] that I have written about, a lot, [internal contradiction: earlier he said the only thing he's written about it is to claim implausibility, etc.] I have no further interest in the assassination [dismissiveness, evasion, minimizing importance of the important] and while I've read a few of the books [internal contradiction: he said he "knows very little:" reading "some books" surely qualifies as more than "very little",] out of curiosity [dismissiveness, suggesting closed-mindedness, not even fake openmindedness] I haven't given the matter any attention [internal contradiction: for someone who "hasn't given the matter any attention" he has arrived at extremely strong and controversial opinions] and have no opinion about how or why JFK was killed." [internal contradiction: he has an opinion, which he has just energetically expressed, that the way JFK was killed was not by a state conspiracy.]

He continues: "People shouldn't be killed, whether they are presidents or kids in the urban slums. I know of no reason to suppose that one should have more interest in the JFK assassination than lots of killings not far from the White House." *obfuscation: comparing a coup by assassination of a head of state that changes history, on the one hand, to a street murder on the other, is a failed parallel; dismissiveness; diminishment of the importance of the important.* In the main, this statement is one long bald assertion, resting on a series of word inflations. It's doublespeak.

You may parse Chomsky's verbiage and conclude I am too hard on him, that some of my attributions of propaganda techniques are questionable. Let's say I'm two-thirds wrong. If only a third of my analysis holds up, then Chomsky's reputation for being evidence-based, logical and consistent does not hold up, in this instance. This instance is not unfairly chosen; it is typical. Here is another, his correspondence with Dr. Robert McFarland of Boulder, Colorado, a retired physician.

McFarland, who served in the US Navy for two years and for 20 years in the Naval Reserve, in 2003 sent Chomsky an article McFarland had written on the relationship between Pearl Harbor and 9/11. In it he quoted the work of Nafeez Ahmed on 9/11. Chomsky in a note thanked McFarland for the article which he said, typically, he "read with interest" but continued, also typically: "I'm frankly unconvinced."

McFarland in a three-paragraph note thanked Chomsky, then drew Chomsky's attention to David Ray Griffin's book *The New Pearl Harbor*, encouraging him to look at the first 33 pages. (These establish the importance of examining evidence on 9/11, provide an intellectual framework for doing so, and begin an examination of Flights 11 and 175, the ensuing collapses of the twin WTC towers, Flight 77 and the damage to the Pentagon.) McFarland concluded: "You have an enormous ability to influence public opinion and I hope you have revised your views since you last wrote me." McFarland did not receive a response. Then, after the report of the

Robert McFarland

9/11 Commission came out in July 2004 McFarland suggested to Chomsky in a telephone voice message that Chomsky look at the photograph at the top of page 313 of *The 9/11 Commission Report*, reproduced here.

It's a picture of the damaged façade of the Pentagon over the legend "The Pentagon, after being struck by American Airlines Flight 77." The pattern of destruction clearly is inconsistent with the building being struck by a Boeing 757.

Chomsky wrote McFarland this note:

MASSACHUSETTS INSTITUTE OF TECHNOLOGY

Department of Linguistics and Philosophy
77 Massachusetts Avenue, 32-D808
Cambridge, Massachusetts 02139

August 5, 2004

Dear Bob,

I haven't read the 9/11 report, and would not be able to have any judgment about the photo you mention if I had.

Sincerely,

Noam Chomsky

This is either an astounding admission of a studied lack of interest in a matter of national, indeed world importance; or of fundamental incompetence; or is a backhanded self-compliment by an overly-specialized academic, or an evasion. The pattern is evasion — and diversion. The pattern goes back to the earliest days after 9/11. One of Chomsky's most complete statements on the events of 9/11:

There's by now a small industry on the thesis that the administration had something to do with 9-11. I've looked at some of it, and have often been asked. There's a weak thesis that is possible though extremely unlikely in my opinion, and a strong thesis that is close to inconceivable.

The weak thesis is that they knew about it and didn't try to stop it. The strong thesis is that they were actually involved. The evidence for either thesis is, in my opinion, based on a failure to understand properly what evidence is. Even in controlled scientific experiments one finds all sorts of unexplained phenomena, strange coincidences, loose ends, apparent contradictions, etc. Read the letters in technical science journals and you'll find plenty of samples.

In real world situations, chaos is overwhelming, and these will mount to the sky. That aside, they'd have had to be quite mad to try anything like that. It would have had to involve a large number of people, something would be very likely to leak, pretty quickly, they'd all be lined up before firing squads and the Republican Party would be dead forever.

That would have happened whether the plan succeeded or not, and success was at best a long shot; it would have been extremely hard to predict what would happen.[43]

The picture Noam Chomsky said he "would not be able to have any judgment about."

In light of the enormity of 9/11, this again is remarkable for its brevity and its tone of dismissiveness, a sort of masked haughtiness, its bald unsupported assertions, shabby logic and its absurdities. He begins with a familiar put-down that there is "a small industry" (usually rendered as "a cottage industry") "on the thesis that the administration had something to do with 9/11." There's an implication behind this worn phrase: it is that those engaged in the "small industry" are a tiny minority of energetically mistaken individuals. There could be the implication that some are making money from this, and perhaps that this is their (disreputable) motive.

But as we saw in Chapter 1, polls show that up to half of New Yorkers, for instance, believe the Bush administration "had something to do" with 9/11. This is not a small minority and its members are not profiting from their suspicions, so both implied slights in the put-down are inapplicable. If anything, the most evident "small industry" — in fact it's quite large — surrounding 9/11 is comprised of apologists for the Administration's official story, such as the "counter-terrorism experts," almost all of whom are being profiting one way or another for promoting the so-called "war on terror" for which the official story of 9/11 is the linchpin.

The Big Standard, Recurring Chomsky Evasion

Then comes the standard Chomsky evasion. "I've looked at some of it …" *What* has he looked at? He *never says*. Check for yourself. I cannot find a single instance in which Noam Chomsky has actually come to grips with how the Twin Towers came down, why WTC7 collapsed, the missing fighter jets, Bush's strange demeanor. Nothing.

Instead, Chomsky sticks to generalizations about abstractions such as theses and theories and experiments (audiences are mesmerized because presumably he has some almost mystical understandings about such things — in fact he's practicing word magic). His central "argument" here (which does not deserve to be called such) is that in both science and ordinary life predictability is virtually unknown and that weirdness, the unexplained and chaos are the norm and "mount to the sky."

His generalization that in "controlled scientific experiments one finds all sorts of unexplained phenomena, strange coincidences, loose ends, apparent contradictions, etc." is completely unsupported. Two reasoned responses would be: "Would you provide a few examples, enough to support your generalization?" and "The majority of controlled scientific experiments result in findings within reasonable parameters of what is expected. Unexplained phenomena are rare. Strange coincidences do not in fact abound." There's a rude response: "Bullshit."

He goes further off the charts when generalizing about the "real world." Chaos in the real world is "overwhelming?" In fact, life proceeds on the basis that mostly life is predictable. That's why the exceptions are called "news."

Then he turns to the standard "arguments" against the idea that the administration could have let 9/11 happen or made it happen. As these have not been dealt with yet in this book, let's deal with them here.

Chomsky's Tired and Unoriginal Arguments Against 9/11 Truth

"They'd have to be quite mad to try it." In that case, most of the rulers of history must have been quite mad in this very respect. In Chapter 7, we list 18 documented cases in which administrations mounted death-dealing fake events to promote their agendas. Suggesting that a reason the administration would be mad to mount such an operation because of a leak about it being "very likely" is to further ignore the history of such operations, in which almost never is there a politically relevant leak, either soon enough to cause anyone to be "lined up before firing squads," or ever. Such "leaking" as there is consists, for the most part, in honest and determined research such as that carried out by Robert B. Stinnett, driven by a desire for truth, starting 44 years after attack on Pearl Harbor to dig into it. Stinnett devotes the next 17 years of his life to finding out everything he can, and then publishes the definitive account of how FDR did all in his considerable power to provoke the attack and make sure that the base at Pearl Harbor was defenseless that day. It's because of this "leak" that a significant number of people, including myself, have learned what is probably fair to call the truth about Pearl Harbor (another topic in which Chomsky has no expressed interest).

The likes of Richard Cheney and those who surround him do not leak. The operatives they direct are loyal and do not leak. The technicians of death who carry out these operations do not leak. Not normally. That's history, as Chomsky would say.

"Success was at best a long shot." This is perhaps the most disingenuous assertion among the many that Chomsky crammed into his brief disquisition on 9/11. False-flag operations are *unopposed military operations,* involving all the resources of the state. Additionally, those who plan them know that if anything goes seriously wrong, corrective actions can be taken, again unopposed. And after the operation is over, all the "loose ends," to use Chomsky's phrase properly, such as the Zapruder film, can be neutralized and explained away during the state-run inquiry. Or in the case of the 9/11 tapes made by FAA employees shortly after the events, destroyed.

"History shows ..." is one of Chomsky's favorite phrases. In this case history shows the opposite of what Chomsky claims: that it would be "extremely hard to predict what would happen." History shows that it is easy to predict what will happen (and is in fact happening). What has happened so far in history is that the perpetrators get away with it, because they control the intelligence agencies, the covert agents of all kinds, most of the police, enough in the judiciary, a sufficient number of legislators, and most of the media.

The Overall Role and Impact of Noam Chomsky

A deconstruction of Chomsky's output reveals a complex and brilliant interplay. It could be characterized as "bait-and-switch." In a bait-and-switch operation, the victim is enticed, then victimized in some way. In this construction, the bait Chomsky offers the Left are his critiques of American foreign policy and the propaganda system of the establishment. These are substantial and continuous offerings that earn him admiration and trust among most on the Left. His "switch" is to redirect his followers on the Left away from questioning particularly toxic and revealing operations of the sinister forces behind the scenes, away from evidence, even, concerning 9/11, and before it the assassinations that decapitated the Left in the 60s.

Obscuring that this is his role are his propaganda techniques, briefly addressed above, and his personal attractiveness. Personality should not be underestimated in any area of life. One US company specializes in assessing the "Q factor" of TV performers and others in the public eye. The measurement is focused purely on "likeability." Not respect, fear, admiration, authenticity — just likeability. TV personalities will kill for a high Q-rating.

Chomsky with his genuine humility and also his fake humility, his fake open-mindedness, his quiet demeanour, rumpled appearance, apparent devotion to people power, his apparent identification with the common man and woman, personal life without blemish, apparent resistance to tyranny, clear personal dedication (to whatever it is he's doing), generosity with his time, his endorsements of the alternative media, expressions of confidence in humanity's struggle for justice, his facility with the language, his prolific output — all this together is seen as remarkable and admirable; a high Q-rating — from the Left.

One of Chomsky's trademark comments is about the power of the people. While appearing to empower dissent, in most of his books and lectures he channels Left energy into a stupor of amazement over past mis-deeds of the Empire and brilliant articulations of the general picture of today's world, which any thinking Leftist can see without the help of Chomsky. His recent comments about Venezuela, again welcome, are nevertheless a case in point.

Some friends of mine on the Left find it difficult to understand that I am not rejecting Chomsky's massive work of critiquing the American Empire. It's not an either/or proposition. One can (and should) critique the Empire vis a vis East Timor, for instance, *and* strive to expose some of its most toxic domestic work, such as 9/11. This toxic work powerfully aids and emboldens the Empire in its drive toward ever more militarism, repression at home, and global domination. The events of 9/11 are *also* the Empire's Achilles Heel, if exposed. The record shows Chomsky strives to prevent the Left from thinking about, let alone exposing, this toxic work. The reality is that Chomsky's ruling out of any investigation into 9/11, which could finally accomplish a real shake-up, is *at odds* with the implied purposes of his foreign policy critiques — to reveal, oppose and displace the Empire.

Germane here is the truism that "the most powerful disinformation is 90 per cent true."

Attacks from the Right are a Major Benefit for Chomsky

Another source of Chomsky's positive reputation on the Left is simply that he is attacked by the Right. The fact that these attacks are overwhelmingly intellectually bereft only adds to his luster. Here his documentations of the perfidy of the American Empire play out well, because his tormentors on the Right really are up against evidence. So the Left awards him major points for valour in the trenches of ideological warfare.

But what points are earned? Since neither Chomsky nor, of course, his Right-wing attackers, question the official stories of 9/11 or the JFK assassination, their internecine warfare is something of a Punch-and-Judy show, essentially a self-serving smokescreen on both sides. Chomsky is well aware of this setup, as proven by his pointing it out during the Vietnam War, when the false adversaries were the alleged "hawks" and the alleged "doves." The former wanted to bomb Vietnam back to the Stone Age. The latter said "We can't win so we should find a way out." Neither side questioned the fundamental immorality of the whole enterprise — win or lose. It was Chomsky who educated some of us about this fake opposition. Now we can apply his lesson to show he is an actor playing out one side in the same kind of debate. The Right says Muslim fanatics did 9/11 because they hate our freedoms; Chomsky says Muslim fanatics did 9/11 because "they draw support from a reservoir of bitterness." Neither confronts the evidence that Muslim fanatics did not do it, that it was an inside job.

Chomsky Fulfills Identical Role to that of Judith Miller or George Bush

In supporting the official story, Chomsky is at one with Right-wing Gatekeepers such as Judith Miller of the *New York Times,* described in the previous chapter. Chomsky's function is identical to Miller's: support the official story. Which is the same as George Bush's function. All function to protect and maintain the Invisible Government. That Chomsky could be fulfilling the same function as Right Gatekeepers seems unthinkable, since he so devastatingly and persistently reveals the structures, operations and hypocrisy of the Right Gatekeepers in particular, and well describes the nature of the American Empire in general. It is a disturbing seeming contradiction that must be confronted.

How to explain this? It is important to touch on some of the other subjects on which Chomsky is either remarkably silent or plays a very misleading role. He has little to say about the centers of immense financial and other power. In his lecture "The New World Order," [44] he manages to say nothing about the Federal Reserve or even the world banking system. He gets a laugh by saying the US "is a country without a banking system." He adds: "The S&Ls [savings and loans institutions which robbed investors of billions] are a small part of the problem. Those are corner banks." He makes little mention the Council on Foreign Relations, Bilderberg Group, or the Trilateral Commission. He has called them "nothing organizations;" has claimed the CIA was never a rogue organization and is an innocent scapegoat; and has rejected any notion there was vote fraud in the US elections of 2004.

His protectiveness about the CIA is curious. During "An Evening with Noam Chomsky, The War on Terror," held at MIT he admitted the CIA was deeply involved in training the *mujahideen* in Afghanistan. (In fact it was the CIA's largest-ever operation). He did so, however, without mentioning Osama bin Laden, with whom the CIA worked closely for years. On other occasions he has admitted an association between bin Laden and the CIA. He has also asserted that connections between bin Laden and the CIA are not "remotely relevant." In *Understanding Power*, Chomsky is quoted:

Or take the CIA, which is considered the source of a lot of these conspiracies; we have a ton of information about it, and as I read the information, the CIA is basically just an obedient branch of the White House. I mean sure, the CIA has done things around the world — but as far as we know, it hasn't done anything on its own.

There's very little evidence — in fact, I don't know of any — that the CIA is some kind of rogue elephant, you know, off on its own doing things. What the record shows is that the CIA is just an agency of the White House, which sometimes carries out operations for which the Executive branch wants what's called "plausible deniability;" in other words, if something goes wrong, we don't want it to look like we did, those guys in the CIA did it, and we can throw some of them to the wolves if we need to. That's basically the role of the CIA, along with mostly just a collection of information.[45]

This is a remarkable misrepresentation. John Stockwell, the highest ranking CIA officer to leave the agency and criticize it, said that the CIA has, conservatively, been responsible for six million deaths since it was formed. Chomsky's characterization should stop us in our tracks. These statements are typical of Chomsky vis a vis the CIA, and they can be taken as nothing less than covering for the agency. Chomsky would have us believe that he does not know that the Bay of Pigs operation, which could have triggered World War III and the end of civilization, was a rogue CIA operation. That's why President John F. Kennedy fired the CIA director, Allen Dulles and his assistant, Richard Bissel, shortly after. Why would Chomsky cover for the CIA?

Chomsky Dispenses Disinformation about the CIA

At another point during "An Evening with Noam Chomsky, The War on Terror," Chomsky said "the Muslim terrorists" work through "leaderless resistance." He says:

> ... the CIA knows about this technique better than anyone else. You have small groups that do things. They don't talk to anybody else. That's how the terrorists go undetected. Actually people in the anti-war movement are very familiar with it. We used to call it affinity groups. If you assume correctly that whatever group you are in is being penetrated by the FBI, when something serious is happening, you don't do it in a meeting. You do it with some people you know and trust, an affinity group and then it doesn't get penetrated. That's one of the reasons why the FBI has never been able to figure out what's going on in any of the popular movements. And other intelligence agencies are the same. They can't.[46]

I'm sorry, this is pure disinformation on Chomsky's part. The CIA and FBI and spy organizations in general have been and continue to be extremely successful at surveilling and penetrating popular movements. Of course they don't want that to be known. But the FBI's infamous COINTELPRO program finally did become well known. So did the FBI's penetration of the Communist Party USA. That was so dense that in some chapters there were more agents than authentic members. An agent from BOSS (the South African intelligence agency) acted undetected as general secretary to the World Council of Churches at its Geneva headquarters for 25 years. Most covert operations remain successful secrets. How could the death squads in Latin America succeed in executing thousands of human rights workers, trade union leaders and peasants who were showing signs of organized dissent? Through spying and penetration. Informers can always be found. The generality is that spying is effective. By claiming otherwise, Chomsky is spreading disinformation that gives his readers and listeners on the left a false feeling of assurance, thereby aiding the work of government spies at the expense of people on the Left — always the targets of surveillance and harassment — that he claims to have an affinity with.

His response on one occasion when he was asked about the possibility that the Bush administration could have had prior knowledge of planned "terrorist attacks" on 9/11:

> Every intelligence agency is flooded, daily, with information of very low credibility. In retrospect, one can sometimes pick out pieces that mean something. At the time, that's a virtual impossibility. By arguments like this we can prove that someone blew up the White House yesterday. [bizarre non sequitur][47]

He starts with the suggestion that intelligence agencies are virtually useless, because they are *all* "flooded daily" with low-credibility information. He *implies* they never receive high-credibility information ("at the time," he says, it's virtually impossible to "pick out pieces that mean something.")

This is ludicrous and also helps guard an important trade secret of the world of intelligence. One of its most brilliant practitioners, British general Frank Kitson, wrote in *Low Intensity Operations*: "Field officers prefer lots of low grade information to a small amount of higher quality." He learned this in the US at a Rand Corporation symposium in 1962.[48] In his book on Pearl Harbor, *Day of Deceit,* Robert Stinett quotes Captain Duane Whitlock, a radio traffic analyst at station CAST in

David Barsamian

Corregidor. Whitlock said he "received stacks of Japanese naval broadcasts" [shortly prior to Pearl Harbor]. "It was not necessary to decipher the coded messages. I was fully convinced that Japan was gearing up for war based on the huge increase of orders transmitted to the warships and military commands." [49] So a flood *can* be meaningful. Short of that, all sorts of patterns in "a flood" are meaningful. Are we to believe Chomsky is ignorant of such information?

The Left Gatekeepers

A surprisingly large number of Left media outlets — most of them, in fact — have adopted the same stance on 9/11 as Chomsky's: refuse to investigate 9/11, and discourage or ridicule those who do. Most wind up using the familiar "wacky conspiracy theorists" putdown to describe others on the Left who want to discuss the evidence of an inside job on 9/11. The almost total uniformity within Left media in sync with the White House and Right media is more than puzzling. In other cases, the Left media pursue questions of malfeasance on the part of the power elites, including some conspiracies such as Iran-Contra.

Individuals and media outlets that have exhibited this stay-away-from-9/11 stance, entirely or in large part, for more than four years now include David Corn and *The Nation;* Amy Goodman of Democracy Now!; Chip Berlet, senior analyst at Political Research Associates in Somerville, Massachusetts; David Barsamian of Alternative Radio; Michael Albert of *Z Magazine;* Alexander Cockburn; Norman Solomon; *The Progressive; Mother Jones;* Alternet.org; Global Exchange; PBS; South End Press; Public Research Associates; FAIR/ Extra!; *Counterspin; Columbia Journalism Review;* Deep Dish TV; Working Assets; Molly Ivins; *Ms Magazine;* Inter Press Service; MoveOn.org; Greg Palast; David Zupan; Northwest Media Project....

Of course, different people can independently or through dialogue arrive at the same or similar conclusions. But it is a startling anomaly for so many organs and leaders of the conscious Left to be seemingly unconscious regarding 9/11. More than a few on the Left share the opinion of progressive film maker Roy Harvey that "the greatest single obstacle to the spread of 9/11 Truth is the Left media." To my mind, the relationship of Chomsky and the Left Gatekeepers on 9/11 is analogous to the relationship of the

White House and the 9/11 Commission. Both relationships are so tight as to invite close scrutiny. Elementary pattern recognition reveals a common agenda among these otherwise well-informed, intelligent, investigative critics of corporate greed, the power elite and US hegemony. The agenda, completely atypical of their approach generally, is to vigorously reject investigation into 9/11. This is *prima facie*. One example, that of perhaps Chomsky's best known protégé and amplifier, David Barsamian, is typical of 9/11 blindness on the Left.

On March 7, 2006, Barsamian spoke at a small event in a church basement in his home city of Boulder, Colorado. He made points about the immorality and wrongness of the war in Iraq, the US imperial project, corporate greed, etc. His audience was appreciative of him, his approach, his knowledge of the territory and his ability to express himself. At the question period, the first hand up was that of a Denver man. It's worth noting that, while Barsamian knew many in the room by name, he did not know who this questioner was except that he was sitting with a 9/11 Truth activist known to Barsamian. Barsamian recognized other hands one after the other, repeatedly ignoring the first hand up. Finally the Denver man's still-raised arm could not be ignored any longer. His question in part: "There's been a lot of research into 9/11 in the four-plus years since it's happened." He then gave examples including the WTC Twin Towers, WTC7, the inadequate military response, the multiple war games. "… my question is this: given this regime is murderous — you have to use that word, you've been talking yourself about what's been going on in Iraq — when are we going to stop calling people 'conspiracy theorists' and dismissing them and be willing to look at 9/11 as an inside job, because it's been the thing that's been galvanizing this fear that's been gripping us?"

Barsamian replied: "I've looked into some of these things and I haven't found any convincing evidence that would persuade me …." He agreed the Bush administration has taken advantage of 9/11. "It's 9/11 24/7. That's their theme song. That their national anthem." Barsamian said Osama bin Laden "took credit for what happened on September 11. Why don't we take him at his word?" This overlooked the first audio tape ostensibly from Osama, in September 2001, denying involvement. The murky December 2001 videotape, allegedly [ostensibly from bin Laden,] found by the US military in Kandahar, "took credit." There are many reasons to believe the second is a fake. Barsamian pointed to statements by Zacarias Moussouai that he had foreknowledge of 9/11 and said famed investigative reporter Seymour Hersh "doesn't find compelling evidence."

Barsmian Says Pursuing the Truth About 9/11 is a "Black Hole"

"If there was a whiff, a whiff ... this would be the greatest story in the history of the world ... bigger than Watergate," Barsamian said. "A whiff." He then said "there's a little bit here and there (which sounds like a whiff) but it doesn't connect. It reminds me of the grassy knoll." He stated: "We know of criminal activities of this administration that can be proven beyond a scintilla of doubt. I think we should concentrate on those things." He did not specify which these were or who would concentrate on them in what ways. He concluded by saying that pursuing the truth about 9/11 is "a black hole," worse than a waste of time. The questioner said later he was "shocked into silence by his response." [50]

Barsamian's response was remarkable for its synchronicity with Chomsky's and for the way it echoed that of David Ray Griffin critics Chip Berlet and Robert Baer, David Corn of *The Nation,* Michael Albert of *Z Magazine,* and Matt Rothschild, editor of *The Progressive.*

That the agenda of Chomsky, Barsamian et al would be so widespread and pursued with such intensity begs explanation. One theory would be incompetence — that for some reason all these thinkers, editors, producers and writers have just lost their curiosity and forgotten how to use the tools of their trade when it comes to 9/11. This theory requires the belief that such widespread persistent incompetence is also coincidental.

Another theory would be that some, perhaps a surprisingly large percentage, of these individuals are following instructions that benefit the national security state; that they are, in other words, agents. The nature and consistency of the anomalies they present prohibit this theory from being rejected out of hand, even though raising it provides a focus for potentially acrimonious debate. This is, indeed, a not unreasonably founded conspiracy theory. The situation brings to mind the line from *The Sign of Four* by Sir Arthur Conan Doyle: "Whenever you have eliminated the impossible, whatever remains, *however improbable,* must be the truth."

Acrimony can be diminished in proportion to facts being brought to bear on the discussion. Because of the suffocating secrecy that attends operations by agents of the state, finding direct evidence is next to impossible. That is why those who want to investigate this intensely troubling and important situation are obliged to turn to circumstantial evidence, intuition and principles of inquiry such as the identification of contradictions, pattern recognition, and the Latin *cui bono?* (To whose benefit? For what purpose?).

There are other possible, and possibly overlapping, explanations for near-uniform 9/11 blindness on the part of Left leaders and Left media. These lead back, in part, to the CIA. Left media increasingly have been seeking and receiving funding from the likes of the Rockefeller Foundation, Ford Foundation, Carnegie Endowment, and MacArthur Foundation. Bob Feldman of San Francisco has been a tireless researcher of Left-foundation connections. His articles paint a picture rarely mentioned because both Left and Right have an interest in keeping quiet about it.

The accompanying chart shows recent money flows from establishment foundations to Left media. In a recent article for *Critical Sociology* entitled "Report from the Field, Left Media & Left Think Tanks: Foundation-Managed Protest?" Feldman begins: "Left media and left think tank staff people generally deny that the acceptance by their organizations of grants from liberal foundations has transformed their organizational priorities, subjected them to elite control, or channeled their energies into safe, legalistic, bureaucratic activities and mild reformism."

However, 5,000 words and dozens of charts later, he concludes: "... there is much evidence that the funded left has moved towards the mainstream as it has increased its dependence on foundations. This is shown by the 'progressive', reformist tone of formerly radical organizations; the gradual disappearance of challenges to the economic and political power of corporations or United States militarism and imperialism; and silence on the relationship of liberal foundations to either politics and culture in general, or to their own organizations."[51]

Specifically on the subject of 9/11, some subtle inducements and pressures on Left media by Right-wing and even CIA-connected foundations have come to light.

For instance Deep Dish TV Inc was given $75,000 in 2002 by the Ford Foundation to enable "the television news series Democracy Now! to continue incorporating the aftermath of the September 11 attacks into future broadcasts." 9/11Truth activist Emanuel Sferios of Seattle, who found the information, commented at the time: "They never told us a reason [that Democracy Now!] refused to consider any programming about 9/11, but it's quite simple. The Ford Foundation, by supplying so much money to Democracy Now! so they can 'continue incorporating' 9/11 into their broadcasts, does not have to explicitly tell Democracy Now! how they want 9/11 to be covered. Democracy Now! will simply self-censor, because they want future money from the Ford Foundation."[52]

A few of the left-wing organizations are primarily concerned about threats to media independence, yet all their attention is focused on for-profit corporate (or government) control; they ignore the possible influence of large subventions from nonprofit institutions such as foundations, says Feldman. Journalist Ron Curran maintains that: "The only money nonprofits can get these days is from private foundations — and those foundations want to control the political agenda."[53] Another critic of the grant system, Brian Salter, makes a strong case against foundation funding of left media and think tanks. After examining the corporate and political connections of Ford and similar foundations' board members, Salter concludes: "The big establishment foundations are likely to seek out 'alternative' media that is more bark than bite, which they can rely on to ignore and dismiss sensitive topics ... as 'irrational distractions' *or 'conspiracy theory.'*"[emphasis added]

"The Kind of Opposition the US Elite can Live with" and Chomsky is its Leader

Salter points out that recipients of funding protest that they are not swayed by any conflicts of interest and don't allow the sources of funding to affect their decisions, "but whether or not these claims are actually true is already somewhat of a red herring. Judging by the journalism being offered (and not offered) by *The Nation*, FAIR, *The Progressive*, IPA, *Mother Jones*, AlterNet.org, and other recipients of their funding, the big establishment foundations are successfully sponsoring the kind of 'opposition' that the US ruling elite can tolerate and live with."[54]

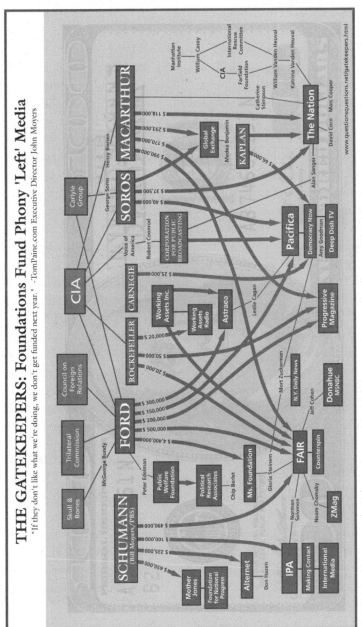

THE GATEKEEPERS: Foundations Fund Phony 'Left' Media

"If they don't like what we're doing, we don't get funded next year." -TomPaine.com Executive Director John Moyers

WWW.QUESTIONSQUESTIONS.NET/FLYER/

www.questionsquestions.net/gatekeepers.html

During the Cold War, the CIA utilized foundations such as Ford "to set up and finance a 'parallel' organization to counter known left-wing bodies.[55] In 1975, the radical US feminist group Redstockings asserted that: "one major CIA strategy" during the Cold War was "to create or support parallel organizations which provide alternatives to radicalism and yet appear progressive enough to appease dissatisfied elements of the society."[56] There are no grounds to imagine the CIA or their partners in the foundations have changed their tune or their methods — except to make them more effective. Chomsky's record shows little or no attention to this kind of subversion.

To conclude, Chomsky, the most quoted "Leftist" in the Left media, systematically engages in deceptive discourse on certain key topics, such as JFK's assassination, 9/11, and with regard to the CIA. In warning the Left against examining the evidence on JFK and 9/11, he lines himself up with George Bush and the corporate media, thereby advancing their agenda — which he otherwise opposes. When he is not appearing to undermine the American Empire, which is the main thing he does, he is buttressing it by undermining the most effective and therefore dangerous foe the Empire faces — the conscious Left.

A study of Chomsky's stands on particularly dreadful actions such as JFK's assassination and 9/11, and the roles of the CIA and FBI, shows Chomsky to be a *de facto* defender of the status quo's most egregious outrages and their covert agency engines. He conducts his *de facto* defense of the Empire he appears to oppose through applying the very propaganda methods against which he has warned, including use of the derogatory phrase "conspiracy theorist," which in one context he has characterized as "something people say when they don't want you to think about what's really going on."

His recommendation that people practice "intellectual self-defence" is well taken. But how many could dream the person warning you is one of the most perilous against whom you'll need to defend yourself? That he is the fire marshal who wires your house to burn down, the lifeguard who drowns you, the doctor with the disarming bedside manner who administers a fatal injection? If Noam Chomsky did not exist, the diaboligarchy would have to invent him. To the New World Order, he is worth 50 armored divisions.

[*POSTSCRIPT: In preparing this book, I contacted Chomsky well in advance and asked him if he would respond to a few questions. No response was received.*]

6

Invisible Government: Manipulator of Events and the Media Gatekeepers

"Behind the ostensible government sits enthroned an *invisible government* owing no allegiance and acknowledging no responsibility to the people. To destroy this *invisible government*, to befoul the unholy alliance between corrupt business and corrupt politics is the first task of the statesmanship of the day." [emphasis added]

—Theodore Roosevelt[1]

"The conscious and intelligent manipulation of the organized opinions and habits of the masses is an important element in democratic society. Those who manipulate this unseen mechanism of society constitute an *invisible government* which is the true ruling power of our country ... We are governed, our minds are molded, our tastes formed, our ideas suggested, largely by men we have never heard of. It is they who pull the wires which control the public mind." [emphasis added]

—Edward Bernays[2]

"There's a power so organized, so subtle, so watchful, so pervasive, so interlocked, that you'd better not speak above your breath when you mention it, in condemnation of it."[3]

— Woodrow Wilson

Philadelphia, August 22, 1934 — Into the lobby of the Bellevue Hotel walks one of the most decorated military men in US history, the respected and charismatic former head of the US Marines Corps, General Smedley D. Butler. It's three days after Adolf Hitler bullied his way to become Fuhrer of Germany.[4]

Butler is keeping an appointment sought by Gerald McGuire, a war veteran and bond salesman with close connections to some of the pillars of the US capitalist establishment. On this occasion he's representing these pillars.

They've assured McGuire that the plan he's about to propose to Butler will be backed up to the tune of $300 million; seed money in the neighborhood of $3 million is already in place. These pillars include Andrew Mellon Associates, Rockefeller Associates, William Knudsen of General Motors and the Du Ponts. One of them is wealthy banker Robert Clark, who told Butler earlier that he was prepared to spend half of his $30 million fortune "to protect the other half from [US President Franklin Delano] Roosevelt."

McGuire leads Butler to a remote corner of the hotel's closed café. There he makes a remarkable proposition: that Butler join a conspiracy to depose Roosevelt and become the first American Fuhrer. As McGuire put it: "If Roosevelt played ball, swell; and if he did not, [we will] push him out." The story is told in Jules Archer's book *The Plot to Seize the White House*.[5] With some differing details but no conflict about the nub of the story, it's told also in *New York Times* correspondent Charles Higham's book *Trading With the Enemy: An Exposé of the Nazi-American Money Plot 1933-1949*.[6] Higham writes that the plotters were ready to kill the president.

But the conspirators picked the wrong man. Whatever his views otherwise, Butler was a Constitutionalist. He gathered information about the plotters and took it to Roosevelt and

General Smedley Butler

the House Un-American Activities Committee. "Roosevelt's state of mind can scarcely be imagined," Higham writes. "He knew that in view of the backing from high banking sources, this matter could not be dismissed as some crackpot enterprise that had no chance of success. On the other hand [he] knew that if he were to arrest the leaders of the houses of Morgan and Du Pont, it would create an unthinkable national crisis in the midst of a depression and perhaps another Wall Street crash. Not for the first or last time in his career, he was aware that there were powers greater than he in the United States."[7]

Roosevelt's decision was to keep quiet publicly about the threat but leak it to the press. "The newspapers ran the story of the attempted coup on the front pages, but generally ridiculed it as absurd and preposterous." Nevertheless when Thomas Lamont of the Morgan Bank arrived from Europe by steamer, he was asked by a crowd of reporters to comment. "Perfect moonshine! Too utterly ridiculous to comment upon!"[8] was his reply. The conspirators knew their cat was out of the bag at the highest levels, knew their invisibility was at risk.

The Un-American Activities committee dealt with the allegations in a secret but farcical executive session in New York City on November 20, 1934. Despite urging by Butler, the committee refused to summon the Du Ponts or anyone from the house of Morgan. McGuire was allowed to get away with saying Butler had "misunderstood" his intentions. Nevertheless the committee could not escape confirming the conspiracy. It submitted its findings to the House of Representatives on February 13, 1935: "There is no question that ... certain persons had made an attempt to establish a fascist organization in this country ... these attempts were planned, and might have been placed in execution when and if the financial backers had deemed it expedient."[9]

Committee co-chair John McCormack recalled in a 1971 interview with Archer: "The plotters definitely hated the New Deal because it was for the people, not for the moneyed interests, and they were willing to spend a lot of money to dump Mr. Roosevelt ... if General Butler had not been the patriot he was, and if they had been able to maintain secrecy, the plot certainly might very well have succeeded ... a well-organized minority can always outmaneuver an unorganized majority, as Adolf Hitler did."[10]

McCormack's phrase "if they had been able to maintain secrecy" could as well be "if they had been able to maintain invisibility." This is a true-life story of conspiracy fact. The dismissive put-down "wacky conspiracy theory" has served as one of the more reliable cloaks to maintain invisibility for ongoing actual factual conspiracies at the highest levels. If the plans of the bankers, the Du Ponts and the others involved had succeeded, the face of the new order in America would have been Butler, an articulate decorated war hero; other willing collaborators would have headed the "patriotic" and "citizen" organizations the behind-the-scenes manipulators were financing.

Much has changed since 1934, but more has not. What I term in this book the Invisible Government has continuity today. "[Seventy] years after the failed coup, a well-organized minority again threatens democracy," writes Joel Bakan in *The Corporation*.[11] "Corporate America's long and patient campaign to gain control of government over the last few decades," Bakan writes, "much quieter and ultimately more effective than the [1934] plotters' clumsy attempts, is now succeeding. Without bloodshed, armies or fascist strongmen, and using dollars rather than bullets, corporations are now poised to win what the plotters [of 1934] so desperately wanted: freedom from democratic control."

The Invisible Government Today: War is its Greatest Need

Today there exist networks: multi-layered relationships between the most powerful owners and strategists on the one hand; and the vast tentacles of the military, covert and propaganda powers that serve them on the other, beside which the machinations of the 1930s appear rudimentary. Probably the most important reality that has not changed is that war — armed conflict as well as psychological and economic warfare — is a necessity for the Invisible Government, no matter how much anguish and waste are suffered by ordinary people and now the planet. "War is the health of the state," Randolph Bourne said, apparently in 1918, more than 200 years after Robert Cecil's War Party fomented the Gunpowder Plot (see Chapter 7). British Prime Minister Benjamin Disraeli said earlier: "The world is governed by very different personages from what is imagined by those who are not behind the scenes." In Disraeli's time (1804-81), the oligarchy was slowly gaining ascendancy over the monarchy.

Probably the second most important reality that has not changed is the manipulation of public opinion. As a result, millions of ordinary people support wars that are contrary to their own interests. As I write this, the *Christian Science Monitor* reports the cost of the Iraq war could "top $2-trillion" if long term costs of health care for wounded soldiers are taken into account.[12]

It is seemingly accepted now, even by the majority of Americans, that the war on Iraq was launched based on lies. The lies were generated by the White House and ultimately by the powers that control the White House. But these lies alone could not have swayed public opinion, especially about alleged WMDs in Iraq, without the complicity of the mainstream media. Disinformation about alleged WMDs was fed into the nation's public address system, especially by the now-disgraced Judith Miller and the agenda-setting *New York Times*, even while the media in general failed to raise even elementary questions.

Augmenting the drive to war was the misbelief, held at one time by 49 per cent of the US population, that Saddam Hussein was one of the plotters behind 9/11. As this and other books seek to establish, 9/11 itself was the most powerful form of lie of all — the "false-flag operation," what Bakunin called "the propaganda of the act," also the most effective tool in the kitbag of manipulation of public opinion.

Personal Profit for the Perpetrators of 9/11

The Invisible Government is a prime beneficiary of 9/11. US vice president Dick Cheney, former head of Halliburton, and who continues to hold stock options in the company, is a member of the Invisible Government. This is as good a point as any to address the apparent paradox of an "Invisible Government" some of whose members are just as visible as Dick Cheney. The paradox is resolved by understanding it is not the body seen in public, making a speech or laying a wreath, that is particularly relevant. The relevant manifestation of the person is behind the scenes. This is where an individual such as Cheney exercises his connections and pursues his hidden machinations, and to some extent, his hidden agenda. Consider for instance Cheney the invisible master of 9/11, in charge of a parallel command and communications system on the day. This according to 9/11 Truth researcher and author Michael C. Ruppert in his book *Crossing the Rubicon*.[13]

Returning to the subject of the benefits of 9/11 for the Invisible Government: the official version of the events of that day have provided a boost into orbit for the arms industry in general and Halliburton in particular, by providing a pretext for the war on Afghanistan directly, and indirectly for the war on Iraq.

By December 12, 2005, Halliburton stock options held by Cheney had risen 3,281 percent over their value in October 2004, according to figures compiled by Senator Frank Lautenberg.[15] In that time, his options worth $241,498 grew to be worth $8 million. "Halliburton has already raked in more than $10 billion from the Bush-Cheney administration for work in Iraq." Lautenberg said, "It is unseemly for the Vice President to continue

Metal Storm: The Ideal Gift for the Empire that has Everything

The planned $11-billion Crusader Artillery System fell victim to a more imaginative toy in 2002, according to an exclusive United Press International story May 12 that year.[14]

A new ballistic technology that can fire burst rates in excess of one million rounds per minute from a 36-barrel weapon was one of the reasons Defense Secretary Donald Rumsfeld canceled the $11 billion Crusader artillery system," UPI reported. The technology is known as "Metal Storm," which is also the name of the Australian research and development company that owns it. Most of Metal Storm's multi-million dollar contracts for the US Defense Advanced Research Projects Agency and the Australian Defense Science and Technology Organization are top secret.

The fastest weapons today are mechanical Gatling gun styles that can fire at the rate of some 6,000 rounds per minute. "Metal Storm's submachine gun will be capable of firing multiple barrel rapid-fire bursts at 45,000 rounds per minute per barrel. Its electronically variable rate of fire has been confirmed to one million rounds per minute."

Under development by Metal Storm is an "area denial weapons system," including an unmanned aerial combat vehicle that will carry twelve ☞

to benefit from this company at the same time his Administration funnels billions of dollars to it."

Media outlets mask Cheney's corruption, by failing to give it the play it deserves, let alone editorializing vigorously against it. They provide complete invisibility for his complicity in 9/11 by failing to ask questions about his role on 9/11, despite anomalies given in testimony before the 9/11 Commission (for instance, testimony by Secretary of Transportation Norman Y. Mineta. Of course, Mineta's testimony did not make it into the commission's whitewash-and-cover-up report.)[16]

The performance of the media in these respects is no more coincidental than was the failure of the fighter jets to show up on 9/11. The Invisible

40-mm mortar boxes comprising a total of 1,200 tubes, and armed with 7,200 grenades. "The system's unprecedented firing capabilities can lay down a continuous 50-meter-wide carpet of grenades for about two miles, firing all its grenades simultaneously with a five-yard separation on impact."

Another gun under development for a small combat aerial vehicle is multi-barreled and can fire 270 rounds onto a target in one one-thousand of a second. The story made no mention of who would be blessed with such instant death. Certainly "terrorists" and "insurgents" should not complain if the Empire has them in mind, and mere dissidents have little to fear. "The weapon will also fire 'less-than-lethal' projectiles for riot control," UPI reported.

Such systems also save taxpayer money. Next to "Metal Storm's" firepower, said a senior Pentagon acquisition official, the lumbering, 45-ton Crusader artillery tube would be obsolete equipment. And then there's the peace dividend. "The technology is not just used for firing projectiles. It is an electronically controlled delivery system that has potential applications in fire fighting, fireworks displays, aerial advertising in the night sky, precision chemical distribution in agriculture, and seismic surveying for minerals and oil."

Your Empire: We do it all for you. ∎

Government is at work making these things happen — or not happen, in the case of the jets and media questioning. The media are owned by giant corporations which are fixtures of the Invisible Government. Some in turn are owned and controlled by other giant corporations deeply into the trough of armaments profits. NBC is owned by General Electric, one of the world's largest arms manufacturers.

The growing concentration of corporate information power is itself rendered largely invisible by the same media that exercise it. Results of a study, published in early 2006 on rense.com, showed that in 1983 the majority of US media were controlled by only 50 corporations. That was already a problem. Today the majority of US media are controlled by *five* corporations. In its report for 2003, Project Censored at Sonoma State University in California named lobbying by global media giants to privatize the entire broadcast system the number one censored story of the year. "One of the longest-lasting censored news stories," wrote Project Censored director Peter Phillips, "is corporate media's failure to cover their own turf."[17]

Another example of the invisibility of the seemingly highly visible: although Australian- born media mogul Rupert Murdoch is one of the most visible members of the international power elite, "there is much more to Rupert Murdoch than meets the eye," writes Bruce Page. Page is a distinguished Australian-raised journalist, highly respected for leading what Alexander Cockburn has called "one of the great investigative enterprises of twentieth century journalism, the Insight team at the (pre-Murdoch) *London Sunday Times*." In 2003, Page published a 580-page book about Murdoch, called *The*

Rupert Murdoch

Murdoch Archipelago.[18] One of Murdoch's behind-the-scenes machinations is to offer ridiculously large advances to politicians for books they would write for his publishing house, HarperCollins. Former British Prime Minister Margaret Thatcher was offered millions of pounds. Her government then, Page notes, "set aside British monopoly law so that [Rupert] could buy the *Times* and the *Sunday Times* ..." Thatcher later handed Murdoch monopoly-control of British satellite television. A similar "book deal" with Murdoch landed Republican Newt Gingrich in hot water.

Mainstream Corporate Media have Become a Privatized State Propaganda Service

But Murdoch delivers to politicians, to governments, something far more valuable than money. The core thesis of Page's book is that Murdoch delivers to governments a privatized version of a state propaganda service, as Alexander Cockburn describes it, "manipulated without scruple and with no regard for truth." Murdoch's price is vast government favors: tax breaks, favorable rulings from "regulatory agencies," and monopoly markets. The incessant pro-Republican propaganda of Murdoch's *Fox News* is a perfect example. One payoff for Murdoch in peddling the Bush White House line was a Federal Communications Commission ruling that gave Murdoch the ability to buy out Direct TV, moving him closer to a monopoly position and the ability to charge consumers accordingly.

The Anti-Murdoch Network,[19] an internet-based activist group whose members include a number of thoughtful if angry journalists, lists almost 20 areas in which Murdoch's record deserves critical scrutiny. The first one is "Murdoch the War Monger." The Network's site quotes a *New York Times* report: "The [Iraq] war has illuminated anew the exceptional power in the hands of Murdoch, 72, the chairman of News Corp .... In the last several months, the editorial policies of almost all his English-language news organizations have hewn very closely to Murdoch's own stridently hawkish political views, making his voice among the loudest in the Anglophone world in the international debate over the American-led war with Iraq."

America: The Fourth Reich

"Media Collusion and the Rise of the Fourth Reich?" was the title of a talk I gave at a conference[1] in Vancouver, BC in 2003. "In a sane and just world," I suggested to the audience, "the title would be 'Media Collision Against the Rise of The Fourth Reich' — and no question mark." Now it seems to me the title should be "The Media: Full Partners in the Fourth Reich."

American Nancy Snow, author of a book on US government propaganda, was a fellow speaker at the conference. She asked me to adapt the talk into a chapter for *War, Media and Propaganda: A Global Perspective*[2] that she was co-editing. For the chapter they chose the title "America: the Fourth Reich."[3] This is an edited version of the chapter.

It should not be denied any longer: America is hurtling along the road to full-fledged fascism. To recognize this is the necessary first step in deflecting the juggernaut and creating the possibility of more peaceful tomorrows. It is not only legitimate but necessary to correctly employ the power of naming.

There is an Invisible Government which through its traditions and current activities is fascistic. Fascism according to the *Collins English Dictionary*[4] is "any rightwing nationalist ideology or movement with an authoritarian and hierarchical structure that is fundamentally opposed to democracy and liberalism." Add racism and brutality.[5] Those eight characteristics define Hitler's Third Reich.

By any sober analysis America has become rightwing and nationalist. At the same time I am soulfully aware of the tremendous numbers of Americans ashamed, appalled, afraid and angry about the direction of their government and too many of their fellow citizens. Signs of growing authoritarianism in the USA are evident especially to those outside the self-absorbed cocoon of U.S. culture. The signs include the supine attitude toward authority of most of the mainstream media.[6] Contrary to incessant rhetoric about democracy, the U.S. power structure is considerably hierarchical. Money power comprises the main rungs of the hierarchy. According to the *New York Times*[7] the Republicans were confident of raising at least $170-million for George W. Bush's 2004 election campaign, redefining what the *Times* called ☞

"standards" for fund-raising. Both the hierarchy of money and the antago-nism to democracy are spelled out in Greg Palast's *The Best Democracy Money Can Buy*.[8] That the U.S. establishment is opposed to liberalism — no matter how you define liberalism — can hardly be debated. We already have six grounds for applying the term Fourth Reich. But consider another 20 parallels between the USA today and Hitler's Germany:

Anti-communism, anti-Marxism, anti-socialism are visceral. The core opposition to the regime is from the strong conscious left. A fundamental-ist faith in capitalism, specifically the systematized form of greed known as monopoly capitalism. Corporations are at the centre of the power structure. Corruption at the top is endemic. The number of people consigned to the grave by military and paramilitary actions in both cases is in the millions.

Backdate the Fourth Reich to the end of the Second World War and the number murdered by U.S. forces equals or outnumbers the toll in the Holocaust. Three million in Vietnam alone. The brutality is a matter of record for those who are willing to look at it. See William Blum's *Killing Hope*[9] for one researcher's record. Most of the Fourth Reich's victims are Asians, indigenous peoples of Latin America, and more recently "towel-heads." The racism is clear.

In each case the leader was illegally installed into power, Hitler in 1933[10], George W. Bush in 2000.[11] The ambition of world domination. The Third and Fourth Reichs invade as many countries as can be gotten away with. A Blitzkrieg approach is favoured. For Hitler: Austria, Czechoslovakia, Poland. For George W. Bush: Afghanistan, Iraq, next? Seizure of other countries' oil. Grabbing Russia's Baku oil fields was a major objective of Hitler.[12]

The "pitiful giant" syndrome is invoked. "Our enemies are powerful," it goes, so we must arm endlessly "in self-defense." Often accompanied with the high-sounding: "Our enemies taunt us, and we are patient, but our patience is not endless." Pre-emptive or "preventive" war is policy and prac-tice. Highly-orchestrated propaganda campaigns are a Reich staple. Hitler's stylized mass rallies come to mind. The propaganda of the Fourth Reich is suited to the TV age: sophisticated and media-savvy deluxe. Embedded ☞

journalists, for instance. An example from the 2003 invasion of Iraq was the much publicized return of petite blonde soldier Private Jessica Lynch to her family, in full uniform. Props included a home town band and Blackhawk helicopters.

Where the media are not sufficiently pro-regime and self-censoring, censorship and intimidation of them. Brutal intimidation under the second Bush regime includes bombing *Al Jazeera* facilities in Afghanistan and Iraq, the latter censorship by assassination.

Use of religion. Invocations of God's approval for the Reich and its works. William L. Shirer in quotes the führer's minister of church affairs as declaring the Nazi party "stands on the basis of Positive Christianity, and Positive Christianity is National Socialism ... National Socialism is doing God's will ..." [13] An ever-encroaching police state is a sure sign you're living in a Reich.

Illegal actions. International and domestic laws are breached, resisted and undermined, along with rejection or subversion of multilateral agreements and organizations. Hitler pulled Germany out of the League of Nations altogether. In America's case the United Nations is sidelined or embraced according to the Empire's needs.

"Terrorism" and terrorism — wholesale and retail [14] — are central to a Reich's operation. The kind in quotes refers to inflated or imagined threats of "terrorism" drummed into the domestic public's mind. Use of fear (orange alerts, etc.) is an important tool of a Reich. Alarms of "terrorism" by a Reich are hypocritical to the nth degree considering the wholesale terrorism a Reich unleashes on others. Third Reich Stuka dive bombers over Spain, V-2 rockets into London. Fourth Reich "daisy cutters," cluster bombs, "bunker busters," dU munitions in Yugoslavia, Afghanistan and Iraq. Skies full of helicopter gunships in a string of countries going back to Vietnam.

Finally there's the actual retail terrorism created by the Reich: the clandestine formation, training, funding and control of functioning terrorists, serving as dark pawns of the Reich. This is one of the lesser known parallels. William Shirer again: "For months prior to July 1934 the Austrian Nazis, with weapons and dynamite furnished by Germany, had instituted a reign of terror, blowing up railways, power stations and government buildings and ☞

murdering …"[15] *Unholy Wars* is a book by British investigative journalist John K. Cooley. He notes close links between the CIA, Pakistan's ISI (virtually an arm of the CIA), Saudi intelligence and the bin Laden family, and that the CIA was deeply involved in the creation and subsequent operations of al-Qaeda.[16]

A preoccupation with secrecy.[17] Secrecy is a precondition for deception.

Deception, above all, is the key to everything for a Reich. The leaders are marinated in a complete obsession with lying and deceiving at every turn.[18] Deceptions are the regime's key to mobilizing public opinion. Deception is needed to fool the citizenry into relinquishing their civil rights and thereby many avenues of dissent. Deception precedes and leads to the police state. Deception precedes and leads to war. At every step deception is required for a Reich's gaining and maintaining power, and carrying out all its other nefarious actions. Without successful deceptions the Reich agenda simply cannot proceed. If the deceptions can be unmasked early enough and sufficiently the Reich collapses. No Reich so far has collapsed this way. In an information age it might be possible. The masterpiece deceptions are those so big that ordinary decent honest people cannot or will not comprehend or face that they exist.[19] They are a species of what the anarchist Bakunin described as "the propaganda of the act." An act such as a bombing or assassination is also a message, is propaganda. A potent version is the fake act, for instance a bombing which the perpetrators make appear to be carried out by others. The gold standard of these is the election-stealing or war-triggering fake event, especially one involving "foreign terrorists."

This makes pivotal the parallel between the Reichstag fire of 1933, on the one hand, and the events of 9/11, on the other. The Reichstag fire of February 27, 1933 was in its day as iconic as were the events of September 11, 2001 in ours. The Reichstag fire was blamed on a communist, subsequently decapitated. And by extension, the fire was blamed on all Communists. The historical evidence is that the Nazis arranged the conflagration. In the *Rise and Fall*, Shirer writes: "… beyond reasonable doubt it was the Nazis who planned the arson and carried it out for their own political ends."[20] The idea for the fire, writes Shirer, almost certainly originated at the top, with ☞

Goebbels and Goering.[21] Vice-chancellor von Papen recalled that when he arrived at the blazing parliament buildings Goering was already on the scene shouting "This is a communist crime..." [22] "Hitler lost no time," Shirer writes, "in exploiting the Reichstag fire to the limit." The very next day he prevailed on the President to sign a decree "for the Protection of the People and the State," suspending the seven sections of the constitution which guaranteed individual and civil liberties. It was described as a "defensive measure against Communist acts of violence against the state." [23]

The parallel with the events of 9/11 is stunning. The official narrative, introduced with Goering-like speed, emerged within two hours: the "attack on America" was portrayed as the work of "terrorists," one evil man, Osama bin Laden, and a small group of co-conspirators, the 2001 equivalents of the 1933 Communists.

The number and magnitude of anomalies surrounding 9/11 can point to only one conclusion: 9/11 was a completely made-in-the-USA inside job, a manufactured incident planned and run by some among the top leadership. Where there's a design there's a designer. One of the most designing groups at the top of the U.S. empire is that clique of neocons who comprise the Project for a New American Century (PNAC). Its members include Paul Wolfowitz, U.S. Deputy Secretary of Defense; Richard Perle, resident scholar at the American Enterprise Institute and William Kristol, editor of *The Weekly Standard*. Key PNAC members — by virtue of this members of the Invisible Government — called for years, even decades, for a muscular expansion of U.S. military and economic might. PNAC in September 2000, one year before 9/11, released a document, *Rebuilding America's Defenses*. The document states[24] that mobilizing the U.S. public behind an imperialist agenda will be long and difficult "absent some catastrophic and catalyzing event like a new Pearl Harbor." You can't get much clearer than that by way of proof that "superhawks" — fascists — at the pinnacle of U.S. power were consciously thinking of the need for something as monstrous as the events of 9/11.

Revealing the fraud of 9/11 in my opinion is the single most important task faced by civilization today. That it was dared is the supreme ☞

Achilles heel of the Fourth Reich. If enough people could be awakened to the enormity of the crime, and who its perpetrators are, they would become a politically-relevant constituency. Then the possibility of a cleansing transformation would emerge. Every worthwhile initiative you can name, be it environmental, social, political or economic, would benefit from politically-relevant exposure of The Great Deception.

In America there's a community of peace and environmental and justice activists, that includes theists, atheists, artists, workers, intellectuals and plain folk, old and young. This community is unidentified, unrecognized and therefore disenfranchised by the mainstream media. It may number 30-million, equal to the population of Canada. It appears to be the responsibility imposed by history on this community to recognize its own existence, importance and power and to exercise that power non-violently before it's too late, to save their country and the world from full-fledged fascism.

Many Americans have told me they're aware of the possibility of the suspension of the U.S. Constitution (there would be a startling, deceptive, pretext of course) and other goose steps toward a führership. Should those steps be taken, it could be too late to prevent awful and perhaps permanent catastrophe.

The Fourth Reich and its outposts, including the ones within each of us, is perhaps humanity's last major challenge. Understanding and sufficiently dismantling it would probably lead to a period of chaos. But from that could emerge another world, still imperfect, but one less in imminent danger of Armageddon. In it we might finally face a reasonable future. ■

Terminology and the Substance of the Invisible Government

Of course, the arbitrary label Invisible Government suggests a neatness and simplicity that is non-existent. Yet we must have a term, a shorthand, to describe players, structures and processes that are very real and very important to the lives of all of us. I'm taken with a description I once heard, "the Permanent Committee." But I settle on Invisible Government because "it" is essentially invisible and it "governs."

A study of the terminology applied to the phenomenon of the Invisible Government suggests the extent of its powers and the nature of its membership. Broadcaster Bill Moyers, former press secretary to US president Lyndon Johnson, uses the term "shadow government" to refer to hidden forces that conspire against the public good. But "shadow government" is a term widely used to describe opposition politicians in a democracy hoping to form a government. Moyers, I take it, means "shadowy government."

Moyers is a member of the Council on Foreign Relations (CFR). The CFR itself has been characterized as an invisible government by the late Georgetown University professor Carroll Quigley, a mentor of future president Bill Clinton. In his book *Tragedy and Hope*,[20] Quigley wrote: "The Council on Foreign Relations (CFR) has come to be known as 'The Establishment,' 'the invisible government' and 'the Rockefeller foreign office.'"

The CFR is generally agreed to be one of the top trio of secretive global-planning bodies. The other two are the Bilderberg Group and the Trilateral Commission. (Different or subsidiary planning bodies, even more secretive, may and probably do, exist.) Murdoch and other media magnates are invited to Bilderberg conferences, for instance, and usually accept. The BBs, as they're known, go to great lengths to be unseen and unheard by the public. Robert Gaylon Ross, Sr. in his book *Who's Who of the Elite*,[21] says "they clear out all people in the buildings where they are to meet, completely de-bug all rooms, bring in their own cooks, waiters, housekeepers, heavily armed security guards, etc." Ross's preferred term is the "worldwide Elite oligarchy," whose members he defines as holding membership in one or more of these three bodies.

The Trilateral Commission was established in 1973, primarily at the instigation of international financier David Rockefeller, longtime chairman of the Rockefeller-family controlled Chase Manhattan Bank and, says Ross, "undisputed overlord of his family's global corporate empire." Ross says Rockefeller was impressed by the book *Between Two Ages*,[22] by Zbigniew Brzezinski, Columbia University professor and advisor to the elite. Brzesinski proposed a vast alliance between North America, Western Europe and Japan. The US government, he wrote, "is compelled … to negotiate, to guarantee, and, to some extent, to protect the various arrangements that have been contrived even by private business."

In 1971, Rockefeller laid out the idea of the Trilateral Commission at the annual meeting of the Bilderberg Group. Named for the city in Germany in which it first met, the Bilderberg membership of top military, media and business figures and covert operatives had been restricted essentially to the elite from NATO alliance countries. With the Trilateral Commission, Rockefeller brought the Japanese into the West's inner sanctums for the first time.

The membership of the Council on Foreign Relations also spans the elite of the corporate world, academia, the military, politics, the covert establishment and the media. It was at a meeting of the CFR in New York City just after the Second World War that the decision was made to create the CIA, building upon the OSS (Office of Strategic Services), a Second World War spy and propaganda organization which was being disbanded. "Gentlemen, we are going to change history," one of those attending the meeting said. He was tragically accurate in his prediction.

There are other organized bodies and regular events at which the most powerful meet out of the limelight to advance their interests. The annual gatherings at the Bohemian Grove club in San Francisco are an example. It has long been rumored that it was at the Bohemian Grove in 1939 that the decision was made for the USA to proceed to build the atomic bomb. General Leslie Groves was chosen to head the Manhattan Project. Those who believe that a major secret project cannot be kept under wraps might ponder this: by the time the world learned of the existence of the Manhattan Project because of the horrific news from Hiroshima, the project employed 43,000 people at 37 facilities in 19 states and Canada.[23] My family was one of those kept successfully in the dark. As far as we knew from his letters, my uncle who worked on the bomb in Los Alamos was living in Albuquerque and doing other things.

For this book it will have to be sufficient to catch the drift of the powers and agenda of these secret organizations. Ross may be right when he says every person on Earth should care about them, because these bodies "decide when wars should start, how long they should last, who should and should not participate," how boundaries will be affected and who will benefit in what ways (for instance who will profit from the destruction caused by the wars, who will lend the money for the reconstruction and who will profit from that). He lists the business of wars as being at the top of their agenda.

The other areas they attend to are how the money supply will be handled, including interest rates, guarantees and so on; who will be "allowed to" run for the offices of president, prime minister, chancellor and so on; how stocks and bonds shall be dealt with; what salary and wage levels will be countenanced and how news and information will be controlled. "They directly or indirectly own all the major news media, and can therefore tell the public exactly what they want [it] to hear, and deny the public what they do not want it to see, hear or read." [24]

Privishing as a Means of Crushing Information and Ideas

The existence of the Invisible Government on a grand scale, then, cannot be denied. But smaller examples can make visible the workings, for instance within the media, of the Invisible Government. Take the intrusion into book publishing of corporate powers in league with covert powers of the national security state, in particular those of the CIA. In *Into the Buzzsaw*,[25] American investigative author Gerard Colby describes how not one, but two books he wrote about the Du Pont family were "privished." This is a relatively new term used in the book industry to mean a book is killed without the author's knowledge or consent. The book's "life support system" is cut off by reducing the initial print run so that the book "cannot price profitably according to any conceivable formula," by refusal to do reprints, by drastically slashing the book's advertising budget, by all but cancelling the book's promotional tour.

Colby's first book was *Du Pont: Behind the Nylon Curtain*.[26] Trouble for Colby began when he was still researching in the early 1970s. He was approached by another "writer" who said he was doing a story for *Ramparts* magazine on then-Congressman Pierre ("Pete") Du Pont IV's presidential ambitions. The "writer" was also a spy reporting indirectly to the Du Pont family elders and had already been commissioned to write a book to answer Colby's forthcoming book. That was just the beginning.

The writer/spy hired Colby's own agent, who failed to tell Colby about the conflict of interest. (Later, Prentice-Hall fired Colby's editor for "non-productivity" and hired Colby's double-crossing agent as a full-time editor.) Along the way there was the Prentice-Hall salesman who, "under orders," leaked the book's unedited manuscript to the Du Pont family. "A series of phone calls ensued," Colby writes. "The first was to the Book-of-the-Month Club (BMOC), whose Fortune Book Club had contracted with Prentice-Hall to sell the book. Du Pont Company officials told BMOC that family members found the book "scurrilous and actionable." BMOC quickly caved in to one of the most powerful corporations in the world and cancelled the book within 24 hours, unprecedented in BMOC's history, according to later court testimony by BMOC.

At this point the book's fate was taken over by the editor-in-chief of Prentice-Hall's trade book division, John Kirk, and the president of the trade book division, Peter Grenquist. They cut the planned press run of 10,000 by a third so that, according to their own documents, the book could not price profitably "according to any conceivable formula." Rather than blow the whistle on Du Pont Company interference, these two cut the advertising budget in half and scaled back promotional efforts to just two cities. Bram Cavin, the book's editor, was ordered to keep these moves secret from the author. One of *Time* magazine's best investigative writers got wind of the interference going on and filed a story. *Time* killed it. The public might never have known any of this had not Prentice-Hall's chief counsel, disgusted, taken his file to

Gerard Colby

Alden Whitman of *The New York Times*. The *Times'* editor, Max Frankel, resisted Du Pont pressure being exerted on him and published Whitman's piece in the Winter of 1975. The book was also getting rave advance reviews. None of this helped, as the cut in the print run meant there were no copies for sale during the crucial Christmas season. One reason there were no copies was because the Du Ponts rented trucks to go to book stores and buy up all copies they could.

The Enemy

On February 17, 2006, the internet service truthout.com published one of a series of "Perspective" columns by William Rivers Pitt, author of *War on Iraq: What Team Bush Doesn't Want You to Know* and *The Greatest Sedition Is Silence*. Following are excerpts:

They called it "Cyber Storm," and it was a war-game exercise run last week by the Department of Homeland Security. The war game had nothing to do with testing the security of our shipping ports, borders, infrastructure or airports. "Cyber Storm" was testing the government's ability to withstand an onslaught of information and protest from bloggers and online activists.

"Participants confirmed," wrote the Associated Press, that "parts of the worldwide simulation challenged government officials and industry executives to respond to deliberate misinformation campaigns and activist calls by internet bloggers, online diarists whose 'web logs' include political rantings and musings about current events."

Say what? Online expressions of political opinion are so dangerous that the Department of Homeland Security must [devise] war-game scenarios to deal with them? Bloggers are potential terrorists now? Bloggers are the enemy? Last week, as far as DHS was concerned, they were ....

We hear a great deal about enemies, both real and contrived. Let us ponder, for a moment, the existence of another enemy so ☞

CIA Role in Privishing is Outed

Colby and his wife decided to take legal action for breach of contract against Prentice-Hall and against the Du Ponts for inducement to breach contract. Their work preparing for court hearings led them to discover that John Kirk, before coming to Prentice-Hall, had worked for two publishers with CIA ties: the Samuel Walker Publishing Company and the Free Europe Press (the publishing arm of the CIA-funded Radio Free Europe). They discovered

insidious that it operates fully in daylight but beyond control. This enemy seeks to destroy the rule of constitutional law in the United States. This enemy seeks to destroy the seed-corn defense against tyranny in this nation, the separation of powers. This enemy gathers more and more power to itself to achieve these goals, and uses fear and division to do so. This enemy will lie with impunity, stonewall endlessly and ruin anyone who might disrupt its plans ....

It is difficult to imagine a more perilous enemy ... than the one operating out of Washington today. The difference between the enemies we hear about and the one in Washington is simple and deadly: only the enemy in Washington can annihilate the constitutional government we have enjoyed for more than two centuries .... America cannot be terminated by terrorists or rogue states. Were the entire nation to be somehow obliterated, the idea that is America would endure. Only its keepers can kill it completely. They are well on their way.

"As nightfall does not come at once," wrote Justice William O. Douglas, "neither does oppression. In both instances, there's a twilight where everything remains seemingly unchanged, and it is in such twilight that we all must be aware of change in the air, however slight, lest we become victims of the darkness."

We must deal with the enemy within the halls of our government, the enemy whose power to destroy far outstrips any enemy beyond our borders. In doing so, we save that which is unique in the world. In doing so, we deal a death blow to all other enemies. In doing so, we save ourselves from that darkness. ∎

Prentice-Hall's close business ties with William Casey, a former officer of the Office of Strategic Services (predecessor of the CIA), and who later would become CIA director. "This all suggested," Colby writes, "the possibility of a network of 'old boys' from the intelligence community within the publishing industry ... who could turn to each other when needed." A major article in *The New York Times* in 1977 confirmed this. The *Times* reported that CIA assets were "positioned throughout the publishing industry."

Eventually the charges went to court. The judge — the fourth assigned to the case — clearly was biased toward the Du Ponts. As Irénée Du Pont Jr. was testifying, the judge suddenly got up from the bench, walked down to Du Pont as he was reading a document, and turned on a light for him. In his account of the trial, Colby — touching on some of the contents of his book — asked: "Was Irénée upset with the book's telling the story of how his family built the gunpowder trust by buying up competitors during the nineteenth century? Or for repeating Secretary of War Newton Baker's denunciation of the family as a "species of outlaws" for overcharging the government and profiteering over $250 million during [the First World War]? Or for reporting how the company helped undermine the 1924 Geneva Disarmament Conference? Or for revealing how it sold munitions to Chinese and South American warlords during the 1920s? Or for quoting Congressional reportage on their smuggling munitions to the Nazis in Cologne in the early 1930s? Or for reporting any of the other revelations of the Senate Munitions Committee? Or for documenting their financing attempts to destroy the New Deal and throw President Roosevelt out of office? Or for citing their profiteering off [the Second World War] and the Vietnam War? Or for their efforts to throttle labor union organizing? Or for their support for the Red Scare and witch-hunts of the 1950s, while helping to build the hydrogen bomb for the military industrial complex? Or for poisoning the environment or helping to destroy the ozone layer that had previously protected us from global warming?"

Apparently not. What concerned Irénée was his children's possible reaction to statements in the book which raised questions about a small event after the Du Ponts arrived on American soil, fresh from fleeing France after the French Revolution. The question was: Had they left a gold coin for a meal they admittedly consumed after breaking into a home in Rhode Island? Colby said "accounts differed." Irénée was pained that the family's version of the story could even be questioned. This minor courtroom drama and Colby's reporting of it speaks volumes about the privateering and value system of these particular members of the Invisible Government. The Du Ponts had been the French king's gunpowder makers. They were the last nobles to defend the king, with drawn swords. Everything surrounding Colby's attempts to publish one investigative book about this family and corporation (there was more to come) speaks to the continuity of the values of the family's — and of the ensuing corporation's — wealth and power. Colby eventually won an only partially satisfactory settlement.

Another Publisher Takes up the Cause of Freedom of Expression

In 1984 another publisher offered to print Colby's book, updated and expanded, with 300 pages of new material on top of the 600 in the 1974 edition. It was slated to be published in October that year under the title *Du Pont Dynasty*. More court cases had to be fought. The book received many favorable reviews. But the *New York Times* chose not to review it, even though the new pages included "revelations of the family's huge contribution to the Reagan presidential campaign, their direct involvement with the CIA in the bombing of Managua International Airport," and much else.

The new book included a lengthy section on the suppression of the first book. During a TV interview, Colby was asked about this suppression. He confidently turned to page 637 where, he explained, he had written 30 pages on this very subject. Imagine his surprise when he found those 30 pages were missing. When he called his publisher he learned that 3,000 of the first print run of 10,000 were similarly damaged by some sort of "accident" on the part of the print jobber, who got 80 percent of his business from Prentice-Hall. Again, it was the Christmas season; there was no time to make up for the books that had to be withdrawn; people could not find the book. It was withdrawn. "The book soon died."

Colby's story comprises the first chapter of *Into the Buzzsaw*, published in 2002. Its editor is Kristina Borjesson, an award-winning CBS producer who was squeezed out of her job at the network as her solid evidence was about to expose military malfeasance in the case of TWA flight 800, which exploded off the coast of Long Island, New York in 1976. "The buzzsaw," writes Borjesson, "is a powerful system of censorship in this country that is revealed to those reporting on extremely sensitive stories, usually having to do with high-level government and/or corporate malfeasance." [28]

An Artist Makes Visible the Invisible

This is why so much malfeasance remains invisible. However, in the work of a remarkable artist, Mark Lombardi, many patterns of malfeasance have been made visible. From about 1977 to about 1981 Lombardi worked as a general reference librarian in the Fine Arts Department of the Houston Public Library. In the text for the printed program of Lombardi's posthumous exhibition "Global Networks," Curator Robert Hobbs writes that Lombardi became fascinated with various financial scandals of the 1990s. He saw them "as ongoing [criminal] conspiracies and he initially wanted to write articles and books about them." Lombardi assembled thousands of three-by-five-inch index cards "covered with handwritten notations about the various scandals, the perpetrators and the people associated with them." The cards eventually came to number 14,500. [29]

The scandals included, for instance, those surrounding Iran-contra, "George [H.W.] Bush and the Palmer National Bank of Washington, D.C. [circa] 1983-86" and "Pat Robertson, Beurt Servaas, and the UPI Takeover Battle, [circa] 1985-91." As an aid to his writing, Lombardi began drawing diagrams on pieces of paper "in order to chart the interrelationships among specific individuals ...." The drawings grew and "became independent entities," a second-level archive. "Although the subject of these works appears to be the unveiling of conspiracies — and certainly the criminal component of the work continued to be an important factor for this politically-motivated artist — his work began to transform his goals from those of a sleuth to those of an architect of knowledge," Hobbs writes.

Lombardi's artistic renderings of networks of the Invisible Government typically came to be done in graphite pencil on Japanese rice paper, with spare but effective means of indicating the nature of the relationships: a straight line with arrows pointing one way would mean "some kind of

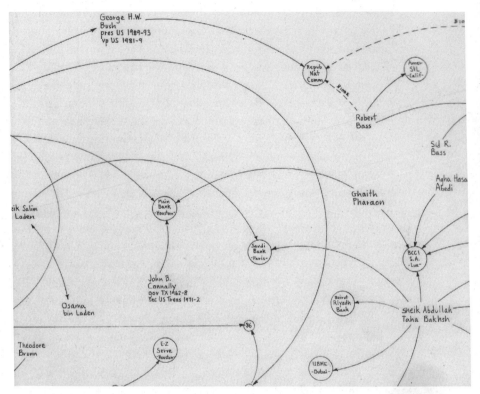

George H.W. Bush, Harken Energy, and Jackson Stephens, ca. 1979-90 (5th version), 1999, 24 1/8 X 48 1/4",
pen on rice paper, Mark Lombardi

influence or control;" a straight line with arrows pointing both ways "some kind of mutual relationship or association;" a broken line a flow of money, loans or credit, and so on. There are only about six of these legends and Lombardi used two colors only: black and red. Lombardi explained: "Black represents the essential elements of the story while major lawsuits, criminal indictments and other legal actions taken against the parties are shown in red. Every statement of fact and connections depicted in the work is [sic] true and based on information culled entirely from the public record." Even though all the lines are fine and the printing small, because of the complexity of the networks some of the works measure five or six feet across. The piece "Oliver North, Lake Resources of Panama, and the Iran-

Contra Operation, [circa] 1984-86," measures five feet, three inches tall and 13 feet across. To encounter these works in person, as I had the good fortune to do at the Art Gallery of Ontario when the "Global Networks" Exhibition visited Toronto, is to experience a gratifying "So here it all is" feeling.

Lombardi rendered these networks of relationships between people, institutions and transactions into art resembling constellations of stars, spheres, ovals, cocoons or butterflies. In a number of the works there are single horizontal lines representing time. Lombardi's work shows that the Invisible Government can be made visible, just as a message written with a pen dipped in lemon juice will become legible when held to a flame. The final public showing of his work during his life was in February 2000 in the first collaboration between the Museum of Modern Art and the P.S. 1 Contemporary Art Center. The exhibition was entitled "Greater New York: New Art in New York Now" and it was received with critical acclaim. A month later, Lombardi's life came to an end at 49 years of age, an apparent suicide.

Hobbs comments: "(Lombardi's) drawings had the great appeal of being practically the first art to visualize the new global order that has seemed to be one of the key sources of power in the late twentieth century and thereafter. They also demonstrated ... [that] this new set of *ad hoc* international alliances was actually made up of a small community of players ... analogous to the intrigues of local scoundrels." An undated news release from The Drawing Center in New York announcing the first leg of the "Global Networks" touring show stated: "Through drawing, Lombardi mapped connections of complicity that traced the flow of capital, the peddling of influence and the construction of invisible power structures."

The CIA is at the Heart of the Invisible Government

One of those structures is the CIA. Although it's well known now, I remember, as a 12-year-old, scoffing at a school chum who told me there was a large American secret spy agency. At the same time it remains Invisible insofar as only glimpses of the extent of its budgets are available. Even the taxpayer-supported budget is subject to secrecy on the grounds of "national security;" these "black budgets" are kept secret because they're illegal. Also unknown are its operations and personnel. One of the earliest and best books on the CIA was *The Invisible Government,* published in 1964.

The CIA long ago infiltrated the media at all levels. This has enabled injection of information and disinformation directly into the arteries of media organizations, management of propaganda campaigns and — as Gerard Colby's books on the Du Ponts — sidelining or obliterating important truths about the ruling elites. The CIA would not do this unless it were itself one of the Invisible Government's tools for full-spectrum dominance.

By the time of the Second World War, the power of information was well understood in the corridors of power. During that conflict, the weapons of secrecy and propaganda were accepted as pivotal for the war effort. William "Wild Bill" Donovan, sent to Europe by then-US president Franklin Roosevelt to assess the situation, came back with a recommendation for the establishment of the Office of Strategic Services (the OSS), predecessor to the CIA. Donovan was a great believer in psychological warfare; to him, this included "propaganda, sabotage, guerilla activities, bribery, blackmail, assassination ...."[31] The majority of Donovan's "assets" were journalists. After the war, separate offices responsible for propaganda, covert action and psychological warfare were merged under Frank Wisner into the Office of Policy Coordination (OPC). This became the fastest-growing unit within the nascent CIA, with staff levels rising from 302 in 1949 to 2,812 in 1952, along with 3,142 overseas "assets." In the same period, Wisner's budget rose from $4.7 million to $82 million.

Wisner kept a highly secret "Propaganda Assets Inventory," known as "Wisner's Wurlitzer," which made "music on demand" through more than 800 news and public information organizations and individuals around the world — "opinion makers that could be called upon at any time to play the tune of Wisner's making."[32] Included were journalists, columnists, book publishers, editors, stringers across multiple news organizations, and entire entities such as Radio Free Europe and Radio Liberty. After the OPC was absorbed by the burgeoning CIA, the propaganda efforts multiplied exponentially. Front organizations such as the Congress of Cultural Freedom were created, enlisting in artists, writers, poets, musicians and intellectuals, some knowing what they were doing and some drawn in unwittingly. The Left-wing intellectual magazine *Encounter* was secretly funded, the aim being to promote anti-Communism and everything American. Wisner himself became "vehemently anti-Communist," legendary CIA operative James

Angleton told Joseph Trento, who reports it in his book *The Secret History of the CIA.*[33]

Wisner was also deeply involved, along with Allen W. Dulles and William Donovan in Operation Paperclip, recruiting former Nazis to work in their anti-Communist crusade. "Donovan and Dulles secretly threw in America's lot with the worst of the Third Reich," writes Trento. The American Army even recruited and evacuated the head of the Gestapo, Heinrich Mueller. Hitler's chief of anti-Soviet intelligence, Reinhard Gehlen, and his associates were brought to an Army base outside Washington, DC for ten months, "laying the groundwork for what was to come," namely the CIA. Nazism was the ideology furtively promulgated through the CIA's media assets.[34]

The CIA: An Arrogant Rogue Organization from the Start

After the war, the CIA immediately moved to influence American opinion about the agency itself, despite prohibitions on it against doing so. "The CIA believed it was not enough to be immune from congressional or judicial control. The agency felt it was also imperative that anti-CIA sentiment and leftist leanings in general had to be defused and combated on every front. To this end, the CIA infiltrated ... the editorial boards of influential journal and book publishers, and any other quarters where public attitudes could be effectively influenced," writes Darrell Garwood in *Under Cover.*[35]

The CIA targeted and infiltrated particular independent publications, such as *Ramparts,* it being one of the few large-circulation magazines to openly publish questions about the official story of the assassination of JFK. At *The New York Times* the technique was pressure at the top. CIA director Allen Dulles complained to the higher-ups that *Times* reporter Sydney Gruson was incapable of reporting "objectively" on the upcoming revolution in Guatemala (which was manufactured and conducted by the CIA). The *Times* complied and kept Gruson away from Guatemala. The CIA nourished high profile "assets," such as columnists Joseph and Stewart Alsop, using them as conduits for "information" it wanted the public to believe.

After a time these efforts were co-ordinated under Wisner as Operation Mockingbird. In this, he enjoyed input from his friend, *Washington Post* publisher Phil Graham. In the operation, writes Deborah Davis in her book

Katherine the Great, about the wife of Phil Graham, "each journalist was a separate 'operation,' requiring a code name, a field supervisor, and a field office, at an annual cost of tens or hundreds of thousands of dollars ...."[36]

Davis wrote that Wisner "owned" respected members of *Newsweek*, CBS, *The New York Times* and many others. Carl Bernstein, in a famous *Rolling Stone* piece in October 1977, "The CIA and the Media," stated that employees of "all the major media in this country owed some allegiance, whether paid or as volunteers, to the CIA." According to Bernstein's article, some who served the CIA wittingly included William Paley, longtime top executive of CBS; Henry Luce of *Time* and Arthur Hays Sulzberger of *The New York Times*. Additionally, Bernstein specified members at ABC, NBC, the Associated Press, United Press International, Reuters, Hearst Newspapers, Scripps-Howard, *Newsweek*, the Mutual Broadcasting System, the *Miami Herald*, and the New York *Herald-Tribune*.

The CIA Stole Marshall Plan Funds

Such a major effort cost big bucks, even by CIA standards. Wisner paid for it by skimming off Marshall Plan funds, which Wisner and his group called "candy." CIA agent Gilbert Greenway recalled: "We couldn't spend it all. I remember once meeting with Wisner and the comptroller. My God, I said, how can we spend that? There were no limits, and nobody had to account for it. It was amazing." [37]

Books — a library — would be needed to record the CIA's influence, manipulation and outright control of and through the media. One example: Trento writes in *The Secret History of the CIA* that President John F. Kennedy's Alliance for Progress in Latin America became "a giant cover operation for [anti-Communist] political activities. Large CIA stations were established in many capital cities. The CIA used an entire news organization, Copley News Service, as a cover for its agents." [39]

References to the close ties between news outlets and spooks are so numerous in Trento's book that most of the news outlets aren't even listed in the index. Some examples: *The People* was a London newspaper "with ties to MI5" (Britain's domestic spy agency); the New York *Herald-Tribune* and the *San Diego Union* were two newspapers with whom FBI director J. Edgar Hoover "had close ties;" *The Empire,* another British newspaper with

Sorrows of Empire

Although tyranny, because it needs no consent, may successfully rule over foreign peoples, it can stay in power only if it destroys first of all the national institutions of its own people.
— Hannah Arendt, *The Origins of Totalitarianism*

In November 2003, Chalmers Johnson, author of *Blowback: The Costs and Consequences of American Empire*, wrote an article for *Foreign Policy in Focus* under the title above. Following are excerpts:

Four sorrows, it seems to me, are certain to be visited on the United States. Their cumulative effect guarantees that the US will cease to resemble the country outlined in the Constitution of 1787. First, there will be a state of perpetual war, leading to more terrorism against Americans wherever they may be and a spreading reliance on nuclear weapons among smaller nations as they try to ward off the imperial juggernaut. Second is a loss of democracy and Constitutional rights as the presidency eclipses Congress and is itself transformed from a co-equal "executive branch" of government into a military junta. Third is the replacement of truth by propaganda, disinformation, and the glorification of war, power, and the military legions. Lastly, there is bankruptcy, as the United States pours its economic resources into ever more grandiose military projects and short-changes the education, health, and safety of its citizens. All I have space for here is to touch briefly on three of these: endless war, the loss of Constitutional liberties, and financial ruin ....

If the likelihood of perpetual war hangs over the world, the situation domestically in the United States is no better. Militarism and imperialism threaten democratic government at home just as seriously as they menace the independence and sovereignty of other countries ....

A year and a half after September 11, 2001, at least two articles of the Bill of Rights were dead letters — the fourth prohibiting unwarranted searches and seizures and the sixth guaranteeing a jury of peers, ☞

the assistance of an attorney in offering a defense, the right to confront one's accusers, protection against self-incrimination, and, most critically, the requirement that the government spell out its charges and make them public. The second half of Thomas Jefferson's old warning — "When the government fears the people, there is liberty; when the people fear the government, there is tyranny" — clearly applies ....

In my judgment, American imperialism and militarism are so far advanced and obstacles to its further growth have been so completely neutralized that the decline of the US has already begun. The country is following the path already taken by its erstwhile adversary in the cold war, the former Soviet Union. The US's refusal to dismantle its own empire of military bases when the menace of the Soviet Union disappeared, combined with its inappropriate response to the blowback of September 11, 2001, makes this decline virtually inevitable ....

There is only one development that could conceivably stop this cancerous process, and that is for the people to retake control of Congress, reform it and the election laws to make it a genuine assembly of democratic representatives, and cut off the supply of money to the Pentagon and the Central Intelligence Agency. That was, after all, the way the Vietnam War was finally brought to a halt ....

John le Carré, the novelist most famous for his books on the role of intelligence services in the cold war, writes, "America has entered one of its periods of historical madness, but this is the worst I can remember: worse than McCarthyism, worse than the Bay of Pigs and in the long term potentially more disastrous than the Vietnam War."[38] His view is somewhat more optimistic than mine .... The US still has a strong civil society that could, at least in theory, overcome the entrenched interests of the armed forces and the military-industrial complex. I fear, however, that the US has indeed crossed the Rubicon and that there is no way to restore Constitutional government short of a revolutionary rehabilitation of American democracy. Without root and branch reform, Nemesis awaits. She is the goddess of revenge, the punisher of pride and arrogance, and the United States is on course for a rendezvous with her. ∎

"close ties to MI5;" super-spy Kim Philby "worked in Beirut undercover as a journalist" for *The Economist* and *The Observer.*

The existence of such a hyper-malignant agency as the CIA has become far too accepted by US society at all levels. In the Valerie Plame affair, a huge stir was caused when a covert operative was outed. This reveals a deeply disturbing characteristic of US society. It is not the "outing" of Plame I refer to. It's the universal agreement that this outing was a breach of some ineffable, almost sacred, value: the inalienable right of the CIA to operate covertly anywhere any time with permanent impunity. This is an agency known — widely known — to torture, assassinate, destabilize societies, overturn governments. To unquestioningly tolerate, even endorse, this right of secrecy for the CIA is a powerful endorsement of all the activities of the CIA. A society that understands the need for decency and accountability would, rather than condoning secrecy by a murdering, deceiving organism, be demanding full investigation of it. The last time anything resembling that was three decades ago with the Church Committee.

It is remarkable that a democracy would place the right to secrecy, especially for such transparently immoral and illegal activities, on such an elevated pedestal. In a true democracy, secrecy is looked upon at best as a necessary evil, always to be held in check. In the socio-political culture of Sweden, for instance, the assumption is that all activities of government should be open and disclosed unless it can be compellingly demonstrated that the contrary is called for. In the US, on the other hand, the socio-political culture — including the journalistic culture — is summarized well in Daniel Ellsberg's compelling book *Secrets: A Memoir of Vietnam and the Pentagon Papers.*[40] The government, according to Ellsberg, was "intoxicated by secrets." He's referring to a series of governments but especially those under Lyndon Johnson and Richard Nixon. Ellsberg said he came to realize that his loyalty to his insider status, career and the president had outweighed what should have been higher loyalties "to the US Constitution, ... to truth, to fellow Americans and to other human lives."

Paul David Collins writes in an article entitled "The Hidden Face of Terrorism," "The public has been systemically conditioned to ignore such patterns, and to condemn those who draw attention to them, derisively calling them 'conspiracy theorists.'"

Gunpowder, Treason and Plot:
From 1605 Through 9/11 to Today

When you only have one act you can do,
you keep on doing it.

— CIA veteran John Sherwood, quoted by Joseph A. Trento
in *The Secret History of the CIA*[1]

LONDON, November 4, 1605 — As midnight approaches on the eve of the traditional opening of Parliament, armed agents of the King raid a basement room of the Houses of Parliament. They discover 36 barrels of gunpowder and a tunnel leading to the room. They apprehend Guy Fawkes, 36, a known agitator for the rights of English Roman Catholics. In Fawkes' possession are a watch, slow matches and touchpaper.

On the throne of England sits James I Stuart, a Protestant, who ordered the translation of the Christian Bible bearing his name. Had Fawkes succeeded, so the King James version of the 11th hour events goes, the next day the King, Queen and members of the House of Lords and the House of Commons would be dead. The Palace of

Guy Fawkes

Westminster complex, including historic Westminster Abbey, would be smoking rubble.

The English public is stunned. It's the equivalent of 9/11 in our day. "A cataclysm," Adam Nicolson describes it in *God's Secretaries: The Making of the King James Bible.*[2] The official story is that upon his arrest, Fawkes admits his purpose was to destroy King and Parliament. By November 8, on the rack, he names 12 co-conspirators. Fawkes and those not killed where they are tracked down (one dies in prison) are later found guilty of treason in a trial lasting less than a day. The are hanged, drawn and quartered.

The following Sunday, November 10, the King James version of the plot begins to be broadcast from the pulpits of the Church of England — the 1605 equivalent of television. William Barlow, Bishop of Rochester, thunders at Paul's Cross church that "the enemy from below is satanic in its wickedness." The king, their hoped-for victim, "is an unqualifiedly good man, the archetype of the good man, virtually a Christ-figure," writes Nicolson. All pulpits echo the palace version. Ten years later "the energy of loathing was undiminished." The palace version becomes historical truth for humankind. Until 1959, it was against the law in Britain *not* to celebrate Guy Fawkes Day.

But Nicolson and others have now cast serious doubt on that version. Many anomalies concerning the events have surfaced. The Royal Chancellor, the wily Robert Cecil, had an efficient network of spies seeded among Roman Catholic dissidents. The authorship of the letter by which the King learned of the plot is murky. The gunpowder was of an inferior nature, unlikely to have achieved much result, if any. Some of the handwriting on Fawkes' confession differed from the rest. There was no tunnel.

Ignored until recently is a book by Jesuit historian John Gerard (1564-1606), *What Was the Gunpowder plot: The Traditional Story Tested by Original Evidence,* finally published in 1897. Gerard writes: "When we examine into the details supplied to us as to the progress of the affair, we find that much of what the conspirators are said to have done is well-nigh incredible, while it is utterly impossible that if they really acted in the manner described, the public authorities should not have had full knowledge of their proceedings."[3]

Overall the evidence points to a false flag operation. US author Webster G. Tarpley writes that James "was considering a policy of accommodation

The "Gunpowder Plotters"

with the Spanish Empire, the leading Catholic power, and some measures of toleration for Catholics in England." But an influential group in London, known as the war party, wanted to push James into a confrontation with the Spanish Empire, "from which they hoped among other things to extract great personal profit." The war party considered it politically vital "to keep persecuting Roman Catholics".[4]

Chief among the war party was Cecil, the Royal Chancellor. He set out, writes Tarpley, "to sway James to adopt his policy, by means of terrorism." It amounts to this: either Cecil and the war party made it happen, or they let it happen. And if they let it happen, they made it happen.

The fallout from the plot is uncontestable. "The English became fixated on homeland security," Nicolson writes. "An inclusive, irenic idea of mutual benefit [between Spain and England, which had recent signers of a peace treaty, between whom trade was growing] was replaced by a defensive/aggressive complex in which all Catholics, of all shades, never mind their degree of enthusiasm for the alleged planned attack, were at least for

The Song is Ended, but the Melody Lingers On

November 6, 2005 — The final item on the late evening radio newscast of the Canadian Broadcasting Corporation (CBC) is about minor vandalism the night before in Newfoundland. Guy Fawkes Day still is celebrated in that province, more so than in the rest of Canada. The CBC, explaining for listeners unfamiliar with the Day, reports: "Guy Fawkes was a plotter who tried to blow up the British Parliament Buildings." Another small proof of the persistence of false official stories, in this case 400 years plus one day later.

a time identified as the enemy ... The state had ... taken over the English conscience."[5]

War with Spain ensues. England's course is set for a century of wars against the Spanish and Portuguese empires, out of which the British Empire emerges. In 1917 the British add Iraq to their Empire after the defeat of the Ottoman Empire; neocolonial turmoil in Iraq continues to this day. The official story of "gunpowder treason" set much in motion, and it would take a foolhardy person to assert that it has all been for the betterment of humankind.

False-Flag Operations as Historical Geostrategy

The Gunpowder Plot false-flag operation hanged and quartered Guy Fawkes and a dozen others, manipulated the British public toward intolerance, and most importantly, contributed significantly to the rise of the British Empire. This is proof that false-flag operations deserve to be far better known and understood than they are. False-flag ops are the least-recognized, highest-impact category of human deceit. In terms of emotional wallop, even the most brilliant lies uttered by the most capable demagogues pale in comparison to the public outcry generated by an outrageous false-flag operation. The false-flag op is the indispensable, most dependable device rulers use to mobilize their populations, especially behind wars the rulers want.

In his book *The War on Truth*[6] Nafeez Mossadeq Ahmed terms the fomenting of terrorism by the state "a strategy of tension" and "historical geostrategy." He quotes Canadian social philosopher and Fellow of the Royal Society of Canada, John McMurtry:

> Shocking attacks on symbols of American power as a pretext for aggressive war is, in fact, an old and familiar pattern of the American corporate state. Even the sacrifice of thousands of ordinary Americans is not new, although so many people have never died so very fast ... The basic point is that the US "secret government" ... has a very long record of contriving attacks on its symbols of power as a pretext for the declaration of wars, with an attendant corporate media frenzy focusing all public attention of the Enemy to justify the next transnational mass murder. This pattern is as old as the US corporate state... Throughout there is one constant to this long record of hoodwinking the American public into bankrolling ever rising military expenditures and periodic wars for corporate treasure.[7]

This technique of stealth, pretense and subversion — for instance the mosque bombings and wanton killings of innocents in Iraq under American and British occupation, blamed on "insurgents" — continues to be the main *modus operandi* of the American and British oligarchies today. In Iraq, it provides a destabilizing campaign of "divide and conquer." It is not an aberrant criminal strategy adopted only by rogue groups. It is established military doctrine and practice — taught in military colleges.[8]

The false-flag operation has been used for decades, if not centuries, by colonial powers; so far, no nation as a whole has wakened up to it sufficiently to escape being bamboozled by it.

False-flag ops are not a side issue. They're at least one key issue. In my view they are *the* central issue of our time because of their *linchpin function*. Repeated false-flag "terrorist" acts are the black lifeblood of the so-called "war on terror," in turn the template for perpetual rule by the oligarchy. It's difficult to think of a more controlling form of deceit. What other form as effectively drives public opinion, empowers the oligarchy, serves aggressive foreign policies, boosts militarism, promotes the squandering of resources, destroys the planet and drastically diminishes hopes of a safe and sane future?

It's a dark tribute to the victors who control so much of what we know as history that while there are thousands upon thousands of books about wars, there are few books about how wars are triggered and not a single book, so far as I can determine, focused only on the most common war trigger: the false-flag op. To grasp how grotesquely out of proportion is our attention to wars, on the one hand, and the means by which they are launched, on the other, consider a fictional parallel. Suppose there were thousands of books about fires and none devoted to their single main cause.

The events of 9/11 marked a significant upscaling and refining of the false-flag op. But in essence it was business as usual for the ruling oligarchy and Invisible Government. We and everything we hold dear are their targets. The events of 9/11 also constitute — if a sufficient number of people of goodwill can only see it — the greatest opportunity ever to launch a new beginning. The reason is that the evidence of an inside job in the case of 9/11 is so obvious that it is susceptible to revelation.

What Is a False Flag Operation?

A false-flag operation is a contrived, staged event, usually shocking, planned by its actual perpetrators to appear to have been done by others. The term comes from naval history: a ship flying a flag not of its true nationality is flying a "false flag." For purposes of this chapter we categorize an event as false flag if it:

(a) Involves significant destruction of life and/or property, or

(b) Is fairly spectacular. The Gunpowder Plot is an example. Although there was no loss of life (until the alleged plotters were executed), it qualifies because of the stunning impact on the England of that time, and

(c) Is used by the perpetrators for a major political purpose, such as to launch or justify war, stage a coup, destabilize a society, subvert a popular movement, round up "undesirables" or cause a major change in policy. Most false-flag ops enable the deceitful rulers who order them to accomplish several aims among those listed.

False-flag ops depend on a contingent of covert operators provided with all the financial and technical resources they require. By definition, a far-from-theoretical conspiracy is involved. If patsies are required, they take time to identify, trick or bribe or blackmail into involvement, and train. False identities and planted trails of "evidence" — such as a Koran in a van — all must be planned with care. All must be in place and orchestrated into a Big Lie event, timed for maximum impact and displayed before an unsuspecting populace.

The British Colonel Who Wrote the Book on Low Intensity Warfare and False-Flag Ops

One of the global masters of the black art of false-flag ops was British Colonel Frank Kitson, also a prolific author. In his books *Gangs and Countergangs* and *Low Intensity Operations*,[9] Kitson boasts that the British covertly led the Mau-Mau uprising in Kenya so that it became warfare between rival factions, thus preventing the rise of nationalism in that British colony. This cost the lives of 18,000 to 30,000 natives, but only 22 whites. It was an anti-nationalist, anti-independentist, racist, genocidal and anti-democratic operation. But Kitson was proud of it.

Such pride is reminiscent of the euphoria expressed by Dr. Donald N. Wilber, the former CIA field agent who in 1954 wrote a document for the CIA's "clandestine service history." The document is entitled "Overthrow of Premier Mossadeq [sic] of Iran, November 1952-August 1953." This coup was made possible by, among other things, false-flag operations. As Peter Scowen puts it in his book *Rogue Nation:*

Clearly, Iran's political life from 1953 on was a creation of the American government, not the Iranian people. Iranians were manipulated into thinking their country was in the midst of a homespun political rev-olution, when in fact it was in the grips of determined CIA agents equipped with a million dollars, a few Photostat machines, and a conscience that allowed them to terrorize people and bomb their homes and make it look like someone else had done it.[10]

Toppling the secular-leaning democrat Mohammed Mossadegh was the CIA's first successful overthrow of a democratic government since the agency's formation six years earlier in 1947. There were many more to follow. Wilber wrote: "It was a day that should never have ended for it carried with it such a sense of excitement, of satisfaction, and of jubilation that it is doubtful whether any other can come up to it." [11]

Kitson's Kenyan black operation was racist, but the CIA's in Iran was not essentially so, although the Iranian people were held in contempt as expendable pawns to be manipulated upon the CIA's grand chessboard. The agents of the oligarchy can be at pains to distance themselves from charges of racism. The captain of a Guatemalan death squad told a freelance radio documentarist for CBC Radio that no one should think the Indians murdered by his death squads were targeted "because they were Indians." He explained: "We only target people who are developing a political consciousness." Of the two evils, racism might be the lesser. Targeting people who are developing political consciousness is tantamount to removing the brightest and most morally advanced individual human beings from our species' gene pool. So in addition to being murderous, the activities of the black operators exterminate efforts at a better future. The murders of President John F. Kennedy, his brother Robert, Dr. Martin Luther King, Jr., and Malcolm X — all false-flag ops in that persons other than the real assassins were blamed — hardly could be said to have improved the future for Americans in general. Such crimes require the invention of new language in order to better resist them. The black operators deal in "killing the future."

Kitson's operation was driven by Britain's trading interests,[12] that is to say, the interests of the British oligarchy. To the Invisible Government of Britain, the colonies were considered sources of raw material and cheap labour. Even within my lifetime I've heard Canada described by British people as "a colony" in tones of condescension. As the people in Britain's colonies grew to understand they were being exploited as raw-material suppliers, unrest developed. To keep the subject populations from uniting against the occupying power, the British sent agents such as Kitson to institute the classic "divide and rule" strategy. The key was to find existing ethnic, racial or other tensions, and exasperate and manipulate them.

The surreptitious nature of the Kenyan operation is reflected in the various terms writers have used to describe it. Kitson and his operatives are variously described as "covertly leading several large scale Mau-Mau units," "leading large-scale units," "manipulating the Mau-Mau uprising," "creating Mau-Mau style synthetic countergangs," "directing" the Mau-Mau and having "created and fostered the Mau-Mau as an unspeakable bloody gang with all manner of atrocities, and these were blamed by many on the

The Devil's Glossary

Black operation (black op): A secret criminal operation by a hidden agency of government or an organization working for the government. Can be a psychological operation and usually has psychological warfare value.

False-flag operation (false-flag op): A black op made to look like the work of others than those conducting it. See "What is a False Flag Operation?" on page 262 for particular criteria used to select examples for inclusion in this book.

Patsies: Convenient or plausible scapegoats to be blamed for the operation. May be unconnected at all, or may be on the payroll of the black operators and sacrificed. Lee Harvey Oswald is a well-known example.

Psychological operation (psyop): An operation, covert or overt, to induce trauma to manipulate public opinion.

Psychological warfare (psywar): Total campaign to frighten, coerce, mislead, etc., a population. Employed are information, disinformation, mixtures of white (truths), black (lies) and grey (half-truths) propaganda, torture, targeted assassinations, coordinated statements of "leaders," exploitation of a variety of forums (such as the UN, NATO, etc.) to megaphone the party line, public relations, black ops including false-flag ops, recruitment of friendly organizations such as corporations and NGOs to augment the campaign, creation and control of front organizations, infiltration and manipulation of existing ones, including "controlled opposition" of the Left, etc. Psychological warfare is pretty much a description of the total operation of the Invisible Government against the people in general, and in particular against individuals and groups that are politically aware and that dissent from the agenda of the Invisible Government.

nationalists, ruining their reputation and scaring the bourgeosie, etc." This latter description is by Webster G. Tarpley, author of *9/11 Synthetic Terror: Made in USA.*[13]

The total operation is also known as low-intensity conflict (LIC), which in turn always involves psywar, although the technicians of death and deception consciously integrate fear and its manipulation with their physical false-flag operations involving bombings, assassinations, and so on. Subsumed within psywar are combinations of elements including very early subversion of the groups resisting exploitation, conventional outreach such as films, articles planted in the media, leaflets, interviews by propaganda agents, economic threats, surveillance, detentions, torture, targeted assassinations, disinformation disseminated in a variety of ways, recruitment of informants, non-violent disorder, manipulated mass meetings, police actions, deployment of "good deed" agents, setting up clinics and job centers, and political moves including some accommodation of the demands of the people, fake strikes and protest marches, bribery, shows of force, military actions short of artillery, tanks and bombers, and, generally, manipulation of whatever needs to be manipulated. The key characteristics, observed Dale Wharton of Montreal in a review of Kitson's *Low Intensity Conflict* are "stealth and fraud." [14]

Diary of 9/11 and the Media

The *Atlantic* Misses the Boat

March 21, 2006 — The top story in the April issue of the *Atlantic* is headlined: "The Infiltrator: How This Man Helped Topple the Most Tenacious Terrorist Organization in History." [15] It's about the Irish Republican Army (IRA), now apparently a spent force. In a "post-9/11 world" it seems any story with "terrorist," "terrorism" or "war on terror" in the headline will attract fearful readers seeking information on how to protect themselves from this insidious threat lurking everywhere.

Most such articles embroider the make believe official line. But this one, by freelancer Matthew Teague, is remarkable in two ways. First, it delivers rarely-published information about false-flag assassinations and bombings carried out by the network of government agents who execute so many "terrorist" outrages. Second, it appears that the editors of the *Atlantic* have very little idea of what they have published. Maybe they are so immersed in the official line that they cannot see what Teague has written. Based on the information in the eight-page article, the headline might read: "I Killed for the British So They Could Blame the IRA."

Teague's main source is ex-British agent Kevin Fulton, who was recruited at the age of 18. For some reason Fulton decided to spill the beans about his career as an informant/killer who infiltrated the IRA in "a cutthroat and secret British effort ... carried out in the shadows ..." Says Fulton: "Darker even than people can imagine."

The article details a convoluted story of double dealing, betrayal, torture and death. British spy services recruited disaffected IRA members who, with relative ease made their way into top positions, including head of internal IRA security. The "ease" part was killing. To rank-and-file IRA members a killing was a bloody badge proving the killer to be an authentic supporter of the IRA cause. The members of this "terrorist" organization were unable to conceive of an infiltrator killing in cold blood just to establish his credentials. This failure of the imagination was the IRA's main Achilles Heel.

In some cases, a lesser British agent under suspicion within the IRA would be killed by another British agent higher up — a "prize" British agent. This would remove the unsatisfactory agent in an extreme way while burnishing, within the IRA, the credibility of the higher-up agent. All agents were, needless to say, indoctrinated. "Each night Fulton rocked himself to sleep," writes Teague, "repeating the mantra his handlers had given him: 'The greater good. The greater good. The greater good.'"

The IRA members also were unable to grasp the extent to which their movement had been infiltrated or for how long. Teague interviewed "folk hero" Denis Donaldson, the "legendary IRA hunger striker." When Teague told Donaldson about Fulton's confessions, "Donaldson's shoulders slumped. 'I still can't believe it,' he said, shaking his head. 'My God.'" After Teague returned to the US he received the news that Donaldson had been found out as a British spy — and that he had been "for two decades." He was killed in early 2006.

The British strategy was laid down and implemented by Brigadier General Frank Kitson in Kenya who, Teague writes, "had recruited locals with money and idealism, and infiltrated the insurgent ranks ... with layer upon layer of sabotage, subterfuge and duplicity ..." Kitson's "principles," adds Teague, now are "being followed by American forces in Iraq."

Much if not most of the terrorism the world news media reported as having been carried out by the IRA was in fact carried out by British agents inside the IRA. The British agents, acting at the behest of the British government, were also largely responsible for the IRA's acquisition of increasingly sophisticated technologies of murder, such as US-manufactured bomb detonators triggered by infrared signals.

A great deal of background about the false flag nature of outrages attributed to the IRA — and to al Qaeda — is contained in the recent book *Spies, Lies & Whistleblowers*,[16] by ex-agents Annie Machon and David Shayler. In it, Machon and Shayler state that "MI5 illegally investigated thousands of UK citizens for their political views," allowed "a known Libyan terrorist into Britain ... and allowed him to set up a terrorist network," and "illegally paid thousands of pounds to al Qaeda to stage a coup in Libya." The last sentence of the 378-page book is: "What you have read in this book is only the tip of the iceberg."

Throughout the *Atlantic* article, Fulton is described by Teague as "a terrorist" and "a bomber for the IRA." Fulton does not deny the accuracy of these descriptions. A fellow agent/killer, Freddie Scappaticci, responsible for killing "dozens of people" — three of them are named — was found out and fled the IRA. Teague does not address, and the *Atlantic* editors apparently did not ask him to address what seems to me an obvious question: how can Fulton, presumably Scappaticci and no doubt many other killers, walk the streets with impunity? In a just and sane world, the article might be headed: "Those Who Torture, Kill and Bomb for an Empire and Survive Will Never be Called to Account."

* * *

Kitson went on to mastermind similar efforts in Malaya, Cyprus and Northern Ireland. Wikipedia, an Internet encyclopedia, states that "Since World War II, the British military has engaged in over 50 low intensity campaigns."[17] The British *Who's Who* states that Kitson's career concluded with his becoming Commander in Chief, United Kingdom Land Forces and Aide-de-Camp General to the Queen (1983-85). In 1985 he was made Knight Grand Cross, Order of the British Empire. His address: c/o Lloyd's Bank, Farnham, Surrey. His club: Boodles. Empires serve the owners of their commercial interests and reward the servants of those owners with the highest accolades, instead of prison terms. It is well to remember on whose behalf the lying, stealth, fraud, torture, killing, destabilization and terror are being carried out.

False-Flag Operation Strategies and Examples

Attacking a second party to frame a third party (for instance blowing up a Sunni mosque with the intention that the Shia will be blamed, and vice versa) is suitable for destabilization purposes. Luring enemies into attacking you is suitable for launching "retaliatory actions" which in fact are aggressive, but you claim their "unprovoked aggression" justifies your "measured response." A variation is simply to claim they've attacked you (as was the case with the Tonkin Gulf resolution). The gold standard is a carefully arranged significant "attack" on yourself and blaming your targeted enemy for it. Such was the 9/11 false-flag op.

History (but not history books, in any coherent way) provides an abundance of examples of false-flag ops, often involving great loss of life. Just a few will be detailed here. It is important that we familiarize ourselves with the sad truth about false-flag ops, so we can try to end them. Meanwhile, we need to build into our reflexes and indeed our very bone marrow just how common and dirty are false-flag operations. The next time we see a news story about some outrage — a bombing or hostage taking or execution — we should reserve judgment about who the true perpetrators are until we learn more.

In fact, I take it further: I believe that we're justified in assuming initially that the latest outrage is a false-flag op, until we are persuaded otherwise, no matter the naïve wall-to-wall bleatings of the incurious establishment-oriented mainstream media or the emotional knee-jerk reactions of our more gullible or incurious fellow citizens. The assumption has proven itself reasonable because of how common false-flag ops have become. The false-flag card is being played repeatedly all over the world, as proven by the sampling of cases that follow. The game is called the "war on terror." We're told "the other side," the "jihadists" and "Islamofascists," are always dealing explosive cards. The record shows otherwise. More like the reverse. The "war on terror" is a dangerous and demeaning illusion fabricated mainly in Washington and London. Now, open the hidden history book and as you read, note the number of times the media swallowed the official story, or fabricated their own, and carried on beating the drums of war. Count the number of times in the following accounts that the media counseled sober second thought, investigated thoroughly and early, encouraged careful debate ....

Provoking the Mexican-American war (1846)

After Mexico's revolution in 1821, Mexico abolished slavery and in 1829 prohibited further US immigration into Texas, then a Mexican state. In 1835, Mexico tried to enforce its authority over Texas but was driven out by Texans who proclaimed their independence and lobbied to be annexed

Zachary Taylor

by the US. Ten years later, new US President James Polk offered to purchase New Mexico and California and set the Rio Grande as the new US-Mexico boundary. Mexico refused. Unable to mobilize support for war against Mexico, Polk sent General Zachary Taylor to parade up and down the disputed border until the Mexicans fired upon him.

When news of this skirmish reached Washington, Polk announced to Congress that Mexico had transgressed the US boundary and shed American blood on American soil. Congress declared war on Mexico and was victorious. Thus in 1847 the US secured more than a million square miles of new territory including what is now the Southwestern US from Texas to

California, with the Rio Grande as the new border. The war mobilized popular support for a weak president, boosted US nationalism and gained vast new territories in which slavery was allowed.[18]

Precipitating the Spanish-American War through the Sinking of the *Maine* (1898)

In 1898, Cuba was poised to win its wars of independence from Spanish colonial rule. The US government agreed to respect Cuba's sovereignty. On the pretext of protecting the safety of US citizens, the battleship *Maine* was sent to Havana Harbor. On February 15, 1898, a huge explosion sank the *Maine*, killing 266 members of its crew. The *Maine's* captain cautioned against concluding this was an enemy attack, because the explosion was internal and probably caused by coal dust igniting weapons stored dangerously near the vessel's coal bunker. But US newspapers seized opportunistically upon the situation, launching an intensive campaign to convince the public the *Maine* had been blown up by enemy agents of Spain. No shred of evidence was produced to prove this, which did not deter stridently escalating calls in the newspapers for war, based on lurid anti-Spain stories of pure invention. On April 25, 1898, the US Congress declared war on Spain. Within four months the US had replaced Spain as the colonial power in the Philippines, Guam and Puerto Rico, and had devised a special status for Cuba. Historian Howard Zinn says the "splendid little war" (as it was dubbed by future secretary of state John Hay) ushered American military and economic power onto the world scene and began the new century of American domination.[19]

The Sinking of the *Lusitania* brings the US into WWI (1915)

In 1915, Europe had been embroiled in war for a year, but the US public did not wish to be involved, and President Woodrow Wilson had declared US neutrality. On May 7, 1915, a German submarine sank a British passenger ship, the *Lusitania*, killing 1,198, including 128 Americans. US newspapers aroused outrage against Germany for ruthlessly killing defenseless US citizens and the US began to be drawn into the war. In April 1917, the US declared war on Germany.

Winston Churchill

Many histories of WWI detailed the ruse. Commander Joseph Kenworthy in his 1928 book *Freedom of the Seas* wrote: "The *Lusitania* was deliberately sent at considerably reduced speed into an area where a U-boat was known to be waiting and with her escorts withdrawn. Patrick Beesly's history of First World War British naval intelligence notes: "No effective steps were taken to protect the Lusitania." The U-boat commanders knew the *Lusitania's* route and that the ship contained six million rounds of US ammunition bound for Britain. Even though two ships had been sunk on its path only days earlier, no escort destroyers were assigned and the *Lusitania* was not specifically warned of any threats. Winston Churchill was leader of the British Admiralty. He wrote in his First World War memoirs, *World Crisis:* "The maneuver which brings an ally into the field is as serviceable as that which wins a great battle."[20]

The German Reichstag Fire (1933)

The "classic" false-flag operation strategy — attack a symbol of your own power and frame your enemy — worked effectively for Adolf Hitler. In the period following its defeat in the First World War, Germany was governed under the constitution of the Weimar Republic. The Nazi party was striving to seize power and Hitler, its leader, had recently been sworn in as Chancellor of a new coalition government.

On the night of February 27, 1933, the Reichstag Building, seat of the German Parliament, erupted in flames, three days before a federal election. The cause appeared to be arson. Police quickly found Marinus van der

Lubbe, an unemployed Dutch Communist brick-
layer who had recently arrived in Germany, cow-
ering naked behind the building. Hitler and
Goering soon arrived, declared at the scene that
the fire had been set by the Communists and had
that party's leaders arrested.

Historians, including William L. Shirer in his
masterpiece *Rise and Fall of the Third Reich,* have
documented that the fire was set by the Nazis
themselves. They set up van der Lubbe as their patsy.
Hitler rapidly took advantage of the situation,
declaring a state of emergency and pressuring
President Hindenburg to sign a decree abolishing
most of the human rights provisions of the
Constitution.

After an unfair trial, van der Lubbe was executed by beheading and the Communist Party
was banned. The public was bombarded with
propaganda, leading most Germans to believe
the Nazi official story: that the Communists had
torched the building. In the political campaign

Adolf Hitler

that followed, Hitler was able to exploit the fear of Communism to eventually seize power, whereupon he proceeded to embark upon preparations to precipitate the Second World War. The technique of deception
used in this false-flag operation has become so paradigmatic that operations in our era, such as 9/11 itself and its spinoffs (including the Madrid
and London train bombings) are sometimes referred to as "Reichstag
Fires."[21]

The Japanese "Sneak Attack" on Pearl Harbor (1941)

US President Franklin Delano Roosevelt personally supported British
Prime Minister Winston Churchill, Canadian Prime Minister Mackenzie
King and others whose countries had declared war on Germany after Hitler
invaded Poland in 1939 (on a false-flag op pretext — that Polish soldiers
had attacked a German radio station). But Roosevelt faced the problem of

fascistic US elites who wanted the US to stay out of the war because they liked Hitler. Also, the majority of the US public for historical reasons — wishing to avoid entanglement in European wars — was also opposed to US involvement. Roosevelt knew a Japanese attack on the US would galvanize his public and bring the US into conflict with Italy and Germany, the other two Axis Powers with which Japan was allied.

The most painstakingly researched book on Pearl Harbor is Robert B. Stinnett's *Day of Deceit: The Truth About FDR and Pearl Harbor.* Based on 17 years' research and tens of thousands of previously unreleased documents, US Navy veteran Stinnett proves that Roosevelt successfully arranged for Japan to strike US facilities at the cost of 2,460 US lives.

Roosevelt secretly assigned a top aide to draw up what became an eight-point plan to provoke Japan. Cutting down Japan's oil supplies was part of the plan and was carried out, as were the other seven points. The keys to the plan were that "the US should not fire the first shot" and that US losses should be great enough to inflame public opinion. By August 6, 1941, Japanese forces were poised to attack the US naval base at Pearl Harbor in Hawaii, where the Pacific fleet had been purposefully exposed to them. The

US high command had broken all the Japanese codes (although the Japanese did not know this) and could have prevented the attack, but Roosevelt made sure it was unopposed.

On December 7, 1941, Japanese bombers attacked Pearl Harbor. This was immediately characterized as a "sneak attack" and by FDR famously as "a day of infamy." The US public was outraged. The day before Pearl Harbor only 14 percent of the US public supported the USA entering the war, according to the Gallup Poll. The day after, one million men volunteered to fight in that war. Two days after that, the

Franklin Delano Roosevelt

US was at war with the Axis Powers.[22]

Canada's Wannabe Pearl Harbor
The Shelling of the Estevan Light (1942)

Canada entered World War II in 1939, but there was little enthusiasm for compulsory conscription (forced service in the armed forces). Canadian Prime Minister Mackenzie King needed soldiers but a significant portion of the Canadian population, especially in the province of Quebec, was opposed to conscription. The conscription controversy was raging in Parliament. King needed a galvanizing event to swing Canadians more fully behind it. There was also some public unhappiness about King's orders for the internment of Japanese Canadians. King believed the patriotism of Japanese Canadians was in question and wanted to cement that idea in the public mind to justify internment.

William Lyon Mackenzie King

King had long enjoyed a close relationship with US President Franklin Delano Roosevelt, who vacationed in Canada. Both were devious and had conspired together on other fronts. Nothing would be written down. By 1942 both US and Japanese submarines were patrolling the US and Canadian West Coasts. On the evening of June 20, 1942, the pastoral peace of Estevan Point, two thirds of the way up the west coast of Vancouver Island, was shattered. The keeper of the Estevan Light lighthouse, Robert Lally, wrote in his log that two "warships" appeared offshore and fired at the structure. About 20 shells landed, all harmlessly. The Canadian commander on the West Coast took 30 minutes to sound the alarm, and Canadian vessels did not reach Estevan Point until the next morning; the vessels involved in the shooting had long vanished. All subsequent Canadian government reports refer to "a lone submarine."

A major anomaly involved the placement of the guns on the one (or two) submarines involved in the attack, which certainly took place.

American subs all had their guns forward of the conning tower; Japanese subs' guns were aft. The guns of the sub or subs involved were forward. News of the attack, the first on Canadian soil since 1812, gave a heartening lift to King's concerns. His illegal and racist internment of Japanese-Canadians was additionally justified in the minds of many, and the argument for conscription was boosted.[23]

Operation Gladio in Post World War Two Europe (1946-)

In August 1990, after the Cold War had ended, Italian Prime Minister Giulio Andreotti confirmed to the Italian Senate that there had been a secret stay-behind army code-named Gladio — the sword — following the Second World War. A June 1, 1959, Italian secret service (SIFAR) document revealed that SIFAR had been running the secret army with the support of NATO in close collaboration with the CIA. These stay-behind armies were all over Western Europe. They originally were supposed to be

A once top-secret Pentagon field manual, *FM 30-31B*, advised US military officers to cooperate with the secret services of European countries in "internal stabilisation operations" and to fight what the Pentagon perceived as the "communist" or "socialist" threat. The manual states: "There may be times when Host Country Governments show passivity or indecision in the face of communist subversion and according to the interpretation of the US secret services do not react with sufficient effectiveness. Most often such situations come about when the revolutionaries temporarily renounce the use of force and thus hope to gain an advantage, as the leaders of the host country wrongly consider the situation to be secure. US army intelligence must have the means of launching special operations which will convince Host Country Governments and public opinion of the reality of the insurgent danger."

The manual concludes, "Only those persons who are acting against the revolutionary uprising shall know of the involvement of the US Army in the internal affairs of an allied country. The fact that the involvement of forces of the US military goes deeper, shall not become known under any circumstances."

in place in case of a Soviet invasion, a trumped-up threat in itself. Later they were employed to mount false-flag operations to demonize Leftists. Italy suffered from numerous "terrorist attacks" during the Cold War, starting on December 12, 1969, when four bombs exploded in public places in Rome and Milan. The terror was deceitfully blamed on Communists and the extreme left. Further bombings followed, culminating on August 2, 1980, when a massive explosion ripped through the Bologna railway station, killing 85 people and seriously wounding a further 200.

Admitted terrorist bomber Vincenzo Vinciguerra, convicted May 31, 1972

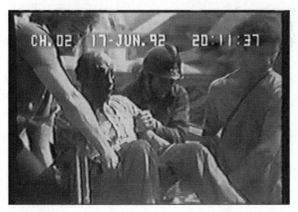

One of the 200 wounded in the bombing (by the right-wing) of a crowded train station in Bologna in 1980. Blamed on the left-wing, the blast killed 85.

Right-wing extremist Vincenzo Vinciguerra was found guilty of a car bomb terror attack in Peteano, May 31, 1972. From behind prison bars he explained: "You had to attack civilians, the people, women, children, innocent people, unknown people far removed from any political game. The reason was quite simple. They were supposed to force these people, the Italian public, to turn to the State to ask for greater security. This is the political logic that lies behind all the massacres and the bombings which remain unpunished, because the State cannot convict itself or declare itself responsible for what happened."[24]

The Pentagon's "Operation Northwoods" (1962)

In 1962, John F. Kennedy was US President, Robert McNamara was Secretary of Defense, and General Lyman Lemnitzer was Chairman of the US Joint Chiefs of Staff. The CIA had just failed in its illegal Bay of Pigs invasion of Cuba and US policy towards Cuba was in public disarray.

General Lyman Lemnitzer

In his book *Body of Secrets*, James Bamford writes: "JFK [decided] to back away from military solutions to the Cuban problem." But Lemnitzer, the CIA and others at the top remained obsessed with Cuba. Writes Bamford, "As the Kennedy brothers appeared to suddenly 'go soft' on Cuba, Lemnitzer could see his opportunity to invade ... quickly slipping away. Lemnitzer and the other chiefs knew there was only one option left that would ensure their war. They would have to trick the American public and world opinion."

Their proposed plan, "Operation Northwoods," which had the written approval of every member of the Joint Chiefs of Staff, contained many "suggestions," all astonishing in their criminality. The plan called for various false-flag actions, including simulated or real domestic terror attacks (such as hijacked planes) on US soil. It called for innocent people to be shot on American streets; for boats carrying refugees fleeing Cuba to be sunk on the high seas; for a wave of violent terrorism to be launched in Washington, DC, Miami, and elsewhere. People would be framed for bombings they did not commit; planes would be hijacked; a plane to be supposedly shot down by the Cubans loaded with US passengers would provide "casualty lists in US newspapers [which] would cause a helpful wave of national indignation." Another suggestion was that, should the rocket due to lift astronaut John Glenn into space on its launch from Cape Canaveral explode accidentally, fake forensic evidence should be in place "to prove the Cubans did it."

Using phony manufactured evidence, all of these atrocities would be blamed on Castro, thus giving Lemnitzer and his cabal the excuse, as well as the public and international backing, they needed to launch their war. President Kennedy, thankfully, did not approve the plan. But such documented history of what the Pentagon is capable of scheming is alone justification for suspicion of US government complicity in the events of 9/11.[25]

The Gulf of Tonkin Incident and the Launch of the Vietnam War (1964)

In 1964, supposedly concerned about the expansion of Communism in Southeast Asia, the US government was looking for a way to justify launching military action to counter it. Once again, they reached for the false-flag strategy. Through the media, the public learned that in the Gulf of Tonkin, North Vietnamese torpedo boats are reported to have attacked the US destroyer *Maddox*. The Associated Press reports that "... three PT boats, identified by Secretary of State Dean Rusk as North Vietnamese, attacked [the US ships] ..."

Later, a second US destroyer was attacked, according to news reports. No US sailor suffers a scratch but the American public is outraged. President Lyndon Johnson goes on television to ask the country to support war action. Two days later the Tonkin Gulf Resolution is approved by the US House of Representatives, unanimously, then by the Senate, 88 to 2. The resolution becomes the entire justification for the United States' war against Vietnam. Before it was over 58,000 American soldiers and 3 million Vietnamese died.

Lyndon B. Johnson

It now is known the Gulf of Tonkin attacks never took place. One source for this is former Admiral James Stockdale, in his book *In Love and War*. On the night in question, Stockdale was at the controls of a fighter jet flying cover for the two destroyers. He saw nothing. Another source is Ben Bradlee, much respected former managing editor of the *Washington Post*. Bradlee at the inaugural James Cameron Lecture in England in April 1987, stated: "The 'facts' behind this critically important resolution were quite simply ... lies." He called the Tonkin Gulf fraud "one of the big lies, that change history."[26]

The *Achille Lauro* Hijacking Incident (1985)

On October 7, 1985, according to what the world was told by officialdom and the media, four heavily armed Palestinian terrorists hijacked the Italian cruise ship *Achille Lauro*, which was carrying more than 400 passengers and crew, off the coast of Egypt. The hijackers demanded that Israel free 50 Palestinian prisoners. They killed a disabled American tourist, 69 year-old Leon Klinghoffer, allegedly simply because he was Jewish, throwing him overboard in his wheelchair. After a two-day drama the hijackers surrendered in exchange for a pledge of safe passage. They were flown towards Tunisia aboard an Egyptian commercial airliner which was intercepted by US jets and forced to land at a NATO base in Sicily. The hijackers were arrested by the Italians after a disagreement between US and Italian authorities.

The episode was part of continuing "low-intensity" warfare between the Palestine Liberation Organization and the state of Israel. Public opinion was very negative towards the actions of the "terrorists." However, in his book *Profits of War: Inside the Secret US-Israeli Arms Network*, former Israeli Defence Force (IDF) arms dealer Ari Ben-Menashe reported that the 1985 hijacking of the Achille Lauro by "Palestinian terrorists" was ordered

Disabled American Jew Leon Klinghoffer was killed in Mossad false-flag operation. Abu'l Abbas was the agent.

and funded by Mossad, the Israeli intelligence service. Ben-Menashe revealed that Israeli intelligence organizations regularly engaged in "black operations," espionage activity designed to portray Palestinians and others in the worst possible light. He wrote that "the 'Palestinian' attack on the *Achille Lauro* ... was, in fact, an Israeli 'black' propaganda operation to show what a deadly, cutthroat bunch the Palestinians were." According to Ben-Menashe, Israeli spymasters arranged the attack through Abu'l Abbas, "who, to follow such orders was receiving millions from Israeli intelligence officers posing as Sicilian dons. Abbas ... gathered a team to attack the cruise ship. The team was told to make it bad, to show the world what lay in store for other unsuspecting citizens if Palestinian demands were not met." In April 1996, Abbas returned to Gaza and apologized for the hijacking. The apology was rejected by the United States government and the family of Leon Klinghoffer, who insisted that he be brought to justice.[27]

The Bombing of the La Belle Discotheque, Berlin (1986)

In 1985, US President Ronald Reagan claimed Libya supported terrorism, especially through the Abu Nidal group purported to be behind the Rome and Vienna airport attacks of December 27, 1985. Reagan wished to intimidate nations that "supported terrorists."

The CIA had failed to assassinate Libyan leader Colonel Moammar Ghaddafi. The US sent carrier forces near Libya in March 1986, attempting to bait Libya into skirmishes, but European reaction to the US aggression was very negative.

Then, on April 5, 1986, a bomb exploded in the West Berlin La Belle discotheque. Two American servicemen were killed and more than 200 other patrons and US servicemen wounded. The US claimed to have intercepted cable transmissions from Libyan agents in East Germany involved in the attack. President Reagan then ordered an air strike against Libya with Gaddhafi the main target. The operation had been planned in advance and was codenamed Operation El Dorado Canyon. Several bombs exploded near Ghaddafi's tent, missing him but killing his 15 month old daughter.

The "Libya did it" theory fell apart years later. A West German intelligence official who later saw the US cable evidence said he and his colleagues were "very critical and skeptical" of US intelligence blaming the Libyans. In November 1997, five defendants were on trial in a Berlin court for their alleged involvement in the La Belle attack. A German Public

Television (ZDF) documentary broadcast August 25, 1998, presented compelling evidence that some of the main suspects worked for American and Israeli intelligence. Many "secret service intrigues" involved in the La Belle bombing presented "a task for the Berlin court that is almost insoluble. But one thing is certain, the American legend of Libyan state terrorism can no longer be maintained," reported ZDF. Stasi (East German police) defector Colonel Frank Weigand reported a phone conversation between a high-ranking West German intelligence officer and the Berlin official responsible for the La Belle investigation. When pressed for his conclusion, Weigand told the West German officer, "Well, when I add it all up, I think the Yanks did this thing themselves." [28]

Ronald Reagan

Kuwaiti Incubator Baby Deception and the Launch of the First Gulf War (1990-91)

On August 2, 1990, Iraq attacked Kuwait, claiming the Kuwaitis were slant-drilling into Iraq's oil fields. US President George Herbert Walker Bush pushed for a land war against Iraq, but polls showed the US public split 50-50 on the idea.

Then in October 1990, came the electrifying eyewitness testimony before a congressional committee, from a 15-year-old Kuwaiti girl called "Nurse Nayirah." The claim was she could not be identified for fear of reprisals. Tearfully, she told the committee, "While I was there I saw the Iraqi soldiers come into the hospital with guns. They took the babies out of incubators, took the incubators, and left the children to die on the cold floor." Her voice cracked as she wiped a tear from her eye.

The US public was outraged. The result? Support for the land war soared. It was a turning point. In January 1991, Operation Desert Storm was launched. An estimated 135,000 Iraqis were killed, and another 1 million Iraqis, many children and the elderly, subsequently died as a result of ten years of economic sanctions imposed by the US. There was only one problem with this. There never were any incubator baby deaths. Not one.

The CBC's flagship investigative program, *the fifth estate*, revealed the girl to be the Kuwaiti ambassador's daughter, given her lines and coached in acting by the giant American public relations firm Hill & Knowlton. This was just one phase in a $10 million joint US-Kuwaiti campaign to deceive the American public into supporting the war against Iraq. The lie was repeated incessantly by President Bush and many others. The telling of this lie was one key element of an out-and-out conspiracy participated in by many people, consisting of fake organizations, false documents, fraud and disinformation. Until *the fifth estate* program, no media exercised skepticism.

Daughter of Kuwaiti ambassador to the US: trained in acting, involved in a major deception, helping trigger operation Desert Storm.

In the January-February 2006 issue of *Extra!*, a journalism review published by FAIR (Fairness and Accuracy In Reporting), the Kuwaiti incubator false-flag op was named one of the top 20 stories of the 20 previous years "that made a major impact on society."[29]

P2OG "Super-Intelligence Support Activity" (2002)

An astonishing admission was buried deep in a story in the *Los Angeles Times* of October 27, 2002. Military analyst William Arkin detailed the vast expansion of secret armies being massed by Defense Secretary Donald Rumsfeld.

Along with other members of the Bush administration, Rumsfeld continually warns there will be more terrorist attacks against the American people, and against civilization at large. These officials can be confident of this because of their plans, as reported by Arkin. These plans are to create a "Super-Intelligence Support Activity" agency that will "bring together CIA and military covert action, information warfare, intelligence, and cover and deception." The "Proactive, Pre-emptive Operations Group (P2OG) "will carry out secret missions designed to 'stimulate reactions' among terrorist groups, provoking them into committing violent acts which would then expose them to 'counterattack' by US forces."

Put into plain language, this would be planning to use "cover and deception" and secret military operations to provoke terrorist attacks on innocent people. Fomenting the deliberate murder of innocent people would be a tactic to further the geopolitical ambitions of the Bush administration. And, after they have successfully provoked "terrorists" into action, the US can justify measures against the "states/sub-state actors accountable" for "harboring" the gangs. As the classified Pentagon program puts it: "Their sovereignty will be at risk." P2OG is, then, a plan and structure to carry out, on a systematic basis, false-flag operations anywhere in the world.[30]

Donald Rumsfeld

The Madrid Train Bombings (2004)

In 2003, the right-wing conservative government of President Jose Maria Aznar threw Spain's support strongly behind the invasion of Iraq, becoming the United States' second most important member, after Great Britain, of the so-called "coalition of the willing." On July 11, 2003, the Spanish cabinet approved the sending of 1,300 combat troops to Iraq. This decision was very unpopular with the Spanish people. As the Iraq war developed, opposition to it mounted, with increasing demands being made for Spain's complete withdrawal. As the general election of March 14, 2004 approached, with the Socialist Party gaining strength because of its clear opposition to the war, the Invisible Government was faced with the prospect of losing its second most important coalition member unless something was done to trick the Spanish people into complying with the Iraq war agenda.

Right on cue, three days before the election, a series of ten coordinated explosions occurred aboard four Madrid commuter trains during the morning rush hour. The "attacks" were the deadliest "terrorist assault" against civilians in Europe since the Lockerbie bombing in 1988, and the worst such event in modern Spanish history. The number of victims — 191 confirmed dead, 1,460 wounded — far surpassed Spain's previous worst

bombing incident at a Barcelona supermarket in 1987, which killed 21 and wounded 40. Responsibility for that bombing was claimed by the Basque separatist group ETA.

The Aznar government initially blamed the ETA for the new bombings, though this accusation was soon dropped when the ETA denied responsibility. On March 12, more than two million people (from a population of four million) took to Madrid's streets to protest the bombings. Soon, a "Muslim connection" was bolstered by the discovery of a van parked outside the rail station of Alcala de Henares containing audiotapes of verses of the Koran, clothes, cell phones and copper detonators. An undetonated bomb was also found in a backpack outside El Pozo station providing clues away from ETA. A London-based Arabic newspaper received an e-mail from someone claiming to be from al Qaeda, and, on March 13, a Madrid television station received a videotape of a man speaking Arabic with a Moroccan accent. Both claimed that responsibility rested with al Qaeda in Europe. On May 24, 2004, seven suspects were arrested, three of them Moroccan citizens. More arrests were made, but on April 3, 2004, as police were moving in to arrest more suspects in an apartment building, the suspects allegedly blew themselves up to avoid apprehension.

The Spanish people, however, delivered the Invisible Government a major blow. Convinced the Aznar government was concealing information, and angry about its support for the Iraq war, voters in the March 14 general election chose a new Socialist government under Jose Luiz Rodriguez Zapatero, who had campaigned to withdraw Spain from Iraq. Some curious anomalies emerged. In April, the Spanish interior ministry said it was investigating reports that two suspects in the train bombings were police informants.

Those skeptical of the official story point out that just as in the 9/11 event, much of the found evidence could have been planted to frame an al Qaeda connection. The bombs were all allegedly placed in backpacks or duffel bags, and systematically loaded aboard the four trains as they passed through the Alcala de Henares station. But no video surveillance has been released or eyewitnesses brought forward to prove this assertion.

No analysis of blast damage patterns has been released, leading to questions as to whether the bombs were in fact placed under the trains while they were in their maintenance yards, rather than in bags dropped inside the carriages. One published photograph of a damaged carriage shows a large section of what appears to be flooring blown upwards, with one end resting on the edge of the roof. Internet writer Joe Vialls reported that the train disabled outside the Atocha station had its back broken in two places. Backpack charges placed on top of the internal floor would be incapable of shattering the strong longitudinal steel support girders running the entire length of the chassis of each carriage.[31]

The Beslan School Massacre (2004)

In 2004, although no longer the Soviet Union, Russia led by President Vladimir Putin is still a world power. It is a fully armed nuclear state, a permanent member of the UN Security Council, and a major world oil producer. It is a dominant influence in the Caucasus region, which is rich in petroleum reserves, and where it also faces a determined Islamic independence movement in the province of Chechnya. Russia is one of only two states (the other being, increasingly, China) capable of limiting or halting the American empire's drive for total world domination. While the Cold War has been officially over since the rapprochement between Ronald Reagan and Mikhail Gorbachev, Russia and America are anything but natural allies, and the unilateralism of America's response to 9/11 is of great concern to Russia.

Beginning in August 2004, Russia experienced a wave of terrorism, including the sabotage of two passenger airliners, the bombing of a Moscow subway station and the Beslan school crisis. On September 1, 2004, at Middle School Number One in the Russian town of Beslan in North Ossetia, a group of about 30 armed terrorists, both men and women, took hundreds of school children and adults hostage, after an exchange of gunfire with police. The attackers moved the hostages to the school gymnasium the first day, and mined the gym and the rest of the building with improvised explosives rigged with tripwires. They threatened to kill hostages and blow up the school if government forces attacked. On the second day, negotiations proved unsuccessful and the terrorists refused even to allow basic supplies to be taken in for the hostages.

On September 3, the third day of the standoff, shots broke out between the hostage-takers and Russian security forces. An unexplained explosion, followed by gunfire, led the hostage-takers to set off their bombs. A chaotic

Evidence indicates that the Beslan slaughter was a US-UK-inspired false-flag operation; a proxy war to neutralize Russia as a world power.

battle broke out and a massive level of force was used, including tanks and flame throwers. According to official data, 344 civilians were killed, 186 of them children, and hundreds more were wounded.

Confusion and contradiction surrounded official accounts of the event, the actual identities of the hostage-takers, their motives for the attack, the identity of their controllers and accomplices, whether any escaped and if so how, and whether there was any government complicity in the attack. The government came under severe criticism for its handling of the crisis.

On September 6, 2004, President Putin met with 30 representatives of the world press. Accounts were published in the *Guardian* of London, *The Independent* and *Le Monde*. Putin denied there was any link between Russian policy in Chechnya and the hostage-taking in Beslan. Rather, he said, the recent wave of terrorism represented proxy warfare against Russia instigated by the governments of the United States and Great Britain, intended to destabilize and neutralize Russia as a world power.

Putin's comments were extended in an interview with his official Chechen adviser, Aslambek Aslakhanov, who said, "The terrorists who seized the school in Beslan, North Ossetia, took their orders from abroad. They were talking with people not from Russia, but from abroad. They were being directed." He said the hostage-takers were not Chechen. When he spoke to them, by phone, in Chechen, they demanded that he speak Russian.

An unsigned commentary by the Russian news agency KMnews.ru blamed the Beslan school massacre squarely on US and British intelligence agencies. Putin accused the United States and Great Britain of a double standard in their "war on terror" in that they harbor individuals from Chechnya that the Russians consider terrorists. In the wake of Putin's remarks, prominent Russian commentators discussed the recent terror campaign against Russia as a possible *casus belli* for a new East-West conflict. Several commentaries reaffirmed the key statement that international terrorism has no independent existence, but functions only as "an instrument," wielded by powerful international circles committed (in part) to the early destruction of Russia as a nuclear-armed power.

These commentators accused the US of conspiring to expel Russia from the Caucasus region so that its oil wealth may be brought under total Anglo-American control. The great Anglo-Saxon fear is that Russia will forge an alliance against US-UK world domination and lead the way to the use of the euro as payment for world oil transactions. This would precipitate an economic collapse in the West and signal the end of US-UK world hegemony.

The attack on the Beslan school, instigated, according to Putin, by Washington and London, may have been a major miscalculation. The Russian press is now openly denouncing Washington and London as centers for terrorist control. The more that is published and broadcast about the nature of false flag operations directed against Russia, the less emotional power future such operations will carry.[32]

London 7/7, Courtesy of
"Her Majesty's Terrorist Network" (2005)

By early summer 2005, the Invisible Government's global agenda was bogging down in England. Pressures for democratic reform of the post-9/11 "endless war" and of the global robbery/domination agenda were filling the headlines.

In January 2005 the BBC re-broadcast its 2004 production of "The Power of Nightmares," a three-part series exposing that the power of al

Qaeda to threaten the West had been greatly exaggerated, and that fear of this "nightmare" had been manufactured for purposes of political manipulation. The series' growing popularity suggested growing public disbelief in the official story of 9/11 and the "war on terrorism."

Opposition to Britain's participation in the Iraq war and disapproval of Prime Minister Blair was becoming a major political force. Organizers of the March 19, 2005 London protest march claimed participation by more than 150,000 people. On July 10, 2005, the *Mail* published a story stating that the Ministry of Defence had been drafting plans which would pull British forces out of Iraq and Afghanistan.

On May 1, 2005, *The Sunday Times* published the "Downing Street Memos" — leaked confidential minutes of the British prime minister's war cabinet meeting of July 23, 2002. These revealed that President Bush had already decided to invade Iraq, despite the complete lack of evidence that Saddam Hussein had any weapons of mass destruction, and that there was no legal grounds for invasion. The memo reported that, to circumvent this, the intelligence and the facts were being "fixed" around the policy to "justify" military action.

The May 5, 2005 general election returned the Labor Party to government, but with a substantially reduced majority.

Meanwhile, in anticipation of the 31st G8 summit meeting in Scotland scheduled for early July, 2005, there was major activism calling for the elimination of African and Third World debt, and massive demonstrations against the G8's economic policies of "structural adjustment," privatization and resource theft. On July 2, 2005 more than 200,000 people marched in Edinburgh to "Make Poverty History," the largest demonstration ever in Scotland. At the same time, the hugely publicized Live 8 concerts focused the campaign to put maximum

Tony Blair

pressure on world leaders to increase and improve aid and negotiate fairer trade rules in the interests of poor countries. Inaction on global warming was another major source of protest.

Just as the forces of global democracy had been "getting out of hand" with the massive anti-corporate globalization protests, the Invisible Government badly needed another 9/11-style "terrorist" attack to clear the headlines of democratic reform pressures besetting them on every side. On July 7, 2005, they delivered.

A series of four blasts struck London's public transport system during the morning rush hour. Three bombs exploded within 50 seconds of each other on three London underground trains, and a fourth bomb exploded less than an hour later on a bus in Tavistock Square. Fifty-six people were killed in the attacks, with another 700 injured. The incident was the deadliest single act of "terrorism" in the United Kingdom since the 1988 bombing of Pan Am Flight 103 and the deadliest bombing in London since the Second World War. It came one month after the terrorist threat level had been lowered and showed similarities in modus operandi to the Madrid train bombing in March 11, 2004.

Diary of 9/11 and the Media

A Tale of Two Londons

July 7, 2005, London, Ontario, Canada — By coincidence I'm in this other London on the day of the London, England bombings. This evening my DVD The Great Conspiracy: The 9/11 News Special You Never Saw will be screened at the public library during a meeting sponsored by four peace and student groups. At 11:10 this morning I'm scheduled to be a phone-in guest on the Morris and Meagan show on London's CJBK news talk radio station. It's a 9 a.m. to noon program. I want to hear the show opening and guest lineup and get a general feeling for their show, so I tune in around 10 after 9. That's when I learn of the London bombings.

An odd thing occurs about 10 minutes into my interview. CJBK lost its transmission signal around the time I was expressing my opinion that the bombings were not the work of al Qaeda or such at all, but most likely the work of black operators in Western intelligence. The show's producer came on the line during a commercial break to tell me of the loss of signal. I asked him how often this happened. "Never," he replied.

(Five days later, on July 12, I was being interviewed by Meria Heller for her webcast program seen in 60 countries. About 10 minutes in, a listener contacted her on Yahoo! Messenger to report that she was "off the air." Meria told me this had not happened in four years, since shortly after 9/11. A few minutes later her Yahoo! Messenger went down.)

This day I place a call to Webster G. Tarpley, author of *9/11 Synthetic Terror: Made in USA* to get some information. While we're on the line he tells me that when he was on Pacifica's WBAI New York for a fund-raising drive, a short time before, "all the telephones went haywire." The station staff had to improvise in order to take calls and pledges. As the "coincidences" piled up I wondered whether covert operators were sending signals to the 9/11Truth movement and to those media that would give us time, that they were monitoring us and letting us know they could escalate from "shots across the bow" to more serious disruption. I took these surveillance and disruption events to be positive. I took them to mean that the dark forces of the Anglo-American establishment now considered the 9/11Truth movement more than a minor irritant to be monitored, but perhaps a major irritant to be disabled. This would mean that their masters, with their superior psycho-political measuring instruments, had begun to see us as a threat. This, if true, would be the equivalent of a campaign victory in a conventional war.

The four bombing attacks had the immediate effect of riveting public attention. On the July 7 edition of *Fox News* "Fox and Friends," host Brian Kilmeade said approvingly, "I think this works to our advantage, in the Western world's advantage, for people to experience something like this together ..." The bombings did indeed completely clear the front pages of any further mention of democratic reform and put the elite's favorite control agenda item, "terrorism," back in the headlines along with the familiar calls to restrict civil liberties to "counter the terrorist threat."

Police investigators immediately identified four young Muslim men, whom they alleged to be suicide bombers, with the attacks attributed to

Islamic paramilitary organizations based in the United Kingdom. Blame and fear of al Qaeda were immediately given blanket coverage.

Contradictions and reversals in the official stories emerged rapidly. First the explosions in the Underground were attributed to a "power surge;" then to bomb attacks. First, visiting Israeli politician Binyamin Netanyahu had been warned to stay in his hotel to avoid the attacks; then he hadn't; and then he had. First, the explosions had been random; then they had been set off with coordinated military precision. First, they had been military grade explosives; then they were home made in a bathtub in Leeds. A previously unknown group, the "Secret Organisation of al-Qaeda in Europe," posted an alleged claim of responsibility on an obscure website forum. But the authenticity of this claim collapsed under scrutiny because of inaccuracy in quotation of the Koran and mistranslation of the message.

The four young men all were British residents of Northern England. All bought return rail tickets; they also paid for and displayed long-term car park tickets before boarding a train for London. They were said to have carried the explosives in backpacks rather than wear them strapped to their bodies, the latter being the usual practice for suicide bombers.

They were not heard to cry "God is Great" in Arabic, usually screamed by suicide bombers as they detonate their bombs. They were claimed to be carrying wallets containing their driving licenses, bank cards and other personal ID, which suicide bombers normally remove completely. The wives of two of them were pregnant, giving those two alleged suicide bombers strong reasons for staying alive. Local residents who knew them expressed astonishment that such ordinary and likeable young men could have been involved in such an atrocity.

The most important evidence to emerge was interviews with eyewitnesses to the explosions, which indicated that the bombs must have been placed under the trains and not detonated within the carriages by suicide bombers wearing backpacks. The first eyewitness report of this was Bruce Lait, a victim of the Aldgate Station bombing, who told the *Cambridge Evening News* on July 25, 2005, "The policeman said, 'mind that hole, that's where the bomb was.' The metal was pushed upwards as if the bomb was underneath the train. They seem to think the bomb was left in a bag, but I don't remember anybody being where the bomb was, or any bag."

Further, *Guardian* journalist Mark Honigsbaum talked to eyewitnesses at the Edgeware Road station bombing who told him that "tiles, the covers on the floor of the train, suddenly flew up, raised up." The victims then heard an almighty crash as a train traveling in the opposite direction collided with theirs, clearly indicating that the train had been derailed due to the bomb being placed under the carriage close to the wheels.

On his website, Prisonplanet.com, Texas anti-globalist talk-show host Alex Jones followed the twists and turns of the contradictory reports about the bombings and their investigation emerging from London on a daily basis. His London Bombings Data Page is a comprehensive compilation of the many anomalies and inconsistencies which emerged in the official attempt to pin the blame on Muslim terrorism and exploit the situation for further repression.

He points out many similarities between the London train and bus bombings and the Madrid train bombings of March 11, 2004, and with the false-flag template event of 9/11 itself. As in Madrid, where the initial media reports blamed Basque separatists, the London attacks were blamed on an alleged but previously unknown al Qaeda group.

Also like the Madrid bombings, it emerged that the bombs were far more likely to have been installed under the trains and coordination timers set for them in advance, than loaded in carry-on backpacks. The only way this could be accomplished would be to obtain secure access to the trains while they were still in their maintenance yards — something clearly beyond the capabilities of alleged individual suicide bombers.

In both cases, the alleged bombers were conveniently blown up (in London) or eliminated (in an apartment building shootout with police in Madrid), so they could not be questioned. It was later revealed that key persons involved in both bombings were informants for the security services. Infiltration by an FBI informant is also known to have occurred in the plot to bomb the World Trade Center in New York City in 1993.

As in the 9/11 aircraft hijackings, there were official terrorist attack simulation exercises taking place at the same time as the real attacks. In London, a security firm called Visor Consultants was running an exercise postulating the bombing of subway cars at exactly the same times and at the very same locations that the real bombs went off. The odds against this being simply coincidence are astronomical. The odds for it being a cover exercise to facilitate the real attacks are very favourable.

Also as in 9/11, there was suspicious stock market activity days prior to the attacks indicating advance knowledge of them and allowing large profits to be made through short selling by insiders. In London and Madrid cases there was no official pursuit of those who had made these trades. Just as with 9/11, there was extreme official resistance to conducting any sort of inquiry into the attacks, with an early announcement, made by the Lord Chancellor, Lord Falconer, that there would be no official inquiry.

There was yet another similarity to the Madrid bombings and their suspicious sequels. Shortly after the Madrid bombings the Spanish people caught on that their own government had been involved in the attacks and in a soon-ensuing general election threw out the Aznar regime and demanded the withdrawal of Spanish troops from Iraq. This was a major backfire for the Invisible Government; the same awareness grew rapidly following the London bombings. So much so that a second event had to be staged on July 21, which was "foiled" because the detonators failed to go off and no one was injured. The "bombers" escaped, but by July 29 four Arabic men had been arrested and charged. Clearly this second false-flag op was an attempt to reinforce the official story of the July 7 bombings — that the bad Muslims did it.

The London train bombings, like the Madrid train bombings, were an escalation of sophistication on the part of the Anglo-American black operators. Unlike the case of 9/11, the British authorities within a week had "identified" the four suicide bombers, finding them to all be "British-born." The psywar implication is that now "the enemy" has infiltrated "our society." This is boogeyman stuff along the lines of "a Communist is under your bed." This encourages people to report on "suspicious activities" by their neighbors, an activity now officially encouraged by the British government.

Identifying the "suicide bombers" so quickly, including where they lived, which happened to be not some esoteric location such as the mountains of Afghanistan but right in Holbeck, Leeds, just a short train ride from London, makes the story much more believable — others factors being equal — than the FBI's list of 19 foreign-born villains, in the case of 9/11. The "firefight" following the Madrid bombings, in which "the perpetrators" were subsequently cornered in an apartment and conveniently all blown to bits also was an escalation in sophistication. This made the Madrid bombings more believable than otherwise might be the case.

For those of us in the 9/11 Truth movement, Madrid and London were more of the same, "inside jobs." If the London bombings were authentic, why would the first naming of suspects come from a suspect website? As David Pallister of the *Guardian* reported on July 8, the first claim of responsibility (apart from vague rumors that there was a new organization called European Jihad) was by "The Secret Organization of the al-Qaeda in Europe," posted on an Arabic website, al-qal3ah.com, registered by Qalaah Qalaah in Abu Dhabi and hosted by a server in Houston.

Pallister writes: "The server in Houston has intriguing connections." It is operated by a company called Everyone's Internet, founded by brothers Robert and Roy Marsh in 1998. By 2002 it had an income of US $30 million. Roy Marsh counts among his friends US President George Bush's former sister-in-law, Sharon Bush, and the President's Navy Secretary."

If the London bombings were authentic, why were we told all the suicide bombers were carrying ID? Why would suicide bombers do that? If the London bombings were authentic, why are we told all the ID survived all the bombing? Is that credible? When a person blows himself/herself up with high explosives, aren't that person's body, clothing and personal effects destroyed beyond any possibility of identification except possibly for DNA? Doesn't the ridiculous claim of ID being found intact, or relatively intact, resonate with the "terrorist" passport reported found intact amidst rubble at the World Trade Center site? If the London bombings were authentic, why were the surviving ID documents not immediately shown to the public? If the London bombings were authentic, why did Prime Minister Tony Blair announce immediately, without the "evidence" the police now have "uncovered," that al Qaeda was involved?

Deeper questions again must be asked. Who benefits? Do Osama bin Laden, al Qaeda, Muslims in general, fanatical Muslims, or Arabs in general, benefit? Do China or India benefit? Does communism benefit? Do any other proven or identifiable or erstwhile critics of monopoly capitalism and the Anglo-American project — such as peace and social justice movements, pro-UN organizations, the 9/11 Truth movement, movements dedicated to less militarism, more restrictions on intelligence agencies' covert activities, opponents of the war in Iraq, proponents of conservation especially of oil, etc. — do any of these benefit? How? I cannot think of any benefits for any of these. On the other hand, all are set back by the latest "terrorist attack." If these were real terrorists they would be very stupid ones, incapable of understanding counter-productive behavior. Can generations of them be that dumb?

On the other hand, do Tony Blair and George Bush benefit politically? Yes. Do arms manufacturers, militarism in general? Yes. Security and police forces everywhere, especially "counter-terrorism units?" Yes. Prime ministers and ministers of justice and defense and security? Yes, they can garner plenty of coverage and extra funds for their ministries by climbing aboard the "national security" bandwagon. Does the Anglo-American alliance benefit? Yes, in relation to Middle Eastern powers and India and China. Do proponents of the so-called "war on terrorism," including the military, intelligence agencies everywhere, legislative committees that oversee them, cabinet members responsible for them, benefit? Yes. Corporations that design and manufacture all manner of security and crowd control and surveillance gear? Yes. So-called terrorism and anti-terrorism and counter-terrorism experts, establishment pundits and columnists in the mainstream media? Yes. Yes to all.

Yes to all. Isn't it passing strange, as *Globe and Mail* editorialists are wont to ask, that there is such a long list of proven beneficiaries, who are not suspected of being involved in any way for these events, while the list of alleged perpetrators is so short, and they are suffering as a result of these events?[33]

British False-Flag Anti-Civilian Car Bombing Attack (2005)

On September 19, 2005, just prior to the Kerbala religious festival, two men dressed as Arabs — disguised as members of the militia of rebel Shia cleric Moqtada al-Sadr, the Mehdi Army — and driving an unmarked Toyota Cressida, were stopped by Iraqi police in Basra, southern Iraq. The men opened fire. One policeman was killed and surrounding civilians injured. They were taken to the Basra police station and questioned by an Iraqi judge where it was discovered that they were in fact British soldiers, members of the Special Reconnaissance Regiment, an intelligence and "black-ops" unit of the SAS.

Diary of 9/11 and the Media ⌐⌐⌐⌐ ✍

Not Even Prime Minister Yet and Already Effectively Covering Up State Terror

January 26, 2006, Ottawa, Canada — Today Stephen Harper held his first press conference since being elected Prime Minister designate of the country on Monday. One of the briefest exchanges was also one of the most revealing. Harper was asked whether his government will recognize a Palestinian government that includes Hamas, when Hamas has not renounced violence. Harper said: "A government cannot be considered democratic unless it has renounced violence."

The governments of the US and Great Britain have repeatedly renounced — and denounced — violence, especially "terrorism." Yet they have practiced and continue to practice violent terrorism covertly. The brevity and lack of follow-up of the exchange reflect a lack of knowledge and curiosity on the part of the media concerning just what's involved. Masked entirely not only in this exchange but in almost all journalism is the fact of Western governments engaging routinely in massive, secret, murderous law-breaking.

The media are complicit in the ongoing cover-up of this reality. They seldom address the hypocrisy inherent in statements such as that made by the Prime Minister designate. Governments such as the one he will shortly form use founded or ill-founded charges of terrorism against groups such as Hamas to justify actions against groups such as Hamas. Enough is known of the covert funding and training of "terrorists," past and present (see examples in this chapter) that the media could address it. In fact the media do address it, if it's "them" doing it (or allegedly doing it), not "us." The media simply do not ask about the realities of covert actions.

Today's small reality-masking exchange, taken together with thousands of others, forms a blanket over essential life-and-death information while reinforcing the superficial impression that exchanges such as this one are truthful and meaningful.

* * *

Sheikh Hassan al-Zarqani, a spokesman for the Mehdi Army, said, "What our police found in their car was very disturbing — weapons, explosives, and a remote control detonator. These are the weapons of terrorists. We believe these soldiers were planning an attack on a market or other civilian targets, and thanks be to God they were stopped and countless lives were saved."

Shortly thereafter, British Army representatives arrived and demanded the men be released. This was refused. A few hours later reportedly up to six British tanks, many troops and a helicopter gunship laid siege to the police station, knocking down the walls of the jail and seizing their two soldiers, in the process releasing 150 other prisoners. That this extreme action was taken underscores how anxious the British were to prevent any further interrogation of their operatives and uncontrolled revelation of their covert false flag mission.

A large crowd of local civilians mobilized to defend the jail. A pitched battle ensued with stones, Molotov cocktails and live gunfire. One British soldier was photographed leaping from his tank engulfed in flames, a picture widely published in the mass media around the world as a battle between local Iraqis and the British occupation forces. Omitted in most of the coverage and underplayed where it was mentioned, was the cause of the confrontation: two undercover British soldiers had been caught in the process of covertly planting a bomb to murder civilians while pretending to be Shia militiamen.

Local Iraqi authorities were outraged by this assault, prompting the governor of Basra to describe the action as "barbaric" and to declare the City Council had unanimously decided to end cooperation with the British military. On October 15, 2005 the British government formally apologized to the Iraqi people and government over "mistakes" made by their army unit which stormed the Basra police station. No mention was made of the arrested undercover British SAS soldiers, however, and no investigation was ordered.

This incident reinforced the view, widely held among Iraqis, that the occupation strategy in Iraq was not to establish a democratically elected government but rather, through incessant false-flag black op murder attacks on civilians and religious institutions, to foment hatred amongst the three major ethnic factions — the Shia, the Sunni and the Kurds — in order to partition Iraq into three separate regions constantly embroiled in civil war,

REUTERS © ATEF HASSAN

A British soldier prepares to jump from a burning tank, set ablaze after local Iraqis in Basra tried to stop the rescue of two black-ops agents, September 19, 2005.

unable to overcome the occupation of their country and theft of its natural resources.

This brings us back full circle to the British Army "counterinsurgency" playbook established by Colonel Frank Kitson in his subversive operations against the Mau-Mau in Kenya in the 1950s, and further refined in false-flag operations conducted through British SAS moles inserted into the Irish Republican Army in Ireland in the 1970s.[34]

Conclusion

Leaders of the so-called "war on terror" tell us we are safer as a result of new laws that further restrict our civil liberties; that we are safer because of greater cooperation between police agencies, and stricter border patrols; because of wider and deeper surveillance. At the same time we are told we can never be completely safe from "terrorist attacks," that "the terrorists" are "cunning" and "resourceful," and "ruthless and determined." Warnings and predictions of more "terrorist attacks" are a drumbeat. "It's not a matter of if, but when." That's the favored phrase. And then the supreme contradiction. The next "terrorist attack" occurs, and is used to promote even more "anti-terrorism" measures which are meant to make us safer — but of course more attacks can never be ruled out. It's perfection itself, if the aim is to keep people afraid and malleable, promote the "clash of civilizations," boost armaments and "intelligence" and surveillance budgets and pass more and more restrictive laws to place more and more power into the hands of the corporate national security state. It is an ever-renewing fear campaign, unanswerable because it is contradictory.

The false-flag operation is the most valuable trade secret of rulers. As such it is protected in perpetuity by the most powerful elements in virtually all societies. Even rulers who have not mounted false flag operations conspire to maintain the secrecy of the technique should they need to employ it. The cover-ups of history taken together amount to "control of the past," needed to ensure control of the present and the future. Because so few of us have sufficient intellectual (and more importantly, emotional) self-defenses in place against the psychological power of false-flag ops, the playing field of the oligarchs and the rest of us is sharply tilted. False flag ops are the mainstay of the super ubiquitous so-called "war on terror."

Prisonplanet.com's final summary of all of the available data on the London 7/7 bombings concluded they were conducted by "Her Majesty's Terrorist Network" — that is, the attacks had to have been orchestrated by or with help from the very highest levels of British intelligence. Their purpose was to suppress growing democratic dissent and to terrorize the populace into accepting yet more draconian police state measure to maintain "security" and tighten the invisible government's grip over captive populations "until all pretences of remaining democracy can be dispensed with completely.[35]

Today's end-to-end false-flag ops constitute a synthetic perpetual reality, what Webster G. Tarpley calls an "over-determined reality." Without the public believing that all these horrific events are perpetrated by the "evil folks" the media report them to be, the "war on terror" could not be sustained.

But the media refuse to allow onto the public's radar more than the slightest hints that there's a giant "dumb show" being presented to the world by the Invisible Government through its covert forces and obedient media. The more that people become familiar with the reality of false-flag ops, the less likely the web of deceit can continue to be maintained. As long as the present situation persists, we're pretty well cooked.

Dr. David Ray Griffin:
Modern Day Prophet

For we wrestle not against flesh and blood, but against
principalities, against powers, against the rulers of the
darkness of this world, against spiritual wickedness in
high places."

— Ephesians 6:12 (King James Version)

What's a nice theologian like Dr. David Ray Griffin doing on the cover of *Hustler* magazine?

He's doing what he can to save the planet. In his own words, he's doing what he can "to get the cabal who engineered 9/11 for imperialist and plutocratic reasons stopped before they do still more damage to our country and our planet."

Call that outspokenness, a characteristic of prophets. Moses was no doubt considered "outspoken." Stopping the members of the cabal at the toxic tip of the American Empire could be called visionary, another core characteristic of an authentic prophet. It's often hard for most of us to believe this cabal can be stopped. Its political, financial,

Dr. David Ray Griffin

303

military and covert powers are immense, entrenched and constrained by none of the usual financial, legal or moral considerations. But prophets are as visionary in their optimism about what can be done as they are convinced about the justice of what they believe *must* be done.

It was not, of course, Griffin's picture that was on the cover of *Hustler*'s August 2005 edition. He has a pleasant face, but that's not the kind of image that appeals to the clientele of *Hustler* (sub-title: *Harder and Raunchier Than Ever*). Griffin's cover appearance was confined to the headline "Omissions & Distortions: What the *9/11 Commission Report* Didn't Tell You," referring to an interview *Hustler* conducted with Griffin. The "Coverbabe" for the August issue was blonde and sultry Malibu. Inside the magazine, the five-page interview with Griffin was as revealing as was the photo of Malibu, in a different way.

Griffin has been generous in responding to requests for essays and interviews about 9/11 in such disparate publications as *Zion's Herald, Global Outlook, LA Times Magazine* and *Conversations in Religion and Theology*. And, of course, *Hustler*.

There's a prophetic dimension to Griffin's co-operating with *Hustler*. A prophet must reach out to the masses. However much its detractors bemoan its very existence, *Hustler* has a circulation of a half million, largely among blue collar American men. If this means Griffin seeing his words in print chockablock with cartoons of busty babes expressing themselves in theologically-incorrect language, so be it, in Griffin's view. And is it any stranger than George Bush quoting The Bible on a military base?

Hustler publisher Larry Flynt's defense of First Amendment rights goes beyond his defending publishing what others call pornography. He also defends publishing editorial material challenging the heights (or depths) of establishment lies and hypocrisy. It's a cause Griffin supports. First Amendment rights are among those under assault by the White House. Remember the infamous quote from former White House spokesman Ari Fleischer on September 26, 2001: referring to news organizations — and all Americans — Fleischer said "people have to watch what they say and watch what they do." This runs sadly counter to the First Amendment.

Griffin is not inclined to take the advice of persons in the White House to watch what he says. And Flynt, while hardly a saint, is on the side of the angels when he risks offending his blue collar constituency by questioning the official story of 9/11. The Griffin interview, even though it involved a kind of undressing, encountered some resistance, as we shall see. In the *Hustler* interview, as good an example as any of his many, Griffin strips the fabric of deceit from the body of the 9/11 official story and the mannekin nature of the *The 9/11 Commission Report*. He reveals the naked truth: the official story consists of contradictions, absurdities and impossibilities and *The 9/11 Commission Report*, in endorsing and excusing and embroidering them, is proof of White House involvement.

Titled "What If Everything You Know About 9/11 Is Wrong?" the *Hustler* interview provides Griffin's responses to 11 questions put by writers Bruce David and Carolyn Sinclair. In their introduction they write: "At *Hustler* we believe the murder of 2,986 innocent people demands hard questions and digging deeper. We're especially troubled by the collapse of Building 7, but we're determined to keep an open mind. As such, we sit down with Griffin to discuss what appear to be disturbing inconsistencies with the government's story."

It's an unabashedly softball interview, with questions such as "What are some of the other problems with the official story?" and "If the government did allow or enable the 9/11 attacks, what is the motivation?" This is a refreshing counterbalance to the Big Cold Shoulder from all other large circulation magazines that 9/11Truth activists have received.

Griffin's cooperation with *Hustler* fits with a strategy he has clarified for advancing the cause of 9/11 truth. He recognizes the mainstream media as the central obstacle to getting that truth out (*Hustler* being an oddly honorable exception). In emails he has said the "key thing...is to focus on the lack of credibility of *The 9/11 Commission Report*." He gives three reasons:

1. The news media and the general public have accepted the *9/11 Report* as definitive. Before people will pay attention to alternative accounts of what really happened on 9/11, the 9/11Truth movement needs to show — not merely say — that *The 9/11 Commission Report* is essentially false.

2. Mainstream reporters will be more likely to cover the glaring omissions and distortions within the *9/11 Report* than deal directly with questions of whether the Bush Administration was complicit.

3. If it becomes widely known that the 9/11 Commission has told even a few lies, this awareness would clearly suggest that it — and the corporate media — are trying to cover something up. If so, what?

Following his own advice in the *Hustler* interview, he notes that one set of contradictions deeply implicating the 9/11 Commission in a cover-up is the way the Commission dealt with a series of explanations trotted out by NORAD as to why no military jet interceptors did their assigned job of protecting US airspace on 9/11. "In the first few days we got three different stories about why there were no interceptions," Griffin tells *Hustler*. He then explains the paths of fictionalization detailed in Jo Lynn Sheane's experience (told in Chapter 4).

Hustler readers, through this interview, learn of the absurdity of the official 9/11 story's claim that the Twin Towers and Building 7 of the World Trade Center collapsed through the effects of fire. (See Chapter 2, Exhibits H-K.) For obvious impossibility Griffin points to the collapse of WTC building 7. He restrains his language, characterizing it only as "particularly unusual," but that's within the surreal official story of all the collapsing towers.

In response to a "large volume of reader response" to the interview, *Hustler* created an ongoing 9/11 Readers' Forum. This is noteworthy. Two besetting sins of the media are lack of sufficient follow-up on particular major issues, and lack of sufficient input from readers, listeners and viewers. Most daily newspapers, for instance, no longer publish a full page of letters. Letters increasingly are edited to "McNugget," or sound-bite, length. The first major contribution to *Hustler*'s new feature was a page-long letter from an Oklahoman who distances himself from "conspiracy theorists." *Hustler* cleared a full page for a response from Griffin. "As I have pointed out, people cannot be divided into those who do and do not accept conspiracy theories," Griffin replied, "as illustrated by the fact that [the Oklahoman] began his letter with his own little conspiracy theory." (That was that Griffin's comments were so far-fetched that perhaps Griffin is an FBI infiltrator into the 9/11 Truth movement, positioned to make the movement "look foolish.") On the question of "conspiracy theories," Griffin concludes: "... anyone who accepts the official theory about 9/11 is accepting a conspiracy theory, according to which all the conspirators were Muslim Arabs."

The Oklahoman also questioned Griffin's credentials: "Griffin is a theologian. Does he also have expertise in aviation, physics, explosives, construction science or demolition?" On the surface it appears a fair criticism. Griffin replied: "In criminal trials, juries are regularly asked to make judgments about matters in which they have no expertise. What is needed is the ability to evaluate evidence and draw logical conclusions." He might have added that in the face of the towering anomalies that populate the official story, the main credential needed is honesty — honest examination of the evidence, *then* the application of logic.

Griffin is considerably more than "a nice theologian." He's Professor of Philosophy of Religion and Theology, emeritus, at Claremont School of Theology and Claremont Graduate University in Claremont, California where he remains a co-director of the Centre for Process Studies. He's one of just 60 theologians in the world named in the most recent edition of the *Handbook of Christian Theologians.* His inclusion in this book does not rest, however, on the more than 25 books and 160 essays he wrote previously in philosophy of religion, theology, and philosophy of science. Nor is it related directly to his serving for 17 years as editor of the *State University of New York Series in Constructive Postmodern Thought,* which published 31 volumes.

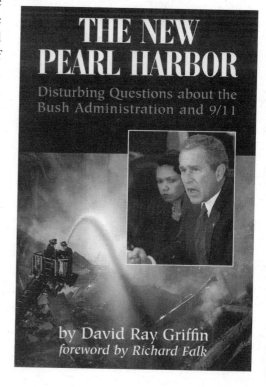

His inclusion is, to begin with, based on the two books he has written about 9/11: *The New Pearl Harbor: Disturbing Questions About the Bush Administration and 9/11,* and *The 9/11 Commission Report: Omissions and Distortions.* These — along with Paul Thompson's *The*

Terror Timeline — have become "Bibles" for the 9/11Truth movement. Griffin's books, because they are relatively compact and organized topically (Thompson's is chronological) are exerting growing influence among reasonable and concerned citizens.

The New Pearl Harbor is so titled for several reasons. A number of publications, such as *Time* magazine, and people, including President Bush (in his diary)[1] have compared 9/11 to Pearl Harbor. Griffin sees another parallel with Pearl Harbor: the restrictions on civil liberties. (Pearl Harbor led to restrictions on the civil liberties of Japanese-Americans and Japanese-Canadians.) As well, those familiar with the call of the neocon Project for a New American Century (PNAC) on page 91 of its September 2000 paper *Rebuilding America's Defenses* for "a catastrophic and catalyzing event — like a New Pearl Harbor" will also see the aptness of Griffin's title.

On the second page of his introduction, Griffin addresses "The Failure of the Press." The public's lack of information about 9/11, noted even by the press itself, is "...due in large part to the fact that [the New York] *Times* and the rest of the mainline press had not authorized investigative reports, through which the public's lack of knowledge might have been overcome." The press, he observes, "has been less aggressive in questioning President Bush about 9/11 than it was in questioning President Clinton about his relationship with Monica Lewinsky, a very trivial matter by comparison."

He also addresses the stance of the Left regarding 9/11, finding it "surprising" that leftist critics of US foreign policy "have for the most part not explored...the possibility of official complicity." In Chapter 5, as we saw, a big part of the explanation is the intransigent refusal by icons of the Left, especially Noam Chomsky, to look at evidence.

By contrast, eight of the 10 chapters of *The New Pearl Harbor* are devoted to evidence. He also lays out eight scenarios to explain 9/11. The most logical scenario, based on the evidence, is that the White House was "a party to planning the attacks." He marshals 24 points of evidence to back that up. The abundance of damning evidence available is reflected in the fact that of the 24 points Griffin lists, 13 are among this book's Exhibits A-Z. (See Chapter 2.) Griffin calls for a full and truly independent investigation.

His second book on 9/11, *The 9/11 Commission Report: Omissions and Distortions,* lays out the case that the makeup of the 9/11 Commission was so manipulated, and the commissioners' report so riddled not only with omissions and distortions but with outright lies that it is *prima facie* evidence in itself of White House involvement in 9/11. He notes that the Commission, contrary to its own stated intention "to provide the fullest possible account of the events surrounding 9/11," instead accepted the official story *a priori* and proceeded to twist, omit, distort and fabricate in order to buttress the official story.

In his introduction, Griffin notes the importance of *The 9/11 Commission Report*. It's widely accepted as providing the definitive story about 9/11. It buttresses the so-called "war on terror." Its recommendations for more money and centralization of intelligence functions have met with considerable success. Griffin says this wide acceptance is unjustified because the Commission was not thorough. It was partisan toward Republicans. An example:

> The Kean-Zelikow Commission, however, could provide this portrayal (of the Bush administration being devoid of the motives below) only by means of numerous omissions and distortions. Besides omitting the Bush administration's reference to the 9/11 attacks as "opportunities," it omitted any discussion of the US Space Command, with its mission to solidify global dominance, and of the PNAC [Project for a New American Century] document, with its suggestion that a new Pearl Harbor would be helpful. It omitted historical facts showing that the Bush administration had plans to attack both Afghanistan and Iraq before 9/11, so that the attacks served as pretext rather than cause. And the Commission distorted US motives in [the attacks on Afghanistan and Iraq], portraying US leaders as interested only in self-defense, human rights, and peace — not oil, bases and geopolitical primacy.[2]

Griffin consistently terms the 9/11 Commission the "Kean-Zelikow Commission" because of the pivotal role of Bush White House insider Philip Zelikow as the Commission's executive director. In Part 2 of his book, Griffin shows, flight by flight, how the military's indefensible non-functionality on 9/11 was defended by the Commission. He shows how the Federal Aviation Administration was chosen to "take the fall." In his final thoughts, Griffin writes:

> In the first part of this [book] I pointed out that the Commission, far from refuting any of the evidence that points in the direction of [complicity by the government] simply ignored most of it and distorted the rest. In the second part, I suggested that the Commission's attempt to defend the US military in particular against this suspicion is at best seriously flawed, at worst a set of audacious lies. Accordingly, the Kean-Zelikow Report, far from lessening my suspicions about official complicity, has served to confirm them. Why would the minds in charge of this final report engage in such deception if they were not trying to cover up very high crimes?[3]

While both of Griffin's books are easy to read, they are also scholarly in the sense of being carefully argued and referenced. Scholarly accomplishment is characteristic of prophets. The four major prophets of the Old Testament, Isaiah, Jeremiah, Ezekiel and Daniel, all have Old Testament books ascribed to them, notes the *Columbia Viking Desk Encyclopedia, Third Edition*. (Over time it will be seen how much similarity there may be between what Griffin and the 9/11Truth movement face, and what Daniel faced in the lions' den.)

Courage is another defining characteristic of prophets. As Orwell wrote: "In a time of universal deceit, telling the truth is a revolutionary act." All the definitions of "prophet" I've been able to find require the candidate be an "inspired teacher." Griffin's colleagues and students at the Claremont School of Theology in Claremont, California, say he's

Dr. Griffin at the National Press Club, July 2005.

that. In the New Testament, *Columbia Viking* has it, "the term prophecy is used of enthusiastic, and presumably inspired, utterance."

Griffin has a knack for hitting the main points of the subject he's addressing in a persuasive, easy to listen to manner, whether he's on campus or community radio, being interviewed by *Hustler,* giving testimony at a session of the annual legislative conference of the Congressional Black Caucus sponsored by Representative Cynthia McKinney (D-GA), or speaking at the National Press Club in Washington, DC. At that event his persuasiveness could not make it to the public through the mainstream media because no mainstream media showed up. (One of the other speakers was Danny Schechter, TV producer, author of *The More You Watch, the Less You Know* and media democracy activist [Globalvision.org]. Danny got a laugh by prefacing his remarks with some requests to imaginary camerapersons at the

back of the room. "Would the cameraperson from CNN please move over a couple of feet? You're blocking the cameramen from NBC and ABC," he quipped, making an important point.)

That was the weekend of the first "DC Emergency Truth Convergence." A rally for those in attendance was held July 23 in Lafayette Park across from the White House. Griffin was the lead-off speaker. "We live in an unprecedented time," he began. "If the present trajectory continues it is almost certain we will see an end of our own species and much of the life of the planet by the end of this century." Also unprecedented, he continued, is that "for the first time we are on the verge of a truly global empire, an empire with no borders. Our own country is involved in what

Dr. Griffin speaking at Lafayette Park, July 2005.

Richard Falk and others call 'the Global Domination Project.' And yet watching the mainstream media you would never guess that these catastrophic events were going on," he said.[4]

Being a theologian, he might have asked whether today's deceptions are of Biblical proportions, and answered that they exceed Biblical proportions. He could have said that the Scriptural warning of "principalities and powers" and "spiritual wickedness in high places" applies today even more than in Biblical times. North American Christians, Griffin said later with typical understatement, "have been insufficiently skeptical about the professed goodness of the US government and the professed independence of the mainstream [media] in America."

Activists for 9/11Truth share a universal concern usually veering toward anger about the height of the obstacle represented by mainstream media collusion in the 9/11 lie. But when I asked Griffin about his worst media experience regarding 9/11, "or your general critical summary of media performance vis a vis 9/11," he replied that he "wouldn't want to say." He prefers to accentuate the positive. His most positive experience in 9/11 activism? "... perhaps the [April 2005] Madison, Wisconsin lecture, '9/11 and the American Empire: How Should Religious People Respond?' partly because of the reception from the audience and partly the fact that, as we had hoped (this was part of my motivation in accepting the invitation) the lecture made it onto C-SPAN."

Dr. Griffin on C-SPAN: "a minor break through."

More specifically, that talk was filmed for C-SPAN's *Book TV*, one of the very few channels in the infamous 500-channel universe that features truly important topics being discussed at length by knowledgeable people, as well as concerned citizens freely asking questions. This made it an exception proving an almost-universal rule, to the time I write this in March 2006: those of us who question the official story find mainstream media interest meager, usually hostile, seldom fair, never sustained. The previous chapters of this book make that clear. Because everything's relative there's a tendency, therefore, for the word "breakthrough" to be applied to Griffin's C-SPAN appearance. My view is that the word "breakthrough" should be reserved for the day that one or more major mainstream media outlets (such as *The New York Times*, *Washington Post*, CNN, ABC, etc.), project coverage that will be startling to the general public, that is followed up doggedly, and that becomes politically relevant. Activists in the 9/11 Truth movement expect the media to pull the movement wagon, but the The movement must pull the media's wagon, through public events and ongoing outreach of all kinds. Griffin, while more hopeful than most that media can play an historic role in 9/11 Truth revelation, shares this sentiment. His greatest disappointment, his "worst continuing frustration" in 9/11 Truth work, is not with the mainstream media per se. It is "cowardice by so many people who should be better." I did not ask him whether he thinks many of these are in the media. I know the answer.

A modern prophet must multiply his message through TV, radio, videos, DVDs, podcasts — through every available means. In Jesus' day "a multitude" was the number of people who could hear one speaker without amplification. Multitudinous audiences today are assembled only through the media. Yet most of these media most of the time censor not only 9/11 truth but the failing vital life signs of our planet. They also broadcast false signals, the equivalent, as Griffin noted in his Lafayette Park speech, of the bread and circuses that distracted the Romans as their empire decayed and then fell. *The Problem of the Media*, to use the title of Robert McChesney's book, is simultaneously the problem of democracy — and the problem of survival.

Richard Falk wrote in the foreword to Griffin's *The New Pearl Harbor*: "It is rare, indeed, that a book has this potential to become a force in history." The key word here is "potential." Prior to that sentence Falk writes: "If the *The New Pearl Harbor* receives the sort of public *and media* [emphasis added] attention that it abundantly deserves, it should alter the general public debate and exert a positive influence on how the future unfolds."[5] Again, the media are key.

Lovers of the planet, democracy, justice, human rights and 9/11Truth must use whatever media they can, and reach out to all identifiable groups, in the intertwined struggle. "My main self-assigned task has been to get more intellectuals involved in the 9/11 truth movement," Griffin says. "Towards that end, I'm arranging for the publication of two volumes in which several intellectuals will speak out about '9/11 and the American Empire.'" One of these is *9/11 and the American Empire: Intellectuals Speak Out*, co-edited with Peter Dale Scott; the other is *9/11 and the American Empire: Christians, Jews, and Muslims Speak Out*, co-edited by Christian theologian John B. Cobb, Jr., Jewish theologian Sandra Lubarsky, and Muslim scholar Kevin Barrett. Griffin secured the agreement of Interlink Books to publish both of these volumes. Griffin also discusses 9/11 in his part of *The American Empire and the Commonwealth of God*, co-authored with Cobb, Richard Falk, and Catherine Keller. His output is prodigious. An intellectual's intellectual, Griffin is at about the same time publishing a collection of his philosophical essays titled *Whitehead's Radically Different Postmodern Philosophy: An Argument for Its Contemporary Relevance*, with SUNY Press.

In two speeches in the prophetic tradition in New York City in October 2005, Griffin issued a challenge to *The New York Times* "to reveal the truth" about the destruction of the World Trade Center.[6]

Griffin concluded that although many questions about 9/11 remain, it is "already possible to know, beyond a reasonable doubt, one very important thing: the destruction of the World Trade Center was an inside job, orchestrated by domestic terrorists." Griffin included quotations from oral histories of 9/11, recorded by the New York City Fire Department, which had recently been released as a result of a prolonged suit against New York City filed by *The New York Times* and victims' families, represented by attorney Norman Siegel. In the quotations, many firefighters and medical workers testified they heard explosions in the Twin Towers. A 12-minute film prepared by New York 9/11Truth activist Les Jamieson was shown for the audiences, who saw for themselves the undeniable evidence of controlled demolition.

Griffin listed characteristics of controlled demolition (see Chapter 2, Exhibits H-K). How can the mainstream US media continue to ignore the story of the century, asks Kevin Barrett in a report on Griffin's talk on rense.com. The conclusion of Griffin's talk addresses that, and is worth quoting verbatim:

The evidence for this conclusion [that many aspects of 9/11 could have been orchestrated only by forces within our own government] has thus far been largely ignored by the mainstream press, perhaps under the guise of obeying President Bush's advice not to tolerate "outrageous conspiracy theories." We have seen, however, that it is the Bush administration's conspiracy theory that is the outrageous one, because it is violently contradicted by numerous facts, including some basic laws of physics.

There is, of course, another reason why the mainstream press has not pointed out these contradictions. As a recent letter to the *Los Angeles Times* said: "The number of contradictions in the official version of ... 9/11 is so overwhelming that...it simply cannot be believed. Yet ... the official version cannot be abandoned because the implication of rejecting it is far too disturbing: that we are subject to a government conspiracy of X-Files proportions and insidiousness."[7]

The implications are indeed disturbing. Many people who know or at least suspect the truth about 9/11 probably believe that it would be so disturbing to the American psyche, the American form of government, and global stability that it is better to pretend to believe the official version. I would suggest, however, that any merit this argument may have had earlier has been overcome by more recent events and realizations. Far more devastating to the American psyche, the American form of government, and the world as a whole will be the continued rule of those who brought us 9/11, because the values reflected in that horrendous event have been reflected in the Bush administration's lies to justify the attack on Iraq, its disregard for environmental science and the Bill of Rights, its criminal negligence both before and after [Hurricane] Katrina, and now its apparent plan not only to weaponize space but also to authorize the use of nuclear weapons in a preemptive strike.

In light of this situation and the facts discussed [here] — as well as dozens of more problems in the official account of 9/11 discussed in my books — I call on *The New York Times* to take the lead in finally exposing to the American people and the world the truth about 9/11. Taking the lead on such a story will, of course, involve enormous risks. But if there is any news organization with the power, the prestige, and the credibility to break this story, it is the *Times*. It performed yeoman service in getting the 9/11 oral histories released. But now the welfare of our republic and perhaps even the survival of our civilization depend on getting the truth about 9/11 exposed. I am calling on the *Times* to rise to the occasion.[8]

That sounds like a prophet calling the powers and principalities to account.

The question most frequently asked about Griffin's deep involvement in the 9/11 Truth issue is the one asked rather flippantly at the opening of this chapter: what does his involvement have to do with his being a theologian? Attempting to answer that sheds considerable light on the factors that can combine to cause anyone to see the issue, to begin with, and then see it as central and requiring action.

As most laypeople understand it, theology would not provide the needed preparation. But most laypeople identify theology with *traditional* theology, based on the authoritarian model ("truth" is handed down). Traditional theologians devote themselves, therefore, to interpreting sacred texts. But there are radically different methods of doing theology. In liberal theology, which Griffin practices, all questions of truth, even in religion, must be decided on the basis of reason and experience.

Further, Griffin was a professor of "philosophy of religion and theology," a field with many branches. One branch grapples with the relationship between science and religion. This leads inevitably into philosophy of science; it has been Philosophy of Science that has been one of Griffin's main interests. In the list of the books he has authored or edited, one finds titles such as *Mind in Nature: Essays on the Interface of Science and Philosophy* (1977) and *Religion and Scientific Naturalism: Overcoming the Conflicts* (2000). Griffin approached 9/11 acutely aware of the nature of belief, the need for evidence, and the relationship between evidence and interpretation of evidence.

In line with his commitment to the scientific method, he knew that prior assumptions must be surrendered if they disagree with the empirical facts. With regard to 9/11, here is where a major separation of sheep from goats takes place. Griffin knows the ideal of the scientific method is seldom followed in practice. "Empirical evidence often takes a back seat to paradigmatic and wishful-and-fearful thinking," he observes.

Even so, a brilliant intellect and deep respect for evidence do not automatically make for an outspoken 9/11 skeptic. If they did, we would have thousands. Griffin, humble theologian, might be lost in the crowd. We encounter here a puzzle that interests me greatly: what combination of personal and cultural heritage, and intellectual and personal influences, coalesce into an ability to *see*, first of all, the brazen outrage apparently unseen by millions? And then to recognize the full significance and the need for action? I pestered Griffin for more personal background. Finally he provided me with information about "early influences," information he had not before committed to paper. Distilling and interpreting very subjectively, I find a number of factors combining to make this modern day prophet.

His early life was happy and secure; the religious faith of his family has provided a framework on which he could build a principled life — and challenge authority. While he was studying psychology his brother-in-law was killed in the Vietnam War. This led him into political activism. Around this time he was introduced to deep ecology, pluralism in religion and elsewhere, the scientific method, and the nuclear peril.

His developing diversified, inclusive outlook expanded further after he founded the Center for a Postmodern World in Santa Barbara, which focused equally on questions of world *view* and world *order*. His goal was to find a position from which churches could realistically advocate the abolition of nuclear weapons. Unable to find a solution, he put the project away. In 1992, however, he found that there *is* a solution: the creation of a global democratic government, which would make war both unnecessary and impossible.

From 1992 until September 11, 2001, Griffin worked on and off on a book manuscript about global democracy. It was about two-thirds finished when 9/11 happened. At first, Griffin reports that he accepted the standard liberal interpretation of 9/11 — that it was "blowback" for US foreign policy. But during his work on the global democracy book, Griffin had learned that the United States, like other imperialist powers, had many times created "incidents" — events that could be portrayed as aggression carried out by another country, to provide a pretext for the US going to war with that country. In other words, false-flag operations. These included the provocation that led to the Mexican-American War, the sinking of the battleship *Maine* which triggered the Spanish-American War, and the enticement and provocation of Japan into attacking Pearl Harbor. (See Chapter 7 for descriptions of 18 false-flag operations.)

Griffin maintains warm relations with colleagues, one of whom, in autumn 2002, encouraged Griffin to look at some websites about 9/11. At that time he "did not find the evidence convincing." (In late 2005 he could not recall which websites these were.) He returned to working on his manuscript. However, when *this* manuscript was about two-thirds finished, he learned from another colleague about Paul Thompson's 9/11 *The Terror Timeline,* at www.WantToKnow. This time Griffin found the evidence for official complicity convincing. This was the moment when his previous life development, in character and intellect, prepared him to see and to take action about the inside job of 9/11. After he read several other sources, especially Nafeez Ahmed's *The War on Freedom* (which he learned about from Gore Vidal's *Dreaming War*), he decided to summarize the strongest evidence in an article, which he hoped to get published in *Harper's* or some other magazine. This manuscript became longer and longer; he realized he was writing a book, which became *The New Pearl Harbor.* Claiming no originality in it, he presented this book as a summary of the best evidence provided by others, especially Ahmed, Thompson, Michel Chossudovsky, Thierry Meyssan, and Eric Hufschmid.

This same background prepared Griffin to be not terribly surprised that Americans tend to reject out of hand, without examining the evidence, the idea that 9/11 was an inside job, that their leaders could "kill other Americans." He describes such rejection as "*a priori,* paradigmatic" thinking (e.g., "US political and military leaders would not commit such a heinous act") or wishful-and-fearful thinking (e.g., "If I knew our leaders had done such a thing, life would be unbearable").

He's prepared to be considered heretical. One of the ideas he developed as a philosopher-theologian is "panexperientialism." In his words, this means following experience "all the way down." He says there is "much evidence for (panexperientialism) and no evidence against it ... (yet) most scientists and philosophers ... will not even give [it] serious attention." Seeing evidence-based positions on 9/11 given the short-shrift even by academics is not a new experience for Griffin.

Griffin understands how strategic 9/11 is and will continue to be, in the struggle to save the planet and humanity. The 9/11 false-flag operation is not just one among others. Griffin is also well aware, like most of the other 9/11Truth activists I know, of the enormity of the "other" major issues humanity faces. I put the worth "other" in quote marks because these issues — ecocide, war, resource depletion, injustice, and the struggles for political, economic and media democracy — thoroughly overlap. Any one person can support any one or any combination of the interwoven struggles. But most of us tend to be more effective when we focus our energies on one. And more effective yet if that one is the weakest link in the chain the oligarchy uses to imprison our minds.

Griffin has become a mentor to the 9/11Truth movement, connecting people to each other, passing about significant information, encouraging effective, principled non-violent action. Without accepting any office within the 9/11Truth movement he's nevertheless a major leader of it.

He's made himself available, as of the time this was written, for more than 130 radio interviews about 9/11 (at first, he refused virtually all invitations to public speaking). When I write "made himself available" I'm thinking of his generosity when I asked if he would participate in a radio program on Toronto's campus and community station CIUT-FM in May of 2004. Although on the date chosen he and his wife were in Europe on a long-deferred, much deserved vacation following his retirement at age 65, and in spite of his having to arrange, on the day, to be in a particular town in Italy with the right kind of phone line, he never complained.

The program was a special two-hour "round table" featuring Griffin and three hosts from CIUT-FM. It was also the launch of "The 9/11 Show," the world's first radio program devoted exclusively to 9/11 truth. The show aired for six weeks in conjunction with the six-day International

Citizens' Inquiry Into 9/11 at the University of Toronto at the end of May 2004. I was the director of the Inquiry and found Griffin to be consistently cooperative and good-natured even in trying circumstances. He has also been exceedingly generous with his time in the preparation of this book.

Finally, prophets are supposed to prophesize, aren't they? Well, yes and no. While people tend to want to be told all will be well, to be given quick and easy answers, and simple rules for salvation, prophets made of sterner stuff are loathe to cater to these simplistic wants. They prefer rather to encourage the multitude to pursue the difficult search for truth, to find the courage to speak it when it's found and the fortitude to persevere when the "principalities and powers" inevitably try to crush justice, democracy, truth, and the people. If there's to be salvation, the only route to it is from here on Earth — while we're here. "Here or nowhere is your America" said immigrants arriving in the US around 1915.

I asked Griffin what he feels the future holds. His response: "The future is open, indeterminate, and hence unknowable." Dr. David Ray Griffin, respecting the limitations of prophecy. A truly modern prophet.[9]

9

You and the Media: Ways Forward

"We have no right to give up. Too many people give up too early. We are in a stream of time, and some progress will take longer; some positive things will happen after our lives. If you are really determined to be on the good side of life, the forces of the universe are there to help you.'
— Robert Muller,
former Assistant Secretary General of the UN

"Be the media."
— Penny Little, California DVD producer,
musician and 9/11 Truth activist

Eugene, Oregon, March 18, 2005 — A lone Marine sits at the back of the recruiting center at the Santa Clara Mall in north Eugene. Someone is knocking on the locked door. Reluctantly the Marine gets up; slowly he goes to the door, unlocks it and stands blocking the entrance.

Facing him is Peter Chabarek, a 51-year-old acupuncturist and member of Eugene's Civil Resistance study group. There are five other members with him. Chabarek introduces himself, shakes the Marine's hand and explains about the group. He says they want to talk with the Marine about the recruitment process and give him a chance to address the group's concerns.

Their concerns are that the government is lying about the realities of the war in Iraq. Members of the group have with them well-researched packets

GORDON STURROCK, SQUADRON13.COM

Peter Chabarek en route to University of Oregon ROTC recruiting office, November 2005.

of written material with photos — of severely injured Iraqi children being held by their anguished parents, American soldiers with missing limbs, anguished relatives of dead GIs at their funerals, and the like.

Chabarek tells the Marine they'd like go over the material with his office and ask the centre to sign an agreement that every potential recruit who comes in will get one of these packets. "We'd like you to raise with potential recruits lack of health care and education benefits for people in the military, the sexual abuse and rape of women in the military, and the lack of a true portrayal of a career that involves killing people, including women, children, and the elderly."

The media had been notified that the group would be there that morning, about 70 resisters and their supporters in all. The media make a beeline for the recruiting office doorway. A half-dozen microphones are thrust between Chabarek and the marine. The marine becomes nervous; he moves to pull the door closed. Chabarek sticks his foot in the door and prevents it from closing. The marine says he will not talk to the group. He wants to close the door. Chabarek continues to explain why he and the others are there. He opens a packet and begins going over the issues involved, the media catching every word. The Marine demands Chabarek get out of the doorway or he will call the police. Chabarek continues talking about the issues.

The Marine declares: "That's it, I'm calling the police." He leaves the doorway to
go to the phone.

While this is happening other members
of the Resistance group are organizing large
placards to which are affixed photographic
enlargements of the pictures in the packets.
The placards bear captions such as "You
won't see this on NBC," and "This is what
collateral damage looks like." It is a dramatic display and the media cameras take it all in.

Peter picks up the narrative:

The first major decision of the action
had arrived — should we, the advance
party of six, take advantage of the
opportunity and enter the office, risking arrest for a federal trespassing
charge, before the main media event we
had planned had a chance to play out?

Media-savvy resistance to dishonest recruitment, November 2005.

We had made the decision beforehand
that we would risk arrest on the shopping center sidewalk for a local
criminal trespass charge, but not occupy the offices or block the
entrances involving a federal charge … I hesitated, thought about our
agreement and the main body of our folks waiting to do the main
part of our action, and decided to step out of the doorway. The
marine immediately ran over and locked the door.

The media asked what would we do now? We were prepared for
this, and told them we would return another time to deliver this
information to the recruiters, "when they would let us in and felt
they did not have to hide from the truth." We then joined the main
group and all marched in single file, our placards turned out of sight,
to the area directly in front of the recruitment center. I saw people
coming out from the shops, curious and a little nervous. We lined up
in a row, and then our media spokesperson Karla Cohen announced
to the press our "human slide show," that would display images of

the war hidden by the mainstream media and the recruiters from the American people and potential recruits.

Silently, one after another, we revealed the images. The public and reporters were visibly shaken. The cameras rolled and clicked. We stood with resolute determination and a solemn respect for the victims of this senseless brutal war. When all of the 32 images were on display, Karla said, "We want the American media to show the truth about the war, and we want the recruiters to tell potential recruits the truth about what they are getting themselves into."

Then we went down the line, and those of us who wished to, made brief personal statements from our hearts about what moved us to be there. Powerful statements came from our deepest feelings and beliefs, tears were shed. All who wanted to speak had the opportunity, and the media paid attention. I remember saying that "We have full faith in the essential goodness and the conscience of the American people, and if these images were shown in America's living rooms every night, the war would be over in a week." Several veterans spoke eloquently, including Hank Dizney, who said the recruitment process was deceptive and dishonorable, and that, as an American citizen, he resented this.

It was time to declare our success. I said to everyone present that we scored two victories today — we had shut down the recruitment center (cheers went up!) and that we had succeeded in establishing our right to protest at a "private property" shopping center where we were told we would be arrested, and had therefore forced the police to yield (more cheers!).

Later we were to discover even more success from the action. It became the lead story on all three major TV networks in Eugene, we received excellent coverage on radio outlets, and we were the cover story in the City/Region section of the following day's *Register Guard*. The TV stations and the *Register Guard* showed some of the graphic images we wanted to get in front of the eyes of the public. And maybe best of all, we built a strong feeling of love and solidarity among the people in our group, made new allies in the public and the media, and experienced a well deserved feeling of standing tall and acting on our convictions in the face of significant risk to ourselves.

The party that night at World Cafe, where we watched a home video of the action made by John Melia, was one of the greatest times I can ever recall. We won a victory today, a badly needed victory in this struggle to save the soul of our nation, and my goodness did it feel good.[1]

Not only did it feel good for those who worked so hard to mount the action, it was, as Peter reported later "a dignified, inspired example of classic non-violent struggle." The story began long before the action of March 18. "A month of meticulous planning preceded it. There were many meetings at the Friends Meeting House, civil disobedience training, copious research and a tremendous amount of hard work and long hours by many of the resisters." The Civil Resistance study group was organized around the idea that the time had come for action, in addition to conventional antiwar work. Members studied successful non-violent resistance movements from the American civil rights struggle, the South African struggle against apartheid, the Indian independence movement under Gandhi's leadership, the Polish Solidarity movement that overthrew the communist regime, and the Danish resistance to the Nazis in the Second World War.

The media strategy of the group was "to present a situation in which the media would be forced to show the violent disturbing images of the war if they wished to cover us." Press releases were sent twice in the week prior to the media and to the three law enforcement agencies in the area. The releases emphasized the group was non-violent but was prepared to be arrested. Organizers met with Lt. Pete Kerns of the Eugene Police Department at his request. They went over their plans and discussed possible police responses, with their attorney present and a tape recorder running. The media, including the *Register Guard*, KUGN, KLCC and KWVA, showed great curiosity and tried to get the organizers to divulge the location, the only information held back until one hour before the action.

The Story Continues in Eugene, OR

November 18, 2005 — Actions must be continuing. Eight months later, 30 war resisters stage a sit-in at the University of Oregon campus ROTC

Profile: Carol Brouillet

"The Truth Matters Now — in Fifty Years Everyone Will Realize 9/11 was an Inside Job"

"I must confess I was born a Republican. My parents were Republicans. My grandparents were Republicans. By the age of seven I was taught how to play the stock market."

From that beginning Carol Liane Brouillet, born in 1957, emerged 49 years and 180 degrees later a mother of three, 9/11Truth activist, and Green Party candidate for Congress whose ticket is "to impeach Bush and cronies, repeal the Patriot Act, extricate the USA from wars throughout the world, redirect resources from killing and controlling people to heal-ing relationships — between people, and people and the planet."

There were several turning points, each of several degrees, which added up to the 180-degree turnaround. "I assumed my childhood, my family, were normal. It came as a bit of a shock to learn in college that some of my fellow students didn't have trust funds and actually had to work to pay their tuitions," she says. On a two-year around-the-world yacht cruise she got to know a man who "liked Democrats more" but "worked for Republicans because they pay more." In China she discovered an artist whose work she loved; back in the USA organizing exhibitions of

Carol Brouillet

his art she discovered her talent for pub-lic relations. "That experience gave me that confidence to become a media activist later." In 1992, when she saw the Oliver Stone film JFK she realized "some-thing was deeply amiss." She began to research the CIA. "When I did figure out what the CIA was up to, and who owned and controlled the mainstream press, I was absolutely outraged and my life changed dramatically." Since then, says

Carol, "I have been trying to make up for all those years when I was happily oblivious to the world's problems."

For the next nine years her activism spanned militarization, nuclear issues, the monetary system and global economics. While initiating three international gatherings on "Strategies to Transform the Global Economy" she found out she had organizing ability.

Then, 9/11. "At first I thought it was too horrible even for the government to dream up. The media coverage was scarier than the attack – the drumbeat toward war. I went to Washington DC to protest the impending war. There I realized the war had nothing to do with 'catching terrorists' but was about geopolitics and oil."

Visits to the offices of Congresspersons, marches and rallies were among Brouillet's earlier activities demanding a full investigation of 9/11. These were followed by her organizing of the San Francisco premiere of the documentary *Aftermath: Unanswered Questions From 9/11,* and the mounting of major public events at San Francisco's downtown Herbst Theatre, including "Behind Every Terrorist There's a Bush" and the International Inquiry Into 9/11, Phase 1. Working with Blaine Machan (see profile, page 334), she suggested to Blaine that if he made a backside to the Deception Dollar they could pass them out at anti-war rallies. She published and distributed eight versions of the Dollar, with print runs of 10,000 to 1,500,000. They were so popular that they helped finance the budding 9/11 Truth movement. There are more than 6,000,000 in print.

What keeps her going? "I love Life. I love my kids, my husband, my friends; I care passionately about now and the future. I also feel connected with all the historical struggles people have engaged in to overcome oppression and liberate themselves from tyranny and injustice." She feels terribly let down by leaders of the Left and, of course, by the media.

"The sooner we can educate people the sooner we can rein in the real criminals, the real terrorists, the ones occupying the White House," says Brouillet. "My hope is that we can expose 'the war game,' expose how just a few people make money off war, but the vast majority of people and the planet pay the price. We must abolish war once and for all by exposing the deceptions used to trick people into supporting wars."

center, and the Army recruitment centre in west Eugene, on the same day. Two waves of resisters are at each site. Again, graphic images are central to the message of peace that the resisters are attempting to get across. There's no violence, but there are seven arrests (for blocking and sitting in). Again, prior discussions had been held with the police, and trained legal observers from the University of Oregon Law School were involved. Media releases · were sent out four days in advance, and again the late afternoon before, stating there would be multiple actions and naming one location, at which the second location would be revealed to media present.

During the actions, media questions were not hostile, as had been the case with a few at the March event. At the campus event, a freelance videographer associated with the resisters complimented one of the Eugene Police officers for being professional, to which the officer responded: "We're glad you guys are here, what you're doing is really important, keep it up." It was an indication of discontent with the Iraq war among some policemen. This was reinforced by one of the resisters, a physician and a Quaker, who said a friend of his who is a Eugene Police officer told him a clear majority of the Eugene Police now opposed the war.

The actions were the top story on the three local TV affiliates of ABC, NBC and CBS as well as Air America Radio. The two college radio stations did stories and the *Register Guard* played the actions on the front page of its City/Region section.

The November actions also showed that even more planning is better. At one point the graphic photo cards happened to face a childcare center next to one of the recruitment centers. An irate mother's comments to *KMTR-TV* that the children may have been exposed to such images became that station's entire story. But it was the only negative coverage.

In an observation that could well apply to 9/11Truth activism, Peter Chabarek commented:

> If the strength of the Empire depends upon the belief system of mainstream Institutions such as the police and the media remaining intact, we most certainly struck a blow against the Empire this day. If the maintenance of conformity with the institutions of war depends on people's fear of sanctions from the government, then by many of us overcoming our fear of being arrested, we most certainly struck a

blow against the institutions of the war machine. By challenging ourselves and doing something that required courage and personal sacrifice, each one became more capable, more powerful, and with that power comes greater responsibility. We look forward to the challenge.[2]

The best success I enjoyed teaching journalism for seven years was with projects — real projects in the outside world. The students and I worked out goals, then tried to achieve them. For instance, we brought in experts on public opinion polling, then under guidance conducted a proper poll in cooperation with a major daily newspaper. The daily published the results. The readers got the information. The students got credits, and the university publicity. We joined a campaign to make *Time Canada* more accountable and less of a Trojan Horse in Canada for the US corporate agenda. We invited nationalist Mel Hurtig to speak. This led to the formation on the Ryerson University campus of a chapter of the Committee for an Independent Canada, precursor of today's influential Council of Canadians. Our Ryerson chapter went on to prepare a paper for a Parliamentary committee holding hearings on Bill C-58, an Act to oblige *Time Canada* to play more by the rules domestic Canadian magazines had to live by. I delivered the paper in Ottawa. The Bill passed. We felt our input made a difference.

We all need to study, to be lifelong students. The events of 9/11 demand study, ideally by every citizen, because the fallout from 9/11 is affecting every citizen. "History is a race between education and catastrophe," wrote H. G. Wells. But studying problems without taking remedial action can leave us frustrated and anxious. Anxiety is a substitute for action. Action is freeing. Action is also educational. We learn by doing. Study and action are not two hermetically sealed categories. We need to learn all we can about 9/11 and all we can about the media, position ourselves for best leverage and take the most effective actions we can imagine.

Acknowledge our power and seize the historic moment

There are ways to impact the future to and through the mainstream media, as we have seen in the example of the Oregon activists. It's vitally important to nurture alternative media, which in turn nurture us. Alternative

Profile: Gabriel Day

"I feel like I'm living in the movie *The Matrix* with Neo and his cadre of underground rebels"

A fulsome smile is the trade mark of 50-year-old entrepreneur and political activist Gabriel Day. His primary motivation is "knowing and feeling the huge silver lining that exists for the transformation of the world by 9/11Truth." He sees 9/11Truth activism as "an excellent path of growth for myself and my family of committed activist friends." He finds "joy in seeing their gradual growth towards their own potential as creative, powerful souls acting courageously in the world." But he is a realist. "As much as I try to keep fear at bay I know the future quality of life for my loved ones and much of the world is at stake."

Day grew up in a "very politically active" conservative Republican family in southern Maine. Day states that the nuclear accident at Three Mile Island "woke me up to the lies of the Republican agenda and caused me to shift across the political spectrum to being passionately involved in progressive causes." That was in 1979. Since then he has been active in the peace, social justice and environmental movements. Until autumn 2002, he had "no idea anything was amiss with the government's account" of the events of 9/11. It was only the "persistent nagging of a couple of friends" that led him to view the video *The Great Deception*. After six months of research he wrote: "Sadly, I am now convinced that rogue elements within our govern-

Gabriel Day

ment committed this vicious criminal act against its own citizens for the larger purpose of swaying us to support both domestic and foreign policies mapped out in the late 1990's by the neocon PNAC."

He sums up: "The so-called the war on terrorism is a cruel hoax on the American people by a small, misguided, out-of-control group of individuals sabotaging the best of American values. We are in the midst of a Constitutional crisis combined with severe domination from an Orwellian corporate media ... serving the true powerbrokers behind the curtain."

He started the Peace Resource Project, a large and growing source for 9/11Truth materials, and he also launched 911sharethetruth.com. In a corporation he'd be National Outreach & Networking Coordinator, and indeed his earlier success in the computer and wireless industries have enabled him to devote himself solely to political activism. Of his role he says: "I feel I'm a cross between Paul Revere and Johnny Appleseed — sounding a warning as well as seeding and networking the courageous actions being taken around the world."

In late 2005, Day committed himself to traveling the US for two years spreading 9/11Truth. As I write this he's the sparkplug behind a 9/11Truth conference to take place in Chicago in mid-2006. "This outrageous criminal act must be brought to justice and our freedoms restored. We need to reach out now to all those who may be willing to hear and break the silence."

Because he worked for so long in peace and social justice, a major frustration for Day has been "the lack of people in the peace and social justice movement willing to look into this issue, willing to see [that] this truth could be a fulcrum for radical political change." The possibilities for the future he sees as "a continuum of outcomes from very dark to moderate success, depending on the collective actions of all involved." But lately he is buoyed by the growing activism he's observed in several US states he's visited. "It's possible we could reach a tipping point," he says. He's clear on his own best contribution: "Building successful strategies, developing infrastructure, media creation, and articulating a positive vision of a post 9/11 truth world." With a smile.

media need encouragement to pay serious and continuing attention to the issue of 9/11 Truth. Those alternative media that resist paying serious attention need to be lobbied as effectively as possible, and that job is up to existing subscribers and supporters. The Winnipeg-based socialist magazine *Canadian Dimension* decided to publish a review of the best material about 9/11 after just one reader bugged them to pay attention to the issue. Alternative media that adamantly resist publishing questions about the 9/11 official story are much less deserving of subscription and support from anyone concerned about the truth of 9/11 than they otherwise would be. As we saw in Chapter 5, the workings of some Left media need to be investigated.

Keep in mind the two characteristics of all successful people. Whatever other characteristics successful people have, they always have these: persistence and flexibility.

The Oregon activists showed flexibility in asking advice from the police. This applies also to media relations. Asking advice from media people can be a very smart thing to do. You'll learn; they tend to be flattered and they remember you. But you have to follow through. These are a few general lessons I've picked up from 50 years in journalism and about as many as a peace and environmental, and now 9/11 Truth, activist.

It's important to "be the media," as California producer and activist Penny Little puts it. Each of us is in fact a medium — a walking, talking receiver, processor and transmitter of information and values. Someone once said that the most important peace talks in the world take place over backyard fences.

The experience we had in mounting the International Citizens' Inquiry Into 9/11, Phase 2, at the University of Toronto in May 2004 was, among other things, a learning and activism workout on the media front. Phase 1 had been a three-day event in San Francisco in March. There were members of our board who believed at the outset of planning that the most important outcome of our Inquiry would be the mainstream media coverage it would attract. They imagined the media "could not ignore" a six-day event on the subject and that we could score a "breakthrough" in consciousness-raising on the 9/11 issue.

As director, I agreed we could not rule out that we might garner priceless publicity, and we had to do everything possible to notify the media, invite them and be helpful to them. (And we did that.) "At the same time," I had to repeat, "the fact of the matter is that regrettably we will probably not get much coverage, if indeed we get any, and such coverage as we get is likely to be negative." As it turned out, it wasn't quite that bad. We enjoyed four good mainstream TV interviews (three of them on *CHCH* Hamilton, because of one interested producer), a good *CBC Radio* interview, although only local, and a fair story in the *Toronto Star*.[4] *NOW* weekly ran an odd piece which oscillated between demonizing "conspiracy theorists" on the one hand, and providing evidence of US government complicity in 9/11 on the other.[5] Alternative weeklies tend to adhere to this waffling approach, as if they're struggling to be included with the mainstream press... which they treat with contempt all the while.

A real breakthrough in "being the media" was in fact scored, thanks to The University of Toronto station, *CIUT-FM* (ciut.fm/). Program manager Ken Stowar gave the green light for "The 9/11 Show," the world's first radio program devoted exclusively to 9/11 Truth. It aired weekly for six weeks — four one-hour and two two-hour programs. We at the Inquiry promised to provide a minimum of two interesting, articulate guests each week. Guests included Republican 9/11 Truth presidential aspirant John Buchanan, the-ologian David Ray Griffin (see profile in Chapter 8), and 9/11 widow Ellen Mariani. I'll never forget the look on Stowar's face early on in the Buchanan phone-in interview. Almost immediately, Buchanan said George W. Bush deserved to be "executed for treason." Stowar's eyebrows almost jumped off his face. There was some concern about adverse listener reaction, which turned out to be groundless; that show and all the editions of the program were a hit with listeners. CIUT also covered the Inquiry sessions extensively and later aired hours of the proceedings. There had been early interest at the station, especially on the part of Jesse Mendes, whose two-hour show *Innovations* used to air Saturday afternoons. She had me on as a guest sever-al times in the previous year and other producers likewise chose to invite local 9/11 Truth activists on air before, during and after the Inquiry.

Looking at the long term, the most important media event of our Inquiry was internal: that we invested the time and money to make every session a three-camera shoot, with a switcher operator on the job. The footage cap-tured on the spot therefore was "pre-edited" with different camera angles,

Profile: Blaine Machan

Deception Dollar Reveals Deceit, Becomes a Collector's Item

Blaine Machan

mysterious billboards appear overnight in Calgary.

Money, everywhere, is a stealth communications medium. Each person, when inflation is running high, is reminded with every purchase that he or she is losing ground financially. It's a very political, if subconscious, reminder. A country's history and power structure tend to be revealed in the choice of artwork for its currency: its official heroes, sacred landscapes, revered flora and fauna and other icons appear there.

Into this economic and political art form steps a 32-year-old Calgary graphic artist, Blaine Machan, who transforms money, infamously the love of which is the root of all evil, for love of the common good. In 2002, he created the Deception Dollar (DD), as this is written in its eighth version, with more than six million in circulation. It has become a collector's item. Proving imitation to be the sincerest form of flattery, Machan's work has been picked up in Iceland, where graphic artist Thorarinn Einarsson, the same age as Machan, has created the Deception Kroner.

Machan "twigged" that 9/11 was an inside job "about a week after. I think it was more the response of the US government to the event than the actual event. I think

I remember watching the towers fall and feeling it looked like a controlled demolition, but I didn't look more closely at that until much later." He's motivated by "the satisfaction of being involved with something I think is extremely important and working with great people who want to make the world better."

The Deception Dollar arose out of his helping publicize a visit to Calgary by Michael Ruppert. Machan, "working on posters for Mike," came up with a graphic using a detailed, politically modified US dollar bill. Carol Brouillet (see profile on page 326) contacted Blaine with the idea of making the dollar two-sided and printing and distributing copies as a means of outreach and fundraising.

Blaine has become the unofficial graphic artist of the 9/11 Truth movement. Besides creating specialized versions of the DD, he has designed many graphics for *Global Outlook: The Magazine of 9/11 Truth,* including most of its covers, and signage for 9/11 Truth events including the international inquiries in San Francisco and Toronto in 2004. He also appears to be connected with some mysteriously-appearing advertising billboards in Calgary, and rendered the basic design for the cover for this book.

He has found it "shocking how well the mainstream media have been able to stay silent on the key questions and issues." As to money, there's little of that for Blaine in 9/11 Truth activism: his day job is with a sign manufacturing company.

close-ups, medium shots, long shots, pans, audience reaction and the like. This footage, finally 45 hours in all, has found its way into a number of 9/11 documentaries including my own *The Great Conspiracy: The 9/11 News Special You Never Saw* (included with this book). It could not have been done without the dedicated interest and hard work of 9/11 Truth activists from both sides of the border. People such as hummux (see profile on page 120) and Ken Jenkins were among the dedicated hard-working volunteer video activists who made it all happen.

So we did it all: cooperated with the mainstream, expecting little and having our expectations slightly exceeded, nurturing the alternative media and "being the media."

The growing concentration of corporate ownership of the mainstream media has become well-known in spite of the details of that story being omitted, by and large, from the pages and airwaves of the corporate media themselves. This means that if you are a progressive person, cause, organization or movement you cannot count on mainstream media pulling your wagon. You have to pull the media's wagon — insofar as it can be pulled — by mounting events, being imaginative, telling your story at every opportunity and trying to establish personal ties of respect with individuals inside the media. It's less than history requires, but we cannot expect magical solutions.

We must persevere and make inroads where we can, using our particular talents, resources and positions in society to best effect. The people in Oregon, and others, are showing what can be done. Whether you're attached to a 9/11 group, outreach opportunities are available. Do you notice sometimes a letter to the editor that pulls the veil off of something the paper itself has not touched? You can try that. You never know your luck. Letters to the editor matter — quite a lot. Typically they're the best or second-best read part of a paper. You read them, don't you? A whole other book could be written about how to increase your chances of getting a letter to the editor published, but one neat turn of phrase will help. One does not have to be a good writer; when you find a compelling quote related to 9/11 in a book or magazine, it's quite legitimate to write a letter that essentially is a vehicle for the quote. It will probably be brief, and it's best to be timely.

Timeliness is important with op-ed page pieces as well. Around the time I submitted, on spec to *Sunday* the article that appears in Chapter 1 pegged to the fourth anniversary of 9/11, I also submitted on spec to the *Globe and Mail* an article about the 1605 Gunpowder Plot false-flag operation, pegged to the 400th anniversary of the plot. That outreach was successful and the piece ran almost word for word.[6] In fact, the editors are encouraging me to submit more pieces for the paper's Comments section.

There are many, many anniversaries. Some are known worldwide, some are national, some regional or local. "Anniversaries are reservoirs of sacred power," an American social critic once said. It's entirely legitimate to leverage some of that power for the cause of 9/11 Truth. Goodness knows many anniversaries — war-related, for instance — are leveraged by the establishment to perpetuate the system that led to the destructive events being commemorated.

In the weeks and days leading up to the fifth anniversary of 9/11, those with a stake in perpetuating the official story of the events will be reinforcing the Big Lie. They have many resources at their disposal. It's entirely likely that Hollywood movies, TV dramas and documentaries and newspapers and magazine articles will feature Arab fanatics, American victims, the "brave resolve" of the "heroes of flight 93" and all those "conducting the war on terror." It will likely be an impressive propaganda onslaught. Reports in 2004 spoke of an eight-hour 9/11 mini-series on the fifth- or sixth-year anniversary. ABC was said to have something in the works. Already the made-for-TV "Flight 93"and "The Last Hour of Flight 11" aired in early 2006. Such programming will dovetail with official commemorations at "Ground Zero" and elsewhere.

The anniversary also will also provide opportunities for those dedicated to 9/11 Truth. It will be a more important time than usual to raise questions that members of the general public may not have considered, or remind them of what they've already considered but have allowed to slip out of their minds. The very one-sidedness that can be expected from the mainstream media should be pointed out and effectively criticized at every opportunity.

Smaller newspapers or TV stations may be willing to open the door to questions, especially if there is a local angle. Letters to the editor, again, come into focus. Use the anniversary as a peg. It's your right and, if you're a 9/11 Truth activist, your duty. The best 9/11 Truth events that can be mounted will carry more power and reach just because of the anniversary. If you haven't yet become active, this is a perfect time to join the 9/11 Truth movement. Existing activists can use all the help they can get to spread the

Profile: Kelly Reinhardt

"I've Never Liked Being Lied To"

"I've never liked being lied to, and my earliest memories, those that affected me permanently, involved deception." This statement by 35-year-old 9/11Truth activist Kelly Reinhardt jumps out for me, as he recounts his remarkable life.

A life that shows Reinhardt also refuses to lie to himself. He expects the future to be "complete ecological collapse and a total global police state with accompanying social chaos." This future is a strong possibility many social and political activists are unable or unwilling to confront as starkly. "We might be able to hold off the global police state," Reinhardt adds, "but our environmental demise is certain."

What is the motivation that drives, or at least keeps going, those of us with such visions of a potentially apocalyptic future? In Reinhardt's case it's the love and support of his partner, Bridget Haworth, and the support and encouragement of others. "The most satisfying experience is to have people thank us for doing the work that we do," he says. That work is producing and promoting educational media that encourage nonviolent activism that might help ameliorate the worst.

Reinhardt was conceived around the time of the world's first Earth

Kelly and Bridget

Day, April 22, 1970. Early on he developed a profound sense of the importance of protecting the global ecosystem. This led him in 1990 to "a conscious decision to dedicate my life's work towards righting some of the wrongs of the world." He studied audiovisual communications and worked in Western

Canada recording the activities of environmental activists, and joining with them. He was one of 900 people arrested on a logging road during the campaign to protect the old-growth forests of Clayoquot Sound in British Columbia.

By autumn 2000, Reinhardt was in Den Hague, the Netherlands, to report on the United Nations Convention on Climate Change, where Canada was voted by the Climate Action Network as "the most obstructive to the climate negotiations." As the talks were collapsing, in protest, he and fellow activist the late Tooker Gomberg burned their Canadian passports in front of hundreds of international media representatives. Briefly, "Activists Without Passports" flourished in Europe. Reinhardt returned to Canada in time for the FTAA Summit in Quebec City in April 2001.

"Then came 9/11." Reinhardt was immediately suspicious. As he and Bridget watched the second plane hit the WTC "I had a strong feeling that plane was under remote control, still one of the more controversial theories associated with 9/11. Then the pitiful reporting and concomitant conclusion that bin Laden was responsible cemented my skepticism. The case closed when it was reported than an alleged hijacker's passport was found intact in the rubble of the WTC complex."

To Reinhardt, "It was clear the rules of the game were changing rapidly." He saw a great need for the promotion and distribution of the media on 9/11Truth that were beginning to appear. Since then, he and Bridget have launched Boilingfrog.ca ,and have hosted more than 200 screenings, launched five film festivals, produced dozens of Internet radio shows and toured Canada three times. They found time in 2005 to produce "Reclaiming Independence," a 74-minute radio play "that connects the dots on the major issues, including 9/11." That play now resides at the *Rabble Podcast Network* (Rabble.ca/rpn).

"Because of the misery around us, there is no shortage of work to do," says Reinhardt. He adds, "Sadly the pay is lousy if at all," further motivation for him to reach some new goals. One is to create "a self-sufficient independent media center, a physical space to include media labs, screening, entertainment, info-shop, library, café, lodging." The payoff should be less misery, more company.

word, mount outreach activities, increase turnouts and generate coverage.

Strategy is important in most endeavors. Presumably, the more limited the resources of a person, organization or movement in relation to its goals, the more important is strategy. Diana Ralph, a former American living in Toronto, is a social justice activist who has written a paper entitled "How to Dismantle the US Empire." She draws on the work of Saul Alinsky and others, and her own experience.

Ralph says: "We need to define where we want to be a year or two or five or more from now. If we are at A, where is B? What exactly do we hope to achieve? What is our vision, our dream?" We then conceive, she says, of steps needed to arrive at B, breaking the work into imaginable chunks. "They need to be realistic and do-able. We need to anticipate reactions from opposition forces." Flexibility needs to be built in. "We need to link with other groups, engage in team efforts wherever possible. Progress needs to be measured. Later on we can notice and celebrate victories along the way."[7]

Diana Ralph says goals should be "simple, winnable, unifying, strongly felt and flexible." She identifies strengths and vulnerabilities of the American Empire, and strengths and vulnerabilities of those opposed to the workings of the American Empire.

Her paper features an "Ally/Opponent Barometer," adapted from David H. Albert's *People Power — Applying Non-Violence Theory*.[8] It's a rainbow chart. Adapting it to the struggle for 9/11 Truth, we see on the far left is a small wedge marked "9/11 activists." The next wedge up represents people opposed to corporate-agenda globalization, militarism, secrecy, covert operations, resource theft — the whole neocon agenda. Then come student and peace groups, religious leaders, unionists — generally progressive people. Next is "the apolitical public," decent citizens who want to feel safe. At this point we're halfway around the rainbow and now move into opposition territory, which includes "much of the public" ("educated by the media," as Ralph puts it, to believe the official story). Then we come to much of big business and government, followed by mainstream media, transnational corporations, rightwing politicians, and finally a small wedge marked "Bush administration, the military, CIA, FBI," completing the rainbow with those who control the pot of gold. The idea is to work on those who are already closest to your position, and try to move every wedge over one space.

The general strategy in Diana Ralph's paper is to expose the US Empire, then block it, then dismantle it. The first step in my adaptation is exposing the truth about 9/11 as the most effective first step in exposing the Empire.

The most effective campaign I know of at the time of writing, as far as organized political action on 9/11 Truth is concerned, is Citizen's Counter-Coup or 3C. Its slogan: "The formula for change now." It's part of 911Truth.org and is on the Internet at 3C.911truth.org/3c_action.htm.

Les Jamieson of New York City is one of the organizers. They believe that legislators can be persuaded and pressured to take meaningful action to reopen an investigation into 9/11. In early 2006, the 3C home page pointed out that by that time "nearly 250 Congressmen had signed a petition to allow a hearing on Able Danger." Able Danger, allegedly a Pentagon "terrorist monitoring" sub-agency, recently became controversial. The 3C organizers infer from the success of the petition process that there "is a growing awareness on the issues of 9/11 and willingness to act." This sounds reasonable but some of the assumptions around Able Danger are themselves dangerous. (See sidebar "Citizen Activists Beware.")

3C cites other reasons for hope, including recent news coverage ranging from comments by a Muslim chaplain with the New York fire department to those of a university professor in the Midwest who stated flatly that his application of science showed him the WTC towers could only have been felled by controlled demolition. This news coverage "is gradually broadening public awareness." A four-step action plan is put forward by 3C.

The first step is to call legislators on the 11th of each month with a particular message. The January 2006 message consisted of five points. One included the results of public opinion polls showing widespread skepticism about the official story.

Step two involves outreach to the media, also with five points selected for each month. For January, one was that "Arab extremists" have been chosen by "the military/industrial/congressional complex to replace our old Cold War foe, Russia, as the new demon."

Step three is to sign up 10 people each month, to become involved in some way. It can be as simple as their agreeing to receive an email.

The fourth step is personal action such as starting one's own 9/11 Truth group or acquiring 9/11 documentaries to show in one's home.

Profile: Paul Thompson

Modest 9/11 Researcher is Author of "Gold Standard" of Truth Research

Paul Thompson

When people think thesaurus, they think Roget's. When they think road atlas, they think Rand-McNally. Those serious about researching 9/11 think Paul Thompson's *The Terror Timeline*.[9] It has become, as an article in *New York* magazine in early 2006 put it, "the undisputed gold standard of Truth research."

Freelance researcher and environmental activist Thompson, as befits the creator of a reference work, remains circumspect about 9/11; he probably has never said it was an inside job. It's an indication of the impoverishment of the official story that this careful compiler of evidence is on record as saying: "Even if — and this is the most charitable explanation — it was only incompetence, then that incompetence was so severe that it should lead to impeachment. How many warnings do you need? Not only that but it was followed after 9/11 by a cover-up, and it is often said that it's not the crime but it's the cover-up that they end up going to jail for. Between the incompetence and the cover-up, that alone should lead to the impeachment of President Bush and all his top people."[10]

The concept and organization of *The Terror Timeline* reflect the mind of its creator. All the information is taken from carefully-identified public sources. There are, therefore, numerous contradictions; the reader is left, by and large, to decide where the truth lies. Thompson is not one to shove a theory down anyone's throat. The unvarnished "facts" with their contradictions constitute a powerful negation of the official story.

Paradoxically *The Terror Timeline,* although composed mainly of information from thousands of mainstream articles and broadcasts, also stands as a stinging indictment of mainstream journalism. Thompson discovered "... many articles ... were simultaneously good and bad. They were good in that they reported the latest news developments. But too often it seemed that the stories were missing important context. It was as if the stories existed in a vacuum." He discovered what long-time media critics call a-historicity and how misleading it can be. "... these articles generally failed to remind the reader ..." Thompson begins a sentence in his introduction. The sentence could have 10,000 endings. "Were the reporters (or their editors) too afraid to publicly contradict the official pronouncements? Whatever the reason, it seemed to me that the reader could not be well-informed unless news stories were put into proper historical context." Thompson also discovered "that new or significant information was often mentioned only in passing, deep within a given article, with little or no follow-up." Instead of just complaining, Thompson built a better mouse trap.

He would be among the first to agree his compendium is imperfect, and readily admits that "of the thousands of facts" he presents, "some will be inaccurate." In my opinion, Thompson's acceptance, in the structure of his book, of the conventional view of the existence of an independent al Qaeda, of hijackers, and of "the attacks," tends to mask the highly dubious nature of these. But such a disagreement with the arrangement of the data under these headings detracts very little from the value of the data.

Thompson's contribution may never achieve the "household name" status of *Roget's* or *Rand-McNally,* but in homes, offices, classrooms or anywhere that people care about getting to the bottom of 9/11, a copy of *The Terror Timeline* is almost certain to be found — and found invaluable. "The quest for the truth is not yet complete, and the work must continue," says Thompson. His past and continuing work are an important part of the quest.

Citizen Activists Beware

In the accompanying text the 9/11Truth citizen initiative Citizen's Counter-Coup (3C), is commended. At the same time, the site's home page contains a couple of seemingly innocuous sentences that are useful reminders of the nature of the psychological warfare we are forced to confront.

The site in early 2006 referred to the willingness of 250 or more Congressmen to sign a petition. This petition was asking that "federal whistleblowers" be allowed to testify about Able Danger, said to be a Pentagon "terrorist monitoring" sub-agency. The wording on 3C's site does not claim that the Able Danger controversy is a politically advantageous opportunity in and of itself for the 9/11Truth movement. What it says is that since this many Congressmen signed such a petition, "it's safe to assume that there is a growing awareness on the issues of 9/11 and willingness to act." A lot depends on what is meant by "awareness on the issues of 9/11."

To 9/11Truth activists, the overriding issue of awareness is that 9/11 was an inside job. Yet in late 2005, some 9/11Truth activists were hopeful that the publicity, and possibly some Congressional action, surrounding Able Danger would help expose the truth about 9/11. It might, but the fallout from Able Danger hearings could well be reinforcement for the official 9/11 story. And planned to be by clever psychological warfare practitioners.

Able Danger, it was claimed by alleged whistleblowers who made public its existence, was a secret Pentagon "intelligence program to monitor al Qaeda networks around the world." It is said to have been ordered set up in autumn 1999 by General Hugh Shelton, Chairman of the US Joint Chiefs of Staff. The alleged whistleblowers said that General Peter Schoomaker, the head of the military's Special Operations Command, was given the responsibility of forming the sub-agency at his headquarters in Tampa, Florida.

By September of 2000, the story goes, Able Danger had information that Mohammed Atta was ringleader of an al Qaeda cell in Brooklyn, NY. Other details "leaked" by the alleged whistleblowers included claims that the Pentagon protected the civil liberties of the "terrorist suspects" in a totally inappropriate way, so as to shield them from other law agencies. Five "insiders" were prepared to come forward and testify on these matters. ☞

Therefore, wrote one 9/11Truth activist on his listserv, "the 9/11 governmental conspiracy is coming apart." The Bush and Clinton administrations can no longer claim, he said, they "had no foreknowledge of the 'who' and the 'how' and the 'when' of the 9/11 attacks."

This wording is unfortunate. Every time the word "attacks" is used in conjunction with 9/11, it reinforces once more the official story. Since 9/11 was an inside job, it should be referred to as a "fake attack" or "a so-called attack conducted by elements of the US government" or a "false-flag operation."

The most fundamental problem with Able Danger is that it buttresses the official story about 9/11 having been carried out by fanatical Muslims. Whatever mini-dramas swirl around Able Danger, however, many people become excited that this or that revelation will show that "the administration had foreknowledge," leaving intact the central lie — and in fact reinforcing it.

It's not that Able Danger presents no opportunities for truth tellers. But these are different from the ones I'm hearing now. One opportunity is to note that the "whistleblowing" in that case would constitute a perfect "limited hangout" smoke screen for the true operation. Since that would be a desirable outcome for the true perpetrators of 9/11, it leads to the question of whether these are authentic whistleblowers. They could be, within their own lights. The psychological warfare operators at the CIA know, and not them alone, that a sincere person saying what you want said is better than an insincere person saying it.

However you cut it, whether the story is that "terrorists" were "discovered" earlier or later or not discovered at all, whether any administration "learned" of the "dangers of al Qaeda" or not, is not real information. It is more deception, to cover larger deception.

Let's keep our eye on the ball. Al Qaeda was from the beginning essentially a creature of the CIA and in general of the Anglo-American covert establishment. Al Qaeda is the engine that keeps the so-called "war on terrorism" running. The managers of the so-called "war on terror" have to keep feeding disinformation into the public arena to maintain the fear and the military and security budgets. Nafeez Mosaddeq Ahmed, in his book *The War on Truth*, "explores in detail," he explains, "the *modus operandi* of the manipulation and subversion of al Qaeda in the Middle East, Central Asia, Asia-Pacific, Caucasus, and Balkans. Al Qaeda is found to be the outgrowth of a ☞

coordinated network of highly secret sub-units of state-intelligence services operating under the overarching strategic direction of the most clandestine parallel structures of western military-intelligence services, especially those of the US and UK."

The Pentagon sees its "total warfare" mandate as including intelligence and all forms of propaganda, what it calls "information war," as well as all the other forms of violence we normally associate with the Pentagon.

General Shelton was quoted in the *New York Times* article by Judith Miller (dissected in Chapter 4), in a way that would suggest he was less than enthusiastic about catching the biggest alleged terrorist of them all, Osama bin Laden. Ms Miller could be said to be pro-military, yet she reported what she was told by former Clinton White House officials about efforts to catch or kill bin Laden: "[They] said the White House pushed the Joint Chiefs of Staff to develop plans for a commando raid to capture or kill Mr. bin Laden. But the chairman, Gen. Henry H. Shelton, and other senior Pentagon officers told Mr. Clinton's top national security aides that they would need to know Mr. bin Laden's whereabouts 12 to 24 hours in advance. Pentagon planners also considered a White House request to send a hunter team of commandos, small enough to avoid detection, the officer said. General Shelton discounted this option as naïve, the officer said. White House officials were frustrated that the Pentagon could not produce plans that involved a modest number of troops. Military planners insisted that an attack on Al Qaeda required thousands of troops invading Afghanistan. 'When you said this is what it would take, no one was interested,' a senior officer said."[12]

The larger picture is that the American Empire recruits, trains, funds and runs "terrorists" all over the world to perform destabilization wherever needed by the Empire, while simultaneously providing the drumbeat of fear so useful in maintaining domestic manipulation and moving further toward a police state. Several indications are that the Able Danger saga is planned to be one of the cleverer parts of the international and domestic deception. Or, if it was accidentally triggered, is being turned to the same purpose. The rules that apply to "information" coming out of government agencies and personnel are the same as those applying to "information" about alleged "terrorist bombings" and other outrages. All thinking citizens, but above all 9/11Truth activists, must pause to relate the "information" to the larger picture and ask the familiar but important question — who benefits? ∎

Reasons for Dedication to 9/11 Truth

Why work so hard to reveal the truth about 9/11? To many, the central importance of this is far from obvious. That's understandable. I've been asked, for instance, if there are not larger issues, such as Peak Oil, resource depletion in general, climate change, pollution, poverty, disease, injustice, civil liberties and media reform that better deserve our attention, time and money.

To begin with, activism for 9/11 Truth is not an either/or proposition. I applaud anyone pitching in on any worthy cause. I've chosen to focus on 9/11 Truth for the rest of my life, but I find some time and money to support environmental, media democracy and other causes as well. But to me, working for 9/11 Truth is the single most effective way for me to work for all the other causes I support.

Everything's relative. These other issues are relatively diffuse and complex. Most are widespread geographically and economically. The events of 9/11, on the other hand, were relatively compact in time and space.

I've met people who might be willing to become involved in 9/11 Truth activism but who fear it will take too much time, and that the time could be wasted. Again, everything's relative. As far as time is concerned, anyone can get up to speed on 9/11 far more quickly than on most other worthwhile causes. The crime of 9/11 is relatively accessible, understandable and, indeed, provable. The literature on 9/11 is not nearly as daunting as that, for instance, on world poverty or on the corporate takeover of the media.

Additionally, the literature of 9/11 Truth, including DVDs, frankly is more fascinating to me in its own right than is the literature on other important issues: 9/11 constitutes a crime mystery with human, military, forensic, political, health, covert and other dimensions.

As for "wasting time," that's always a risk when it comes to large causes. There's no guarantee we will "win," or that truth and justice will prevail. But nothing in the universe is wasted. Rather than being a waste, devoting one's self to a cause greater than one's self — win or lose — is one of the most important and meaningful time investments any person can make.

As with other causes, there are people who say "it's no use," because the forces of the establishment are overwhelming. That is what is known as "surplus powerlessness," or sometimes "the counsel of despair." Surely we

Profile: Jimmy Walter

The One in a Million Millionaire who Invests in the Truth

A small burden Jimmy Walter Jr. bears is that people mistakenly call him Jimmy Walters. In a way the error is correct: he's living more than one life. He's a venture capitalist, philosopher, writer, political activist, patriot, practical utopian and philanthropist.

Those who "put their money where their mouth is" are all too rare, and rarer still are those among the wealthiest who put both their mouth and their money behind a search for difficult truths that may point back to the wealthiest. Walter is offering $1 million to anyone who can prove explosives were NOT used at the World Trade Center on 9/11. The contest rules are posted on his website at Reopen911.org/Contest.htm

Jimmy Walter

The number "one million" applies to another feature of Jimmy's 9/11 Truth activism. Almost that many copies of Walter's DVD *Confronting the Evidence: A Call to Reopen the 9/11 Investigation,* in ten languages, have been given away. And they're having an impact. I've met quite a few people whose first encounter with the lies of 9/11 was through one of Jimmy's DVDs.

I've always had a soft spot in my heart for what used to be called "eccentric millionaires." One was Marshall Field III, who bankrolled New York's *PM,* a legendary paper that investigated what others would not. Jimmy Walter is cut from the same cloth, and he has a newspaper connection, too. In his quest to spark interest in the truth about 9/11 he has invested millions on full page advertisements with headings such as "Are We Safer Now?" in *Business Week, Forbes, Newsweek, The New York Times, Washington Post, Readers Digest, The New Yorker, The Observer, The Guardian, Le Monde* and more. These ads offer free copies of his DVD.

He sponsored a "9/11Truth tour" in Europe in May 2005, of which I enjoyed the privilege of being part. Meeting Jimmy in person is an experience most people will tell you is unforgettable. He's unpredictable in thought and actions. He's been known to hire someone quickly, fire them as quickly, and sometimes hire them again. He can be contradictory: on the European tour he said publicly he would never return to the US, but return he did. With Jimmy it's never a dull moment. What finally comes through to me is his sincerity, his drive to make the world a better place, and his activism-oriented intellectual curiosity. In February 2006, Jimmy traveled with William Rodriguez (see profile, page 76) to Venezuela hoping to meet President Hugo Chavez on the 9/11 issue.

Jimmy is a son of James W. Walter, Sr., of Florida, who started Walter Homes and Walter Industries in 1946 with a borrowed $1,000. He sold the company in 1986 for $2 billion. Son Jimmy's IQ tested at the genius level. He was Cum Laude at Asheville Prep School and winner of the prestigious Morehead Scholarship at University of North Carolina. Until 9/11, he was devoting his knowledge of business, finance, psychology, economics, behavior management, religion, computer science, and philosophy, to promote the creation of eco-friendly, utopian societies. He still does, but he sees the fraud of 9/11 as an outrage that threatens existing societies, let alone utopian ones. He believes "the world economy and environment are being wrecked by Bush's fanatical actions." He believes "the facts present incontrovertible proof why a new, real and unbiased 911 investigation must take place."

have to do what we can. In the eighteenth century, Edmund Burke said: "Nobody made a greater mistake than he who did nothing because he could do only a little." I would add, from life experience, that you never know your luck. Repeatedly I've seen seemingly lost causes, small and large, won. One example of the potential for rapid change in today's historical terms is seen in the fall of the Berlin wall.

It could be that "history is with us." There's nothing as powerful as an idea whose time has come. The record crowds that demonstrated before the invasion of Iraq (an unprecedented outpouring of peace sentiment *before* a war), the election of leftwing governments across Latin America, the worldwide antipathy to the US military colossus and other indicators show the world is getting ready for something better. It has been said that there's "second superpower" — world public opinion. Many are the signs that the second superpower is growing with a strength that is benign. We could be approaching a tipping point.

Many of our elders are telling us that a new world is emerging. Eco-theologian Thomas Berry in his book *The Dream of the Earth*[13] says, "It's all a question of story. We are in trouble just now because we do not have a good story. We are between stories. The old story, the account of how the world came to be and how we fit into it, is no longer effective. But we have not learned the new story."

Jean Houston, author of *A Mythic Life*,[14] writes: "Myth is important because we're at a time of the changing of the story. We're at the end of one era and not quite at the beginning of a new one. We do not yet see it, but we can feel a new story in our bones. The hound of heaven is going 'woof, woof, woof!' at our ankles in the morning."

The new story will be the path followed once humankind finds the collective will to survive. Each person who comes to that consciousness is contributing what he or she can, in a sustained way, to a new dream of the Earth.

We are Powerful

We should remember how powerful we are. In this particular instance, by "we" I mean average North Americans. Just 150 years ago, our horses tethered outside, consider how relatively powerless we'd be. We would not have the power to be in touch instantly with events and individuals around the world. We would not have the power to summon up most of the knowledge accumulated by our species. Nor would we be living in a time when that store of knowledge is as great as is today, and growing exponentially. Each of us has far more knowledge power than did any king in history. Never has the capacity for humankind to learn from past mistakes been greater.

The current system of the rich getting obscenely richer while more and more people starve, and diminishing resources are squandered on armaments is unsustainable. This very unsustainability contributes to the world being in its current multi-dimensional crisis. Its most important dimension by far is the environmental one. We're destroying the Earth's life support systems; of that there is abundant evidence. There are also growing economic crises, building like earthquake pressures. Millions are shielded from awareness of our precarious situation by the mass media, which function to anesthetize, distract, confuse and mislead on most major issues most of the time.

But crisis is a powerful teacher. Rumi, the Sufi mystic, said: "To increase your knowledge, increase your necessity." Our necessity is being increased for us. Crisis wakes up people who otherwise would not wake up. This presents people already awake with more and more "teachable moments."

There's a personal payoff in 9/11 activism. Responses to a questionnaire I sent to about 20 9/11 Truth activists showed that the most satisfying aspect of the struggle for most was the warm camaraderie of joining like-minded others in a common goal. I recognize this is not unique to 9/11 activism, but that doesn't make it any less true. I continue to enjoy the privilege of talking on the phone with hundreds of people deeply concerned about the crime of 9/11. This is because I take orders for my DVD personally. Most of these people are Americans. These people as a group are — hands down — more widely knowledgeable, passionate, concerned, patriotic and just plain decent than are the people in any other group I have ever encountered. And they usually have a good sense of humor, too. Working with colleagues in a common worthwhile goal is intensely satisfying and gives us energy.

The little paperback *The 100 Simple Secrets of Happy People*,[16] by David Niven, is instructive here. Secret number 100 is headed "What does it all mean? You decide." The truth, writes Niven, "lies not within someone else, but within you. You have been given life, and with it you have been given an

Profile: Ian Woods

"The Crime of 9/11 — If Solved Soon — Will Usher In a Thousand Years of Peace"

Ian Woods set out to be a landscape architect in 1977 but switched careers several times before entering the world of alternative media and communications. Currently, the 56-year-old publishes *Global Outlook,* which helps 9/11Truth activists get their message out, as well as educating those with an open mind to the truth about what really happened on 9/11.

In 1996 he began his first publishing venture, *Monetary Reform* magazine which tackled the corrupt debt-based money system. It reached a total circulation of 3,000 before it ceased publication in 2001. *Global Outlook* soon followed in the spring of 2002, reaching a circulation of 12,000. His self-proclaimed job description is "to help improve the human condition" by revealing the political and corporate corruption in high places and offering positive solutions.

As the events of 9/11 unfolded, Woods felt what he was seeing and hearing in the mainstream media "was too much like Hollywood to be true." At a dinner party in October 2001 Woods found many in agreement. One of those attending suggested Pearl Harbor "was not a surprise attack." Woods checked out two books on the subject[15] that "proved conclusively [to him] that Pearl Harbor had, in fact, been orchestrated by the US government." Using that as a starting point and putting in many hours of research, he deduced that "9/11 was a gigantic hoax perpetrated on the modern world by the Bush administration (among others), as part of a hidden agenda." Woods has become determined to do what he can to reveal "the enormity of this lie and all its potential outcomes."

Ian Woods

Woods says he has always been inspired by the life and work of Mahatma Gandhi, who once said of his local paper that its purpose was to unite their community under one cause. It is Woods' hope that *Global Outlook* will do the same, and in so doing, break the truth about 9/11 into full public view.

Publishing a magazine is a full-time job, but Ian still finds time to be the inspiring and well-organized president of Skeptics' Inquiry For Truth (SIFT), the incorporated nonprofit organization which hosted the six-day International Citizens' Inquiry into 9/11 held in Toronto, May 2004 (www.911Inquiry.org). He's attended most of the major 9/11Truth events in North America as a speaker and promoter of 9/11Truth resources. His high energy and enthusiasm makes it unsurprising that he ran for federal public office three times, as well as in three marathons, including in Boston, in 2001.

His professional and personal lives are characterized by vision, thoughtfulness, attention to detail and generosity. Elsewhere in this book I pay tribute to the hundreds of hours Ian devoted to helping with this book, which highlights perhaps his most notable characteristic: dedication. "My main inspiration," he says, "comes from my fellow truth activists — people who really are making a difference." He names a long list.

Woods sees our challenge as "primarily a psychological battle in which we need to use our wits and brains in delivering the right message, at the right time, to the right people, with pinpoint accuracy, similar to how an acupuncturist heals a patient. That way we can break the collective trance the mainstream corporate media has imposed on us." Woods believes that strategic thinking and truth activism are the keys to unraveling this nefarious web of deceit and corruption in which we find ourselves. "There is a way out. All we have to do is take it."

opportunity to define it. Your life's purpose will be drawn on a map created by you." He refers to a study of 100 adults over two years which found the effect of "good" and "bad" events quickly faded; the subjects' happiness "was not dependent on the sum of events but on what they made of those events."

I believe exposing 9/11 Truth is the single most important task we face. It can be the catalyst that releases the full potential of the second superpower. The key ruling trick of all oligarchies would be revealed. The political impact on the general public would be enormous. As we saw at the end of Chapter 3, it could be the psychological and emotional equivalent of a war. It could have more impact than the original events of 9/11. Those at the Project for a New American Century (PNAC) who conceived the massive deception said their agenda required "a catastrophic and catalytic event such on the scale like a new Pearl Harbor." It worked. Exposing their deception could unleash the massive power of public opinion against the conspirators and finally clear the way for a sane, peaceful agenda.

The truth about 9/11 made known to the populace could start a transformation leading more quickly to the solution of those other large issues than, paradoxically, can struggling with them directly. The events of 9/11 are the potential Achilles Heel for the whole system of oligarchy, the Invisible Government that deceives people into wars for the profit of the few, that sustains international injustice and inequalities of many kinds.

9/11 Truth marchers in Toronto, Canada

My father, before Diana Ralph, said: "Decide where you are, which is A, and then decide your goal, which is B." We're at A, which clearly is, more and more, a dangerous place. The minimum goal, the B of all people of goodwill, surely is a safer, saner and more just world. I believe the shortest distance from A to B is through 9/11 Truth.

Diary of 9/11 and the Media ~~~✍

The Movie *United 93* will Crash and Burn

April 28, 2006 — In the beginning was 9/11. Then the 9/11 official story. The Big Lie. Then three years of reinforcement of the lies within the official story by mainstream and alternative media, leading up to the release of the 9/11 commission "report" — the official lies in book form. Today I see the movie *United 93* on the day it opens. I see the lie about Flight 93 in cinema verité

This version, like the others, is easily demonstrable as a falsification. It features the same impossibilities, absurdities and contradictions as the official lie about Flight 93 in its other forms. As such it contains the seeds of its own destruction.

The official story makes the FAA the fall guy for the "failures" that day. This is embellished in celluloid in *United 93*. "We're getting no clearance from the FAA to get those birds over Manhattan," complains a NORAD commander playing himself. Since when do the military await orders from civilian authorities?

United 93 trots out anomalies that should make audiences laugh out loud, but the frenetic pace of the hand-held camera work precludes critical thought by the unprepared. At one point we meet a passenger who says: "I'm a pilot. I've been flying all my life. There's something wrong here." This would make sense except that his line comes after the plane has been hijacked by a screaming man baring a home made bomb strapped to his abdomen and holds aloft a detonator switch with wires running to the bomb. Yep, something's not right here — this pilot, the dialogue, the whole movie. We see four cell phone calls made, none of which would be possible. The fact that debris from Flight 93 was found over 13 square kilometers cannot be allowed in this movie, which has the plane going straight down into that "crash site" too small for such a plane, where no bodies and not a drop of blood were found.

According to executive producer Paul Greengrass *United 93* is "based on fact" and spun out in the "real time" Flight 93 was aloft. This combination will prove its Achilles heel. For instance, long after all the four airliners have allegedly been hijacked by terrorists, the FAA and the military are engaged in patently absurd discussions about "getting some birds up there." In the real world, interceptors are scrambled in three minutes or so.

United 93 is a particular form of psychological warfare. The night I saw it, the stunned silence that followed the end of the movie suggested that perhaps the audience had swallowed it hook, line and sinker. If so they have swallowed state-sponsored propaganda. Is it coincidence that the alleged conversations captured from the cockpit voice recorder of Flight 93 were released 1,670 days after the events of 9/11, but just 15 days before release of this movie? That they were released at the show trial of Zacarias Moussaoui, and that the movie's dialogue follows the released alleged conversations perfectly? This is high-level scripting.

As usual, the mainstream media remain oblivious to such facts and questions. Mainstream reviewers universally praised the movie for its verisimilitude, thus themselves becoming effective tools of the state psywar planners. Maclean's magazine movie critic Brian D. Johnson accepts *United 93* as a documentary, something even the movie doesn't claim. "There's something reassuring to have the pieces of the puzzle put together. It's very true to reality," he said on TVO's current affairs program Studio 2.

United 93 presents another opportunity for the 9/11 Truth movement to reveal another pastiche of lies and thereby a cover-up, this one produced by Hollywood. *United 93,* the movie, will eventually be shot down as Flight 93 was. It's up to us to shoot the movie down, using ammunition drawn from the flick itself. "Nobody's going to help us. We've got to do it," says one passenger. That's right. It's us against the government, the media, the courts and Hollywood. Let's roll.

Diary of 9/11 and the Media: June 15, 2006 ～～✍🗐

Conversation With A Senior Editor

Barrie Zwicker: Could I ask you a few questions?

Senior Editor: Shoot

BZ: Do you consider yourself an honest person?

Ed: I do, yes.

BZ: Do you think of yourself as alert and well-informed?

Ed: I'm not sure where you're going with this but yes, if I have to say so, I think I'm fairly well informed. And, to use your word, alert.

BZ: So you know about 9/11?

Ed: What do you mean?

BZ: That the official story is, to say the least, obviously laden with large unanswered questions?

Ed: Such as?

BZ: Such as that if one looks coldly at the evidence — utter failure of the US Air Force that day, controlled demolition of World Trade Center Building Number 7 later that day, stonewalling of Bush Administration for 441 days before appointing a commission of inquiry, to cite just three pieces of evidence — that these alone point to an inside job directed by the White House.

Ed: That's quite a charge.

BZ: It's not a charge, it's a look at evidence.

Ed: Your evidence.

BZ: What do you mean?

Ed: Well, what you call evidence I call conspiracy theory.

BZ: That's a putdown phrase. Let's go back to evidence. Have you checked out any?

Ed: You mean on the Internet?

BZ: Yes, and in books such as the ones written by Webster Tarpley, Michael Ruppert, David Ray Griffin and Nafeez Ahmed. Both Griffin and Ahmed have written two books on 9/11.

Ed: Well, I don't tend to read books that haven't been reviewed by respected newspapers.

BZ: Okay, the Internet. Have you ever sat down and just using your honesty, your alertness and your wish to be well-informed — I'm not being disrespectful or facetious here — done searches for, say, WTC 7?

Ed: No, I have better things to do.

BZ: But doesn't that put you in conflict with your belief that you're fairly well informed? We're talking about very large, life-and-death issues here. We're talking about the basis for the so-called war on terrorism and for hot wars in Afghanistan and Iraq.

Ed: You say "so-called war on terrorism." Look, there's such a thing as terrorism. Either you're out of your depth, or out of your mind, or for some reason you get your jollies from hectoring editors. Or maybe all three.

BZ: How am I out of my depth?

Ed: You apparently don't understand how the world works or how the news business works. The war on terror has some warts, granted. The people in the slammer for years without charges being laid, I don't agree with that. But as an editor there's only so much you can do. There are limited resources, there's resistance from readers, there are deadlines. An editor has to balance all these.

BZ: Okay, but you're evading my question.

Ed: I think I'm answering it.

BZ: Okay, let me re-state it: Do you, personally, as an editor, feel any responsibility for investigating those anomalies I mentioned about 9/11, about the air force going AWOL, about WTC Building 7, about the resistance of the White House to a so-called independent investigation until the families forced it?

Ed: There you go, you call the investigation of the 9/11 commission "so-called." As far as I can see, that report of that commission put "paid" to all your conspiracy theorizing.

BZ: I think you'd find it difficult to say that if you'd read David Ray Griffin's book *The 9/11 Commission Report: Omissions and Distortions.*

Ed: Well I haven't. And I don't intend to. As I mentioned I don't read books on current affairs that no mainstream media see fit to review.

BZ: You said near the outset that you didn't see where I was going. I think at this point I see where you're coming from. And I'm guessing you're thinking you have better things to do right now.

Ed: For the first time, I'm in agreement with you.

BZ: So thank you for your time.

Ed: You're welcome, and good luck.

Diary of 9/11 and the Media: September 11, 2020

Conversation With A Senior Editor

Leah (author's granddaughter, age 17): May I ask you a few questions?

Senior Editor (just retired): Shoot

L: What do you think about the treason convictions of George Bush and the others?

Ed: Clearly overdue.

L: How much overdue?

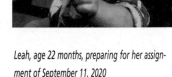

Ed: Well, once the special prosecutor, the one who went to work after the rigged election of 2008, once he essentially had the goods on them in early 2011, they

Leah, age 22 months, preparing for her assignment of September 11, 2020

should have 'fessed up and saved their country and the world the next five years of agony.

L: It would have been better if their treason trials had been much sooner than 2016?

Ed: Absolutely.

L: How early do you think definitive steps could have been taken to bring this crowd to justice?

Ed: As I say, 10 years ago.

L: Did you ever read a book titled *Towers of Deception*, that came out in 2006?

Ed: I heard of it but I never read it.

L: Why?

Ed: Well, as I recall it wasn't reviewed and was one of those conspiracy theory books.

L: But now conspiracy has been proven…

Ed: I suppose. But until it's proven in a court of law, it's still theory.

L: The Kucinich Administration is re-opening the investigation into 9/11.

Ed: Yes…and?

L: *Towers of Deception* and a dozen other books published between 2002 and 2009 spelled out unmistakably even then the criminal conspiracy that already existed behind 9/11.

Ed: Well, now we can see that's very likely. But back then, the mainstream did not believe that.

L: Reading at least one of those books is required in our History classes.

Ed: Is that so?

L: Yes. *Towers of Deception* is the one that focuses on the role of the media, and within the media people like you — called gatekeepers. The author says you functioned as de facto censors, covering up the truth about 9/11 that even then, he says, was "hidden in plain sight."

Ed: So what, exactly, has this to do with me?

L: I think you're the editor Barrie Zwicker had in mind when he wrote *Towers of Deception*. He was my grandfather. He's gone now, and he said that it would be bad form for him to become too personal when he wrote the book. But he was really angry about the way the mainstream media, as he put it, "stymied justice and history by remaining autistic" about these widely-accepted facts. The dirty tricks, the rigged elections and especially the fraud of 9/11 that kept them in power, as you say, far too long.

Ed: Well, well.

L: So what do you say?

Ed: I say you're a very sassy young miss. You probably get it from your grandfather, and I say that it wasn't that simple, not by a long shot. Essentially we didn't know, even if your granddaddy claims we did.

L: He actually predicted you'd say that. He said it reminded him of all the Germans who claimed they didn't know a thing about the Holocaust.

Ed: Young lady, I think, with all due respect, that you've about worn out your welcome. My conscience is clear.

L: He predicted you'd say that, too.

Ed: How's school going?

L: Very well, thank you. This interview will help me finish my History assignment, "What was the role of the mainstream media in the aftermath of 9/11?" And our school has a lot of terrific archival resources now that more and more funds are being diverted from the military, spy agencies and state surveillance.

Ed: Well good for you. Now if you'll excuse me...

L: Actually, I won't.

Ed: You really are nervy.

L: Not really. It's just that I owe it to my grandfather's memory. He said if we don't get our priorities straight, if we don't ask ourselves every day "What can I do for my planet?" we will have to make excuses for ourselves at the end of our lives. I've decided I don't want to do that.

Senior Ed., Ret'd: Goodbye, Ms Zwicker.

L: Goodbye, and good luck.

What is your take on the events of 9/11?

Back on page vi, the "Four Box 9/11 Questionnaire" I developed in early 2002 is first offered. You may have chosen to fill it in. Here it is again if you want to compare your responses now against your responses then. Or you can fill it in here for the first time, for your interest. Below it I offer background on the questionnaire and comments on the responses to it that I've encountered.

The Four-Box 9/11Questionnaire

Check the box that comes closest to your take on 9/11:

[   ]1. I believe that 19 fanatical Muslim terrorists, members of Al Qaeda led by Osama bin Laden, caught all of the US intelligence, military and political establishments totally off guard.

[   ] 2. I believe that enough advance information had been received by U.S. agencies that the "attacks" could have been prevented or ameliorated, but that incompetence at various levels enabled the events to proceed as they did.

[   ] 3. I believe that a great deal of advance information had been received by US agencies, enough that the events could have been prevented, but that people at the top deliberately allowed the events to unfold as they did.

[   ] 4. I believe that the alleged 19 hijackers, if there were that many, were dupes and patsies, that the events of 9/11 were planned at the highest levels in and around the White House, that it was an inside job.

* * *

If you've read the book, you'll recall the above four "takes" on 9/11 are described in more detail in chapter 1, within the article submitted to the newspaper *Sunday*. The choices equate this way:

Box 1 equates to The Official Story of 9/11
Box 2 equates to The Incompetence Theory
Box 3 equates to the Let It Happen On Purpose (or LIHOP) theory and
Box 4 equates to The Inside Job theory

Starting in early 2002 I've asked for hands-up responses to this questionnaire from dozens of audiences, mainly in Toronto, the U.S. West Coast and Midwest and New York City as well as in Western Europe and Iceland. I asked the questions prior to screenings of the DVD enclosed in this book (or its predecessor video The Great Deception) before the screenings and again after.

Over the 2002-2006 time period, patterns became evident. In early 2002, up to a third of those in audiences, when first asked, indicated a belief in the official story. Sometimes as few as one in ten chose inside job as their take on 9/11. The others were divided between boxes two and three, with box two, the "incompetence theory," heavily represented. As time passed, fewer and fewer people chose the official story box to start, and more and more chose box four, and there was a trend out of box two and into box three.

At individual screenings at any time, when the pre- and post-screening responses are compared, without exception what happens is a migration of responses up through the boxes. Typically audiences shift along these lines: box one will drop by two-thirds or more; box two will drop by half; box three will double and box four will quadruple.

By late 2004, with an audience of 200 at the Tattered Cover Bookstore in Denver, Colorado, not a single hand went up to in belief of the official story and almost a third went up to favor 9/11 being an inside job, prior to the DVD screening. Afterwards, more than half voted that 9/11 was an inside job. By early 2006, three-quarters of audiences would be clustered in boxes three and four and frequently half or more members of all audiences would already believe 9/11 to be an inside job out the outset.

There's no question that people attending events advertising that there are serious questions about the official 9/11 story are not average. They have a heightened consciousness or concern about the subject. But it's fair, I think, to extrapolate somewhat from the numbers who turn out for such events and the patterns of belief they express, especially in light of the poll results reported in the article within chapter one. I think these patterns show that views within the general public are trending in the same direction.

This underscores for me the tragic sabotage the mainstream media engage in when they cover up not only the evidence that 9/11 was an inside job, but the extent of public understanding and intuition on this subject. If just one significant mainstream medium would initiate a public "hands up questionnaire" about 9/11 and stay with it long enough to beget a serious public discussion, it could be a society-wide eye opener. This eye opening is what I and everyone I know associated with the 9/11 Truth movement are working toward by every non-violent means we can think of.

A final note, relating to Chapter 5: If Noam Chomsky had been at the Tattered Cover Bookstore in November 2002, or others like it, his would have been the only hand among an audience of 200 Americans to be raised in support of the official story. For shame.

I welcome your feedback about this questionnaire or anything else in the book. Especially welcome are corrections of fact, or new or added information on any aspect of 9/11, as well as your thoughts and interpretations surrounding 9/11, the so-called "war on terror," and the interests behind these. Email bwz@rogers.com.

Barrie Zwicker
May, 2006

Notes

Chapter 1

1. These colleagues included Ian Woods, editor and publisher of *Global Outlook: The Magazine of 9/11 Truth;* Webster Griffin Tarpley and David Ray Griffin, US authors of books exposing the truth about 9/11; Carol Brouillet of Palo Alto, California, 9/11Truth activist and newsletter publisher; Nafeez Ahmed, UK author of three books on 9/11 and the sham of the so-called "war on terrorism;" Peter Phillips, Executive Director of Project Censored at Sonoma State University in California; David McFadden, Canadian author and poet; and Dr. Terry Burrows, psychologist and 9/11Truth activist.

2. PNAC, p. 91.

3. At the time, the intended title of this book.

4. Published in French in 2002 by Les éditions des Intouchables of Montreal, and in English in 2003 by McClelland & Stewart of Toronto. ISBN 0-71710-8005-0.

5. A book by Clyde Prestowitz of the same title, but with the sub-title *American Unilateralism and the Failure of Good Intentions,* was reviewed by *BusinessWeek.* But the same October 2005 search that found that review found no reviews for Peter Scowen's *Rogue Nation,* apart from one in the *Star* itself.

6. It's been suggested that it looks as if I was setting Peter up so that his rejection of the article would be fodder for this book. Nothing could be further from the truth. My aim was crystal clear: I really wanted to see this article published. Part of my brief initial email to Scowen read, typically: "As you'll see, this article is intended for publication Sunday, Sept 11 (the fourth anniversary of 9/11), with *Sunday* specifically in mind (the piece contains early germane references to earlier work published in the Sunday *Star*)....I dare to think I have a completely different, and frankly an important, 'take' on the events of 9/11, for a mainstream medium. (Yes, new and important — for mainstream media — facts and interpretations remain unpublished.) And I think I have the bona fides to justify my tackling this subject. Anything else I can learn from you that will increase the chance of this article at least being seriously considered for publication will be appreciated..." I dared to believe there were rational grounds for cautious optimism. I did everything within my power to get it published and still grieve it wasn't, in small part for reasons of ego, but for the largest part by far because it was such an opportunity lost for 9/11Truth and indeed for *Sunday.* I still believe, and I said this to Scowen, that the major mainstream media outlet that does a "takeout" on the anomalies of 9/11 will be in line sooner or later for every major journalistic award the world has to offer. However, I understood that my working on this book at that time could be a factor in the way an editor would think about my submission. It was clear to me I must disclose the book project, and I did so in the "shirt tail" to the article, just as I did with an article I submitted to *The Globe and Mail* around the same time, that was published on November 5, 2005. That article comprises the opening example of false-flag operations, in Chapter 7.

7. Scowen, Peter. *Rogue Nation: The America the Rest of the World Knows,* McClelland & Stewart, 2003, p. 5.

8.   Ibid, p. 55.
9.   Ibid, p. 67.
10. Ibid, Chapter 8.
11. Ibid, p. 148.
12. Ibid, p. 112.; from a CIA manual for so-called "contras" undermining the democratically-elected government of Nicaragua.

Chapter 2

1.   David Ray Griffin, *The New Pearl Harbor: Disturbing Questions about 9/11,* Olive Branch Press, 2004.
2.   Noel Twyman, *Bloody Treason: On Solving History's Greatest Murder Mystery — The Assassination of John F. Kennedy,* Laurel Publishing, 1997.
3.   *Black's Law Dictionary,* 4th Edition, 1957.
4.   William J. Caughlin, *Shadow of a Doubt,* G.K. Hall & Co., 1992.

EXHIBIT A

5.   Larry Silverstein — Profile in Wikipedia encyclopedia. Cited at En.wikipedia.org/wiki/Larry_Silverstein
6.   "America Rebuilds," PBS documentary, September 2002.
7.   *The 9/11 Commission Report: Final Report of the National Commission on Terrorist Attacks Upon the United States,* W.W. Norton & Company, July 2004, mentions WTC 7 five times, on pages 284, 293, 302 and twice on page 305. Use the search engine at Vivisimo.com/911
8.   NIST (National Institute of Standards and Technology) "Final Report on the Collapse of World Trade Center 7." Cited at Wtc.nist.gov/NISTNCSTAR1-1J.pdf
9.   FEMA Report #403, *World Trade Center Building Performance Study,* Federal Emergency Management Agency, May 2002: "The specifics of the fires in WTC 7 and how they caused the building to collapse remain unknown at this time. Although the total diesel fuel on the premises contained massive potential energy, the best hypothesis has only a low probability of occurrence. Further research, investigation, and analyses are needed to resolve this issue." Cited at Fema.gov/fima/mat/fema403.shtm
10. USinfo.state.gov/media/Archive/2005/Sep/16-241966.html
11. Prisonplanet.com/articles/january2006/050106silversteinanswers.htm
12. Table 5.1 WTC 7 Tenants as reported by Jim Hoffman at WTC7.net/articles/FEMA/WTC_ch5.htm

Floor	Tenant
46-47	Mechanical floors
28-45	Salomon Smith Barney (SSB)
26-27	Standard Chartered Bank
25	Inland Revenue Service
25	Department of Defense (DOD)
25	Central Intelligence Agency (CIA)
24	Inland Revenue Service
23	Office of Emergency Management (OEM)
22	Federal Home Loan Bank of New York
21	First State Management Group
19-21	ITT Hartford Insurance Group
19	National Association of Insurance Commissioners (NAIC)
18	Equal Opportunity Commission (EEOC)
14-17	Vacant
13	Provident Financial Management

11-13	Securities and Exchange Commission (SEC)
9-10	US Secret Service
7-8	American Express Bank International
7	OEM generators and day tank
6	Switchgear, storage
5	Switchgear, generators, transformers
4	Upper level of 3rd floor, switchgear
3	Lobby, SSB Conference Center, rentable space, management
2	Open to first floor lobby, transformer vault upper level, upper level switchgear
1	Lobby, loading docks, Con Ed transformer vaults, fuel storage, lower level switchgear

EXHIBIT B

13. David Ray Griffin, "Flights of Fancy — Flights 11, 175, 77 and 93: The 9/11 Commission's Incredible Tales," *Global Outlook,* No.11, Fall-Winter 2006; Lecture, December 4, 2005. Cited at 911truth.org/index.php?topic=911commission

14. Congressional testimony by NORAD's commander, General Ralph E. Eberhart, made in October 2002, and *Slate* magazine, January 16th, 2002. Source: David Ray Griffin, *The 9/11 Commission Report: Omissions and Distortions,* Olive Branch Press, 2005, p. 140.

15. Paul Thompson's "Complete 9/11 Timeline — The Failure to Defend the Skies on 9/11," cited at Cooperativeresearch.org/essay.jsp?article says: "These planes within NORAD's system routinely scrambled after other aircraft. Often the goal was drug interdiction. General Ralph Eberhart, NORAD Commander-in-Chief, said that before 9/11, 'Normally, our units [flew] 4-6 sorties a month in support of the NORAD air defense mission.'" [Federal News Service, October 25, 2001.] In 2000, there were 425 "unknowns" — pilots who didn't file or who diverted from flight plans or used the wrong frequency. In 2000, NORAD scrambled fighters 129 times. (*Calgary Herald,* October 13, 2001.)

16. *The 9/11 Commission Report,* op. cit., Paragraph #2246 (p. 459) states: "In response to allegations that NORAD responded more quickly to the October 25, 1999, plane crash that killed Payne Stewart than it did to the hijacking of American 11, we compared NORAD's response time for each incident. The last normal transmission from the Stewart flight was at 9:27:10 A.M. Eastern Daylight Time. The Southeast Air Defense Sector was notified of the event at 9:55, 28 minutes later. In the case of American 11, the last normal communication from the plane was at 8:13 A.M. EDT. NEADS (NORAD's Northeast Air Defense Sector) was notified at 8:38, 25 minutes later. We have concluded there is no significant difference in NORAD's reaction to the two incidents. See NTSB memo, Aircraft Accident Brief for Payne Stewart incident, Oct. 25, 1999; FAA email, Gahris to Myers, 'ZJX Timeline for N47BA accident,' Feb. 17, 2004."

17. The FAA reported that NORAD scrambled fighter jets 67 times between September 2000 and June 2001. (FAA News Release, August 9th, 2002; Associated Press August 12, 2002.)

18. *The 9/11 Commission Report,* op. cit., Paragraph #127 (p. 20) reads: "In summary, NEADS received notice of the hijacking nine minutes before it struck the North Tower. That nine minutes' notice before impact was the most the military would receive of any of the four hijackings."

19. David Ray Griffin, *The 9/11 Commission Report: Omissions and Distortions,* Olive Branch Press, 2004, p. 187.

20. FAA clarification memo by Laura Brown, the FAA's Deputy in Public Affairs (dated May 21, 2003) posted at911truth.org/article.php?story=2004081200421797. Brown's

memo reads: "Within minutes after the first aircraft hit the World Trade Center, the FAA immediately established several phone bridges that included FAA field facilities, the FAA Command Center, FAA headquarters, DOD, the Secret Service, and other government agencies. The US Air Force liaison to the FAA immediately joined the FAA headquarters phone bridge and established contact with NORAD on a separate line. The FAA shared real-time information on the phone bridges about the unfolding events, including information about loss of communication with aircraft, loss of transponder signals, unauthorized changes in course, and other actions being taken by all the flights of interest, including Flight 77. Other parties on the phone bridges, in turn, shared information about actions they were taking. NORAD logs indicate that the FAA made formal notification about American Flight 77 at 9:24 a.m., but information about the flight was conveyed continuously during the phone bridges before the formal notification."

EXHIBIT C
21. *The 9/11 Commission Report,* op. cit., Paragraph #99 (p. 17). According to the *Report,* 100 other facilities not "on alert" would need time "to arm the fighters and organize crews."
22. Ibid., Paragraphs #123-124 (p. 20).
23. Paul Thompson, *The Terror Timeline,* Regan Books, 2004, pp. 380-381. (Quoting from many mainstream media sources and official documents.)
24. *The 9/11 Commission Report,* op. cit., Paragraph # 125-126 (p. 20).
25. Ibid., Paragraph # 149 (p. 24).
26. Some researchers, such as David Ray Griffin, aren't so sure *any* jets took off from Otis that day.

EXHIBIT D
27. *The 9/11 Commission Report,* op. cit., Paragraph #150 (p. 24): "Because the Otis fighters had expended a great deal of fuel in flying first to military airspace and then to New York, the battle commanders were concerned about refueling. NEADS considered scrambling alert fighters from Langley Air Force Base in Virginia to New York, to provide backup. The Langley fighters were placed on battle stations at 9:09. NORAD had no indication that any other plane had been hijacked."
28. Ibid., Paragraph #166-167 (p. 26): "The NEADS technician who took this call from the FAA immediately passed the word to the mission crew commander, who reported to the NEADS battle commander. Mission Crew Commander, NEADS: 'Okay, uh, American Airlines is still airborne. Eleven, the first guy, he's heading towards Washington. Okay? I think we need to scramble Langley right now. And I'm gonna take the fighters from Otis, try to chase this guy down if I can find him.'"
29. Ibid., Paragraph #221 (p. 37): "Inside the NMCC [National Military Command Center in the Pentagon], the deputy director for operations called for an all purpose 'significant event' conference. It began at 9:29, with a brief recap: two aircraft had struck the World Trade Center, there was a confirmed hijacking of American 11, and Otis fighters had been scrambled. The FAA was asked to provide an update, but the line was silent because the FAA had not been added to the call. A minute later, the deputy director stated that it had just been confirmed that American 11 was still airborne and heading toward D.C. He directed the transition to an air threat conference call. NORAD confirmed that American 11 was airborne and heading toward Washington, relaying the erroneous FAA information already mentioned [in Footnote 2 above]. The call then ended, at about 9:34." According to this Commission account, the military brass believed "American 11" (which had already crashed at 8:46 in NYC) was the flight heading toward the Pentagon an hour later, and that the reason the

NMCC believed this was because of faulty information from the FAA. This could be construed as gratuitous overkill in a detail to further scapegoat the FAA.

30. Ibid., Paragraph #169 (p. 27): "At 9:36, the FAA's Boston Center called NEADS and relayed the discovery about an unidentified aircraft closing in on Washington.... This startling news prompted the mission crew commander at NEADS to take immediate control of the airspace to clear a flight path for the Langley fighters: "Okay, we're going to turn it ... crank it up ... Run them to the White House." He then discovered, to his surprise, that the Langley fighters were not headed north toward the Baltimore area as instructed, but east over the ocean. "I don't care how many windows you break," he said. "Damn it.... Okay. Push them back."

31. Nafeez Mosaddeq Ahmed, *The War on Freedom: How and Why America was Attacked on September 11,* Media Messenger Books, 2002, p. 168, quoting Jared Israel in the *New York Press.*

EXHIBIT E

32. Illarion Bykov and Jared Israel, "Guilty For 9-11: Bush, Rumsfeld, Myers," November 17th, 2001: "Andrews Air Force Base is a huge installation. It hosts two 'combat-ready' squadrons: the 121st Fighter Squadron (FS-121) of the 113th Fighter Wing (FW-113), equipped with F-16 fighters; the 321st Marine Fighter Attack Squadron (VMFA-321) of the 49th Marine Air Group, Detachment A (MAG-49 Det-A), equipped with F/A-18 fighters"; emperors-clothes.com/indict/indict-1.htm

33. Paul Thompson's "Complete 9/11 Timeline," op. cit., posted at Cooperativeresearch.org/essay.jsp?article states: "There are dozens of other air force bases on the East Coast. How quickly other bases could get fighters into the air varied from base to base. Before 9/11, the web sites of many of these bases used terms like 'combat ready,' 'five minute alert,' 'highest state of readiness,' and so on, indicating they should have been able to quickly respond as well. For instance, the web site for Andrews Air Force Base next to Washington boasted that it hosted two 'combat ready' squadrons, 'capable and ready response forces for the District of Columbia in the event of a natural disaster or civil emergency.' The District of Columbia Air National Guard was stationed at Andrews, and its web site claimed its mission was 'to provide combat units in the highest possible state of readiness.' Both web sites changed on September 12, 2001, and the phrases suggesting such quick response capability were removed. Bases at Westfield, Massachusetts; Syracuse, New York; and Hartford, Connecticut, also promised high readiness status, and these bases would have been in good positions to defend the skies on 9/11."

34. Ibid.

35. *Aviation Week and Space Technology,* September 9, 2002.

36. David Ray Griffin, *The 9/11 Commission Report,* op. cit., p. 257.

37. Paul Thompson, *The Terror Timeline,* op. cit., p. 459.

38. David Ray Griffin, *The 9/11 Commission Report,* op. cit., p. 159.

39. David Ray Griffin, "Flights of Fancy," op. cit.

40. Paul Thompson, *The Terror Timeline,* op. cit.

EXHIBIT F

41. *The New York Times,* October 14, 1961.

EXHIBIT G

42. Edited excerpt from a speech by Michael C. Ruppert at the Commonwealth Club, San Francisco, August 31, 2004, reprinted in *Global Outlook,* No. 9, pp. 46-47. The seven following footnotes are sourced from Ruppert's book, *Crossing the Rubicon: The Decline of the American Empire at the end of the Age of Oil* (New Society Publishers, 2004, pp. 641-642).

43. Hart Seely, "Amid Crisis Simulation, 'We Were Suddenly — No Kidding — Under Attack,'" Newhouse News Service, January 25, 2002.

44. Forces.gc.ca/dcds/dir/dpdt/j7Ex/pages/exercises_e.asp
Globalsecurity.org/military/ops/vigilant-guardian.htm

45. William B. Scott, "Exercise Jump-Starts Response to Attacks," *Aviation Week and Space Technology,* June 3, 2002; ABC News, September 11th, 2002.

46. Mike Kelly, "NORAD confirmed two mock drills on September 11," NJ.com, December 5, 2003.

47. Richard A. Clarke, *Against All Enemies,* Free Press, 2004, p. 5: "Not a pretty picture, Dick. We are in the middle of Vigilant Warrior, a NORAD exercise ..."

48. Scott Simmie, "'Northern Guardian:' The Scene at NORAD on September 11," *Toronto Star,* Ontario edition, December 9, 2001.

49. John J. Lumpkin, "Agency Planned Exercise on September 11 built around a plane crashing into a building," Associated Press, August 21, 2002 7:45 p.m. EST.

50. There are conflicting reports about how many jet fighters were on alert on 9/11. See StandDown.net's "33 USAF Bases Were Within Range On 911 — 7 Air Stations Were On Full Alert Covering The Continental United States (5 of these 7 Air Stations were within range of the four airliners hijacked on 9/11) — 28 More Air Stations Were In Range Of The 4 Hijacked Airliners On 9/11," at Standdown.net/USAFbases.htm

51. *The 9/11 Commission Report,* op. cit., Paragraph #2241 (p. 458), states: "On 9/11, NORAD was scheduled to conduct a military exercise, Vigilant Guardian, which postulated a bomber attack from the former Soviet Union. We investigated whether military preparations for the large-scale exercise compromised the military's response to the real-world terrorist attack on 9/11. According to General Eberhart, 'it took about 30 seconds' to make the adjustment to the real-world situation. Ralph Eberhart testimony, June 17, 2004. We found that the response was, if anything, expedited by the increased number of staff at the sectors and at NORAD because of the scheduled exercise."

EXHIBIT H

52. Jim Hoffman, *Global Outlook,* No. 10, Spring-Summer 2005, p. 35.

53. Note that Building 7, however, imploded inwards, typical of a different style of demolition.

54. *The New York Times* Online, 2005. "The September 11 Records" (9/11 Oral Histories). Cited at
Graphics8.nytimes.com/packages/html/nyregion/20050812_WTC_GRAPHIC/met_WTC_histories_full_01.html

55. James Williams, "WTC a Structural Success," *SEAU NEWS: The Newsletter of the Structural Engineers Association of Utah,* October 2001.

56. David Ray Griffin elaborates in his essay "The Destruction of the World Trade Center: Why the Official Account Cannot Be True" (Paul Zarembka, ed., *The Hidden History of 9-11-2001,* Elsevier, 2006; also published at 911Review.com): "If all these firefighters and medical workers witnessed all these phenomena suggestive of controlled demolition, it might be wondered why the public does not know this. Part of the answer is provided by Auxiliary Lieutenant Fireman Paul Isaac. Having said that 'there were definitely bombs in those buildings,' Isaac added that 'many other firemen know there were bombs in the buildings, but they're afraid for their jobs to admit it because the "higher-ups" forbid discussion of this fact' (Lavello, Randy, n.d. "Bombs in the Building," at Prisonplanet.com/analysis_lavello_050503_bombs.html). Another part of the answer is that when a few people, like Isaac and William Rodriguez, have spoken out, the mainstream press has failed to report their statements."

EXHIBIT I

57. Steven Ashley, ScientificAmerican.com, In *Focus*, "When the Twin Towers Fell," October 9, 2001. Cited at Sciam.com/article.cfm?articleID=000B7FEB-A88C-1C75-9B81809EC588EF21&sc=I100322

58. MIT Dept. of Civil and Environmental Engineering, "CEE and Industry Panelists Discuss World Trade Center Collapse at Huge Lecture," October 3, 2001. More than 450 people crammed into Rm. 54-100 to hear "Structural Engineers' Perspective on the World Trade Center Collapse." An extensive summary by Steve Ashley, "When the Twin Towers Fell," appears on the Scientific American website, Siam.com for October 10, 2001. Cited at Cee.mit.edu/index.pl?iid=3742&isa=Category

59. "World Trade Center, New York, Engineering Aspects" from posting at US Search and Rescue Task Force website: Owners: Port Authority of New York and New Jersey. Architect: Minoru Yamasaki, Emery Roth and Sons. Consulting Engineers: John Skilling and Leslie Robertson of Worthington, Skilling, Helle and Jackson. Ground Breaking: August 5, 1966. Ribbon cutting: April 4, 1973. Cited at Ussartf.org/world_trade_center_disaster.htm

60. See "The Fall of the World Trade Center," BBC 2, March 7, 2002, transcript at Bbc.co.uk/science/horizon/2001/worldtradecentertrans.shtml. For a comparison of the 707 and the 767, see "Boeing 707-767 Comparison," at Whatreallyhappened.com/boeing_707_767.html

61. Norman Glover, "Collapse Lessons," *Fire Engineering*, October 2002.

62. Jim Hoffman, "Twin Towers' Designers Anticipated Jet Impacts Like September 11th's." Cited at 911research.wtc7.net/wtc/analysis/design.html

63. Thomas Eagar and Christopher Musso, "Why Did the World Trade Center Collapse? Science, Engineering, and Speculation," *JOM: Journal of the Minerals, Metals & Materials Society*, 53/12, pp. 8-11.

64. National Institute of Standards and Technology Report 2005, pp. xliii and 171.

EXHIBIT J

65. Environmental Health Laboratories is a division of Underwriters Laboratories.

66. November 11, 2004. Gayle was deputy chief of the Metallurgy Division at NIST. See "NIST Scientist says Jet Fuel Couldn't Possibly Melt Steel in Twin Towers," by Nicholas Levis, *Global Outlook*, Issue 9, Fall 2004/Winter 2005, p. 5.

67. Nick Levis, ibid., and "Letter from Kevin R. Ryan to NIST's Frank Gayle," *Global Outlook*, No. 9, Fall-Winter 2005, pp. 5-6.

68. Kevin Ryan, "A call for a Personal Decision," *Global Outlook*, No. 10, Spring-Summer 2005, p. 96.

69. NIST describes the collapses of the towers as instances of "progressive collapse," which happens when "a building or portion of a building collapses due to disproportionate spread of an initial local failure" (NIST Report, p. 200). NIST even claims that the collapses were eventually "inevitable." Cited at Wtc.nist.gov/pubs/NCSTAR1ExecutiveSummary.pdf

70. Federal Emergency Management Agency (FEMA), 1988.

71. FEMA, 1991.

72. Robin Nieto, "Fire Practically Destroys Venezuela's Tallest Building," Venezuelanalysis.com, October 18, 2004.

73. David Ray Griffin, "The Destruction of the WTC: Why the Official Account Cannot Be True," a series of lectures in West Hartford, Connecticut; Manchester and Burlington, Vermont and New York City in October 2005. Cited at 911review.com/articles/griffin/nyc1.html

74. NIST claimed the towers collapsed because the planes knocked the fireproofing off the

steel columns. If this has validity it should apply to the Philadelphia and Caracas buildings; the steel in those buildings was directly exposed to raging fires for 14 or more hours, yet the steel did not buckle.

EXHIBIT K

75. Represented by Norman Siegel, former head of the New York Civil Liberties Union.
76. *New York Times* reporter Jim Dwyer explained that the materials "were originally gathered on the order of Thomas Von Essen, who was the city fire commissioner on September 11th, who said he wanted to preserve those accounts before they became reshaped by a collective memory." The 9/11 oral histories are available at the *New York Times* website: graphics8.nytimes.com/packages/html/nyregion/20050812_WTC_GRAPHIC/met_WTC_histories_full_01.html
77. Greg Szymanski, "NY Fireman Lou Cacchioli Upset that 9/11 Commission 'Tried to Twist My Words,'" *Arctic Beacon*, July 19, 2005. Cited at Arcticbeacon.com/ articles/article/1518131/29548.htm. A briefer account of Cacchioli's testimony was made available in the September 24th, 2001 issue of *People* magazine.
78. *The New York Times,* 2005, "The September 11 Records" (9/11 Oral Histories Rivera, p. 9). Cited at graphics8.nytimes.com/packages/html/nyregion/ 20050812_WTC _GRAPHIC/met_WTC_histories_full_01.html
79. *New York Times,* Banaciski, pp. 3-4
80. Alicia Shepard and Cathy Trost in *Running Toward Danger: Stories Behind the Breaking News of 9/11,* Newseum, 2002, Rowman & Littlefield.
81. As reported in *Washington Free Press* (#63 May/June 2003): "On September 11, the British Broadcasting Corp. (BBC) interviewed one of its New York-based reporters, Steve Evans." Cited at washingtonfreepress.org/63/mysteriesOfTwinTowers.htm
82. *The Chief Engineer,* 2002: "We Will Not Forget: A Day of Terror." Cited at chiefengineer.org/article.cfm?seqnum1=1029
83. Mitchell Fink and Lois Mathias, *Never Forget: An Oral History of September 11, 2001,* HarperCollins, 2002, p. 82.
84. Julian Borger, Duncan Campbell, Charlie Porter and Stuart Millar, "Special Report: Terrorism in the US," London *Guardian,* September 12, 2001. Cited at Guardian.co.uk/september11/story/0,11209,600839,00.html
85. "The Destruction of the World Trade Center: Why the Official Account Cannot Be True" Paul Zarembka, ed., *The Hidden History of 9-11-2001* (Elsevier, 2006; also published at 911Review.com. This talk by theologian David Ray Griffin, given to audiences in New York City in October of 2005, is a comprehensive run-down of the evidence of controlled demolition of the World Trade Center Twin Towers and Building 7. Griffin includes a number of excerpts from the oral histories of emergency responders, which had been released only a few months earlier.
86. The official investigators found that they had less authority than the clean-up crews, a fact that led the Science Committee of the House of Representatives to report that "the lack of authority of investigators to impound pieces of steel for examination before they were recycled led to the loss of important pieces of evidence." Cited at house.gov/science/hot/wtc/wtc-report/WTC_ch5.pdf
87. "Baosteel Will Recycle World Trade Center Debris," Eastday.com, January 24, 2002. Cited at china.org.cn/english/2002/Jan/25776.htm.
88. This removal was, moreover, carried out with the utmost care, because "the loads consisted of highly sensitive material." Each truck was equipped with a vehicle location device (VLD), connected to GPS. "The software recorded every trip and location, sending out alerts if the vehicle traveled off course, arrived late at its destination, or deviated from expectations in any other way. One driver ... took an extended lunch break of an hour and a half. ... [H]e was dismissed." Jacqueline Emigh, "GPS on the

Job in Massive World Trade Center Clean-up," in *Access Central and Security Systems,* July 2002.

89. This protest was echoed by Professor Abolhassan Astaneh-Asl, Professor of Civil Engineering at the University of California at Berkeley, who said: "Where there is a car accident and two people are killed, you keep the car until the trial is over. If a plane crashes, not only do you keep the plane, but you assemble all the pieces, take it to a hangar, and put it together. That's only for 200, 300 people, when they die. In this case, you had 3,000 people dead. You had a major ... man-made structure. My wish was that we had spent whatever it takes. ... Get all this steel, carry it to a lot. Instead of recycling it. ... After all, this is a crime scene and you have to figure out exactly what happened." (CBS News, March 12, 2002)

90. Bloomberg was thereby recommending precisely what Bill Manning, the editor of *Fire Engineering,* had warned against when he wrote: "As things now stand ... the investigation into the World Trade Center fire and collapse will amount to paper-and computer-generated hypotheticals." (Bill Manning, editor-in-chief, *Fire Engineering,* January 4, 2002.) Griffin notes that "what Bloomberg desired and Manning feared is exactly what we got with the NIST report. It is, in fact, even worse. Physicist Steven Jones, after pointing out that there are 'zero examples of fire-caused high-rise collapses' and that even NIST's 'actual [computer] models fail to collapse,' asks: 'So how does the NIST team justify the WTC collapses?' He answers: 'Easy, NIST concocted computer-generated hypotheticals for very "severe" cases,' and then these cases were further modified to get the desired result. The NIST report, Jones adds, admits this..." The NIST report states on page 142: "The more severe case ... was used for the global analysis of each tower. Complete sets of simulations were then performed for [these cases]. To the extent that the simulations deviated from the photographic evidence or eyewitness reports [e.g., complete collapse occurred], the investigators adjusted the input." (Paper by Prof. Steven E. Jones, Dept. of Physics and Astronomy, Brigham Young University, March 19, 2006.)

91. "Baosteel Will Recycle World Trade Center Debris," op. cit.

92. FEMA Report, Appendix C., "World Trade Center Building Performance Study," May 2002. Cited at fema.gov/library/wtcstudy.shtm

93. See the section headed "The ASCE's Disclosures of Steel Sulfidation" in Jim Hoffman, "Building a Better Mirage: NIST's 3-Year $20,000,000 Cover-Up of the Crime of the Century," 911 Research, August 21, 2005. Cited at 911research.wtc7.net/essays/nist/index.html

94. Bill Manning, the editor of *Fire Engineering* magazine wrote: "The structural damage from the planes and the explosive ignition of jet fuel in themselves were not enough to bring down the towers. *Fire Engineering* has good reason to believe that the 'official investigation' blessed by FEMA ... is a half-baked farce that may already have been commandeered by political forces whose primary interests, to put it mildly, lie far afield of full disclosure. Except for the marginal benefit obtained from a three-day, visual walk-through of evidence sites conducted by ASCE investigation committee members — described by one close source as a 'tourist trip' — no one's checking the evidence for anything." (Bill Manning, *Fire Engineering,* January 2002)

95. Cited at Boston.com/news/daily/26/photo_ban.htm

Exhibit M
96. Paul Thompson, *The Terror Timeline,* op. cit., 381-382.
97. *Christian Science Monitor,* September 17, 2001; *Time,* September 12, 2001.
98. Associated Press, August 19, 2002.
99. Paul Thompson, *The Terror Timeline,* op. cit., pp.385-390.

100. Wikipedia, "September 11, 2001 attacks — Timeline for the day of the attacks" states: "09:06: After brief introductions to the Booker elementary students, President Bush is about to begin reading with the students when Chief of Staff Andrew Card interrupts to whisper to the president, 'A second plane hit the other tower, and America's under attack.' The president stated later that he decided to continue the lesson rather than alarm the students." Cited at En.wikipedia.org/wiki/September_11,_2001_attacks_timeline_for_the_day_of_the_attacks

101. As dramatically shown in the movie *Fahrenheit 911,* directed by Michael Moore, Alliance Atlantis Films, 2004.

102. Section 202 of theUS Code (as of 01/06/03) specifies that the Secret Service "shall [protect] the President and members of his immediate family..."

103. John Cochrane of *ABC News* had told Peter Jennings on air about 8:30 a.m. on 9/11 that the president would be at an elementary school in Sarasota one half-hour later.

104. According to Michael C. Ruppert in *Crossing the Rubicon,* p. 355: "During the 2000 presidential campaign, George W. Bush vowed that he would not tap into the Social Security trust fund except as a result of war, recession, or a national emergency. On September 11, 2001, shortly after the attacks, President Bush turned to his budget Director, Mitch Daniels, and said: "Lucky me. I hit the trifecta." Trifecta is system of betting in which the bettor must pick the first three winners in the correct sequence.

105. Brad Carlton, "How Bush Hit the 'Trifecta' on 9/11 — and the Public Lost Big-Time," *Baltimore Chronicle and Sentinel,* June 12, 2002. Excerpt: "Then, on the morning of September 12, Bush announced his very first post-9/11 policy move. Because the attacks were 'more than acts of terror; they were acts of war, this morning I am sending to Congress a request for emergency funding authority.' On cue, pundits like Tim Russert chirped, 'Suddenly the Social Security lockbox seems so trivial.' Since then, the trust fund has been stripmined to subsidize pork barrel and deficit spending with no political fallout for the president. These extraordinary coincidences have gone unremarked in the media, who have entirely missed that the terms of the 'trifecta' — note that the word connotes something you bet on — was never mentioned until two-and-a-half weeks after Bush's August 6 briefing and days before 9/11. ... First and most obviously, defense contractors contributed more than $8.7 million to Republican campaigns in 2000. They stood to gain billions from the fallout of a successful terrorist strike. Second, Treasury Secretary Paul O'Neill advocated the abolition of Social Security and Medicare in a May 20, 2001 interview with the *Financial Times.* 'Able-bodied adults should save enough on a regular basis so that they can provide for their own retirement, and, for that matter, health and medical needs,' he said, adding, 'The president is also intrigued about the possibility of fixing this mess.' Third, and by far most importantly, Bush needed to save his presidency, which by August was already in serious danger of sinking into fiscal chaos and one-term ignominy. This is a viable motive. Whether or not Bush or someone in his administration acted on it by winking at hijacking threats remains to be seen."

EXHIBIT N

106. *The 9/11 Commission Report,* op. cit., p. 34: "NEADS never received notice that American 77 was hijacked. It was notified at 9:34 [a.m.] that American 77 was lost. Then, minutes later, NEADS was told that an unknown plane was six miles southwest of the White House. Only then did the already scrambled airplanes start moving directly toward Washington, D.C."

107. FAA clarification memo by Laura Brown, the FAA's Deputy in Public Affairs (dated May 21, 2003.) Posted at 911truth.org/article.php?story=2004081200421797

108. David Ray Griffin, *The 9/11 Commission Report* op. cit., p. 197.
109. Quoting "Statement of Secretary of Transportation Norman Y. Mineta before the National Commission on Terrorist Attacks upon the United States, May 23, 2003." Cited at Cooperativeresearch.org/timeline/2003/commissiontestimony052303.htm

EXHIBIT O
110. "A Trainee Noted for Incompetence," *New York Times,* May 4, 2002, p 10. Cited at Query.nytimes.com/gst/abstract.html?res
111. "DCANG Yanks its Mission Statement," 911review.com/coverup/dcang.html. This refers to the deletion, on September 12, 2001, from the Andrews Air Force Base website, of reference to 2 fighter squadrons based at Andrews. These were the 121st Fighter Squadron (FS-121) of the 113th Fighter Wing (FW-113), equipped with F-16 fighters; the 321st Marine Fighter Attack Squadron (VMFA-321) of the 49th Marine Air Group, Detachment A (MAG-49 Det-A), equipped F/A-18 fighters. The mission of 121 Fighter-Wing reads, in part, "provide capable and ready response forces for the District of Columbia in the event of a natural disaster or civil emergency." Cited at Emperors-clothes.com/indict/indict-1.htm
112. According to *CBS News* (transportation correspondent Bob Orr), September 11, 2001: "The plane flew several miles south of the restricted airspace around the White House. At 9:33, [it] crossed the Capital Beltway... flying at more than 400 mph, [which] was too fast and high when it neared the Pentagon at 9:35. The hijacker pilots were then forced to execute a difficult high-speed descending turn. Radar shows Flight 77 did a downward spiral, turning almost a complete circle and dropping the last 7,000 feet in two-and-a-half minutes. The steep turn was so smooth, the sources say, it's clear there was no fight for control going on. And the complex maneuver suggests the hijacker had better flying skills than many investigators first believed."
113. Danielle O'Brien, *ABC News,* October 24, 2001.
114. *The 9/11 Commission Report,* op. cit., p. 34, "Nor did the military have 47 minutes to respond to United 93, as would be implied by the account that it received notice of the flight's hijacking at 9:16. By the time the military learned about the flight, it had crashed."
115. *The 9/11 Commission Report,* op. cit., p. 29.
116. FAA clarification memo by Laura Brown, the FAA's Deputy in Public Affairs (dated May 21, 2003), to the Kean-Zelikow Commission concerning FAA Communications with NORAD on September 11, 2001.
117. Richard A. Clarke, *Against All Enemies,* op. cit., p. 2, "On my way through the Operations Center of the Situation Room, Ralph Seigler, the longtime Situation Room deputy director, grabbed me. 'We're on the line with NORAD, on an air threat conference call.'"
118. David Ray Griffin, *The 9/11 Commission Report,* op. cit., p. 237-244.

EXHIBIT Q
119. According to software engineer Jim Hoffman, "... there were a number of alleged voice communications from pilots, flight attendants, and passengers on the doomed flights. However, as of July 2005, it does not appear that any recordings of these calls have been made public except for 4 1/2 minutes of Betty Ong's call from Flight 11, which supposedly lasted 23 minutes. See "Missing Evidence About the September 11th Flights" at 911research.wtc7.net/planes/evidence/phonecalls.html
120. *The 9/11 Commission Report* mentions the use of cellular phones at least once, on page 12: "Shortly thereafter, the passengers and flight crew began a series of calls from GTE AirFones and cellular phones. These calls between family, friends, and colleagues took

place until the end of the flight and provided those on the ground with firsthand accounts. They enabled the passengers to gain critical information, including the news that two aircraft had slammed into the World Trade Center."

121. The experimental results of Professor Dewdney which determine the ability of cell phones to transmit or not aboard high-flying passenger aircraft are summarized here and reported in full at the website, Physics911.net

A. February 25, 2003. Diamond Katana: A total of 32 calls were attempted using three cell phone types. At steps of 2,000 feet (altitude), the calls had success rates that decayed from 75 percent at 2,000 feet to eight percent at 8,000 feet.

B. April 19, 2003. Cessna 172-R: In steps of 2,000 feet, 32 calls were attempted, using the same experimental protocol as February 25. The success rates in this aircraft decayed from 75 percent at 2,000 feet to 13 percent at 8,000 feet.

C. A third experiment, conducted under the scrutiny of a camera crew from ASAHI (Japan's second largest TV network) used a Piper Apache, the first twin-engine aircraft employed in these experiments. On this occasion a cell phone expert made the calls to a ground operator. Following essentially the same protocol, a lower "operational ceiling" for cell phones was encountered. The success rate decayed from 95 percent at 2,000 feet to 44 percent at 5,000 feet, 10 percent at 6,000 feet, and 0 percent at 7,000 feet.

122. A comment from Dewdney: "It is unclear why the FCC instituted a law banning the use of cell phones aboard commercial aircraft in 1991. The main reason for the law (interference with avionics equipment aboard the aircraft) is completely inconsistent with two easily verified facts: 1. All aircraft avionics are heavily shielded against stray EM radiation (i.e., radio waves); 2. The presence of powerful antennae in the belly of commercial aircraft with a power output more than 1,000 times the feeble (0.2 watt digital, 0.6 watt analog) signal from a cell phone."

123. According to an American Airline / Qualcomm announcement in 2005, the technology for cell phone transmission at high altitude will only be available aboard commercial aircraft in 2006.

124. Michel Chossudovsky, "More Holes in the Official Story: The 9/11 Cell Phone Calls," August 10, 2004. Cited at Globalresearch.ca/articles/CHO408B.html

EXHIBIT R

125. Interview on September 11, 2003 with Thomas Kimmel, a former FBI agent and retired Navy captain, on *The Current*, a daily public affairs program on CBC Radio One. Kimmel is a grandson of Admiral Husband E. Kimmel, commander-in-chief of the US Pacific Fleet during the Pearl Harbor attack.

126. Jim Marrs, *Inside Job: Unmasking the 9-11 Conspiracies*, Origin Press, 2004. Appendix B-23: Questions presented by the Family Steering Committee to Kean-Zelikow Commission on February 16, 2004.

127. New York Times, November 29, 2002. According to author David Ray Griffin, "Skepticism about Kissinger's capacity to run an independent investigation was based in part on evidence that he was receiving consulting fees not only from corporations with heavy investments in Saudi Arabia but also from Unocal, the oil company that wanted to build a pipeline through Afghanistan — if only the Taliban could be replaced by a government that would provide the needed stability. When there were cries that Kissinger needed to reveal his business clients, the President said that this would not be necessary. The Congressional Research Service declared, however, that Kissinger had to reveal his clients. Kissinger resigned rather than do so." (MSNBC, December 13, 2001.)

128. Time.com, "9-11 Commission Funding Woes," March 26, 2003; FloridaToday.com, February 21st, 2004, "NASA gets $50 million for shuttle investigation;" NYTimes.com, National News Briefs; Outside Assistance Cost Starr $4.2 Million, August 29, 1999.

EXHIBIT S
129. Thomas Hansen, Ph.D., "A Conversation with Philip Zelikow," *Global Outlook*, No. 10, Spring-Summer 2005, pp 43-44. Cited at Septembereleventh.org/newsarchive/2005-06-07-outrageous.php

130. C. Rice and P. Zelikow, *Germany Unified and Europe Transformed: A Study in Statecraft*, Harvard University Press, September, 1995.

131. Griffin elaborates: "Let me give you one tiny example of how important that is. There is a new book out by Peter Lance, called *Cover-Up: What the Government is Still Hiding about the War on Terror*, [Regan Books, 2004] and Peter, good patriot that he is, went to testify because he had some important information about Ramzi Yousef — remember the mastermind of the 1993 bombing of the World Trade Center? He was also the mastermind of the Bojinka Project which they discovered in Manila. Yousef also was the one who came up with the planes idea, that is, of using planes for weapons. So he was the mastermind. Peter went to give testimony and his testimony was going to contradict some of the things that were in the prosecution's case in 1996 when they prosecuted Ramzi Yousef. Who took Peter Lance's testimony? Dietrich Snell, one of the two prosecutors of that trial. So that is an example of how the executive director could skew the proceedings. Peter said he had a mole inside the Commission, somebody who was very unhappy with the staff, who was unhappy with the way things were going, and they would meet and he would tell Peter what was going on. He said that Zelikow just ran the whole Commission — that there were these leadership teams and seven out of the eight teams were completely controlled by Zelikow. Only one team (run by John Farmer) was not and they were butting heads all time."

EXHIBIT T
132. Jim Hoffman, in "Popular Mechanics' Assault on 9/11Truth — Facts Ignored by PM," *Global Outlook*, No. 10, Spring-Summer 2005, pp. 28 & 41, gives four mainstream references: "Revealed: Men with Stolen Identities," Telegraph.co.uk, September 23, 2001; "Hijack 'Suspects' Alive and Well", BBC, September 23, 2001, news.bbc.co.uk/1/hi/world/middle_east/1559151.stm; "Dead Saudi Hijack Suspect Resurfaces, Denies Involvement," AllAfrica.com, September 24, 2001, allafrica.com/stories200109240325.html; "'Suicide Hijacker' is an Airline Pilot Alive and Well in Jeddah," Independent.co.uk, September 17, 2001, news.independent.co.uk/world/middle_east/story.jsp?story.

133. David Ray Griffin "*The 9/11 Commission Report:* A 571 Page Lie", posted at 911truth.org/article.php?story=20050523112738404

EXHIBIT U
134. Michael J. Springman, "The Agency's Visa Machine: Most of the 911 Hijackers Got Their Visas in Saudi Arabia," *Covert Action Quarterly*, Winter, 2001-2002.

135. According to Webster Griffin Tarpley in *9/11 Synthetic Terror — Made in USA* (Progressive Press, 2005, p. 16), these guys were used as patsies: "We have no illusions about the psychotic Arab patsies whose antics are being used to cover up what was in reality a coup d'état made in the USA."

136. CBC Radio One program *Dispatches*, July 3, 2002, Excerpt of interview with J. Michael Springmann, posted at cbc.ca/dispatches/summer2002.html

EXHIBIT V

137. Edmonds' website is Justacitizen.com. She was featured in an article, "An Inconventient Patriot," by David Rose in the September 2005 issue of *Vanity Fair.*

138. *The 9/11 Commission Report,* op. cit., p. 453, Footnote 25 in the Notes to Chapter 3: See DOJ Inspector General report, "A Review of the FBI's Actions in Connection with Allegations Raised by Contract Linguist Sibel Edmonds," July 1, 2004; Sibel Edmonds interview (February 11, 2004)."

139. Public letter, August 1, 2004, to 9/11 Commission Chairman from FBI whistle blower, cited at Commondreams.org/views04/0802-06.htm; *Global Outlook* No. 9, Fall-Winter 2005, pp 33-37.

140. *60 Minutes,* October 25, 2002. See cbsnews.com/stories/2002/10/25/60minutes/main526954.shtml

141. The Arab hijacker patsies had to be protected by the FBI to fulfill their role on 9/11. The superior exposition of patsies, moles and operators can be found in *9/11 Synthetic Terror: Made in USA,* by Webster G. Tarpley.

EXHIBIT W

142. "CIA worked with Pakistan to create Taliban," *Times of India,* 2001. Cited at Emperors-clothes.com/docs/pak.htm

143. Information in this Exhibit is based on parts of an article by David Ray Griffin, "Truth and Politics of 9/11," *Global Outlook,* No. 10, Spring-Summer 2005, p. 53.

144. Michel Chossudovsky, *America's "War on Terrorism,"* Global Research, p. 54; "Political Deception: The Missing Link behind 9/11", *Global Outlook,* No. 2, Summer 2002, pp.68-70.

145. Asia Times Online April 8, 2004, "9/11 and the Smoking Gun, Part 2: A real smoking gun," By Pepe Escobar. Cited at atimes.com/atimes/Front_Page/FD08Aa01.html

146. *USA Today* "Goss to be new CIA chief," October 8, 2004.

147. *Asia Times* Online, op. cit. Pepe Escobar went on to corroborate both stories in this report: "If the 9/11 Commission is really looking for a smoking gun, it should look no further than at Lieutenant-General Mahmoud Ahmad, the director of the Pakistani Inter-Services Intelligence (ISI) at the time. In early October 2001, Indian intelligence learned that Mahmoud had ordered flamboyant Saeed Sheikh — the convicted mastermind of the kidnapping and killing of *Wall Street Journal* reporter Daniel Pearl — to wire US $100,000 from Dubai to one of hijacker Mohamed Atta's two bank accounts in Florida. A juicy direct connection was also established between Mahmoud and Republican Congressman Porter Goss and Democratic Senator Bob Graham. They were all in Washington together discussing Osama bin Laden over breakfast when the attacks of September 11, 2001 happened. Mahmoud's involvement in September 11th might be dismissed as only Indian propaganda. But Indian intelligence swears by it, and the US Federal Bureau of Investigation (FBI) has confirmed the whole story: Indian intelligence even supplied Saeed's cellular-phone numbers. ... Goss spent as many as ten years working on numerous CIA clandestine operations. He is very close to Vice President Dick Cheney. It's interesting to note that [at the end of March 2004] Goss suggested the Justice Department bring perjury charges against the new Cheney nemesis, [Richard] Clarke."

148. *Times of India,* October 9, 2001

149. *The 9/11 Commission Report,* op. cit., Paragraph #800, p. 172, "The Funding of the 9/11 Plot. As noted above, the 9/11 plotters spent somewhere between $400,000 and $500,000 to plan and conduct their attack. The available evidence indicates that the 19 operatives were funded by al Qaeda, either through wire transfers or cash provided by

KSM [Khalid Sheikh Mohammed], which they carried into the United States or deposited in foreign accounts and accessed from this country. Our investigation has uncovered no credible evidence that any person in the United States gave the hijackers substantial financial assistance. Similarly, we have seen no evidence that any foreign government — or foreign government official — supplied any funding."

EXHIBIT X

150. Michael C. Ruppert, *Crossing the Rubicon: The Decline of the American Empire at the End of the Age of Oil*, New Society Publishers, 2004, p. 238.
151. Dylan Ratigan of Bloomberg News, ABC World News Tonight, September 20, 2001.
152. This makes sense when you realize that according to Michael C. Ruppert, "Morgan Stanley saw, between September 7 and September 10, an increase of 27 times (not 27 percent) in the purchase of put options on its shares" and Morgan Stanley occupied 22 floors of the WTC. Also, Merrill-Lynch saw a jump of more than 12 times the normal level of put options in the four trading days before the attacks" with headquarters near the Twin Towers. (*Crossing the Rubicon*, op. cit., pp 239, 246.)
153. Ibid., page 244.
154. *The 9/11 Commission Report*, p. 499, Footnote 130 in Notes to Chapter 5 states that: "Highly publicized allegations of insider trading in advance of 9/11 generally rest on reports of unusual pre-9/11 trading activity in companies whose stock plummeted after the attacks. Some unusual trading did in fact occur, but each such trade proved to have an innocuous explanation. For example, the volume of put options surged in the parent companies of United Airlines on September 6th and American Airlines on September 10th — highly suspicious trading on its face. Yet, further investigation has revealed that the trading had no connection with 9/11. A single US-based institutional investor with no conceivable ties to al Qaeda purchased 95 percent of the UAL puts on September 6th as part of a trading strategy that also included buying 115,000 shares of American on September 10th."
155. Ibid, pp. 171-172: "There also have been claims that al Qaeda financed itself through manipulation of the stock market based on its advance knowledge of the 9/11 attacks. Exhaustive investigations by the Securities and Exchange Commission, FBI, and other agencies have uncovered no evidence that anyone with advance knowledge of the attacks profited through securities transactions."
156. Michael C. Ruppert, *Crossing the Rubicon*, op. cit., p.242.

EXHIBIT Y

157. Nafeez Mosaddeq Ahmed, *The War on Truth: 9/11, Disinformation, and the Anatomy of Terrorism*, Olive Branch Press, 2005, p. 91. He elaborates: "The *Village Voice* reported that Helms described one incident after another in which, she claimed, the Taliban agreed to give up bin Laden to the US, only to be rebuffed by the State Department. On one occasion, she said, the Taliban agreed to give the US coordinates for his campsite, leaving enough time so the Yanks could whack al Qaeda's leader with a missile before he moved. The proposal, she claims, was nixed. The State Department denied receiving any such offer."
158. Bin Laden on FBI's *Ten Most Wanted Fugitives* (as of June 1999) — Bounty increased (November 2001) to $25 million.
159. Michel Chossudovsky, "Who is Osama bin Laden?" *Global Outlook*, No. 1, Spring 2002, pp. 3-5.
160. Richard Labeviere, editor-in-chief of Radio France Internationale, on November 1, 2001, writing in *Le Figaro*.
161. *Le Figaro*, October 31, 2001 and London *Guardian*, Anthony Sampson, November 1,

2001 as quoted by Nafeez Ahmed in *The War on Truth,* p. 91; the London *Guardian* [Ibid., p. 92].

162. Reuters, January 19, 2002, CBS *Evening News* with Dan Rather; CBS, January 28, 2002.

163. Bob Graham, *Intelligence Matters: The CIA, the FBI, Saudi Arabia, and the Failure of America's War on Terror,* Random House, 2004.

164. David Ray Griffin, "Truth and Politics of 9/11," *Global Outlook,* No. 10, Spring-Summer 2005, p. 51.

EXHIBIT Z

165. Senate Foreign Relations Committee Chair Joe Biden (D-DE), as reported in zmag.org/Zmag/Articles/nov01boeing.htm

166. PNAC website: newamericancentury.org

167. "Rebuilding America's Defenses: Strategy, Forces and Resources for a New American Century," Sept. 2000, Project for the New American Century, pp. 14-16, 51, available at newamericancentury.org

168. Chalmers Johnson, *The Sorrows of Empire: Militarism, Secrecy, and the End of the Republic,* Metropolitan Books, January, 2004.

169. "Strategy for Victory," White House paper, November 30, 2005.

170. David Ray Griffin, "The 9/11 Commission Report: A 571-Page Lie," May 22, 2005, Omission #58. Cited at septembereleventh.org/newsarchive/

171. Zbigniew Brzezinski, *The Grand Chessboard,* Basic Books, 1997.

CLOSING ARGUMENT

172. See listserv.cc.kuleuven.ac.be/cgi-bin/wa?A2=ind0110&L=natopres&T= 0&F=&S=&P=361

173. See also archives.cnn.com/2001/WORLD/europe/10/02/inv.nato.if/

174. Nicholas DeMasi and Mike Bellone, *Ground Zero: Behind the Scenes,* TRAC Team Inc. (Trauma Response Assistance for Children), 2003, p. 108. tracteam.org

175. Michael C. Ruppert, "2004 — The Year of the Law and of Living Dangerously," *From the Wilderness,* December 31, 2003. Cited at fromthewilderness.com/free/ww3/123103_danger.html

176. "National Priorities Project," as of January 25, 2006, gives a figure of approximately US $236 billion for the cost of the war in Iraq. Cited at nationalpriorities.org/index.php?option=com_wrapper&Itemid=182

177. "Calendar of US Military Dead during Iraq War," as of January 17, 2006, lists a total of 2,357 deaths, including 149 in Afghanistan in the period of the Iraqi war and one at Guantanamo of non-hostile cause. Not included are civilian casualties in Iraq and Afghanistan. See Cryptome.org/mil-dead-iqw.htm
Officially acknowledged as of May 1, 2006: 2,400 miliary dead. See Casualties.org/oif/

178. See Informationclearinghouse.info/article11674.htm

Chapter 3

1. Steven Pinker, *How The Mind Works,* W. W. Norton & Co. Inc., 1997.

2. Steven Pinker, *The Blank Slate: The Denial of Human Nature and Modern Intellectual Life,* Viking Adult, 2002.

3. Rita Carter, *Mapping the Mind,* University of California Press, 2000.

4. The series of experiments was conducted by Michael S. Gazzaniga. See *Nature's Mind: The Biological Roots of Thinking, Emotions, Sexuality, Language and Intelligence,* Harmondsworth, Penguin Books, 1992.

5. *New York Times*, Science Section, January 24, 2006: "A Shocker: Partisan Thought Is Unconscious," by Benedict Carey. Cited at nytimes.com/2006/01/24/science/24find.html?ex=1138338000&en=4c18dcb8b0d1 8950&ei=5070

6. Rita Carter, *Mapping the Mind*, op. cit., p. 61.

7. Douglass Rushkoff, *Coercion: Why We Listen to What "They" Say*, Penguin, 1999.

8. Ibid., p. 64.

9. Kevin Barrett, "Apocalypse of Coercion: Why We Listen to What 'They' Say about 9/11," December 2005. Cited at mujca.com/apocalypse.htm

10. Ibid., p. 2.

11. Ibid., p. 3.

12. Ibid., p. 3.

13. Ibid., p. 3

14. Rita Carter, *Mapping the Mind*, op. cit., p. 153.

15. Ibid, p. 151.

16. Ibid, p. 155.

17. Kevin Barrett, "Apocalypse of Coercion," op. cit., p. 3.

18. Ibid., p. 1.

19. Gregory W. Lester, "Why Bad Beliefs Don't Die," in the *Skeptical Inquirer*, Vol. 24, November/December 2000.

20. E. Martin Schotz, *History Will Not Absolve Us: Orwellian Control, Public Denial, and the Murder of President Kennedy*, Kurtz, Ulmer, & DeLucia Book Publishers, 1996.

21. Ibid, p. ix.

22. Ibid., p. 283.

23. Matt Everett, "The New 9/11 Scandal," in *The Journal of Psychohistory*, Vol. 32, No. 3, Winter 2005.

24. Lloyd deMause, quoted in "The New 9/11 Scandal," ibid.

25. Tracy L. Dietz, "Disciplining Children: Characteristics Associated With the Use of Corporal Punishment," *Child Abuse & Neglect* # 24, 2000, pp. 1529, 1536.

Chapter 4

1. Several passages in the account given here are from a story prepared by Nick Levis, a New York City-based 9/11Truth activist, posted on August 1, 2004 on 9/11Truth.org. The information squares with other accounts provided by researchers and writers Michael C. Ruppert, David Ray Griffin, Nafeez Ahmed, and others. Levis's article was headed "Senator Dayton: NORAD Lied about 9/11."

2. Paul Thompson, *The Terror Timeline*, op. cit., p. 376

3. Ibid.

4. "The CBC crew was told," Sheane said in the email, "that in the month after 9/11, several things had apparently changed and we talked about them at length in our item." She agreed her crew might have "been misled" but said "the record and our story did support that monumental changes had happened at NORAD immediately following 9/11. Whether they had previously actively monitored US airspace ... is a question someone else will no doubt explore." The information given to the CBC was that "FAA's radar images were unavailable to NORAD before 9/11 ... they were made available through computer programs immediately after 9/11." In her email she says: "We had no reason to disbelieve this and in fact, the FAA confirmed this to us when I got a CD copy of the North American radar image from that day that showed the airspace emptying of all airplanes — the FAA's radar image appears in our item. Second, the FAA now had one person physically sitting in the command centre inside Cheyenne Mountain, connected by phone and computer directly to the FAA. That was

new after 9/11. This was confirmed through the FAA, NORAD and NAVCAN and we included this in our story. Third, at the time NORAD had asked for and received the help of NATO to fly AWACS missions over the USA."

5. David Ray Griffin, *The 9/11 Report*, op. cit., p. 259.

6. The *Posse Comitatus Act* is a United States federal law passed in 1878, intended to prohibit Federal troops from supervising elections in former Confederate states. It generally prohibits Federal military personnel and units of the United States National Guard under Federal authority from acting in a law enforcement capacity within the United States, except where expressly authorized by the Constitution or Congress. *The Posse Comitatus Act* and *The Insurrection Act* substantially limit the powers of the Federal government to use the military for law enforcement.

7. Steven Komarow and Tom Squitieri, "NORAD had Drills of Jets as Weapons," in *USA Today*, April 18, 2004. Cited at usatoday.com/news/washington/2004-04-18-norad_x.htm

   In the case of the Pentagon, Komarow and Squitieri reported, "that drill was not run after Defense officials said it was unrealistic, NORAD and Defense officials say." The newspaper reported: "NORAD, in a written statement, confirmed that such hijacking exercises occurred. It said the scenarios outlined were regional drills, not regularly scheduled continent-wide exercises."

8. Sheane, in an email to the author, notes "We DID include mention of it (Vigilant Guardian) by the way, in passing, in the full one-hour *Newsworld* [the all-news channel of the CBC] documentary (so I suppose it's possible CBC was first to talk about and name the exercise Vigilant Guardian!). Sheane added: "By the way, my interest (for better or for worse for the purpose of your book) in the Russian war games over the NORAD games in the documentary ... was that it underscored for me after doing (seven) on-camera interviews and several other off-camera interviews that NORAD was still mired in old cold war thinking."

9. William B. Scott, "Exercise Jump-Starts Response to Attacks." Similar information was reported by *ABC News* on Sept. 11th, 2002 and by Newhouse News Services January 25, 2002.

10. NJ.com quoting from Rap Basement message board, February 11, 2005.

11. In author's DVD *The Great Conspiracy: The 9/11 News Special You Never Saw*, 2004, included with this book.

12. Ibid.

13. Michael C. Ruppert, *Crossing The Rubicon*, op. cit., p. 591.

14. In May 2003, Laura Brown of the FAA attended hearings of the 9/11 Commission that bore witness to the aviation aspects of the day. Embarrassed by previous non-forthcoming testimony about the FAA's role, she sent an email to members of the media whose business cards she had collected. "Within minutes after the first aircraft hit the World Trade Center," she states in her email, "the FAA immediately established several phone bridges that included FAA field facilities, the FAA Command Center, FAA headquarters, DOD, the Secret Service, and other government agencies. The US Air Force liaison to the FAA immediately joined the FAA headquarters phone bridge and established contact with NORAD on a separate line. The FAA shared real-time information on the phone bridges about the unfolding events, including information about loss of communication with aircraft, loss of transponder signals, unauthorized changes in course, and other actions being taken by all the flights of interest, including Flight 77."

15. John Pike, director of Globalsecurity.org, a Virginia-based intelligence research firm, noted that an obscure line item hidden in the Air Force budget calls for an additional $1.9 billion in spending on "selected activities" — language that he said has previously

served as budgeting code for the CIA, according to a story by Greg Miller and John Hendren in the *Los Angeles Times* on February 5, 2002. In an Associated Press story on February 5, 2002 by John J. Lumpkin, titled "CIA gets big spending boost in president's proposed budget, Defense Increase Biggest Since '66" the proposed 2003 budget contains an increase, estimated to be between $1.5 billion and $2 billion, that would bring the [VIA's] budget to above $5 billion annually. Precise figures were unavailable; intelligence spending is classified. The CIA's annual budget was previously believed to be around $3.5 billion."

16. "Who Bombed the U.S. World Trade Center?Growing Evidence Points to Role of FBI Operative," by Ralph Schoenman, *Prevailing Winds*, Number 3, 1993.

17. "Visas for Terrorists," Michael Springmann, *New York City 9/11 Citizens' Commission: An Open Inquiry into the Attacks of September 11th* (conducted on) September 9, 2004, sponsored by 911CitizensWatch.org, 911Truth.org and NewYork911Truth.org, pages 37-39, transcript published by *Global Outlook*. Springmann was the State Department Visa Officer in Jeddah, Saudi Arabia.

In an interview on CBC Radio's program *Dispatches* on July 3, 2002, this exchange took place between Springmann and the program's host, Rick MacInnes-Rae:

MacInnes-Rae: If what you say may be true, many of the terrorists who allegedly flew those planes into those targets, got their US visas through the CIA and your US consulate in Jeddah. That suggests a relationship ongoing as recently as obviously September. But what was the CIA presumably recruiting these people for as recently as September 11th?

Springmann: That I don't know. And that's one of the things that I tried to find out through a series of Freedom of Information Act requests starting ten years ago. At the time the State Department and the CIA stonewalled my requests. They're still doing so

MacInnes-Rae: If the CIA had a relationship with the people responsible for September 11th, are you suggesting therein that they are somehow complicit?

Springmann: Yes, either through omission or through failure to act... By the attempts to cover me up and shut me down, this convinced me more and more that this was not a pipedream, this was not imagination...

18. Nafeez Mosaddeq Ahmed, *The War on Truth,* op. cit. "Al Qaeda," says Ahmed, "is found to be the outgrowth of a coordinated network of highly secret sub-units of state-intelligence services operating under the overarching strategic direction of the most clandestine parallel structures of western military-intelligence services, especially those of the US and UK." The best books on this reality are his *The War on Truth: 9/11, Disinformation, and the Anatomy of Terrorism;* Michel Chossudovsky's *War and Globalization: The Truth Behind September 11,* and David Ray Griffin's *The New Pearl Harbor: Disturbing Questions about the Bush Administration and 9/11.*

19. William A. Swanberg, 22. Douglas Herman, "911 — Too Hot To Handle?" www.rense.com/general69/hot.htm. December 8, 2005.

Luce and His Empire, Scribner, 1972.

20. Stewart Bell, *Cold Terror: How Canada Nurtures and Exports Terrorism Around the World,* John Wiley & Sons; New Ed edition, 2005.

21. James DiEugenio and Lisa Pease, eds., *The Assassinations: Probe Magazine on JFK, MLK, RFK and Malcolm X,* Feral House, 2003, p. 304.

Chapter 5

1. Peter R. Mitchell and John Schoeffel, eds., *Understanding Power: The Indispensible Chomsky,* The New Press, 2002, p. 26.

2. Daniel L. Abrahamson, commentary, September 27, 2005, on Rense.com

3. Jim McIlroy and Coral Wynter, "Venezuelan Humanism vs. US Terrorism," *Green Left Weekly,* February 19, 2006.

4.   Dan Ackman, "Bernie Ebbers Guilty," Forbes.com, March 15, 2005.

Indictment "Count One" (Conspiracy to Obstruct Justice, Make False Statements, and Commit Perjury), United States of America v. Martha Stewart and Peter Bacanovic, Defendants. United States District Court Southern District of New York, S1 03 Cr. 17 (MGC).

US Department of Justice, "Former Enron Chairman and Chief Executive Officer Kenneth L. Lay Charged with Conspiracy, Fraud, False statements," Press Release, July 8, 2004.

5.   National Security Archive, The George Washington Univeristy Gelman Library, "Chile: 16,000 Secret US Documents Declassified," Press Release, November 13, 2000. These relate to the "Washington's role in the violent overthrow of the Allende government," nsaarchive.org

6.   Webster Griffin Tarpley, *9/11 Synthetic Terror: Made in USA,* Progressive Books, 2005, pp. 333-343.

7.   Ibid., p. 335.

8.   Webster Griffin Tarpley and Anton Chaikin, *George Bush: The Unauthorized Biography,* Executive Intelligence Review, 1991.

Webster Griffin Tarpley, *Surviving the Cataclysm,* Washington Grove Books, 1999.

Webster Griffin Tarpley, *9/11 Synthetic Terror,* op. cit.

Since 1996, *George Bush: The Unauthorized Bibliography* has been available for free download on Webster Tarpley's website. See www.tarpley.net.

9.   David Ray Griffin's response to Baer review of *The New Pearl Harbor.*

10. Floyd Rumin, Professor, Psychology Department, University of Tromsø, Tromsø, Norway, writing on www.NewDemocracyWorld.com, April 2003.

11. Ibid.

12. Ibid.

13. Peter R. Mitchell and John Schoeffel, eds., *Understanding Power,* op. cit. This book is an important resource because it is not produced by an acolyte of Chomsky, and because it is well-organized and -edited.

14. Ibid., p. 389.

15. Ibid., p. 390.

16. Ibid., p. 390.

17. Ibid., p. 390.

18. Ibid., p. 390.

19. Ibid., p. 390.

20. Ibid., p. 391.

21. Ibid., p. 391.

22. Ibid., pp. 394-395.

23. E. Martin Schotz, *History Will Not Absolve Us,* op. cit.

24. Ray Marcus, *Addendum B: Addendum to the HSCA, the Zapruder Film, and the Single Bullet Theory,* self-published, 1995.

25. Ibid.

26. Martin Schotz here inserts an Editor's Note: "To be more accurate, what Chomsky has done of late is to claim agnosticism on the question of whether there was a conspiracy to kill President Kennedy, but has insisted that if there was a conspiracy it was of no political significance, since there is no evidence of any shift in policy following the assassination. In addition to this Chomsky has played an important role in the *orchestrated debate* [emphasis added] which has focused the significance of the murder of Kennedy around the issue of the escalation of US involvement in the war in Vietnam. As discussed elsewhere in this volume, the function of this debate has been to *divert public attention* [emphasis added] from Kennedy's important movement against the cold war, for peace, for rapprochement with the USSR and toward normalization of relations with Cuba."

27. Noam Chomsky, *Rethinking Camelot*, Black Rose Books, 1993.
28. Ibid., p. 97.
29. Michael Parenti, *Dirty Truths: Reflections on Politics, Media, Ideology, Conspiracy, Ethnic Life and Class Power*, City Light Books, 1996.
30. Ibid., pp. 180-181.
31. *The Pentagon Papers*, Gravel edition, "Phased Withdrawal of U.S. Forces, 1962-1964," vol. 2, pp 160-200
32. Michael Parenti, *Dirty Truths*, op. cit., p. 177.
33. Ibid., p. 185.
34. "An Evening With Noam Chomsky: The New War on Terrorism," October 18, 2001, transcribed from audio recorded at the Technology and Culture Forum, Massachusetts Institute of Technology.
35. Zpedia.org/Noam_Chomsky
36. Michael Parenti, *Dirty Truths*, op. cit., p. 188.
37. Richard Falk, in Foreword to David Ray Griffin, *The New Pearl Harbor*.
38. Noam Chomsky, *9-11*, Seven Stories Press, 2002.
39. Ibid., p. 120.
40. Noam Chomsky and Edward S. Herman, *The Washington Connection and Third-World Fascism: The Political Economy of Human Rights*, Black Rose Books, 1979.
41. Michael Parenti, *Dirty Truths*, p. 183.
42. Daniel Abrahamson, Ibid., p. 3.
43. Comment posted by Noam Chomsky from an e-mail response to a query, in "On the War in Iraq: Noam Chomsky interviewed by David McNeill," on Znet, January 31, 2005.
44. Noam Chomsky, lecture delivered at Bates College, Lewiston, Maine, January 30, 1991, and published in *The New World Order*, Open Magazine Pamphlet No. 6, Second Printing, April 1991, p. 22.
45. Peter R. Mitchell and John Schoeffel, *Understanding Power*, op. cit.
46. Noam Chomsky, "An Evening With Noam Chomsky," op. cit.
47. An email from Noam Chomsky sent to Daniel L. Abrahamson in 2005, a copy of which is retained by Abrahamson. See rense.com/general67/noam.htm
48. Frank Kitson, *Low Intensity Operations: Subversion, Insurgency, Peacekeeping*, Faber & Faber, 1971.
49. Robert Stinnett, *Day of Deceit: The Truth about FDR and Pearl Harbor*, Free Press, 2001.
50. Timothy C. Boyle, of Denver, CO, in an e-mail to Barrie Zwicker, April 2006.
51. Bob Feldman, "Report from the Field: Left Media & Left Think Tanks: Foundation-Managed Protest?" in *Critical Sociology*, Winter 2006.
52. Emanuel Sferios, January 2005, in an email to Charles Shaw, founder and editor of *Newtopia Magazine*.
53. Ron Curran, "Buying into the News," *San Francisco Bay Guardian*, October 8, 1997.
54. Brian Salter, "'Alternative' media paymasters: Carlyle, ALCOA, Xerox, Coca Cola?" posted on questionsquestions.net, September 29, 2002. Cited at questionsquestions.net/docs/0209/0929_ford_trustees.html
55. Joan Coxsedge with Ken Coldicutt and Gerry Harant, *Rooted in Secrecy: The Clandestine Element in Australian Politics*, self-published by the Committee for the Abolition of Political Police (CAPP), p. 70.
56. Ibid., p. 74.

Chapter 6

1. Roosevelt was 26th President of the United States, 1901-9. this quotation is from *Progressive Covenant with the People*, excerpt from *A Confession of Faith*, an address

originally delivered to the national convention of the Progressive party in Chicago on August 6, 1912. See *Social Justice and Popular Rule: Essays, Addresses, and Public Statements Relating to the Progressive Movement (1910-1916)*, Theodore Roosevelt, Arno Press, New York, 1974. Cited at memory.loc.gov/ammem/collections/troo-sevelt_film/trfpcp.html#pcp

2. From *Propaganda*, first published by Horace Liveright, New York, 1928, reprinted by Ig Publishing, New York, 2004.

3. Woodrow Wilson *The New Freedom: A Call for the Emancipation of the Generous Energies of a People*, Doubleday, Doran & Company, Inc., 1913, pp. 13-15. Also quoted in *Secret Records Revealed*, by Dr. Dennis Cuddy, p. 24.

4. "On Saturday, January 28, 1933, [Hitler] had been abruptly dismissed by the aging President of the Republic, Field Marshal von Hinderberg. Adolph Hitler, leader of the National Socialists, the largest political party in Germany, was demanding for himself the chancellorship of the democratic republic he had tried to destroy," writes Shirer in *The Rise and Fall of the Third Reich*. (Simon & Schuster, p.3). "After secret negotiations with [Franz von] Papen and other leaders of the Conservative Right," he got his way and was sworn in January 30, 1933. Less than 19 months later, democracy was dead in Germany and Hitler became the sole dictator, the Fuhrer.

5. Jules Archer, *The Plot to Seize the White House*, Hawthorn Books, 1973.

6. Charles Higham, *Trading With the Enemy: An Expose of the Nazi-American Money Plot*, Delacorte Press, 1983.

7. Ibid.

8. Ibid., p. 164.

9. Joel Balkan, *The Corporation*, op. cit., p. 94.

10. Jules Archer, *The Plot to Seize the White House*, op. cit.

11. Joel Balkan, *The Corporation: The Pathological Pursuit of Profit and Power*, Free Press, Simon and Schuster, 2005. Bakan is a law professor at the University of British Columbia, a Rhodes Scholar, and is co-creator and writer of the film, *The Corporation: An Inquiry into the Dominant Institution of our Time*, based on the book.

12. Tom Regan, writing at csmonitor.com, January 10, 2006.

13. Michael C. Ruppert, *Crossing the Rubicon*, op. cit., pp. 591-592.

14. The UPI story was distributed by Antiwar.com and by the Global Network Against Weapons & Nuclear Power in Space (Space4Peace.org), who provided the following "Space War Links" on US military plans for global control through, in the words of the US military, "full spectrum dominance:" (1) US Space Command's LONG RANGE PLAN: spacecom.af.mil/usspace/LRP/cover.htm (2) af.mil/vision (3) dtic.mil/jv2020 (4) spacecom.af.mil/usspace (5) Report of the Commission to Assess United States National Security Space Management and Organization. See defenselink.mil/pubs/space20010111.html

15. Senator Frank Lautenberg (D-NJ), reported by the Executive Intelligence Review News Service (EIRNS), rawstory.com and rense.com

16. Quoting "Statement of Secretary of Transportation Norman Y. Mineta before the National Commission on Terrorist Attacks upon the United States, May 23, 2003." Cited at cooperativeresearch.org/timeline/2003/commissiontestimony052303.htm

17. Peter Phillips and Project Censored, *Censored 2004*.

18. Bruce Page, *The Murdoch Archipelago* Gardeners Books, 2004.

19. See bloggerheads.com/archives/2004/11/the_antimurdoch.asp

SIDEBAR

1. Adapted from remarks delivered to the World Association for Christian Communication, North American Region, University of British Columbia, Vancouver, BC July 30, 2003.

2. Yahya R. Kamalipour and Nancy Snow, eds., *War, Media and Propaganda: A Global Perspective*, Rowman & Littlefield Publishers, 2004.
3. Alternative and some mainstream media are increasingly applying the "f word" (fascism) to the US. See, for instance, "Is America Becoming Fascist?" in *Adbusters* magazine, Sept/Oct 2003, p. 33.
4. Third edition.
5. Ibid., p. 1,042.
6. Most especially seen in the coverup, rather than coverage of, the most overarching crimes of the power elites.
7. June 15, 2003.
8. Greg Palast, *The Best Democracy Money Can Buy*, Peguin, 2003.
9. William Blum, *Killing Hope*, Black Rose Books, 1998.
10. William Shirer, *The Rise and Fall of the Third Reich*, op. cit., pp. 199.
11. See Michael Moore, *Stupid White Men*, Regan Books, 2001.
12. William Shirer, *The Rise and Fall of the Third Reich*, op. cit., p. 798.
13. Ibid., p. 239.
14. To my knowledge, the terms "wholesale terrorism" (meaning state-sponsored) and "retail terrorism" (meaning acts of terrorism committed by non-government-sponsored individuals or groups), were originated by Noam Chomsky and Edward S. Herman in the 1970s.
15. William Shirer, *The Rise and Fall of the Third Reich*, op. cit., p. 280.
16. John K. Cooley, *Unholy Wars: Afghanistan, America, and International Terrorism*, Pluto Press, 2000, pp. 107, 120-121, 225.
17. For an exploration of the deeply corrosive effects of obsession with secrecy, see Daniel Ellsberg, *Secrets: A Memoir of Vietnam and the Pentagon Papers*, Viking, 2002.
18. Ian Kershaw, *Hitler 1889-1936: Hubris*, and *Hitler 1936-1945: Nemesis*, Peguin, 2001. Kershaw details dozens of Third Reich deceptions. In *Nemesis:* "Distortions of the truth were built into the communications system of the Third Reich at every level — most of all in the top echelons of the regime." (p. 549)
19. It was part of the evil genius of Hitler that he knew, as he wrote in Chapter 10 of *Mein Kampf,* "The broad mass of a nation ... will more easily fall victim to a big lie than to a small one."
20. William Shirer, *The Rise and Fall of the Third Reich*, op. cit., p. 192.
21. Ibid.
22. Ibid.
23. Ibid., p. 194.
24. PNAC, "Rebuilding America's Defenses," PNAC website, p. 91. To purchase this video (US$32.00), call (416) 651-5588.

20. Carroll Quigley, *Tragedy and Hope: A History of the World in Our Time*, MacMillan, 1966.
21. Robert Gaylon Ross, Sr., *Who's Who of the Elite: Memebers of the Bilderberbergs*, CFR, and *Trilateral Commission*, R.I.E., 2000.
22. Zbigniew Brzezinski, *Between Two Ages: America's Role in the Technetronic Era*, Viking Adult, 1970. Reprinted by Greenwood Press, 1982.
23. Joyce Nelson, *The Perfect Machine: Television and the Bomb*, New Society Publishers, 1991, p. 30.
24. Robert Gaylon Ross, Sr., op. cit.
25. Kristina Borjesson, ed., *Into the Buzzsaw: Leading Journalists Expose the Myth of a Free Press*, Prometheus Books, 2002.
26. Gerard Colby, *DuPont: Behind the Nylon Curtain*, Prentice-Hall, 1974.

27. Gerard Colby, *DuPont Dynasty: Behind the Nylon Curtain*, L. Stuart, 1984.
28. Kristina Brojesson, *Into the Buzzsaw*, op. cit., p.12.
29. Independent Curators International (ICI), New York, 2003.
30. David Wise and Thomas B. Ross, *The Invisible Government*, Random House, 1964.
31. James DiEugenio and Lisa Pease, eds., *Assassinations*, Feral House, 2003, p. 300.
32. Ibid., p. 300.
33. Joseph Trento, *The Secret History of the CIA*, Carroll & Graf Publishers, 2005.
34. Ibid., p. 23.
35. Darrell Garwood, *Under Cover: Thirty-five Years of CIA Deception*, Grove Press, 1985, p. 250.
36. Deborah Davis, *Katharine the Great: Katharine Graham and her Washington Post Empire*, Sheridan Square Press, 1991, p. 130.
37. Frances Stonor Saunders, *The Cultural Cold War: The CIA and the World of Arts and Letters*, The New Press, 2000, p. 105.
38. John le Carre, "The United States of America has Gone Mad," *The Times* (London), January 15, 2003. Cited at timesonline.co.uk
39. Joseph Trento, *The Secret History of the CIA*, op. cit., p. 205.
40. Daniel Ellsberg, *Secrets: A Memoir of Vietnam and the Pentagon Papers*, Viking Adult, 2002.
41. Paul David Collins, "The Hidden Face of Terrorism: The Dark Side of Social Engineering, from Antiquity to September 11," *Nexus*, Vol. 10, No. 3, April-May 2003.

Chapter 7

1.   Joseph J. Trento, *The Secret History of the CIA*, op. cit.
2.   Adam Nicolson, *God's Secretaries: The Making of the King James Bible*, HarperCollins, 2003.
3.   John Gerard, *What Was the Gunpowder Plot? The Traditional Story Tested by Original Evidence*, Osgood, McIlvane, 1897. (Out of print)
4.   Webster Griffin Tarpley, *9/11 Synthetic Terror*, op. cit., p. 68.
5.   Adam Nicolson, ibid.
6.   Nafeez Ahmed Mossadeq, *The War on Truth*, op. cit.
7.   Ibid., quoting John McMurtry in reply to ZNet Commentary of May 22, 2002: "What Did Bush Know?" ZNet, June 8, 2002. Cited at Zmag.org/content/TerrorWar/mcmurtry.cfm.
8.   Lawrence E. Cline, *Pseudo Operations and Counterinsurgency: Lessons from Other Countries*, Strategic Studies Institute of the US Army War College, June 2005. Cited at Carlisle.army.mil/ssi
9.   Frank Kitson, *Gangs and Countergangs*, Barrie & Rockcliffe, 1960.
     Frank Kitson, *Low Intensity Operations: Subversion, Insurgency, Peacekeeping*, Stackpole Books, 1971.
10. Peter Scowen, *Rogue Nation*, op. cit. p. 148.
11. Dr. Donald N. Wilber, "Historian's Note," in *Overthrow of Premier Mossadeq of Iran: November 1952- August 1953.*
12. See Defencetalk.com
13. Webster Griffin Tarpley, personal communication.
14. Dale Wharton, 40@dale.cam.org, Jan. 11, 1966. Cited at Hartford-hwp.com/archives/27/054.html
15. Matthew Teague, "The Infiltrator: How this man helped topple the most tenacious terrorist organization in history," in *Atlantic*, April 2006.
16. Annie Machon and David Shayler, *Spies, Lies and Whistleblowers: MI5, MI6 and the Shayler Affair*, The Book Guild Ltd., 2005.

17. Wikipedia.org/wiki/Low-intensity-conflict

18. Sources:
Press for Conversion, Issue #50, January 2003, page 4. Cited at
Coat.ncf.ca/our_magazine/links/issue50/issue50.htm
History of Mexico, Empire and Early Republic, 1821-55, Area Handbook, US Library of
Congress, June 1996.

19. Sources:
Press for Conversion, op. cit., p. 6.
"Emergence of the U.S. as a World Power," editorial in *Granma*, August 7, 1998.
Michael Rivero, "Dictatorship through Deception," in *New Republic Forum*, December 24,
1999.
Howard Zinn, "History as a Political Act," in *Revolutionary Worker*, December 20, 1998.

20. Sources:
Gwpda.org/naval/lusika04.htm
Press for Conversion, op. cit., p. 8.
J.M. Kenworthy and George Young, *Freedom of the Seas*, Hutchinson & Co., 1928.
American edition published in New York by Horace Liveright.
Patrick Beesly, *Room 40: British Naval Intelligence 1914-18*, Harcourt Brace Jovanovich,
1982.
Winston Churchill, *World Crisis*, Thornton Butterworth, 1923.

21. Sources:
En.wikipedia.org/wiki/Reichstag_fire
William L. Shirer, *Rise And Fall Of The Third Reich*, Simon & Schuster, 1990.
Press for Conversion, op. cit., p. 11. Cited at
En.wikipedia.org/wiki/Attack_on_Pearl_Harbor
Robert B. Stinnett, *Day of Deceit: The Truth About FDR and Pearl Harbor*, Free Press, 1999.

22. *Press for Conversion*, Issue #50, January 2003, page 11.
En.wikipedia.org/wiki/Attack_on_Pearl_Harbor
Robert B. Stinnett, *Day of Deceit*, op. cit.

23. Sources:
En.wikipedia.org/wiki/William_Lyon_Mackenzie_King#Second_World_War
"Did You Know Why Canada Fought in WWII?" Cited at
Poormojo.org/pmjadaily/archives/000807.html
"Lighthouse Attack Was Staged by US to Trick Canada Into War." Cited at
Prisonplanet.com/articles/april2004/040204lighthouseattack.htm

24. Sources:
Daniele Ganser and Frank Cass, *NATO's Secret Army; Operation Gladio and Terrorism in
Western Europe*, ISN Security Watch, Dec. 15, 2004.
Daniele Ganser and Christian Nuenlist, eds., *Secret Warfare: Operation Gladio and NATO's
Stay-Behind Armies, Parallel History Project on NATO and the Warsaw Pact*, Synopsis
and documents cited at Isn.ethz.ch/php/collections/coll_gladio.htm.
Chris Floyd, "Terror Intel Style: Sword Play and Operation Gladio," in *Moscow Times*, Feb.
19, 2005. Cited at Boston.indymedia.org/newswire/display/33482/index.php

25. Sources:
En.wikipedia.org/wiki/Operation_Northwoods
James Bamford, *Body of Secrets: Anatomy of the Ultra-Secret National Security Agency*,
Doubleday, 2001.

26. Sources:
En.wikipedia.org/wiki/Gulf_of_Tonkin_incident
Jim Stockdale and Sybil Stockdale, *In Love and War: The Story of a Family's Ordeal and
Sacrifice During the Vietnam Years*, HarperCollins, 1984.

Ben Bradlee's Speech on the Tonkin Gulf, April 29, 1987. Cited at
Emperors-clothes.com/archive/bradlee.htm.
27. Sources:
En.wikipedia.org/wiki/Achille_Lauro
"Was the *Achille Lauro* another Zionist 'Black Op?'" Cited at
The7thfire.com/new_world_order/zionism/abu_nidal-mossad_terrorist.htm
28. Sources:
Press for Conversion, op. cit., p. 27.
En.wikipedia.org/wiki/Operation_El_Dorado_Canyon
"German TV exposes CIA, Mossad links to 1986 Berlin disco bombing," World Socialist
Web Site, August 27, 1998. Cited at Wsws.org/news/1998/aug1998/bomb1-
a27.shtml
29. Sources:
Press for Conversion, op. cit., 31.
En.wikipedia.org/wiki/Nurse_Nayirah
"To Sell a War," *the fifth estate,* documentary, 2002. See cbc.ca/fifth/
30. Sources:
Press for Conversion, op. cit., p. 39.
En.wikipedia.org/wiki/P2OG
William Arkin, "The Secret War," in Los Angeles Times, Sunday, October 27, 2002. Cited at
Commondreams.org/views02/1028-11.htm.
31. Sources:
BBC News, April 29, 2004. Cited at News.bbc.co.uk/go/pr/fr/-
/1/hi/world/europe/3670627.stm
En.wikipedia.org/wiki/Image:Ac.madrid2.jpg
En.wikipedia.org/wiki/Madrid_train_bombings
En.wikipedia.org/wiki/Aftermath_of_the_March_11%2C_2004_Madrid_attacks
Joe Vialls, "Myahudi Monsters Maul Madrid," March 15, 2004. Cited at
Joevialls.co.uk/myahudi/madrid.html
"Madrid bombing suspects kill themselves," CBC.CANews, April 4, 2004. Cited at
Cbc.ca/stories/print/2004/04/03/world/spain_blast040403
"Madrid Bombers Linked to Spanish Security Service," London Times, June 21, 2004. Cited
at Avantgo.thetimes.co.uk/services/avantgo/article/0,,1150429,00.html.
32. Sources:
En.wikipedia.org/wiki/Beslan_school_hostage_crisis
Webster Griffin Tarpley, "Putin Exposes US-UK Terror Strategy Behind School Atrocity;
Russian Press Blasts Anglo-Saxon Terrorist Controllers," Washington DC, September
14, 2004. Cited at Inn.globalfreepress.com/modules/news/article.php?storyid=793
Alex Jones, "Beslan School Massacre: Inside Involvement" (Data Page). Cited at
Prisonplanet.com/articles/march2005/240305beslanmassacre.htm
"Terrorists Got Orders From Abroad; Did Not Speak Chechen," RIA Novosti, September 7,
2004. Cited at
Prisonplanet.com/articles/september2004/070904ordersfromabroad.htm
33. Sources:
Ralph Schoenman, "Who Bombed the US World Trade Center in 1993? Growing Evidence
Points to Role of FBI Operative," in *Global Outlook,* Issue 9, Fall 2004/ Winter 2005.
Prisonplanet.com/archives/london/index.htm
"'No internal inquiry' into blasts," BBC July 17, 2005. Cited at
Prisonplanet.com/Pages/Jul05/170705inquiry.html
Steve Watson, "New Stasi style UK Anti-Terror campaign encourages reporting your neigh-
bours," January 4, 2006. Cited at

Infowars.net/articles/january2006/040106Stasi_London.htm

En.wikipedia.org/wiki/7_July_2005_London_bombings

Bill Van Auken, "Washington in crisis over opposition to Iraq war,<i> June 28, 2005. Cited at Wsws.org/articles/2005/jun2005/iraq-j28_prn.shtml

Glenn Frankel and Josh White, "U.K. Memo Cites Plans For Troop Reduction," *Washington Post* Foreign Service, July 11, 2005. Cited at Washingtonpost.com/wp-dyn/content/article/2005/07/10/AR2005071000725_pf.html

Glenn Frankel, "London Subway Blasts Almost Simultaneous, Investigators Conclude Timing Devices, High Explosives Used," *Washington Post,* July 10, 2005. Cited at Washingtonpost.com/wp-dyn/content/article/2005/07/09/AR2005070901248_pf.html

Paul Joseph Watson and Alex Jones, "London Underground Bombing 'Exercises' Took Place at Same Time as Real Attack: Culpability cover scenario echoes 9/11 Wargames," July 13, 2005. Cited at Prisonplanet.com/articles/july2005/090705bombingexercises.htm

"Phony 'Al-Qaeda' Responsibility Claim a Proven Hoax," July 8, 2005. Cited at Prisonplanet.com/articles/july2005/080705provenhoax.htm

Jeff Edwards, "Exclusive: Was It Suicide?" in *Daily Mirror,* July 16, 2005. Cited at Mirror.co.uk

"Bomb Was UNDER the Train Says Eyewitness Closest To It," in *Cambridge Evening News,* July 11, 2005. Cited at Cambridge-news.co.uk/news/region_wide/2005/07/11/83e33146-09af-4421-b2f4-1779a86926f9.lpf

Who shorted British pound? Currency fell 6% in 10 days before London terror attacks, *World Net Daily,* July 16, 2005. Cited at Wnd.com/news/article.asp?ARTICLE_ID=45312

34. Sources:

Paul Joseph Watson, "British Special Forces Caught Carrying Out Staged Terror In Iraq?" September 20, 2005. Cited at Prisonplanet.com/articles/september2005/200905stagedterror.htm

C.L. Cook, "Basra Bizarre: SAS Commandos Arrested and Sprung," *PEJ News,* September 19, 2005. Cited at Pej.org/html/modules.php?op=modload&name=News&file=article&sid= 3331&mode=thread&order=0&thold=0

Michael Keefer, "Were British Special Forces Soldiers Planting Bombs in Basra? Suspicions Strengthened by Earlier Reports," September 25, 2005. Cited at Globalresearch.ca/index.php?context=viewArticle&code=KEE20050925&articleId=994

Kim Sengupta, "Basra governor ends co-operation with British," *London Independent,* September 23, 2005. Cited at News.independent.co.uk/world/middle_east/article314500.ece

Michel Chossudovsky, "Britain 'apologizes' for terrorist act in Basra: Rescue of SAS men who were planning to place bombs in Basra City Square," October 15, 2005. Cited at Globalresearch.ca/index.php?context=viewArticle&code=20051015&articleId=1094

Kurt Nimmo, "British 'Pseudo-Gang' Terrorists Exposed in Basra," September 20, 2005. Cited at Kurtnimmo.com/?p=32

35. Paul Joseph Watson and Alex Jones, "7/7 Bombings Final Word: Her Majesty's Terrorist Network," August 7, 2005. Cited at Prisonplanet.com/articles/august2005/070805finalword.htm

Chapter 8

1. Before going to sleep around 11:30 p.m., Bush wrote in his diary, "The Pearl Harbor of the 21st century took place today.... We think it's Osama bin Laden." Washington Post, January 27, 2002. Cited at Washingtonpost.com/ac2/wp-dyn/A42754-2002Jan26

2. David Ray Griffin, *The 9/11 Commission Report: Omissions and Distortions,* op. cit, p. 135.
3. Ibid., p. 291.
4. David Ray Griffin, from a talk at Lafeyetter Park, recorded by B. Zwicker.
5. Richard Falk, in Foreword to David Ray Griffin, *The New Pearl Harbor,* op. cit.
6. David Ray Griffin, "The Destruction of the World Trade Center: A Christian Theologian Speaks Out." The lecture has been published as "The Destruction of the World Trade Center: Why the Official Story Cannot Be True," in Paul Zarembka, ed., *The Hidden History of 9-11-2001,* Elsevier, 2006, and is also available at 911review.com/articles/griffin/nyc1.html
7. Letter to the *LA Times Magazine,* September 18, 2005, by William Yarchin of Huntington Beach, California, in response to an interview with Griffin in that magazine, conducted by Mark Ehrman, titled "Getting Agnostic about 9/11," published August 28th, 2005.
8. David Ray Griffin, "The Destruction of the World Trade Center", op. cit.
9. Sources:
Bruce David and Carolyn Sinclair, "What if Everything You Know about 9/11 is Wrong?" in *Hustler* magazine, August 2005. Cited online at 911truth.org/article.php?story=20050604140153943
Paul Thompson, *The Terror Timeline,* op. cit.
David Ray Griffin, *The New Pearl Harbor,* op. cit.
David Ray Griffin, *The 9/11 Commission Report,* op. cit.
Allan Wood and Paul Thompson, "An Interesting Day: President Bush's Movements and Actions on 9/11," May 9, 2003. Cited at Cooperativeresearch.net/essay.jsp?article=essayaninterestingday
Thomas Berry, *The Dream of the Earth,* (paperback), Sierra Club Books, 1990.
David Ray Griffin, "9/11 and the American Empire: How Should Religious People Respond?" Speech given to the University of Wisconsin, Madison WI, and broadcast on C-SPAN *Book TV,* April 30, 2005. DVD available from *Global Outlook,* Globaloutlook.ca.
Robert W. McChesney, *The Problem of the Media: U.S. Communication Politics in the Twenty-First Century,* (paperback), Monthly Review Press, New York, 2004.
David Ray Griffin and Peter Dale Scott, *9/11 and the American Empire: Intellectuals Speak Out,* Interlink (in press). See Interlinkbooks.com
David Ray Griffin, John B. Cobb, Jr., Sandra Lubarsky and Kevin Barrett *9/11 and the American Empire: Christians, Jews, and Muslims Speak Out,* Interlink (in press). See Interlinkbooks.com
David Ray Griffin, "The Destruction of the World Trade Center: Why the Official Story Cannot Be True," in *The Hidden History of 9-11-2001, Research in Political Economy,* Volume 23, Spring 2006, Elsevier. Also available at 911review.com/articles/griffin/nyc1.html
MUJCA-NET: Muslim-Jewish-Christian Alliance for 9/11 Truth, Kevin Barrett, coordinator, kevin@mujca.com, mujca.com/
Mark Ehrman, "Getting Agnostic About 9/11: A society of nonbelievers questions the official version," in *Los Angeles Times Magazine,* Friday, August 26, 2005 (dateline Aug. 28). Cited at LAtimes.com and reproduced at 911truth.org/article.php?story=20050826125021191
Gore Vidal, *Dreaming War: Blood for Oil and the Cheney-Bush Junta,* Thunder's Mouth Press, Nation Books, 2002.

Chapter 9

1. Peter Chabarek, Personal Communication.
2. Peter Chabarek, Personal Communication.
3. Barrie Zwicker, "9/11: What Really Happened?" in *Canadian Dimension*, Volume 39, Number 6, November/December 2005.
4. Antonia Zerbisias, "Poking Holes in the Official Story of 9/11," in the *Toronto Star*, May 26, 2004.
5. Stephen Humphrey, "Whodunnit? They Know. Inquiry Wades into Swamp of Conspiracies and Everyone Follows," in *NOW* magazine, June 10-16, 2004. Cited at NOWtoronto.com/issues/2004-06-10/news_story11.php
6. Barrie Zwicker, "Was Guy Fawkes just a victim of an earlier WMD scheme?" *The Globe and Mail*, November 5, 2005, Page A23.
7. Diana Ralph, Diana Ralph, "How to Dismantle the US Empire," self-published.
8. David H. Albert, *People Power: Applying Non-Violence Theory*, New Society Publishers (Philadelphia), 1985. (Out of print)
9. Paul Thompson, *The Terror Timeline*, op. cit.
10. Paul Thompson, in a presentation at the International Citizens' Inquiry Into 9/11 at The University of Toronto, May 2004.
11. Nafeez Mosaddeq Ahmed, *The War on Truth*, op. cit.
12. Judith Miller, op. cit.
13. Thomas Berry, *The Dream of the Earth*, Sierra Club Books, 1990.
14. Jean Houston, *A Mythic Life: Learning to Live Our Greater Story*, HarperCollins; New York, 1996.
15. John Toland, *Infamy: Pearl Harbor and its Aftermath*, Anchor (rep edition), 1992. Robert Stinnett, *Day of Deceit*, op. cit.
16. David Niven, *The 100 Simple Secrets of Happy People: What Scientists Have Learned and How You Can Use It*, HarperCollins, 2000.

Index

Fleischer, Ari, 304
Flight 11, 76, 174, 207, 337
Flight 77, 47, 83-85, 151, 207, 208
Flight 93, 47, 86-91, 174, 337, 355-356
Flight 175, 207
Flynt, Larry, 304
Forensic evidence, 79
Fourth Reich, 234-235
Fox News, 233
Free Europe Press, 245
Freedom of Information Act, 73
French documentary film crew, 25
Full Spectrum Dominance, 2, 109
Fulton, Kevin, 267-268

Ganor, Boaz, 168
Gatekeepers, 43, 141ff, 177, 179-224, 225, 360
Gayle, Frank, 69, 71
Gehlen, Reinhard, 252
General Electric, 232
General Motors, 226
Gerth, Jeff, 153
Ghaddafi, Moammar, 282
Gibson, Charles, 172-174
Gingrich, Newt, 233
Giuliani, Mayor Rudolph, 51, 79
Global Domination Project, 312
Global Networks, 248-250
Global Outlook, 13, 22, 304, 335, 352-353
Globe and Mail, 9-12, 34, 154, 337
Goebbels, Josef, 238
Goering, Hermann, 238, 273
Gonzales, Attorney General Alberto, 164, 166
Goodman, Amy, 218
Goodspeed, Peter, 167-168
Gorelick, Jamie, 145-146
Goss, Porter, 102-103
Graham, Phil, 252
Graham, Senator Bob, 102-103, 107
Great Conspiracy, xiv, 51, 291, 336, inside back cover
Grenada, 8
Griffin, David Ray, 27, 29, 43, 47, 59, 87, 95, 96, 97, 105, 107, 109, 121, 145-146, 162, 188, 207, 220, 303-320, 333, 357
Ground Zero, 72
Gruson, Sydney, 252
Guantanamo Bay, 114, 165
Gulf of Tonkin incident, 16, 269, 279-280
Gulf War (1991), 283-284
Gunpowder plot, 257-260, 337

Halliburton Corporation, 229-231
Hamas, 298
Hamburg cell, 115
Hamilton, Lee, 93, 157
Hanjour, Hani, 26, 85, 131
Harper, Stephen, 298
Harris, David B., 163
Harvey, Roy, 218
Helms, Leili, 106-107
Helms, Richard, 106-107
Herman, Douglas, 176-177
Hersh, Seymour, 220
Higham, Chalres, 226-227
Hijackers, 97, 114, 202, 343
Hijackings, procedures for, 53, 146, 148
Hill & Knowlton, 31, 283
Hitler, Adolf, 226, 227, 235, 236, 238, 272-273
Hopsicker, Daniel, 174
House of Morgan, 227
House Un-American Activities Committee, 227
Houston, Jean, 350
Hugo, Victor, 4
hummux, 117-121, 336
Hurricane Katrina, 36, 38, 315
Hussein, Saddam, 109, 157-158, 229, 290
Hustler, 303-306, 311

Ignatieff, Michael, 34
Incompetence theory, vii, 21, 220, 342, 362
Incubator baby deception, 31, 283-284
Indirect evidence, 45, 221
Industrial Military Academic Intelligence Media complex (I MAIM), 3
Inside Job theory, vii, 22, 24, 110, 176, 209, 238, 308, 314-315, 318, 344, 357, 362

Intelligence agencies, 44, 153, 217
Intelligence failures, 217
Inter Services Intelligence Agency (ISI), 47, 102-103, 237
Intercepts by jet fighters, 53-55
International Citizens' Inquiry Into 9/11, 13, 24, 91, 121, 319-320, 332, 335, 336, 353
International Policy Institute for Counter-Terrorism, 168
Into the Buzzsaw, 242, 247
Invention of reality, 30
Invisible government, 3, 30, 133, 214, 225-256, 264, 265, 286, 295, 302, 354

About the Author

In January 2002, Barrie Zwicker became the first journalist in the world to deeply question the official story of 9/11 on national TV, in seven commentaries released as the video *The Great Deception*. He was director of the six day International Citizens' Inquiry Into 9/11 at The University of Toronto in 2004, then produced the DVD The Great Conspiracy: *The 9/11 News Special You Never Saw*. An environmentalist and long distance cyclist, he gave up car ownership in 1966.

Global Outlook
The Magazine of 9/11 Truth

P.O. Box 222, Oro, Ontario L0L 2X0 Canada
Phone: 1-705-720-6500
Toll-Free: 1-888-713-8500
E-mail: info@GlobalOutlook.ca
Website: www.GlobalOutlook.ca
ISSN: 1499-7754
Copy price varies: $4.95 to $5.95 Cdn/US
Subscription (Individuals):$20.00 Cdn/US
Subscription (Libraries): $40.00 Cdn/US

> Available at: Chapters, Indigo, Borders,
> Barnes & Noble, and specialty
> bookstores across North America.

Global Outlook is the only magazine in the world devoted to investigating, reporting and commenting on the events of 9/11 and the so-called war on terrorism for which 9/11 is the linchpin. Begun in early 2002, (just after September 11, 2001), *Global Outlook* has been tracking the implementation of the "Project for the New American Century" (PNAC) organized by Dick Cheney, Donald Rumsfeld, Paul Wolfowitz and Jeb Bush among other neo-cons, since 1997.

Every issue of *Global Outlook* offers the latest evidence, illustrations and commentary about the events of 9/11 and everything related to them. It includes discussions on foreign policy, military, covert, financial and psychological warfare dimensions of the US domination project, as well as articles on domestic spying, repression and the increasing criminalization of dissent. *Global Outlook* has a circulation of approximately 12,000 to 15,000 copies. It is an anti-war, propeace magazine that gives you the truth behind the headlines.

Start your subscription now. Order by Phone, Fax, E-mail or on-line using PayPal at www.GlobalOutlook.ca. Back Issues and other 9/11 resources are available.

If you have enjoyed *Towers of Deception*
you might also enjoy other

BOOKS TO BUILD A NEW SOCIETY

Our books provide positive solutions for people who want to
make a difference. We specialize in:

Environment and Justice • Conscientious Commerce
Sustainable Living • Ecological Design and Planning
Natural Building & Appropriate Technology • New Forestry
Educational and Parenting Resources • Nonviolence
Progressive Leadership • Resistance and Community

New Society Publishers

ENVIRONMENTAL BENEFITS STATEMENT

New Society Publishers has chosen to produce this book on Enviro 100, recycled
paper made with **100% post consumer waste**, processed chlorine free, and old
growth free.

For every 5,000 books printed, New Society saves the following resources:[1]

45	Trees
4,041	Pounds of Solid Waste
4,446	Gallons of Water
5,799	Kilowatt Hours of Electricity
7,346	Pounds of Greenhouse Gases
32	Pounds of HAPs, VOCs, and AOX Combined
11	Cubic Yards of Landfill Space

---

[1]Environmental benefits are calculated based on research done by the Environmental Defense Fund and
other members of the Paper Task Force who study the environmental impacts of the paper industry.

For more information on this environmental benefits statement, or to inquire about environmentally
friendly papers, please contact New Leaf Paper – info@newleafpaper.com Tel: 888 • 989 • 5323.

For a full list of NSP's titles, please call **1-800-567-6772** *or check out our website at:*

www.newsociety.com

NEW SOCIETY PUBLISHERS